THE
ENVIRONMENT
PROBLEMS AND SOLUTIONS

A Collection of New Studies and Outstanding
Dissertations on Current Issues

STUART BRUCHEY
Allan Nevins Professor Emeritus
American Economic History
Columbia University
GENERAL EDITOR

A GARLAND SERIES

PROTECT AND ENHANCE

"Juridical Democracy" and the Prevention of Significant
Deterioration of Air Quality

A. STANLEY MEIBURG

Garland Publishing, Inc.
NEW YORK & LONDON 1991

Library of Congress Cataloging-in-Publication Data

Meiburg, A. Stanley
Protect and enhance : juridical democracy and the Prevention of Significant Deterioration of air quality / A. Stanley Meiburg.
p. cm. — (The Environment : problems and solutions)
Includes bibliographical references.
ISBN 0-8240-4049-X (alk. paper)
1. Air—Pollution—Law and legislation—United States. 2. Air—Pollution—Government policy—United States. 3. United States. Environmental Protection Agency. I. Title. II. Series: Environment—problems
and solutions.
KF3812.M43 1991
344.73'046342—dc20
[347.30446342]   91-6852

PRINTED IN THE UNITED STATES OF AMERICA

To
_____

CATHERINE, JONATHAN, AND DOROTHY

CONTENTS

Chapter

Chapter

PREFACE

This work was inspired when I attended a session
in 1980 in which staff from the Environmental
Protection Agency's Office of Air Quality Planning
and Standards (OAQPS) were explaining to a skeptical
audience of EPA Regional employees just how the
"final" version of the regulations on preventing
significant deterioration were supposed to work.
The sincerity and good intentions of the presenters
were obvious; yet the material being presented was
so confusing and complex that I began to wonder just
how regulations like this could have come into
being.
Though I had been working at EPA for two years,
my experience had been primarily in the area of
water pollution control. Since the field of air
pollution control was new to me, I assumed that my
confusion was largely the result of ignorance.
However, as I learned more about "PSD", as the
program was universally called, its complexities
seemed to grow rather than diminish. At the same
time, it became apparent that despite the seemingly
unobjectionable policy objective of keeping clean
air clean, PSD was unpopular with the States which
were supposed to implement it, and even within EPA
it had many detractors. These observations
increased my curiosity about why PSD had gotten so
complicated and how a program with so little
apparent support was established as law.
While I would still not make the claim that I
fully understand PSD, the story set out in the

following pages provides some insight on how and why
these results occurred. PSD's complexities are not
accidental, but spring from a theory which holds
that if public administration is to serve the public
interest, it must be guided by very specific laws
and regulations which limit the discretion of
individual officials. In its strongest form, this
argument holds that since public officials cannot be
trusted to act in the public interest, mechanisms
must be established in the laws and through the
courts to compel officials to do the "right thing."
In the case of PSD, the outcome which was most
feared was that industry would be able to avoid
stringent air pollution controls on new sources in
clean air areas if the requirements for such
controls depended to any substantial degree on the
discretionary judgments of EPA or State officials.
Avoiding this outcome meant that PSD's requirements
had to be spelled out, first in law and then in
regulation, in excruciating detail.

This approach reflects an ongoing debate in
public administration about how to control the abuse
of discretion by public agencies. The phenomenon of
"capture" has been identified in the traditional
literature as one of the pathologies to which
regulatory agencies are subject, and both the law
and regulations on PSD were structured to eliminate
future opportunities for capture by specifying in
great detail how individual decisions were to be
made. While PSD is intrinsically interesting, this
perspective on its development led me to examine
whether PSD might usefully be viewed as a test of
the proposition, put forth by Theodore Lowi, that
greater specificity in drafting laws and greater
reliance by agencies on formal rulemaking in
establishing policies would produce outcomes which
were more consistent with the needs of a democratic
society.

While only I am responsible for the shortcomings
of this effort to address these issues and tell why
PSD wound up as it did, any work of this sort
requires the assistance and encouragement of many
people. As acknowledged in the Bibliography, I
formally interviewed several current and former EPA

officials and other participants as part of my
research, and their insights and contributions were
extremely helpful. Also valuable, though, were the
informal conversations with countless other people
inside and outside EPA who were willing to spend
time in informal conversation about their
experiences with and perspectives about PSD.

In the mid-1980's, when the dissertation on
which this book is largely based was written,
efforts to amend the Clean Air Act had reached an
impasse in the Congress. As is discussed in great
detail in Chapters 5 and 6, Congress amended the
Clean Air Act in 1977 to give legislative form to
PSD. However, EPA's regulations to implement the
1977 PSD amendments were extremely controversial,
and by 1981 had prompted calls by industry for
further legislative amendments to PSD. This effort
failed in 1982, and further attempts by either
industry or environmental groups to amend the Clean
Air Act were effectively stalemated for many years.

In 1989, however, the new Administration of
President Bush made amendment of the Act a high
priority, and put forward a proposal to the 101st
Congress which, together with especially strong
support from new Senate Majority Leader George
Mitchell, broke the long logjam. Congressional
debate over the 1990 Clean Air Act Amendments
extended throughout the entire session, and their
passage and enactment into law on November 15, 1990
was hailed as one of the signal accomplishments of
the 101st Congress. However, from the standpoint of
this study, the most striking aspect of the 1990
Amendments was that despite the intense controversy
and criticism which PSD attracted throughout the
1970's and early 1980's, the 1990 Amendments contain
virtually no amendments to PSD.

This does not to me seem to have been an
accident, and is consistent with my thesis that
excessive detail in law and regulations can hinder
rather than help the establishment and
administration of policy in a democratic society. I
have attempted to detail some of my reasons for this
conclusion in some new material in Chapter 6, which
reviews events both at EPA and in the Congress since

the time the original dissertation was completed.
Time and space constraints preclude as extensive or
well documented a discussion of these topics as I
would have liked, but they should be helpful for the
reader who would like to see how the story has been
brought up to the present day.

While I have benefitted enormously in my
understanding from my work over the course of my
career with many outstanding people at EPA, I wish
to be emphatically clear that this work was written
by me in my private capacity, and that no official
endorsement by the Environmental Protection Agency
or any other agency of the Federal Government is
intended or should be inferred. The views and
opinions expressed in it are strictly my own and do
not represent official Agency policy in any way.

Several people offered essential support in
preparing this manuscript. The most important was
my academic adviser, Professor Francis E. Rourke,
who continued to encourage me to press on when he
had precious little evidence that anything at all
was being accomplished, and whose gentle yet
persistent encouragement is for me a model of how a
mentor ought to be. Of my colleagues at EPA, I am
especially indebted to Ronald Brand and Jerry
Emison, who pushed me to finish the work I had
started at a time when this objective seemed far
beyond my grasp. Virginia Neely did outstanding
work in helping me compensate for late production by
typing Chapters 4, 5, and 6 in record time from
barely legible handwritten drafts. My mother also
helped out by typing Chapters 1 and 2, but her
greater role, along with my father, was in providing
a constant supply of affection and assistance in
doing whatever needed to be done. I owe an
overwhelming debt to all of these people.

My deepest gratitude goes to my wife, Catherine.
She more than anyone else caused this work to be
written by giving me the opportunity to do it and
the incentive to struggle on during the years when
my own initiative seemed to fail. Along with my
children Jonathan and Dorothy, she paid the price of
the missed vacations, the late nights, and the
weekends away from home, but never gave up on the

idea that I would someday finish.   It is a pleasure
to dedicate this work to her.

PROTECT AND ENHANCE

"Juridical Democracy" and the Prevention of Significant Deterioration of Air Quality

CHAPTER I

PUBLIC ADMINISTRATION AND AIR POLLUTION CONTROL

A chief theme in the traditional literature of
public administration concerns the "capture" of
government regulatory agencies by the interests
which they are supposed to be regulating. In its
most blatant form, this "capture" is thought to
result in a regulatory process that enhances the
profits and power of the regulated community. The
larger concern of the literature on "capture,"
however, is not with the conduct of particular
individuals or even agencies. Rather, it is with
the detrimental effect of this phenomenon on
democratic government in America. Thus, for
example, Grant McConnell concluded after an
extensive analysis of several areas of public policy
that "a substantial part of government in the United
States has come under the influence or control of
narrowly based and autonomous elites."[1]
One of the most persuasive and influential
critics of the capture phenomenon in public
administration has been Theodore Lowi. In his
widely-read book, The End of Liberalism, Lowi
attacked what he called "interest group liberalism"
for adopting a philosophy of government which held
that successful government required only that the
interests of all parties concerned with a particular
problem be accommodated. In the political/social

sphere, Lowi argued, this meant that government
would refrain from resorting to coercion even when
coercion was needed to achieve legitimate social
ends in the public interest (i.e., social justice).
The reason for this, in Lowi's view, was that the
use of coercion implied the existence of
unaccommodated interests---something which the
"liberal" world view could not legitimately accept.
The result was to render the state impotent in the
face of challenges to its authority and ineffective
in achieving necessary social objectives.[2]

Lowi's indictment of the effect of liberal
philosophy on public administration flowed from his
critique of the liberal view of government's role.
Lowi charged that the discomfort of interest group
liberalism with the use of coercive power led to
government agencies which shrank from the
application of that power when needed to sustain the
values that the agency was expected to promote.
Left to their own devices because of unduly broad
grants of discretionary power by the Congress and an
abdication of responsibility by the courts,
government officials usually sought to accommodate
effectively organized interest groups rather than
properly pursue the public interest, whether it was
represented by organized groups or not. This
pattern of accommodation had four consequences: it
led to the treatment of all values as having
equivalent weight; it left government unable to plan
for the future since goals had to be continually
renegotiated with interest groups; it denigrated the
use of general rules of law or principles of justice
by making all outcomes depend on ever-flexible
"accommodations;" and it weakened government's
ability to establish and live by formal processes
which were set up precisely to prevent the arbitrary
conduct of government for the benefit of the
powerful at the expense of the weak.[3]

Lowi and Juridical Democracy

Lowi did more than just attack the failures of
interest group liberalism; he proposed reforms that
would make government simultaneously more democratic
and more effective. Saying that "a good cry is half
the battle," he called his proposals "juridical
democracy." While stating that the proposals were
both "deceptively simple" and "politically extremely
difficult to accomplish," he also argued that they
would be "enormously effective" and that "once the
first step is taken, the rest suddenly seems no
longer radical."[4]
Lowi focused on two strategies for reforming the
way in which the administrative sector of government
operated. First, he argued that statutes should do
a better job of specifying explicit standards of
implementation so that the discretion of
administrators in carrying out programs would be
substantially reduced. Since much of the "capture"
problem, in Lowi's view, resulted from excessively
vague delegations of authority by Congress to
administrative agencies, strong clear statutes would
reduce the likelihood of agency capture by making
decisions dependent on the outcome of laws passed by
democratic institutions (Congress, in the Federal
case) and not on agency-client bargaining.[5]
This would not be the only effect of improved
statutory construction. Freed from the case by case
bargaining which Lowi saw as the heart of interest-
group liberalism, administrative agencies would find
themselves invigorated by statutes which clearly
laid out their responsibilities. Lowi argued that
"law begets law," and that "agencies that begin in a
context of statutes that associate guidance with
power are agencies that begin with legal integrity
and have histories of greater legal integrity,"
while "agencies that begin with little or no
integrity are very unlikely to develop any along the
way."[6] The corollary of strong, clear statutes
would be agencies that were "more effective than
ever."[7]

Lowi was skeptical that Congress would act on its own initiative to reassert this authority. Therefore, his first proposal was that the Supreme Court revive the practice of invalidating Congressional acts when these acts delegated authority to administrative agencies without adequate guidance as to the scope or exercise of this authority. Lowi argued that this would be tantamount to an order "for Congress to do its own work." He argued further that this practice would be a restraint on the judicial function rather than an expansion, since by failing to remand statutes the courts ended up effectively rewriting them in the process of finding "an acceptable meaning of a statute in order to avoid invalidating it."[8]

Lowi's second major proposed reform recognized that even the best statutes could not completely eliminate vagueness in the delegation of powers. To allow for this, he proposed that when taking actions consistent with delegated legislative authority, agencies should make extensive use of formal administrative rulemaking. Formal rulemaking would provide an alternative to the undesirable patterns of interest group liberalism. By increasing the use of formal administrative rulemaking, agencies would reinforce greater legislative specificity by promoting bargaining on the rule rather than on the decision.[9]

This is a critical distinction. Lowi refers to bargaining on the decision as "logrolling", in which the facts and stakes of a particular case are at issue in a dispute over how administrative authority will be applied. In contrast, bargaining over a rule involves a debate over the general set of constraints which will apply to a class of affected parties.[10] Without the discipline imposed by formal, specific rules, Lowi argues, "logrolling" on the decision will invariably become the pattern of administration, leading to a growing disrespect for laws which in any event have little practical impact because their effects can always be avoided.[11] In contrast, formal rules would force bargaining to occur at points in the political process where it was appropriate in a democratic state for such bargaining to occur--in open forums, whether they be the notice and comment provisions of administrative rulemaking or the drafting of legislation by Congress. Moreover, Lowi argued that formal rulemaking would also have the effect of leading agencies back to Congress more frequently for guidance, as well as making it easier for Congress to evaluate the results of legislated programs. Finally, formal rules were more likely to receive early judicial evaluation, before agencies were "too committed" to their positions.[12]

Environmental Protection and Administrative Reform

Most reformers, especially academic advocates of change, have to wait many years for an opportunity to see their proposals put into practice. However, the thinking of scholars in the late 1960's and early '70's on the problems of bureaucratic capture coincided with the establishment of a number of new regulatory agencies to respond to pressures for expanded Federal intervention in areas which had formerly, if regulated at all, been primarily the responsibility of State and local governments.[13] This was particularly true in the case of the Environmental Protection Agency (EPA), created in 1970. The growth of the environmental movement in the late 1960's[14] was fueled in part by the growing belief that the government organizations which might otherwise have acted to control pollution were failing to do so in large measure precisely because of the capture phenomenon.[15] Even where capture of agencies had not occurred in the sense that policy-making was overtly controlled by private organizations, there was widespread suspicion that business groups had been able to forestall effective government action to reduce pollution, or had even been able to keep the problem of pollution from surfacing as an actionable issue on government's

agenda. This could be true even when this outcome
resulted from a large number of collective small
decisions rather than the action of a specific
individual or group.[16]
     In the deliberations about EPA's creation, two
arguments were made in favor of the establishment of
a separate environmental agency (as opposed to its
incorporation of such an agency in a larger
Department of Natural Resources). The first was the
need to foster integrated environmental planning to
control "the unwanted byproducts of an 'affluent'
society."[17] The second, which spoke directly to the
need to prevent capture, was that the regulatory
function of protecting the environment would be
swallowed up in a department which also contained
programs aimed at natural resources development. At
the very least, such an organization would contain a
permanent conflict of interest. This problem would
not arise, however, if a separate organization
headed by a single Administrator were established
with the sole mission of pollution control.
Interestingly, there is no record that a commission
form was ever seriously considered for EPA when it
was first established.[18]
     By accepting the arguments in favor of the
creation of a separate EPA, the Nixon Administration
provided an organizational focus for advocates of
pollution control, one which was relatively free
from the need to satisfy individual client groups
(with the possible exception of environmentalists).[19]
Moreover, just after the Agency was formed in
December, 1970, it was given a statutory mandate in
the Clean Air Act which included a very specific set
of standards, deadlines, guidelines and procedures.[20]
     Yet as EPA has implemented the Clean Air Act
over the past twenty years, a reaction has set in
which goes beyond the predictable calls for its
revision from private parties who feel that they
have been adversely affected by the Act's
provisions. This reaction is best symbolized by two
critiques which argue that neither the specificity
of the Act nor the single administrator model of a
regulatory agency have produced "good" public policy
with respect to clean air.[21]

These critiques differ somewhat in their focus and conclusion. The first, offered by Bruce Ackerman and William Hassler, argues that EPA has read the statute and its accompanying legislative history too literally. To be sure, in their view, Congress was not wrong in drafting a statute which was "agency forcing" in character and was considerably more specific than the earlier, vague regulatory laws of which Lowi was so critical. However, Congress erred in requiring, in excessive detail, the means which were to be used to attain the specific ends established by the Clean Air Act. Ackerman and Hassler use the example of the emissions standard for new coal-fired power plants to make their case that a small, determined coalition of environmental and coal-producing interests was able to effectively force a means-oriented solution on the Agency by manipulating obscure provisions of the Act and its associated legislative history. This solution, in their view, ran contrary to the basic ends of the Clean Air Act. EPA, while saved from the worst excesses of rigidity in applying the law by virtue of its single Administrator structure and by counterattacks from the White House and Executive Branch, nevertheless failed by "arbitrarily constricting the range of policy choices left open by the statutory test."[22]

R. Shep Melnick, in his recent book, Regulation and the Courts, is also critical of the way in which the Clean Air Act has been carried out over the past twelve years. Unlike Ackerman and Hassler, however, he saves his strongest criticism for the courts. Under a specific agency-forcing statute, he points out, the courts are asked to resolve disputes between the agency and outside parties over whether or not EPA has properly carried out its responsibilities under the law.[23]

The demands for adjudication of disputes through the courts have led to what Melnick refers to as "the new administrative law." Its effects, in his view, have been to increase (1) the ability of groups to bring their complaints to court; (2) the burden faced by agencies in justifying their actions; and (3) the willingness of courts to

"second guess" the interpretation of statutes by
Federal agencies. These developments have been
based on the fundamental premise that
"Administrators could not be trusted to carry out
the mission assigned to them by law"--a presumption
which reflected the academic critiques of the 1950's
and 1960's which Lowi and others exemplified.
However, in Melnick's view, "the consequences of the
new administrative law in general and court action
under the Clean Air Act in particular are neither
random nor beneficial." He writes:

> The courts have pushed the EPA in two directions
> at once, extending the scope of its programs
> while diminishing its already inadequate
> resources for achieving publicly proclaimed
> objectives. Court action has encouraged
> legislators and administrators to establish
> goals without considering how they can be
> achieved, exacerbating the tendency of these
> institutions to promise far more than they can
> deliver. The policy-making system of which the
> federal courts are now an integral part has
> produced serious inefficiency and inequities,
> has made rational debate and conscious political
> choice difficult, and has added to frustration
> and cynicism among participants of all stripes.[24]

Both Melnick and Ackerman/Hassler propose
essentially the same solution to these problems:
the greater use of discretion by Agency officials in
interpreting the provisions of the Act. They differ
in one important respect: Ackerman and Hassler
believe that EPA already had such discretion (at
least in the case they reviewed), while Melnick
argues that EPA cannot exercise significantly more
discretion without further action on the part of the
courts and the Congress.[25] In either case, the irony
of these recommendations is that they endorse
precisely what Lowi and others had so actively
condemned.
    This analysis will explore these conflicting
perspectives through an examination of one of the
most controversial disputes over the Clean Air Act

during the 1970's: the issue of whether the Act
required EPA to prevent the significant
deterioration of air quality in areas of the country
where air quality is better than that required by
the health-protective national standards established
by the Act. The conventional wisdom is that the
prevention of significant deterioration (PSD)
program was imposed on a recalcitrant EPA by the
courts during the Nixon Administration. While legal
scholars have disagreed about its merits, many
commentators have agreed with Melnick's assertions
that the 1972 <u>Sierra Club v. Ruckelshaus</u> court
decision on significant deterioration "was the most
important decision issued under the Clean Air Act.
Without it there would be no PSD program today."[26]
In applying a statutory requirement to force the EPA
to act on behalf of a "public interest," the court
in the <u>Sierra Club</u> case would seem to have been
behaving precisely as Lowi and others would have
liked. Moreover, one element of the decision was
that the court required EPA to engage in formalized
rule-making about PSD--a requirement in keeping with
Lowi's prescriptions.
    As described above, Lowi predicted that two
effects would occur when courts required
administrative agencies to adhere to clear standards
of law through formal rulemaking. First,
administrative power would become more efficient in
that general rules would cover large numbers of
individual cases and reduce the tendency for
agencies to engage in case by case bargaining.
Second, administrative power would become more
responsible, in that formal rules would lend
themselves more readily to judicial and legislative
review than large numbers of case by case decisions.
This study will examine not only whether such
patterns occurred in this instance, but more
importantly whether they in fact led toward greater
efficiency and responsibility or (as
Ackerman/Hassler and Melnick would argue) away from
it. Here is where the case study approach has a
comparative advantage. While it is not well-suited
for drawing large scale generalizations about the
validity of a general hypothesis, it can allow us to

see whether the behavior of organizations reflects the pressures which are supposedly at work on them.

Lowi's predictions, of course, would not be not fully discredited by the failure of events in one instance to conform to them. Events rarely offer pure test cases, and PSD is no exception. However, PSD seems to be a relatively good test. Many of the actions which occurred in the course of considering PSD--including the passage of the Clean Air Act and the formation of EPA--were intended in part to respond to the criticisms of reformers such as Lowi. Moreover, enough time has now passed so that some of the ramifications of the original court actions can be seen more clearly. If Lowi's expectations are not met, it at least should raise questions about the validity of his underlying assumptions, notably the proposition that directive legislative rule-making and aggressive judicial review has beneficial effects on public policy.

What is the "Prevention of Significant Deterioration of Air Quality?

In order to understand why the PSD program is controversial, it is necessary to give a brief description of PSD's place in the regulatory scheme established by the Clean Air Act. It is not the purpose of this section to discuss PSD's provisions in detail, as this will occur in later chapters. However, some sense is needed of what portion of the air pollution "universe" PSD occupies and how it relates to the other parts of that universe.

As will be described in the following chapters, "prevention of significant deterioration" as a concept predates the landmark Clean Air Act Amendments of 1970. Yet since most of the contro-versy about PSD occurred after the passage of the 1970 Amendments, PSD is best understood in the context of the regulatory system set up by these Amendments.[27]

The cornerstones of the Amendments are the National Ambient Air Quality Standards (NAAQS). These represent standards for specific air pollutants which, in the judgment of the Administrator of EPA, are needed to protect the public health or welfare from the harmful effects of air pollution.[28] The Clean Air Act Amendments of 1970 required the Administrator to set these standards within 120 days of the passage of the 1970 Amendments. Standards were set for six pollutants: sulfur oxides, nitrogen oxides, photochemical oxidants, hydrocarbons, carbon monoxides, and particulate matter.[29] These are the "criteria pollutants," so called because prior to setting standards, the Administrator must publish air quality criteria which describe the effects of the pollutant on public health or welfare.[30]

Two types of ambient air quality standards were authorized in the 1970 Amendments: primary and secondary standards. Both were to be based on the criteria, but they were to be aimed at different effects of air pollution. Primary standards were to be aimed at the protection of public health, and were to be set at levels which not only reflected the information supplied by the criteria, but also allowed an adequate margin of safety. Secondary standards were to be set at a level requisite to protect the public welfare from any known or anticipated adverse effects associated with the presence of such air pollutant in the ambient air. While "primary" and "secondary" were not defined in the Act, the presumption of its authors and those who were called to implement it appears to have been that the secondary standards would be more stringent than the primary standards, and that they would, in one official's words, "protect against all other adverse effects" of air pollution, including such things as vegetation damage and visibility reduction.[31] The distinction between primary and secondary standards was given additional weight in that the statute recognized that different urgency should be given to the programs to attain the different standards. Primary standards were to be

attained within three years. Secondary standards
were to be attained within a "reasonable time."

The NAAQS were to define what constituted
healthy air quality. Designating certain levels of
air quality as healthy or unhealthy was important
because many areas of the country had (and still
have) air quality poorer than the level of the
standards. In places where this was the case, the
1970 Amendments specified that States were to
develop implementation plans which would result in
the attainment of the primary standards by 1975.
The law listed a number of very specific conditions
which these State implementation plans (which
quickly became known as SIP's) had to meet. Among
other things, the plans required major changes in
State legal authorities, enforcement practices, air
pollution control personnel and staffing, and
emissions limits from particular sources of air
pollution such as factories or power plants.[32] If a
State failed to submit an acceptable implementation
plan, the 1970 Amendments required EPA to promulgate
a plan of its own for that State.[33] The requirements
of the 1970 Amendments with respect to
implementation plans represented both a response to
the perceived failures of past Federal clean air
statutes and an attempt to force States to upgrade
their own efforts.

As such, these requirements generated a whole
host of controversies. For our purpose, what is
important is that the SIP requirements in the 1970
Amendments were all aimed at areas where existing
air quality was worse than the ambient standards,
and where real actions by polluters to reduce or
eliminate emissions would be required if areas were
to meet the NAAQS by 1975 or even show improvement
in air quality. However, this left open a large
question which the statute did not explicitly
address and which is at the heart of the PSD
controversy: what is the Federal responsibility
toward areas where air quality is better than the
national ambient standards?

One section of the 1970 Amendments did appear to
address this question directly: Section 111, which
set up a new requirement for national emissions

standards for new stationary sources of air
pollution. The Administrator of EPA was given the
responsibility of identifying "categories of
stationary sources" which "may contribute
significantly to air pollution which causes or
contributes to the endangerment of public health or
welfare," and for publishing emission standards for
new sources in such categories which "reflect the
degree of emission limitations available through the
application of the best system of emission reduction
which (taking into account the cost of achieving
such reduction) the Administrator determines has
been adequately demonstrated."[34] The effect of this
section was to mandate that large new polluting
facilities, which would presumably be listed by the
Administrator, would be required to meet that same
emissions standards everywhere <u>regardless</u> of the
ambient air quality in the area where the new plant
was being built. Since these standards would be
based on the "best demonstrated system of control,"
one could assume from this language that such
controls would be sufficient to prevent significant
deterioration in air quality.[35]

This basic structure--primary and secondary
ambient standards, State implementation plans to
achieve these standards, and new source performance
standards for large new sources--formed the
background for the controversy which would develop
over what authority EPA could and should exercise in
the "clean air" areas of the country.

The Critique of PSD

As a concept, the prevention of significant
deterioration of air quality is deceptively simple:
it holds that air which is relatively clean should
stay that way. Yet this simple concept gave rise to
a program which both supporters and detractors alike

have declared to be among the most complex in all of
government.

How and why did this occur? Past attempts to
answer this question have attributed the complexity
which now affects PSD to some particular "devil",
with environmental groups, bureaucrats, or industry
being the leading candidates.[36] A more cautious
approach would point to the difficulties inherent in
implementing any governmental policy of the scope
and magnitude of PSD.[37]

Melnick argues that courts bear a major share of
the responsibility for the PSD's problems because
the courts cannot perform the balancing among
conflicting goals which is necessary in making
public policy.[38] In Melnick's view, PSD's defects
resulted because the court which initiated the PSD
program in the Sierra Club case issued a sweeping
order requiring EPA to produce a comprehensive
program without explaining the expected goals of
this program and without considering the
administrative shape such a program might take."[39]
He argues that this failure to select among
competing goals left EPA at the mercy of those who
sought to use PSD to further their own objectives,
so that PSD "became a political Christmas tree on
which supporters of new environmental protective
efforts hang their pet projects."[40] In this view,
EPA officials were victims of courts and
Congressional staff who had run away with the
program, interpreting statutory provisions on the
one hand without regard to their administrative
feasibility, and making cavalier assumptions on the
other as to the ability of a single program to
achieve an often divergent set of environmental
goals.

EPA officials and staff have some sympathy with
this analysis.[41] As the following discussion will
indicate, it has considerable validity. Yet it
leaves three questions unanswered. First, the
failure of the court to initially define just what
"significant deterioration" meant gave EPA a greater
degree of flexibility than was available in
implementing many other parts of the extremely

detailed Clean Air Amendments of 1970. How did the
Agency use this flexibility? Why did it select
certain choices and foreclose others? While
recognizing that both Congress and the courts placed
real constraints on EPA's implementation of the PSD
program--as they should, according to Lowi's model--
this review will examine just how these constraints
affected official behavior and how EPA officials
used their discretion in designing a program which
responded to their own concerns as well as to their
constraints. Such an investigation requires an in-
depth examination of just how these concerns and
constraints shaped the outcome of EPA's rules on
PSD.

The second unanswered question is equally
important. Even those who denounce the current PSD
program most strongly would not deny that it has had
an effect. What has this effect been? Was it what
the original proponents and opponents of the policy
expected? Did the process by which PSD was
developed have any effect of the outcomes of the
policy? While it is perhaps still too early to
assess the full range of effects of PSD as a policy,
there have been enough studies done to allow for at
least some conclusions about these questions.

The third question directly addresses Lowi's
prescriptions for how public policy should be
articulated and implemented. Have fifteen years of
legislation, regulation, and court suits produced
"better" public policy than a program which would
have relied more on the greater use of discretion of
administrative agencies? While this is a difficult
question, it seems a fair one in light of the
substantial public investment in both arguing about
PSD and carrying it out. Lowi would argue that
there is a public return on the investments in
changed policy processes which he would advocate, in
that the public interest is better served. If the
process used to develop the PSD program is a
relatively good example of the kind of policy
process which Lowi would advocate, with detailed
legislation, formal rulemaking and extensive
litigation over the particulars of these rules, it

is reasonable to ask how the public interest
benefitted from its use.

The following chapters will attempt to describe
and assess PSD's development. It is most definitely
not the objective of this review to re-analyze and
evaluate the legal arguments of PSD's supporters and
opponents or to discuss the politics of the Clean
Air Act. This job has been more than adequately
done by others.[42] However, PSD offers an opportunity
to test the belief that a directive and very
specific legal/regulatory system is beneficial for
public policy, and to examine how organizations
respond to the kinds of constraints which such a
system imposes.

NOTES

1. Grant McConnell, <u>Private Power and American
    Democracy</u> (New York: Alfred A. Knopf, 1966), p.
    339. Marver Bernstein, <u>Regulating Business By
    Independent Commission</u> (Princeton: Princeton
    University Press, 1955) is usually cited as the
    seminal work on this point. However, the
    concern over the relationship between the
    regulators and the regulated is part of a much
    older tradition in American life--that though
    Americans over time have assigned more and more
    responsibility to government, they have harbored
    great mistrust about the way in which that
    responsibility will be carried out. This theme
    can be traced back at least to Madison's and
    Hamilton's arguments in the <u>Federalist</u> <u>Papers</u>
    (especially numbers 10 and 51).

    James Q. Wilson notes the expansion to the
    general public of the belief that agency capture
    is a routine phenomenon of government in James
    Q. Wilson, ed., <u>The Politics of Regulation</u> (New
    York: Basic Books, 1980), pp. vii-xii.

2. Theodore Lowi, <u>The End of Liberalism</u> (New York:
    W. W. Norton, 1969), especially chapters 2, 3, 4
    and 10. Lowi defines interest group liberalism
    as a philosophy whose key points were: 1) use
    of government in a positive and expansive role;
    2) motivation by high sentiments; 3) faith that
    what is good for government is good for society;
    and 4) that the policy agenda and public
    interest must be defined in terms of the
    organized interests of society (p. 71).

3. Ibid., pp. 288-293.

4. Ibid., p. 297.

5. Ibid., pp. 154-56.

6. Ibid., p. 154.

7. Ibid., p. 299.

8. Ibid., p. 298.

9. Ibid., pp. 299-300.

10. Ibid., p. 147.

11. Ibid., pp. 154-55.

12. Ibid., p. 301.

13. Alfred Marcus, <u>Promise and Performance</u> (Westport, Conn.: Greenwood Press, 1980): p. xi.

14. For more on public involvement in environmental issues, see Anthony Downs, "Up and Down With Ecology--The Issue Attention Cycle," <u>The Public Interest</u> 28 (Summer, 1972): pp. 38-50.

    Charles Jones reviews some of the polling data associated with the rise of pollution as a public issue in the late 1960's in <u>Clean Air: The Policies and Politics</u> of Pollution Control (Pittsburgh: University of Pittsburgh Press, 1975), pp. 152-154.

15. An example of this particular strain in the early environmental movement can be seen in the article by Harrison Wellford, a "Nader's Raider" (and later a Carter Administration reorganization official) entitled "On How To Be A Constructive Nuisance," in Garrett de Bell, ed., <u>The Environmental Handbook</u> (New York: Ballantine Books, 1970), pp. 268-284. The strongest attack along these lines, which played an important role not just as a critique but as a political event, is the Ralph Nader-sponsored study on air pollution control, John C. Esposito, <u>Vanishing Air</u> (New York: Grossman Publishers, 1970). The impact of this study is discussed in Jones, <u>Clean Air</u>, pp. 191-92.

16. Matthew Crenson, The Un-Politics of Air
Pollution (Baltimore: Johns Hopkins University
Press, 1970). For a review of the theoretical
literature on "decisions" and "nondecisions,"
see Mark V. Nadel, "The Hidden Dimensions of
Public Policy: Private Governments and the
Policy Making Process," Journal of Politics,
Vol. 37, no. 1 (February, 1975), pp. 9-11.

17. Marcus, Promise and Performance, p. 37.

18. Ibid. Marcus elsewhere writes that "it was
thought that fixing responsibility in one person
and equipping him with authority over many
different industries would minimize the chances
that EPA would become the tool of any single
source of influence." Alfred Marcus,
"Environmental Protection Agency", in Wilson,
ed., The Politics of Regulation, p. 267.
However, it is not clear whether the commission
idea was explicitly rejected because commissions
were felt to be prone to capture, or because
commissions were regarded as an inefficient form
of government in a Nixon Administration which
was interested in applying private-sector models
to centralize rather than share administrative
power. Whether true at the time or not,
however, most observers looking back at the
creation of the new social regulatory agencies
of the late 1960's and early 1970's have
discerned a pattern of creating single-headed
units directly within the Executive Branch. On
this point, also see R. Shep Melnick, Regulation
and the Courts: The Case of the Clean Air Act
(Washington: Brookings, 1983), p. 8; and Bruce
Ackerman and William Hassler, "Beyond the New
Deal: Coal and the Clean Air Act," 89 Yale Law
Journal 1466 (1980), p. 1476. Two exceptions to
this trend are the Consumer Product Safety
Commission and the Nuclear Regulatory
Commission. In 1983, during the tenure of Anne
Burford as EPA Administrator, a proposal did
surface in Congress to turn EPA into a
commission. The proposal was widely seen as an

attack on the Reagan Administration's
environmental policy. After Mrs. Burford's
departure, this proposal disappeared.

19. This raises the question of whether "public
interest groups" can be said to be "clients of"
or to "capture" an agency. Rather than try to
address this question in the abstract, it is
enough to note that in this case, environmental
groups certainly do not believe they have
"captured" EPA. The Agency, however, has
generally shown a particular interest in the
views of these groups. However, this is also
attributable in part to the statutory tools
given such groups to block or compel Agency
action (e.g., citizen suits). On President
Nixon's concerns about EPA's possible "capture"
by environmental groups, see Marcus, Promise and
Performance, pp. 44-46.

20. Melnick, Regulation and the Courts, pp. 7-8.
The requirements of the Clean Air Act, and some
of the changes that occurred in the making of
the 1970 Act, are discussed in much greater
detail in chapter 2. A full account of the
drafting and provisions of the 1970 amendments
can be found in Jones, Clean Air, pp. 175-210.
The 1970 Amendments were generally seen at the
time as a watershed in regulatory legislation.
This impression has not changed over time, which
accounts in part for the continuing high
symbolic value attached to the Clean Air Act by
both its supporters and opponents.

It is interesting to contrast the specific
requirements of the 1970 Amendments, which ran
to more than 60 pages, with the rather vague
language of the supposedly broader 1969 National
Environmental Policy Act, which is a mere six
pages long. The change of philosophy in the
1970 Amendments is also immediately apparent
when it is compared to its predecessor
legislation, the 1967 Air Quality Act.

21. Melnick, <u>Regulation and the Courts</u>, and Ackerman and Hassler, "Beyond the New Deal." Ackerman and Hassler have expanded their Yale Law Review article into a book, <u>Clean Coal/Dirty Air</u> (New Haven, Conn.: Yale University Press, 1981).

22. Ackerman and Hassler, "Beyond the New Deal," pp. 1556-71.

23. Melnick, <u>Regulation and the Courts</u>, pp. 9-13, 393. It is interesting to note in passing that Lowi's analysis fails to discuss what the role of the courts would be in "enforcing" the terms of "specific" statutes. Instead, Lowi appears to assume that such laws would be self-executing.

24. Ibid., chapters 1, 3 and 10 (quote is from p. 344).

25. Compare "Beyond the New Deal," pp. 1566-71 with <u>Regulation and the Courts</u>, pp. 387-393. These difference are somewhat lessened by Ackerman/Hassler's stress on the need for Congressional action to increase the <u>ends</u>-forcing (as opposed to the <u>means</u>-forcing) character of the Clean Air Act. It remains true, however, that Ackerman/Hassler have more faith in the ability of the courts to "force" EPA to do the "right thing," while Melnick is sharply critical of the effect of past attempts by the courts to do just that.

26. Melnick, <u>Regulation and the Courts</u>, pp. 345-46. For different assessments of Judge Pratt's decision by legal scholars, compare Marc B. Mihaly, "the Clean Air Act and the Concept of Non-Degradation," 2 <u>Ecology Law Quarterly</u> 801 (1973) and Hines, N. William, "A Decade of NonDegradation Policy in Congress and the Courts," 62 <u>Iowa</u> <u>Law Review</u> 643 (1977) with Richard Stewart, "The Development of Administrative and Quasi-Constitutional Law in Judicial Review of Environmental Decision-

Making: Lessons From the Clean Air Act," 62 <u>Iowa Law Review</u> 713 (1977), pp. 740-50. Melnick agrees with those who argue that the 1970 Act did <u>not</u> require PSD (see <u>Regulation and</u> <u>the</u> <u>Courts</u>, pp. 76-80).

    Although much time and effort has been devoted to legal arguments over <u>Sierra Club vs.</u> <u>Ruckelshaus</u>, the original decision itself is only four pages long.

27. Public Law 91-604, the Clean Air Amendments of 1970, was an amendment to the Clean Air Act, which was first codified by the Clean Air Act of 1963 (P.L. 88-206), and modified by subsequent amendments in 1965, 1966, and 1967. It is codified at 42 U.S.C. 1857 <u>et</u> <u>seq</u>. All citations which follow will refer to sections of the Clean Air Act as they were numbered in the public law version, since this is the way they are commonly referred to within EPA and by outside parties.

28. Clean Air Act §109.

29. 36 <u>Federal Register</u> 22384, codified in 40 CFR 50. Standards for lead were added in 1978; in 1979 the photochemical oxidant standard was changed to ozone and raised from .08 parts per million (ppm) to .12 ppm.

30. Clean Air Act §108(a). At the time the 1970 Amendments were passed, the widespread expectation existed that criteria would be developed for a large number of additional pollutants. See, for example, U.S. Senate, <u>Clean Air Amendments of 1970</u>, S. Rpt. 91-1196 to accompany S. 4358, 91st Congress, 2nd sess., 1970, p. 9 (hereafter referred to as <u>1970 Senate Report</u>). This has not occurred, and the criteria pollutants today are (with the exception of lead) the same ones which were first established in 1971.

31. Clean Air Act §109(b)(1) and (2). The quote is by Acting Administrator John Quarles in U.S. Congress, House, Committee on Interstate and Foreign Commerce, <u>Clean Air Act Oversight--1973, Hearings Before the Subcommittee on Public Health and Environment of the Committee on Interstate and Foreign Commerce</u>, 93rd Congress, 1st sess., pp. 14-15 (hereafter cited as <u>1973 House Hearings</u>).

32. Clean Air Act, §110.

33. Ibid.

34. The language cited is from §111 as written in the 1970 Clean Air Act. This section was altered substantially by the 1977 amendments to require the use of "scrubbers" (also known as flue gas desulfurization units) on new coalfired power plants, so that this language now reads rather differently. The controversy over the regulations implementing this section of the 1977 Amendments is the main focus of the Ackerman/Hassler article and book.

35. This was the basic argument which EPA adopted in defending itself in the later court suits over this issue. See the Brief for the Petitioners in <u>Sierra Club vs. Ruckelshaus</u>, No. 72-804, Supreme Court, October term, 1972, pp. 12-13.

36. See, for example, the comments in the Clean Air Act oversight hearings held in 1981. U.S. Senate, <u>Clean Air Act Oversight, Hearings Before the Committee on Environment and Public Works</u>, 97th Congress, 1st sess. 1981 (hereafter cited as the <u>1981 Senate Oversight Hearings</u>). To cite only one example of the comments by someone who was generally supportive of clean air programs, consider the following exchange between Senator Gary Hart of Colorado and Richard Ayres of the Natural Resources Defense Council.

> Senator Hart: It was suggested to me that
> there may be only one person in the
> country, Mr. David Hawkins, who so fully
> understands the PSD program that he could
> carry on an intelligent conversation about
> it for an hour . . .
>
> Mr. Ayres: He will be pleased to have that
> praise.
>
> Senator Hart: He may or may not. If it is
> true, I think it is an abomination . . . .

37. See Jeffrey Pressman and Aaron Wildavsky,
     Implementation (Berekley: University of
     California Press, 1973) and Jones, Clean Air.

38. Melnick, Regulation and the Courts, chapter 4.

39. Ibid., pp. 111-12.

40. Ibid., p. 111.

41. Interviews with EPA officials.

42. See note 14 above.

CHAPTER II

BIRTH OF AN IDEA: PSD FROM 1966 - 1972

This chapter will examine how "significant
deterioration" changed from a concept advocated by a
few officials buried in the Department of Health,
Education and Welfare to a requirement, imposed by
the D.C. District Court on the fledgling
Environmental Protection Agency, to promulgate
regulations that would prevent significant
deterioration of air quality in any portion of the
United States. This development occurred in concert
with the expansion of the Federal role in air
pollution control in the late 1960's and early
1970's. Yet PSD spoke to somewhat different public
concerns than those which were reflected in the
landmark Clean Air Amendments of 1970. Moreover,
PSD's initial consideration in official Washington
was accompanied by a clash between the legal and
technical staff about just what the law both before
and after the 1970 Amendments authorized the Federal
government to do. Finally, the treatment of PSD by
the bureaucracy and the Congress in the late 1960's
and early 1970's laid the groundwork for the
successful suit against the EPA by the Sierra Club
in 1972. This suit forced the Federal government to
be specific about what had, until then, been a vague
statement of desirable social policy. However, the
suit did not "invent" PSD as is often claimed. The
"invention" of the policy had been underway for many
years.

Round 1:   Emissions Standards and Air Quality

The goal of keeping clean air clean has probably
occurred to anyone who has ever looked around on a
clear day. Its immediate appeal is aesthetic, but
it also is connected to a basic American belief
that technological solutions to social problems can
be found.[1] According to this belief, for any
industrial activity which causes pollution, there
ought to be some form of technology which could
reduce or eliminate it given the will to develop and
apply the technology.

However, there is little evidence of organized
thinking in the Federal government about clean air
areas (as opposed to those where air was already
dirty) until the mid-1960's. Such thinking first
appeared as part of an ongoing dispute between
President Johnson's Department of Health, Education,
and Welfare and the Senate Subcommittee on Air and
Water Pollution, chaired by Senator Edmund Muskie.

In 1966, the Johnson Administration developed
legislation which would have established national
standards for permissible emissions of air pollution
from different types of industrial operations (e.g.,
power plants, steel furnaces and coke ovens, etc.).
This legislation was prepared in the Department of
Health, Education and Welfare, which at that time
was responsible for national air pollution control
programs under the Clean Air Act of 1963. White
House staff members, particularly President
Johnson's special assistant Joseph Califano,
initiated and took a keen interest in the
development of this legislation. Vernon McKenzie,
head of what was then called the National Center for
Air Pollution Control in HEW, was the chief sponsor
of this approach to controlling air pollution.
William Goodman of the HEW General Counsel's office
also participated in developing the proposed
legislation.[2]

However, this approach (which will be referred
to below as the "emissions standards approach") did
not sit well on Capitol Hill, particularly with the

Muskie Subcommittee. At the Third National
Conference on Air Pollution, Muskie clearly and
forcefully announced his opposition to an approach
which focused on emissions standards for particular
industries, saying that, "With the exception of
moving sources of pollution [for example,
automobiles], I do not favor fixed national
emissions standards for individual sources of
pollution." What Muskie did favor was an approach
which focused on <u>ambient</u> standards, set in
accordance with criteria to be developed by HEW.
Ambient standards referred not to concentrations of
air pollution given off by a particular industrial
operation, but to the concentrations which the
individual emissions from many such operations would
produce in the ambient air. Muskie suggested that a
more aggressive ambient standards approach would
improve the air pollution control efforts going on
at that time.

> "We need to set a national clean air goal
> which says that, as far as it is within our
> control, no emissions will be permitted which
> cause the quality of air to deteriorate below
> acceptable health standards.
> What this suggests is that we no longer
> limit our efforts by trying simply to set
> emission standards on a plant-by-plant basis,
> hoping that the result will be reduced air
> pollution.
> This will require a reorientation of our
> efforts. Frankly, I think one of the
> shortcomings of our air pollution control
> program to date has been our failure to move
> ahead on the development of air quality
> criteria. Such criteria need to go beyond
> questions of clinical injury or gross insults
> from specific pollutants. They need to include
> considerations of subtle, long-term effects of
> pollutants on our health and welfare."[3]

Muskie's proposal was to use national
"criteria," which showed the adverse health effects
resulting from ambient concentrations of air

pollution, to set ambient air quality standards
which could be applied in "meteorological airsheds."
Once criteria were developed, and standards set,
<u>then</u> emissions limits could be established for
sources in an airshed to insure the attainment of
the ambient standards. Since, in Muskie's view,
"community or State jurisdictions bear little or no
relationship to the geographic spread of air
pollution," then "effective regional institutions"
would have to be developed which overcame the
limitations of present arrangements.[4]

In the abstract, the focus on <u>air quality</u>
criteria and standards had one major political
advantage over a focus on emissions standards. As
Senator Muskie was to explain later, ambient
criteria and standards, based on health effects,
allowed those in favor of air pollution control to
point to specific health benefits from controlling
down to a certain level.

> "The health basis has never been challenged
> on the floor--so it's been a useful political
> tool . . . The big struggle . . . was the notion
> that you couldn't move any faster than was
> economically or technologically feasible. And
> both of these are peculiarly within the control
> of the industry that is being regulated."[5]

In other words, criteria which showed harmful
health effects at low pollutant concentrations might
lead to stringent standards, which in turn might
lead to more stringent pollution controls than might
otherwise have been politically achievable using
technology-based standards.

In the consideration of legislation by Congress
in 1967, it quickly became apparent that the Muskie
opposition to the emissions standards approach
effectively killed any chance it might have had of
being established as law.[6] One internal result of
this within HEW was Vernon MacKenzie's replacement.
Though the exact reasons are unclear, his aggressive
support for national emissions standards appeared to
have damaged his relations with the Muskie
Committee, and been a factor in his being "kicked

upstairs" to a Deputy's job. MacKenzie's
replacement at the National Center for Air Pollution
Control (soon to be renamed the National Air
Pollution Control Administration, or NAPCA) was Dr.
John T. Middleton of California. Dr. Middleton was
more supportive of the air quality
criteria/standards approach favored by Senator
Muskie, and quickly established a close working
relationship with the Senate committee staff.[7]

Round 2:   Air Quality Criteria and Air Quality Standards

The 1967 Amendments to the Clean Air Act,
otherwise known as the Air Quality Act of 1967,
passed Congress and were signed by President Johnson
on November 21, 1967. They followed the approach
laid out by Senator Muskie in every significant
respect.[8]

Like most legislation, the Air Quality Act of
1967 contained an opening preamble stating the
findings and purposes of the legislation. Such
preambles generally exist to lay out the broad goals
set for the law, with the specifics which follow
representing Congress' more detailed directions for
what it wants. However, one element in the preamble
of the 1967 Act, section 101(b), would later take on
a greater importance. It read:

> The purposes of this title are: (1) to protect
> and enhance the quality of the nation's air
> resources so as to promote the public health and
> welfare and the productive capacity of its
> population . . .

The 1967 Act had added the words "and enhance
the quality of" to the existing language of the 1963
Clean Air Act. From the context of the bill and its
accompanying committee reports, it appeared that

this "purpose" addition was intended to reinforce
the authority contained in the Act for State and
local governments, or HEW, to require improvements
in air quality in areas where the air was dirtier
than the ambient standards set for the area.[9]

There is no indication that this phrase had any
special meaning to the authors of the bill at the
time it was drafted. The only reference in the 1967
Senate report to the problem of preventing
deterioration of (as opposed to forcing improvement
of) air quality is in a section which discusses the
potential environmental problems associated with
economic growth. In this reference, the Senate
report states:

> The fact that an area is not now a problem
> area will not mean that controls will never be
> required. When the air quality of any region
> deteriorates below the level required to protect
> health and welfare, the Secretary is required to
> designate that region for the establishment of
> air quality standards, enforceable by the
> Federal Government if the states fail to act.[10]

This suggests only that the process established by
the 1967 Act was expected to handle problems of
growth as well as clean up existing polluted areas.

Implementing the Air Quality Act of 1967

The 1967 Air Quality Act was doomed almost from
the time it was passed.[11] In particular, it quickly
became clear that the structure established by the
1967 Act was cumbersome at best. Dissatisfaction
with this structure was expressed at Congressional
oversight hearings in the years between 1967 and
1970.[12]

Officials at NAPCA, however, struggled to
implement the provisions of the 1967 Act, though

many regarded it as an "awful, unworkable" piece of
legislation."[13] In brief, the 1967 Act required that
a four step process occur before actual emissions
standards could be established for sources of
pollution in a given area. The first step was the
designation of air quality control regions (AQCR's)-
-areas of the country "necessary to provide adequate
implementation of air quality standards." This was
interpreted to mean areas of the country which, in
the judgment of NAPCA, were experiencing air
pollution problems. They could lie entirely within
a single state or include portions of two or more
states. Though the political problems of such an
approach were recognized, it was hoped that while
air pollution "didn't respect state lines," it could
be usefully dealt with by looking at meteorological
airsheds and assuming relatively little pollutant
transfer among the airsheds.[14] Yet for this approach
to succeed, NAPCA would have had to create
institutions of regional government. This proved to
be difficult, especially in interstate areas, with
the result that the designation process was much
delayed.

At the same time as it was trying to designate
AQCR's, NAPCA was struggling to develop the air
quality criteria required by the 1967 Act. These
criteria were not in themselves legally binding, but
were to serve as guides for areas designated as
AQCR's to use in adopting their own air quality
control standards. The Clean Air Act of 1963 had
contained the initial requirement for the
development of "criteria documents," though their
purpose under that statute was mainly to catalogue
effects, with no particular action required to
follow from the documents.[15] An initial document on
sulfur oxides had been issued in early 1967, but the
1967 Act required its revision, largely for
political reasons.[16]

Once air quality control regions were designated
and criteria documents developed, the third step in
the process was for the affected area to "adopt,
after public hearings, ambient air quality standards
applicable to any designated air quality control
region . . ." Within 180 days after adopting air

quality standards, a state was also to adopt "a plan for the implementation, maintenance, and enforcement of such standards."[17]

Air quality standards were supposed to differ significantly from air quality criteria. In Dr. Middleton's words (which the Senate and House Committees both wrote into their reports), the criteria "describe the effects that can be expected to occur whenever and wherever the ambient air level of a particular pollutant reaches or exceeds a specific figure for a specific time period."[18] In contrast, air quality standards, though expressed similarly as a concentration of pollution per volume of air, were fundamentally different legal creatures. They were "prescriptive," and set "pollutant levels that cannot be exceeded during a specific time in a specific geographic area." As such, they were to be "an expression of public policy rather than scientific findings . . . influenced not only by a concern for health or welfare, but also by economic, social, and technological considerations." The Senate report went on to assert that "protection of health should be considered a minimum requirement, and wherever possible standards should be established which enhance the quality of the environment."[19]

Since the air quality standards were to apply throughout discrete (in theory) meteorological airsheds, and since they were as much "policy choice" as science, they could clearly differ from one area to another. Presumably, some level deemed acceptable by HEW "to protect health" would serve as a baseline for approval, but any more stringent air quality standard was not only acceptable, but was encouraged by the language of the Senate report and explicitly sanctioned by §109 of the 1967 Act.

However, to speak of an air quality standard as legally binding missed an important connecting step. Since air quality worse than a given standard resulted from emissions above some acceptable level, then clearly control of air quality could only be achieved by control of emissions. Thus, the approach of the 1967 Act led eventually back to the question of emission controls, yet by a circuitous

route. Only after the complicated process of area
designation, criteria development, and standard
setting was completed could a State or local agency
focus on what emissions controls would be required
to achieve air quality consistent with the ambient
standards "within a reasonable time."[20] These
emission limits were to be a part of the
"implementation plan" adopted by the State, local or
regional organization designated as the responsible
actor in the air quality control region. HEW would
assist in plan development by providing guidelines
on possible control techniques, but the initiative
was to be with State and local governments.

Charles Jones has described the 1967 Act as "an
effort . . . to <u>create</u> national standards from the
ground up . . . based on another vision of how a
federal system should work. In this vision, regions
would be identified that made sense in terms of air
quality, with traditional jurisdictional boundaries
being ignored if necessary."[21] This approach created
problems almost immediately in trying to implement
the Act, in that it placed a tremendous burden of
responsibility on State and local agencies to carry
out complex and controversial standard setting and
enforcement responsibilities which they had never
assumed before.

NAPCA and the 1969 "Guidelines"

Officials within NAPCA knew that, given the
complex structure of the 1967 Act, some sort of
further guidance on the development of the standards
and implementation plans called for in the Act would
be needed. The purpose of this guidance was to
interpret the requirements of the Act to the State
and local governments that would have to satisfy the
new Federal requirements.

Work on the guidance commenced in 1968, shortly
after the Act's passage, but it quickly became

controversial. For one thing, as others have noted,
the 1967 Act represented a stage in the
transformation of NAPCA from a "distributive" to a
"regulatory" agency.[22] However, the culture of the
organization did not automatically change in concert
with the new Act. NAPCA in the late 1960's
experienced conflict among several competing
perspectives in the organization. One group, headed
by Thomas Williams, emphasized public information,
awareness, and participation as the most effective
way for NAPCA to proceed in building support for the
broad goal of reducing air pollution. A second
group, headed initially by Smith Griswold and later
by William Megonnell, argued that a more vigorous
use of the abatement conference provisions of the
Clean Air Act was needed to compel compliance. Yet
a third group argued that the provision of technical
support to State and local air pollution agencies
was, over time, the most effective way to bring
about improvements in air quality. Dr. John
Middleton, the head of NAPCA in the 1967-70 period,
appears to have been sympathetic to both the public
information and the technical support arguments. He
was less sympathetic to the arguments of the
abatement conference advocates, who fell out of
official favor at this time.[23]

These splits within NAPCA were compounded by a
dispute between NAPCA officials and officials in the
Office of General Counsel (OGC) in HEW. HEW
attorneys in the Office of General Counsel had
played a strong role in drafting the original
Johnson Administration proposal for a national
emissions standards bill, and felt rebuffed when
this approach was rejected by Senator Muskie's
subcommittee.[24] Personality conflicts appear to have
exacerbated the tension between HEW-OGC and NAPCA
officials.[25]

In brief, the dispute between the two offices
focused on the nature of the authority granted to
NAPCA by the 1967 Act. Attorneys in HEW-OGC pushed
for NAPCA to prepare an enforceable guideline which
would have put more teeth in the provisions of the
Air Quality Act which required approval of State
plans by the Secretary of HEW. Under this approach,

State plans inconsistent with the provisions of a
very specific guideline would have been found
inadequate: this would have initiated the complex
procedures in the Act which in theory could have led
to Federal promulgation of standards.[26] NAPCA
officials, in contrast, favored an approach which
relied heavily on a combination of "voluntary" State
actions and a public education campaign designed to
encourage State officials to adopt relatively
stringent air quality standards. In the view of
these officials, the entire philosophy of the 1967
Act was based upon a premise of State action, and
the idea of an enforceable guideline leading to a
Federal promulgation was anathema to this premise.
Instead, a public information unit was established
in NAPCA to disseminate information about the
effects of air pollution and to encourage attendance
at the public hearings which the 1967 Act required
before air quality standards could be adopted.[27]
     The protracted battle between these two groups
ultimately resulted in a NAPCA publication entitled
"Guidelines for the Development of Air Quality
Standards and Implementation Plans" in May, 1969.
The "Guidelines" laid out the requirements of the
Air Quality Act, drawing heavily on the reports of
the Senate and House Committees for explanatory
language where it was available. NAPCA described
its purpose as "to furnish state governments
guidelines in performing the functions assigned to
them under the [1967 Air Quality] Act." However,
while the document spoke of "steps that State
governments are expected to take" and
recommendations for States to follow in developing
standards and plans "that can be considered
consistent" with the Act, the "Guidelines" had no
legal status and very carefully avoided any mention
of what consequences would befall a State which
failed to act in accordance with their provisions.
The closest the "Guidelines" came to doing so was
the observation that the 1967 Act authorized HEW "to
take steps to insure adoption of appropriate air
quality standards" if the State failed to do so.
The tool available to the HEW Secretary was "to
establish or designate a planning commission for

this purpose." However, the "Guidelines" were quick
to note that such action would be taken "only where
there is evidence that one or more of the states
involved is not making satisfactory progress toward
establishment of standards."[28]

This hesitant, vague language is typical of the
1969 NAPCA Guidelines. The HEW-OGC attorneys were
critical of NAPCA for issuing these guidelines,
arguing that they had little practical regulatory
value.[29] On the other hand, the responsible NAPCA
officials do not appear to have thought of
themselves as "regulators" in the sense of being
personally responsible for the adoption of legally
enforceable, source specific rules. In fact, the
adoption of such a set of rules would have been
quite alien to much of NAPCA's culture at that time.

The "Guidelines" in fact had little practical
utility except that they did repeat and reinforce
the 1967 Act's requirement that States hold public
hearings on the proposed ambient standards to be
adopted in each control region.[30] It is likely that
the Guidelines would have passed unnoticed into
bureaucratic history when the 1967 Air Quality Act
was superseded by the 1970 Clean Air Amendments.
However, one paragraph in the Guidelines was to
achieve a status which its authors did not expect at
the time. It is worth repeating in full.

> "In addition, as indicated earlier in this
> chapter, an explicit purpose of the Act is to
> protect and enhance the quality of the Nation's
> air resources. Air quality standards which,
> even if fully implemented, would result in
> significant deterioration of air quality in any
> substantial portion of a air quality control
> region clearly would conflict with this
> expressed purpose of the law."[31] [emphasis added]

No one at NAPCA had any specific idea what this
paragraph meant. It was crafted by an Assistant
Commissioner of NAPCA whose responsibility it was to
get the Guideline out regardless of the internal
bureaucratic controversy within NAPCA and with the
HEW lawyers. To be sure, the paragraph was

consistent with the general philosophy that the best
cure for pollution was its prevention. In a more
immediate way, the statement appears to have been
directed at any possible attempts to set air quality
standards which permitted air quality worse than
already existed.[32] Whatever its purpose, though the
paragraph cites as its statutory base the words in
the preamble of the 1967 Air Quality Act, neither
the Act nor either Committee report had made any
mention of "significant deterioration."

Some importance could be attached to the phrase
"in any substantial portion of an air quality
control region." NAPCA officials recognized that,
especially with respect to particulate matter and
sulfur oxides pollution, the boundaries of an air
quality control region (AQCR) would likely encompass
areas with substantially different air quality.
AQCR's were to be designated where air was "dirty;"
however, it was likely that "clean pockets" would
exist within the AQCR. NAPCA officials did not want
the existence of an AQCR and the accompanying
standards to encourage pollution increases in the
clean pockets; thus the phrase in the "Guidelines"
could be construed to apply only to these "clean
pockets." However, this was not clear from the text
of the "Guidelines" themselves.

Though confusing, this paragraph did not seem
very important at the time. For by the time the
"Guidelines" were issued, it was already clear that
the 1967 Act was collapsing under its own cumbersome
weight. Moreover, aided by NAPCA's public
information efforts, public support was beginning to
build behind more aggressive efforts to control air
pollution. While these public concerns were largely
directed towards the cleanup of existing air
pollution problems rather than the prevention of new
ones, they were nevertheless to leave their mark on
the "significant deterioration" question.

Significant Deterioration and the 1970 Amendments

The story of the enactment of the 1970 amendments to the Clean Air Act is well documented elsewhere.[33] The most important point about this activity as it relates to "significant deterioration" is that most observers agree that the issue was not considered in the deliberations over the 1970 Amendments.[34] However, the 1970 Amendments were to be important for "significant deterioration" in three respects. First, by establishing national standards and requirements, they eliminated one of the most cumbersome elements of the 1967 Act and provided a uniform yardstick for distinguishing between "dirty" and "clean" air areas. Secondly, the passage of the 1970 Amendments, combined with the creation of the new Environmental Protection Agency, elevated the visibility within and outside government of environmental regulation and increased both the resources and the legal tools available to regulators who sought to give the new laws real teeth. Finally, the 1970 Amendments contained a new legal experiment -- the "citizen suit" provision -- which greatly eased the burden otherwise faced by outside groups which sought to compel the government to act under the new law.

In the debate over the 1970 Amendments, questions related to significant deterioration were seriously discussed only twice, and both times before the Senate Subcommittee on Air and Water Pollution. The first time was at a hearing on March 17, 1970. The hearing was well attended, with seven Senators present, all of whom appear from the record to have joined actively in the discussion.[35]

The primary witness at this hearing was HEW Undersecretary John Veneman, substituting for Secretary Robert Finch. Veneman's testimony was intended to support the Nixon Administration's 1970 proposal to amend the Clean Air Act. The highlight of this proposal was the replacement of the regional air quality standards mandated by the 1967 Air Quality Act with national ambient air quality

standards set by the Federal government. Moreover,
while the 1967 Air Quality Act had specified that
regional standards were to be achieved "within a
reasonable time," it had failed to place any
intermediate requirements on State or local agencies
to submit implementation plans stating how this
result was to be achieved. The proposed
administration bill would have required a State to
specify its intent to adopt a plan within 90 days of
the bill's passage, and to actually submit such a
plan six months later. In the event that a State
failed to take action to develop and submit a plan,
the Federal government was authorized to develop one
for the area. However, the administration bill did
not propose to change the "reasonable time" criteria
specified in the 1967 Act for actually achieving air
quality levels consistent with the standards.[36]

In addition, the Administration proposed to
establish two new sets of national standards. In a
return to the approach advocated by HEW in 1966,
these standards were to govern <u>emissions</u> rather than
ambient air quality. However, the 1970 proposals
were more restricted in application. One set of
emission standards, known as "New Source Performance
Standards" (NSPS), were to apply to "new, stationary
sources of air pollution that would contribute
substantially to endangering public health or
welfare." A second set of emissions standards,
later referred to as "National Emissions Standards
for Hazardous Air Pollutants" (NESHAP), were to
apply to any stationary source, whether new or
existing, which emitted pollutants which were
"extremely hazardous to health."[37]

One paragraph of Veneman's statement repeated
the provisions of the "Guidelines" on significant
deterioration.

> As you know, one of the express purposes of
> the Clean Air Act is 'to protect and enhance the
> quality of the Nation's air.' Accordingly, it
> has been and will continue to be our view that
> implementation plans that would permit
> significant deterioration of air quality in any
> area would be in conflict with this provision.

We shall continue to expect states to maintain air of good quality where it now exists.[38]

Later in the statement, he repeated this paragraph almost word for word, adding, for emphasis, that "we do not intend to condone backsliding." He also stated that "if an area has air quality which is better than the national standards, they would be required to stay there and not pollute the air further, even though they may be below national standards."[39]

These were strong statements. They vigorously expressed the position taken by NAPCA in the 1969 "Guidelines," which is surprising in light of the opposition to this provision with the HEW Office of General Counsel. One possible explanation for this can be found in the process by which Veneman's testimony was prepared and approved. While NAPCA had the lead in preparing this testimony, it, like all other testimony, was screened by the Legislative Division of HEW-OGC prior to being released for delivery. In this case, it appears that the staff in the Legislative Division who did the screening were relatively inexperienced in the subtleties of the debate between NAPCA and HEW-OGC on the importance of the significant deterioration issue. Consequently, no one who looked at the statement had any reason to think that these phrases signified anything other than support for a concept, unassailable in principle, that areas with relatively clean air should keep it clean. This is consistent with the overall lack of attention and thought which senior officials gave at that time to the "significant deterioration" question. However, the practical consequence of this lack of review was that NAPCA officials were able to get their opinion on significant deterioration included as a position of the HEW Secretary without his being aware of what was happening. As one official later noted, "We had a lot of fun with Finch."[40]

Veneman's statement provoked considerable questioning from the Senators in attendance at the hearing. Unfortunately, this questioning was marred by confusion among the Senators about whether

ambient standards, ambient criteria, or emissions
standards were the subject of discussions at any
given time.

Senator Muskie, the chief advocate of the
ambient criteria/standards approach, opened the
discussion on this point by questioning Veneman
about whether State and local agencies would be able
to set air quality standards more stringent than
those of the Federal government. He criticized the
Administration proposal because it would not require
public hearings on the national ambient standards.
Such hearings, in Muskie's view, were needed "to
screw up the local courage, to stiffen the standard
as it may be necessary in a community . . ."
Veneman replied that States would always have the
freedom to set more stringent air quality standards
if they desired to do so, but that the focus of
public participation would be shifted from debating
levels of air quality to discussing the
implementation plan by which this air quality was to
be achieved. Muskie responded by noting his view
that "standards" included the implementation plan,
which provoked an extended and confused discussion
of the difference between air quality criteria, air
quality standards, and plans. Muskie's statement
precisely matched the contorted interpretations of
"standards" which NAPCA had been forced to adopt
under the 1967 Air Quality Act.[41]

Muskie again and again returned to the question
of "the machinery or the process of setting higher
standards by the States." Undersecretary Veneman
and Charles Johnson, Administrator of HEW's
Environmental Health Service (parent agency of NAPCA
at that time) responded that the setting of national
ambient standards would not restrict States from
setting more stringent ambient standards if they so
desired. This did not satisfy Senator Muskie, who
said that by asking only for implementation of
national standards in the law, "you open up the
possibility that the States may be satisfied with
something less than they ought to be in the given
problem area." In Muskie's opinion, "a loophole here
needs to be closed."[42]

Senator John Sherman Cooper of Kentucky, the
ranking Republican member of the Committee, picked
up on this line of questioning. After stating his
opinion that the idea of national ambient standards
"had value," and would "set a level below which no
region in the country could pollute the air," Cooper
asked whether "there might be other areas in the
country where higher standards could be
established." When Veneman affirmed that this could
occur, Cooper asked whether criteria could still be
provided to allow areas to set higher ambient air
quality standards. Veneman replied that he thought
that national standards themselves would be "tough
enough standards," though he did suggest a
"maintenance of effort" provision so that "a state
or locality that is above the national minimum
standards that were adopted would not be permitted
to go below what they have presently in effect."[43]
Senator Muskie reentered the hearing at this
point, and the questioning moved on to other topics.
The subject of whether some areas might be subject
to "different" standards came up only once more in
this hearing. In the middle of a series of
questions over whether public hearings would be
required before national ambient standards would be
issued, the following exchange occurred between
Senator Caleb Boggs of Delaware and Undersecretary
Veneman.

> Senator Boggs: In other words, a cement plant
> near Wilmington, Delaware might have to meet
> more rigid requirements than a cement plant in a
> rural area of Missouri in order that the area's
> air meets the national air quality standards.
> There wouldn't be any comparison in the
> emissions levels each would have to achieve; is
> that right?
> Mr. Veneman: Unless it is in excess of national
> standards.
> Senator Boggs: As the air in Delaware or any
> industrial area might be already loaded up with
> pollutants, a plant in a rural county in
> Missouri might be allowed to emit a whole lot of

things that you couldn't emit in Delaware; that
would be the difference, wouldn't it?
Mr. Veneman: I think that there would be
different judgmental factors that go in. I
think you would have to recognize there would be
national emission standards for certain
stationary facilities as defined in the bill. It
wouldn't be all of them.
Senator Boggs: Therefore, there wouldn't be any
uniform restrictions on emitters under the
national air quality standards. Their emission
levels would depend on their location in the
country?
Mr. Veneman: That is true as to old plants,
particularly, unless they emitted extremely
hazardous pollutants. The old ones would all be
controlled by the state. They would implement
and enforce.[44]

In this brief exchange, Senator Boggs and
Undersecretary Veneman captured both the tension
between the emissions standards and air quality
approaches and a problem that was to become a focal
point in the debate over "significant
deterioration." An emission standard approach could
be applied with relative uniformity across the
country; however, at least in theory, such uniform
standards would result in overcontrol in some places
and undercontrol in others as compared to the level
of control needed to produce air quality which would
protect health. However, though it was not brought
out in this hearing, it would quickly become
apparent that (again in theory) the ambient
standards approach would discriminate against
already "dirty" areas, by requiring both existing
and new sources in such areas to put on more
stringent -- and costly -- air pollution controls.
Some of these implications came out at a
subsequent hearing held by the Senate Subcommittee
on May 27th. This hearing was held in executive
(closed) session; a transcript was not released
until July 8th. Instead of the entire HEW policy
bureaucracy present at the earlier hearing, only
NAPCA Commissioner Middleton and his special

assistant Irwin Auerbach represented the Executive
Branch; they presented no formal testimony which
would have had to be cleared. While six Senators
were present for the hearing, Senators Muskie and
Eagleton dominated the discussion to a much greater
degree than in March.

Senator Muskie, in particular, was more focused
in his concerns about ambient standards.

> I would like to start by outlining what I
> think troubles all of us about the concept of
> national standards...the question is whether
> these areas which are above (the national
> standard) are required only to come down to that
> standard -- regardless of local requirements --
> and any areas which are below that standard in
> effect are permitted to allow pollution up to
> that standard, whatever it is."

> "The objective that we all have clearly in
> mind is to see that there be some acceptable
> national uniformity of approach, with variations
> reflecting local conditions."[45]

Muskie clearly assumed that the regional
standard setting process of the 1967 Air Quality Act
would produce standards better than existing air
quality--in some cases much better--because of
public pressure. This process, however, had been
discredited both because of the time it took to set
these standards and because the standards, in the
absence of a specified means to achieve them, meant
very little. In reaction, the Administration,
seizing upon the popularity of the environmental
movement as expressed in events such as "Earth Day,"
had proposed to speed up the process by both setting
national ambient standards and by resurrecting
national emissions standards, albeit only for
certain new sources or hazardous pollutants.
Muskie, however, believed that national ambient
standards would have a "levelling" effect, and that
polluting industries would be able to use lowest
common denominator national standards to override
local desires for cleaner air. The burden of proof

would be shifted to local project opponents to demonstrate why any further control beyond this level was reasonable.

Reasonable as this argument may have seemed in theory, in 1970 Muskie's approach had shown few benefits, as the practical problems of getting regional standards and implementation plans had proved overwhelming. Moreover, despite the appeal of the regional air quality standards approach to Muskie, the Clean Air Act at this time was undergoing what Charles Jones has referred to as "speculative augmentation." Mounting public concern over air pollution, combined with a savage attack by the Ralph Nader organization which threatened his prospects as a Presidential candidate, Muskie found himself engaged in a serious campaign of "one-upmanship" with both the Administration and the House committees reviewing the 1970 Amendments.[46]

John Middleton was one of Senator Muskie's allies in this effort. Middleton's arrival at NAPCA in 1966-1967 had coincided with the defeat of the national emission standards bill. Relations between Middleton and Muskie, as well as with Muskie's chief staff aide, Leon Billings, were by all accounts close.[47] This was to be reflected in the May 27th hearing.

After Senator Muskie's opening remarks, Dr. Middleton engaged several of the Senators in a colloquy over just how national ambient standards would work. Muskie continued his persistent questioning about whether the standards were "going to be tough enough in a lot of places" and would "permit pollutants up to that level across the country." Dr. Middleton responded to this concern by asserting that the national standards would protect "against the minimum adverse health effect." Muskie finally got to the point.

> Senator Muskie: What you are saying in that language is that this would be public health effects standards?
> Dr. Middleton: Yes. Let's take the example of the standards being adopted for sulfur oxides. The standard being adopted by the States which

are acceptable to the Secretary are less than
0.04 parts per million (p.p.m.) as an annual
average...The State standard in the Denver area
is 0.009 p.p.m. as an annual average, but other
states are adopting standards that are higher.

The difference in standards largely reflects
the differences in public sentiment, attitude,
for example, recreation being particularly
important in the State of Colorado . . .

While States must have standards that are
protective of health, they are free to do
better.   It depends on what they want in their
particular area.
Senator Muskie: Let me ask you this based on
the .009 and .03.   Which of those figures would
be the national health effects standard?   Would
it be the .009 or the .03?
Dr. Middleton: I would say that insofar as the
national air quality standards concept is
described if it were to be based on health, we
would be likely to promulgate a standard of .03
p.p.m.
Senator Muskie: That would not protect health
in Colorado.
Dr. Middleton: It would protect the public
health in Colorado.   It would protect public
health in every community.
Senator Muskie: Let me put it another way.
Would the national health effects standards be
the one which would be the lowest common
denominator? . . .
Dr. Middleton: The number that would be applied
would have to be protective of health
everywhere.
Senator Muskie: So it would be more stringent
in many areas of the country than it needs to be
in terms of those areas.
Dr. Middleton: I can't answer you in regard to
a specific area.[48]

Muskie's discussion continued to focus on health
based standards.   NAPCA staff intervened by pointing
out that the very low Denver standards were based on
considerations other than public health--e.g., the

desire for very clean air, and the relatively "small
use of high sulfur fuel."[49]

The questioning then turned to other topics,
including the Administration's proposal for national
emissions standards. Middleton observed that the
goal of these standards was for large new pollution
sources to be "as clean as they can be." Muskie
asked whether a plant which met such emissions
standards could be excused from violating ambient
standards. Middleton responded that the ambient
standards would prevail, and that the purpose of the
new source emissions standards was "to assure that
everybody must meet the same performance
requirements for new plants wherever they are built,
that requirement being the best possible control, so
that we begin to do more than just talk about
protection and enhancement of air quality."[50]

Dr. Middleton returned to this theme of
"protection and enhancement" in response to Senator
Muskie's question about whether new sources of air
pollution could delay attainment of air quality
standards. Middleton strongly endorsed the NAPCA
"Guidelines" philosophy, saying that "the implementation plans that we expect from the States, for
which NAPCA has issued guidelines, must have an
accountability for areas that now have acceptable
air and what plans are being laid to keep it that
way." Middleton did allow that "perhaps there is
some desirability in having a statement, in the
implementation sections of the Act, to emphasize the
overall policy of the act, namely, the protection
and enhancement of the air resource as a goal"
[emphasis added]. Still, Middleton asserted that
air quality standards, emissions standards, and
implementation plans were "all designed to provide
air quality protective of health and the flexibility
for making decisions on whether a region wants the
air to be just healthful or whether it wants to have
a fully liveable environment."[51]

Middleton, with encouragement from the Senators,
was breaking new ground. This discourse with the
Senators ended with Middleton making a strong
assertion that if a new plant conflicted with an

area's proposed implementation strategy, the Federal
government would not allow the plant to be built.

   Dr. Middleton: All implementation plans must
   take into account the normal growth pattern in
   the area. In some cases, these plans will not
   allow for the introduction of major new
   pollution sources. These decisions will be made
   as part of the implementation plan approved and
   covered in our monitoring of progress under the
   plan.
   Senator Muskie: Unless the procedure for
   handling these licenses includes you, you are
   going to be dealing with a lot of horses gone
   before you can lock the door.
   Senator Eagleton: Mr. Chairman, if he is
   included he has the responsibility to protect.
   Is the Federal Government to issue a Federal
   order for every new plant built in this country?
   Dr. Middleton: No. At most, only for those
   industries covered by national emissions
   standards.
   Senator Eagleton: In a region that is already
   "over sulfured," if it adds one microcosm of new
   sulfur, it is further endangering that region.
   You would want to stop it?
   Dr. Middleton: Every implementation plan is
   subject to the Department's review and approval.
   Any alterations in that plan are subject to
   review and approval.
        So, in my mind, there is not any doubt as to
   who gets to look at them.
   Senator Muskie: I think that all they will say
   is, "We have looked at this and it does not
   change the implementation plan, so we don't have
   to take this to Washington."
   Dr. Middleton: We will have news for them. . .
   Senator Muskie: In your concept of the
   legislation, do you have a clear handle on the
   construction of new powerplants, new industries
   of any kind in these control regions?
   Dr. Middleton: We would expect, Mr. Chairman,
   to have State and local jurisdictions make a
   judgment for our review.

Senator Muskie: It would still have to come to
you as a matter of routine if you are to have
effective control? If local agencies decide
whether or not you are to review their decision,
that gives you no control.
Dr. Middleton: If it is that loose, that is not
the way we want it, and had not intended it that
way.[52]

As Senator Muskie left the hearing, he thanked
Dr. Middleton for a "very informative, educational
afternoon." Indeed it had been. The exchanges
between the Senators and Dr. Middleton laid out a
new framework for Federal/State/local government
relationships in the area of regulating construction
and land use--one which would involve prior approval
by the Federal government before construction of at
least some new sources of air pollution would be
allowed. Though this is only one example of the
overall trend toward greater Federal authority in
the development of the 1970 Clean Air Act, it is
striking in that it represents the first real
articulation of the view that the Federal government
could exercise prior restraint upon new construction
in furthering air quality goals.

The departure of the Senators did not end this
hearing, as the Subcommittee staff remained behind
to continue questioning Dr. Middleton. As their
exchange is recorded in the record, it documents a
well-known Washington phenomenon: the symbiotic
Congressional staff/agency official relationship.

This record contains the most explicit evidence
that the concept of "significant deterioration"
received at least staff attention at the time the
1970 Amendments were considered. One staff member
suggested that the authority of States or localities
to "require more stringent control than the national
standard" should be explicitly written into the act;
Dr. Middleton agreed that "local decisions are
necessary on what kind of environment they wish to
have."[53] Another staff member asked whether land use
controls should be required to achieve air quality
and offered to include such a requirement "as a
guideline in the development of implementation

plans.[54] Then, immediately following, came this
question:

> Mr. Brayman: Would it be practical to require
> that a nondegradation plan be incorporated into
> every State's implementation plan? To put it
> another way, each State would have to establish
> a policy of nondegradation in certain areas.
> Dr. Middleton: Since the Clean Air Act states,
> in section 101, that it is national policy to
> protect and enhance air quality, I think it
> would be very appropriate to have this policy
> reiterated in the other sections, where action
> is prescribed.
>
> I am sort of against the word,
> 'nondegradation.' I think there is a more
> positive way to say it--protection and
> enhancement.[55]

It would be unproductive to infer too much from
this brief exchange. At least some of the
committee, members and staff, had some concern that
the promulgation of national standards, based on
health effects, would undercut the more stringent
regional standards already approved in some areas
which were based more on public outcry than on
demonstrable health threats. As a practical matter
this fear was wellfounded.[56] However, it must be
recalled that the slow pace of establishing regional
standards contributed to the push for 1970
Amendments. Also, there is a telling point in Dr.
Middleton's response; without answering the question
("would it be practical"), he called for some
reiteration of the policy of §101 in other sections
of the Act, "where action is prescribed." This
acknowledged that while the words of §101 set forth
a bold philosophy of air resource management
and conservation, they had no practical meaning in
the statute absent a more fully prescribed course of
action. This point would be the subject of a heated
dispute in the later debate over significant
deterioration.

The Senate report on the 1970 Amendments which
emerged from Public Works Committee was a remarkable

piece of work. Its most memorable phrase was the
assertion "that existing sources of pollutants
should meet the standards of the law or be closed
down, and in addition that new sources should be
controlled to the maximum extent possible to prevent
atmospheric emissions."[57] Land use planning,
transportation controls, automobile emissions
control, direct Federal enforcement and citizen
suits were only a few of the dramatic policies
envisioned in this far-reaching report. Moreover,
the report and the bill specified that areas had to
meet the national standards within three years from
the approval of implementation plans. When combined
with deadlines for the establishment of national
ambient air quality standards (NAAQS) and the
approval of implementation plans, and the
requirement that States submit the plans within nine
months from the time the NAAQS were established, the
Senate report established a national deadline of
1975 for all areas of the country to have healthy
air.[58]

The report also spoke to the concerns about
regional air quality standards by assuring "an
opportunity for a region to adjust standards."[59] The
language of the bill was somewhat stronger,
requiring each State to "consider adoption of
ambient air quality standards more stringent than
the national ambient air quality standards" at a
public hearing.[60] However, the Senate bill endorsed
the Administration's proposal for national ambient
air quality standards based on health (hereafter
referred to as "NAAQS") "to expedite the
establishment and implementation of ambient air
quality standards.[61]

In this discussion of the ambient standards,
there occurs the only discussion of "deterioration"
in the report. Interestingly, the paragraph in which
the discussion occurs starts off by noting that the
Senate bill "does not require attainment of the air
quality goals within a specified time period."
(This would change by the time of the final bill.)
Nevertheless, the report states, "progress in this
direction should be made as rapidly as possible."
The report goes on to note that "in areas where air

pollution levels are already relatively low, the
attainment and maintenance of these goals should not
require an extended time period."[62]
With this as preamble, the report stated:

> In areas where current air pollution levels are
> already equal to, or better than, the air
> quality goals, the Secretary should not approve
> any implementation plan which does not provide,
> to the maximum extent practicable, for the
> continued maintenance of such ambient air
> quality. Once such national goals are
> established, deterioration of air quality should
> not be permitted except under
> circumstances where there is no available
> alternative. Given the various alternative
> means of preventing and controlling air
> pollution--including the use of the best
> available control technology, industrial
> processes, and operating practices--and care in
> the selection of sites for new sources, land use
> planning and traffic controls--deterioration
> need not occur.[63]

This section of the Senate report resembles the
NAPCA "Guidelines," in that while it is bold it
contains no guidance on how to prevent deterioration
other than asserting that with technology and
"planning", deterioration "need not occur." This
assertion seems to have been based on the exchange
between Middleton and the Committee staff. The
paragraph itself is not clear on whether all
deterioration was to be prevented, or just
deterioration which would create air quality worse
than the "national goals." The latter
interpretation seems more persuasive, in that the
paragraph occurs as part of the discussion on the
proposed new air quality standards, rather than in
the section dealing with implementation plan, where
measures for carrying out such a requirement might
have been specified. Given the loose understanding
of standards, goals and criteria displayed in the
Committee's hearings, it is hard to say anything
more definitive just what this paragraph was

intended to convey. Yet it is the only reference in
the legislative history of the 1970 Act to the
deterioration question.

Two conflicting explanations have been offered
for why there was no further discussion of
"deterioration" in connection with the 1970
Amendments. Neither has been recorded in any
official manner, and it is probably impossible to
tell which is more nearly correct. Both were
probably at least partly true.

The first explanation is that no further mention
was made of significant deterioration because no one
regarded it as an important issue. Many other
momentous questions were at stake in the 1970
Amendments, and "deterioration" seemed to be a
relatively minor issue when compared to the problems
of cleaning up dirty areas and putting controls on
automobiles. Moreover, NAPCA officials who sat in
on the markup meetings with committee staff during
the summer of 1970, when the Senate report was being
drafted, do not recall that significant
deterioration was ever discussed in a meaningful way
in the committee markups.[64]

The other explanation is that Senate committee
staff members were quite aware of the "significant
deterioration" issue at the time of the 1970
amendments, but deliberately chose not to bring the
issue up. According to this interpretation, the
Senate staff felt that the law already provided
adequately for "significant deterioration" because
of the modification made to Section 101(b) of the
Act in 1967. Moreover, the Senate staff felt in
1970 that the agenda for Act amendments was already
more than full. The Committee and the Congress as a
whole would simply have been unable to address what
"protect and enhance" would mean if it had required
greater detail about just what steps would have to
be taken to prevent "significant deterioration of
air quality" in practice. Therefore, while some
language could be added to the Committee report to
bolster the philosophical position which Dr.
Middleton and NAPCA had taken in the 1969
"Guideline," the Senate staff opposed the addition
of any statutory language to the 1970 Amendments to

strengthen the interpretation of "protect and enhance."[65]

The Senate committee report effectively ended the 1970 discussion of "significant deterioration." There are a few passing references to the concept of protecting clean air areas in the Senate debate. Senator Baker probably made the most thoughtful observation, looking back to the emissions standard/air quality standard debate in 1967. He noted that while "the ambient air concept implies that it is possible or desireable to accept a certain amount of pollution," the emission standard theory contains the implication "that we will not permit a degree of pollution in the atmosphere of those areas that have relatively clean air, which is probably the more idealistic and probably less attainable objective." Baker noted that while in the 1967 Act, "the policy of ambient air quality was adopted and became the law of the land," the 1970 legislation set new precedents by requiring uniform emissions controls on cars regardless of air quality where the cars were used. This, in his judgment, would be "the forerunner of other efforts to establish particular standards for particular sources of pollution into the atmosphere"--a situation already borne out by the provisions of the 1970 Amendments authorizing emissions standards for large new pollution sources and for sources of hazardous pollutants. However, Baker did not mention these provisions explicitly.[66]

All other references to the protection of clean air (as opposed to cleaning up dirty air) in the Senate debate refer to the provisions which would establish emissions standards for new sources. These new source performance standards, or NSPS, were described by Senator Randolph as meant to "insure that when an industry moves into an area with low pollution levels, that this new facility does not appreciably degrade the existing air quality."[67] Earlier in the debate, Senator Dole from Kansas had made essentially the same point, saying that "passage of this bill will assist in remedying the problems which do exist and insure the preservation of the high quality of air Kansas

presently enjoys . . . Under this bill, we can
continue to encourage the location of new industry
in Kansas and other rural unspoiled regions without
fear of polluting the high quality of air found
there.[68]

These general statements add nothing to the
committee's action in reporting S.4358. With the
possible exception of Senator Baker's statement,
they are little more than the standard rhetoric of
almost any Congressional debate. The real argument
over the 1970 Amendments in the Senate was over the
1975 deadline established by the Amendments for
requiring emission controls on cars in the face of
claims by the manufacturers that such controls did
not exist and could not be produced by 1975.[69] None
of the further debate on the 1970 Amendments in
either the Senate or the House further clarified
Congressional intent on air quality deterioration.

Both Senator Muskie and his aide Leon Billings
later stated that the Congress had intended a policy
of "nondegradation," and based their claim on the
1967 change in Section 101(b) of the Clean Air Act
which was affirmed by default in 1970.[70] However,
the legislative history and the recollection of
individuals involved at that time suggest that if
this kind of policy decision was made, it was
certainly not widely advertised. Most of the active
Congressional participants in the debate over the
1970 Amendments had other primary concerns--national
ambient standards with fixed deadlines which would
require major social changes, or technology-forcing
emissions standards for automobiles. In this heady
atmosphere of legislating the impossible, the
concept of nondegradation was unlikely to attract
meaningful attention.

This neglect enabled officials within NAPCA, who
believed in prevention of significant deterioration
as an ideal, to persist in stating that it was an
objective of the Clean Air Act. Such attitudes were
reinforced by the inclusion of the phrase in the
official Administration testimony on the proposed
1970 Amendments, which gave legitimacy to
"significant deterioration" even though no one had
seriously questioned what the phrase meant. NAPCA's

views were reinforced by Senators such as Muskie who
expressed concerned about the effect of national
ambient standards in sanctioning worse air quality
in some parts of the country. These actions by
program advocates in both NAPCA and the Senate
created a basis for the future expansion of a
nondegradation program.

The Aftermath of the 1970 Amendments

     The Senate bill passed by a unanimous vote of
73-0 on September 22, 1970. The House had approved
their version of the bill on June 10th. The
resulting conference was difficult, and focused on
the wisdom of the 1975 deadline for automobile
emissions reductions. In the end legislation
similar to the Senate bill passed both Houses on
December 18th, and was signed into law by President
Nixon on December 31, 1970.[71] "Significant
deterioration" was not discussed in the closing
debates on the Amendments.
     At about the same time, an event occurred which
would have a profound effect on the further
development of policy on significant deterioration.
In July, 1970 President Nixon had proposed the
creation of a new Federal organization, the
Environmental Protection Agency, to consolidate
pollution control authorities which were scattered
across a multitude of Federal agencies. Among other
things, this step served the political need of the
Administration for action in the wake of the massive
Earth Day rallies of 1970. The proposal, presented
to Congress as a reorganization plan, met with no
significant objections and on December 2, 1970, EPA
was established with William D. Ruckelshaus as its
first Administrator.[72] Ruckelshaus had been an
Assistant Attorney General in charge of the Civil
Division of the Justice Department; before that, he
had been majority leader of the Indiana State Senate

and an unsuccessful Republican candidate for the
U.S. Senate in 1968.

This reorganization meant that NAPCA was
transferred into an organization of which it was a
substantially larger component than it had been of
HEW. Moreover, the high visibility given to
environmental issues in 1970 which led to the
passage of the 1970 Clean Air Amendments meant that
NAPCA itself was much more visible than ever before.
These circumstances caused its actions to come under
much closer scrutiny by both the public and, of more
immediate significance, by the senior political
officials of the new EPA. This scrutiny, combined
with the formal legal mandates and deadlines given
to the Administrator of EPA by the 1970 Amendments,
put pressure on NAPCA officials to give greater
meaning to "significant deterioration."

DEVELOPING REGULATIONS FOR STATE PLANS IN 1971

The passage of the 1970 Amendments was a
landmark event. However, President Nixon was
unintentionally prophetic when he remarked upon
signing the bill that the legislation was "only a
beginning."[73] As both EPA and other affected parties
began to implement the new law, many of the issues
which had been glossed over in the push to pass the
Amendments began once again to demand attention.
For "significant deterioration," this would take the
form of charges that EPA had bowed to pressure from
industry to ignore the Act's requirements and result
in an order by the D.C. District Court in May, 1972
that EPA develop regulations within six months to
prevent "significant deterioration."

While the 1970 Amendments did not directly
address significant deterioration, they were one of
three key elements in the events which followed.
The other two were the creation of EPA as a focal
point for environmental activism, and the growth of
sophisticated environmental groups with the desire
and ability to use litigation as an agency-forcing

tool. These factors were interdependent: in the absence of any of the three, it is unlikely that "significant deterioration" would have received the attention it did. Therefore, before moving on to discuss the period between January 1, 1971 and May 31, 1972, a brief description of the three key elements of legal requirements, agency position, and interest-group concern is needed.

Requirements of the 1970 Amendments

    As discussed above, the Clean Air Act contained a number of very specific deadlines by which the new EPA had to take certain actions. The following schedule lays out the key required actions:[74]

Action	Timing
Propose national Ambient Air Quality Standards (NAAQS).	30 days from passage of the Amendments.
Publish final NAAQS.	90 days from proposal.
States submit implementation plans to EPA.	9 months after publication of final NAAQS.
EPA reviews plans and approves or disapproves them.	4 months after plans submitted by states.
If EPA disapproves a state's plan, EPA promulgates its own plan for the state unless the state submits an adequate plan.	6 months from date of disapproval or failure by the state to submit an adequate plan.

All areas of the State attain ambient air quality standards for all pollutants.	3 years from date of EPA approval of the state plan (with a very restrictive provision allowing for an additional two years if the Governor requested it and if the state demonstrated that the necessary technology was not available and that the state was applying all reasonably available alternative means of attaining the standard.)

The "deadline" philosophy of the 1970 Amendments would have been an administrative challenge for a smooth, well-functioning, established agency. To the one-month old EPA, this was asking the impossible. Yet Ruckelshaus felt "for the purposes of Agency credibility, it was important to meet these deadlines." Doing so in the early months of EPA's existence, however, left Ruckelshaus very much dependent on the advice of the NAPCA staff which EPA had inherited from HEW. Moreover, it increased the likelihood that in the rush to meet the deadlines, some of the finer points of what the regulations said and meant were bound to be overlooked.[75]

EPA: New Kid On the Block

As with any new agency, EPA was experiencing both physical and organizational birth pangs. The Agency was scattered in several buildings around Washington, and the diverse components which had been brought together in EPA were still trying to figure out just what their new role should be. EPA had been created, as one writer put it, "on the crest of a wave of public concern over environmental

degradation."[76] Ruckelshaus' task was to translate
the generalized support of mass public opinion into
the kind of effective support by the "attentive
public" which the Agency would need to function
effectively.[77]

While Ruckelshaus deliberately set out to
establish a sense of rapport and mutual trust with
officials such as Middleton who headed up the large
"blocks" of the new EPA, tensions within the new
organization soon became clear. For one thing,
Ruckelshaus felt an early need to establish EPA's
credibility as an agency which would not simply
continue business as usual. This meant, among other
things, taking dramatic actions to enforce pollution
control laws--a step which was alien to the existing
organizational culture within NAPCA. Middleton
himself had been part of the struggle during an
earlier attempt by NAPCA officials to conduct
aggressive (by 1960's standards) enforcement
actions, and the 1967 Air Quality Act had increased
the difficulty of Federal enforcement. Now armed
with the new 1970 Act, EPA's enforcement staff were
looking for opportunities to demonstrate the
Agency's "tough" attitude toward pollution
violations. Yet while most of EPA's dramatic early
enforcement actions were in the water pollution
area, tensions arose quickly between EPA enforcement
officials who wanted dramatic action on the air
front as well, and officials from NAPCA who, while
pleased at the new level of attention being paid to
air pollution control, were not comfortable with the
aggressive posture proposed by enforcement
officials.[78]

Moreover, the new EPA was clearly to be a
regulatory agency. The more traditional forms of
technical assistance, public education, guidance,
conferences, and negotiation on which NAPCA had
traditionally relied were to be replaced by a new
ethos of regulation and litigation. This new
approach substantially enhanced the position of the
attorneys in EPA's new Office of Enforcement and
General Counsel. In contrast to the situation in
HEW, the attorneys now had substantially more access
to and control over agency decision-making

authority, since the form of agency action was more
clearly in the legal realm. In addition, the staff
of this office tended to be young, bright, and
aggressive, and they embraced the activist
philosophy of the new EPA. It was inevitable that
conflicts would arise between these attorneys and
former NAPCA officials.[79]

Environmental Interest Groups: A New Clientele

     As a new agency, EPA was faced with the
traditional interest group, Congressional and
Executive Branch pressures faced by any large
Federal organization. However, EPA's set of
"attentive publics" included a relatively new one--a
collection of public interest groups focusing on
environmental protection. While the origins and
specific interests of these groups varied, they had
collectively helped to generate the popular
enthusiasm behind Earth Day, and had moved to
capitalize on it by setting up more "official"
structures which would enable them to keep close
tabs on EPA's implementation of the new Clean Air
Act. These groups included both units of older
organizations such as the Sierra Club, the National
Audubon Society and the National Wildlife
Federation, as well as organizations founded in the
late 1960's such as the Natural Resources Defense
Council (NRDC) and the Environmental Defense Fund
(EDF).[80]
     Most of these organizations did carry out some
traditional lobbying of Congress to pass desireable
legislation. However the usual lobbying of agency
officials was less important to some groups because
of three legal innovations in the Clean Air Act
which enabled these groups to make extensive use of
the Federal courts to force EPA to take actions
which they favored. First, the specific deadlines
of the Clean Air Act were a great help because, in
specifying exactly what EPA had to do and how long
the Agency had to do it, they set up clear, explicit
criteria for agency failure. Secondly, in what is
know as the "citizen suit" provision, §304 of the

Act gave any person the right to file suit in
Federal court against the Administrator for failure
to meet these deadlines or otherwise perform duties
which were not discretionary in the statute. This
made it easier for environmental groups to
successfully sue EPA, and the likelihood of such
suits increased the pressure on Agency officials to
proceed with regulatory actions required by the
statute in the face of uncertain data or
assumptions. Finally, §307 of the Act required that
all challenges to EPA regulations which were
"nationally applicable" or "based on a determination
of nationwide scope and effect" were to be heard
before the Court of Appeals for the District of
Columbia Circuit (hereafter referred to as the D.C.
Circuit). Proponents of this provision had argued
that it would limit the practice of "court
shopping," and that the D.C. Circuit has relatively
greater expertise in regulatory matters. However,
this provision was highly significant to
environmental groups, industry and EPA because the
D.C. Circuit was widely perceived as more
sympathetic to environmental suits than other
Circuit Courts of Appeal.[81]

This background will help to clarify some of the
forces at work which helped to influence EPA's
actions over the next eighteen months.

EPA'S Actions After January 1, 1971

The first decision which EPA faced under the new
Clean Air Act was the establishment of the new
national ambient air quality standards (NAAQS).
Under the law, EPA had to propose them by January
31, 1971 and publish them by April 30, 1972.

Under these circumstances, and given the self-
imposed constraint of meeting the statutory
deadline, Ruckelshaus had little practical choice
but to accept the recommended levels for the NAAQS

which the NAPCA staff had developed. Reportedly, this situation had two substantial effects on Ruckelshaus' thinking. First, it caused him to recognize the specificity of the Clean Air Act's requirements and the degree to which his flexibility was constrained by the Act. Second, he came to believe that the degree of analysis and preparation which had occurred prior to issuing the standards was substantially inadequate and inconsistent with their potential impact.[82] Therefore, though Ruckelshaus did agree to the NAPCA recommendations on the ambient standards, the seeds of later skepticism were sown.

Ruckelshaus soon had another opportunity to express these views. The next step in the timetable laid out by the 1970 Act was for the States to develop and submit implementation plans by the end of January, 1972. Yet though §110 of the Act contained many specific requirements for these plans, it did not cover all of the necessary details. Therefore, just as NAPCA had done with the 1967 Act, EPA began preparing "guidance" to the States on what these implementation plans should look like.

However, this time there was an important difference. The new Act allowed the EPA attorneys to argue, successfully, that this "guidance" should take the form of regulations promulgated by the Administrator. This prevented the air program from unilaterally issuing "guidance" which had not first been cleared by EPA's Office of General Counsel (OGC). One effect of this procedure was to enable attorneys within EPA to renew the attack upon "significant deterioration."[83]

This question came up quickly. A March 11, 1971 "memorandum of law" from Robert Baum, EPA's Associate General Counsel for Air, to the air program office concluded that the primary and secondary ("welfare") NAAQS, together with the new source performance standards (NSPS) constituted the "maximum practicable" controls which could be applied and that these would satisfy the requirements of the Act. EPA, according to Baum, had no further authority to require air to be any

cleaner; any such authority was expressly reserved
to the States under §116 of the Act.[84]

Notwithstanding this memorandum, the regulations
promulgating the NAAQS on April 30, 1971 contained
the following provision: "standards shall not be
considered in any manner to allow significant
deterioration of existing air quality in any portion
of any State."[85] It may be that EPA's attorneys
accepted this phrase because they did not want to
imply that areas with more stringent standards under
the 1967 Act were automatically forced to raise them
to the level of NAAQS. A more likely explanation is
that in the rush to get the standards out by the
deadline, the phrase was simply not worth arguing
about.

However, at about the same time as the final
NAAQS regulations came out, EPA was proposing the
regulations for the preparation of implementation
plans. These regulations (which will be referred to
below as the "Part 51 regulations" after their
location in volume 40 of the Code of Federal
Regulations), were supposed to have the same effect
as the 1969 "Guidelines." That is, they were
supposed to spell out the details of what the 1970
Amendments actually required States to do in their
implementation plans. In accordance with OGC's
arguments, they were established as formal
regulations rather than informal "guidelines."
However, in a striking difference from the 1969
"Guidelines", the proposed Part 51 regulations were
silent on the question of "significant
deterioration."[86]

The absence of provisions dealing with
"significant deterioration" attracted the attention
of the environmental groups, who argued with EPA
that the failure to include specific requirements to
use "the best available control measures to prevent
degradation of air quality" was contrary to
Congress' intent in passing the 1970 Amendments.
Environmentalists also noted an inconsistency in
EPA's inclusion of a statement on significant
deterioration in its regulations governing the NAAQS
while failing to include one in the Part 51
regulations.[87]

These comments from the environmental groups on
the proposed Part 51 regulations gave air program
officials an opportunity to reinsert the significant
deterioration language before publication of the
final rules. Dr. Middleton's June 28, 1971
memorandum transmitting the air office's final
version of the regulations to the Administrator
indicated that the insertion had been made.

> Environmental groups, in particular, urged that
> EPA establish a non-deterioration policy
> applicable to clean air areas (those places
> where air pollution levels are below national
> secondary ambient air quality standard).
> Accordingly, the regulations have been modified
> to include the following statement, which is
> similar to one that appeared in the Federal
> Register notice setting forth the national
> standards: 'Approval of a plan shall not be
> considered in any manner to allow significant
> deterioration of existing air quality in any
> portion of any State.'
>
> This statement does not go as far as the
> environmental groups would have us go, in that
> it does not oblige the States to have an action
> program to prevent deterioration. In the
> opinion of the General Counsel, the Clean Air
> Act, as amended, does not authorize EPA to
> impose such a requirement...(emphasis added).[88]

John Middleton, who had remained the head of the
air program during the organization of EPA, sent
these regulations forward for Ruckelshaus' signature
on June 28, 1971. However, they were not published
in the Federal Register until August 14, 1971. In
the meantime, the regulations were changed in
several ways. Among these changes was one which
dropped the "significant deterioration" phrase and
replaced it with one which read that nothing in the
Part 51 regulations should be construed to
"encourage a State to prepare, adopt, or submit a
plan which does not provide for the protection and
enhancement of air quality so as to promote the

public health and welfare and productive capacity"--
the very language of Section 101(b)
of the Act which was supposed to be the basis for
the significant deterioration provision.[89]
    This and other changes in the regulations
quickly became the subject of controversy, which
stemmed in part from the context in which the
changes occurred. Apart from the deterioration
issue, the most notable and substantive change from
the June 28th version of the Part 51 regulations was
its treatment of the emissions limitations in an
"Appendix B" to the regulations. Appendix B had
originally been intended as a set of guidelines for
what EPA considered to be "reasonably available
means of attaining the ambient standards." As such,
it amounted to a presumptive set of national
emissions standards for areas with poor air quality.
The August 14th regulations "recast" Appendix B "as
a series of statements setting forth emissions
limitations achievable through the application of
reasonably available control technology," without
requiring States to adopt any particular means of
attaining the NAAQS. Along with other changes in
operating permit requirements, enforcement
provisions, and public information requirements,
environmental groups saw the changes as part of a
concerted effort by the Nixon Administration to
undermine the implementation of the Clean Air Act.[90]
    This charge surfaced publicly at a hearing of
the House Subcommittee on Public Health and
Environment on January 28, 1972. Chairman Paul
Rogers asked Ruckelshaus whether the language on
significant deterioration was changed by the White
House, specifically, the Office of Management and
Budget (OMB). Ruckelshaus responded that "like all
these other changes, Mr. Chairman, it was made by
me. The way we first had them, frankly, went beyond
our authority given us under the Act." Rogers was
not convinced, but let the matter drop.[91]
    The Rogers' hearing did occasion a brief notice
in the newspapers.[92] However, much greater attention
would be focused on Ruckelshaus at a hearing before
the Senate Subcommittee on Air and Water Pollution
on February 17-18, 1972.

This hearing was the first general oversight
hearing on air pollution held by the Senate
Subcommittee since the passage of the 1970
Amendments. It had several interesting features.
First, the chairman, Senator Muskie, was not
present. Second, as befitted an election year and
in sharp contrast to the hearings on the 1970 Act,
it was fiercely partisan, with Democrats generally
attacking Ruckelshaus and Republicans defending him.
The strongest attacker was Senator Thomas Eagleton
(D-Mo.). In the hearings on the 1970 Amendments,
Senator Eagleton had pressed Dr. Middleton on the
significant deterioration question, and Eagleton was
to assume this role once again. Finally,
Ruckelshaus' testimony was preceded the day before
by testimony from Richard Ayres of the Natural
Resources Defense Council (NRDC). Ayres, with the
help of Senator Eagleton and the Committee staff,
launched a volley of charges to the effect that the
White House was interfering with the operation of
EPA and, by implication, with air quality and public
health. This testimony received extensive media
coverage.[93]
It is neither possible nor necessary here to go
into all the charges raised at the hearing, only
those related directly to the significant
deterioration question. However, it is important to
remember that criticism by environmental groups of
EPA's actions with respect to significant
deterioration was only one item in their indictment
of the Nixon Administration's implementation of the
1970 Amendments.

THE FEBRUARY, 1972 SENATE HEARINGS

Prior to the hearings, the staff of the
Subcommittee on Air and Water Pollution had prepared
a staff paper which summarized the charges against
EPA. Copies of the staff paper were not made
available to EPA until the day of the hearing. The
paper laid out three specific areas of inquiry in

addition to the general charges of OMB interference.
These had to do with changes to language concerning
the economic feasibility of implementation plans,
the use of emission limits, and nondegradation.[94]

Richard Ayres from NRDC was the opening witness.
He used, as the focus for his testimony, copies of
internal EPA briefing memoranda of June 28 and
August 2, 1971 which he had obtained. These
memoranda, he charged, revealed that OMB had been
exercising its power of review to "press for major
weakening changes in the guidelines." The effect,
charged Ayres, was to incorporate "the demands of a
few powerful interested parties" and impose "OMB's
will on those who are empowered by law and qualified
by expertise to carry out the Clean Air Amendments."
Ayres attacked Ruckelshaus's insistence that the EPA
was responsible for the changes from the June 28th
version, saying "this strains credulity" and
suggesting that Ruckelshaus was at best only trying
to "cover up for OMB."[95]

These were dramatic charges. Yet with respect
to significant deterioration, Ayres' testimony was
somewhat ambivalent. His written statement
condemned OMB's alleged deletion of the "significant
deterioration" phrase from the Part 51 regulation,
saying that the new version was "worse than
meaningless" in that it reinserted the phrase
"productive capacity" into the regulations--a phrase
which in the environmentalists' eyes was a code word
"used to hinder pollution control on economic
grounds."[96] However, when asked by Senator Boggs
what States were doing "to prevent degradation of
the air in those regions where ambient air is more
pure than the secondary standards," Mr. Ayres
replied:

That is a very interesting question,
Senator. The act itself doesn't require
nondegradation in terms, as you know, but the
legislative history of the Clean Air Amendments
is very strongly in favor of preserving above
standard air.

EPA's revised version of its June 28th
guidelines contained provisions requiring
nondegradation or encouraging it very strongly.

OMB cut these or garbled them so badly you
could no longer recognize them. As a result,
almost no States have included nondegradation.[97]

This answer provoked a remarkable response from
Senator Eagleton, who was presiding at the hearing
in the absence of Senator Muskie.

"I don't agree with you when you say that
nondegradation is not a part of the 1970 Clean
Air Amendments. I think it very much is."

Eagleton, obviously prepared, went on to quote
Section 101(b)(1), the 1969 HEW guideline, and the
1970 testimony of HEW Secretary Finch in support of
his contention. He concluded:

"So I think that nondegradation was in the
1970 law, very much is in the 1970 law, and has
to be part of the implementation plan submitted
by a State."

Ayres replied, "I was being an overcautious
attorney, I am afraid, Mr. Chairman. I stand
corrected."[98]

Other witnesses at the hearing took up the theme
that EPA was being forced to knuckle under to
pressure from the White House, with special emphasis
on the difficulties this was causing States which
were attempting to apply strict pollution control
requirements to industry. The most forceful
statement was made by Benjamin Wake, head of
Montana's environmental program, who described "a
deterioration in resolve at the Federal level to
develop and sustain strong, aggressive air and water
pollution [control] programs." Wake specifically
criticized "the deteriorated stance taken by EPA in
the formulation of standards which do not protect
air quality better than the standards." He attacked
the implication that allowing air quality to

deteriorate up to the level of the ambient standards
was acceptable in a State where air quality
generally was much cleaner, and argued that EPA
should give greater support to the establishment of
source-specific emissions limits and constant
pollution controls in such areas.[99]

In questioning the next day, Senator Eagleton
returned to the significant deterioration issue.
The three State environmental officials present
(Kentucky and Ohio were represented as well as
Montana) continued their advocacy for some sort of
Federal nondegradation policy, though none specified
what that might be other than to generally endorse
emissions limits for existing sources and stringent
controls for new sources. Senator Eagleton summed
up the questioning as follows:

> Senator Eagleton: As to nondegradation, would
> it be helpful in enforcement and attainment of
> cleaner air if the Federal Government had a
> nondegradation requirement in its guidelines?
>
> Mr. Pointer [Kentucky]: Yes, I believe it
> would.
>
> Mr. Wake [Montana]: Yes, it would.
>
> Mr. Josselson [Ohio]: Yes.[100]

This questioning set the stage for Ruckelshaus'
appearance. He was accompanied by John Middleton
and Dr. Bernard Steigerwald, director of the Bureau
of Stationary Source Control and the effective day
to day manager of the activities under question by
the Subcommittee. Ruckelshaus was very conscious of
the political overtones of the hearing, and had made
the decision that these officials would accompany
him only when it became clear that Senator Muskie
would not be present at the hearing.[101]

In his opening statement, Ruckelshaus strongly
defended himself against all the charges raised by
Senator Eagleton. He denied that OMB had exerted
any improper influence on the Part 51 regulations,
describing the charge that EPA had given up its

decision-making authority to OMB as "categorically
false." Ruckelshaus said that the Senate
Subcommittee itself had prodded EPA into making many
of the changes in the regulation, citing letters
from Senators Muskie and Cooper which called for
such changes. However, he asserted that while he
would listen to "anybody in this society who can
give me some guidance . . . the final decision on
the issuance of these regulations is mine alone."[102]
    Eagleton and Ruckelshaus then engaged in an
extended debate about the various charges raised in
the earlier parts of the hearing. After first
discussing OMB review and requirements for emission
limits, the argument turned to nondegradation.

> Senator Eagleton: Why was the nondegradation
> requirement . . . dropped out in the August 14
> final guidelines?

> Mr. Ruckelshaus: In my opinion it was not . . .
> I don't know what nondegradation means, and
> since it was pointed out to me that this is the
> section (101(b)(1)) from which nondegradation
> comes, then I said, 'Let's quote the section and
> put it in the guidelines,' and that is what we
> did . . .[103]

Ruckelshaus went on to assert his central point-
-that in the absence of an explicit, defined
requirement that implementation plans include a
nondegradation requirement, he had to approve an
implementation plan regardless of whether it
contained such a provision, as long as it provided
for attainment of the standards. The mere fact that
air quality deteriorated was not, in itself, grounds
for disapproval in the absence of a standards
violation. Ruckelshaus argued that any further
responsibility for protecting cleaner air lay with
the States--a response Senator Eagleton was unhappy
with because of the earlier State testimony that
States would inevitably fall back on the lowest
common Federal denominator.[104]
    Senator Boggs followed by complimenting
Ruckelshaus on his answers, and asked him to restate

his views on degradation once more. Ruckelshaus
repeated that EPA's standards were intended to
protect against all known or anticipated effects of
air pollution, and that States could, if they
wished, set stricter ones. He noted:

> "I don't know how you could degrade much
> from (this) standard . . . It is true any
> pollution in the air arguably degrades it, but
> if that is the way you interpret an
> antidegradation standard, that would mean you
> could not locate any more industry that emits
> anything in the air where that degradation
> standard existed. I don't think that is what it
> means. I have had a lot of difficulty
> understanding what it does mean."[105]

In response to a follow up question from Senator
Buckley, Ruckelshaus expanded this point somewhat.
After first agreeing with Buckley that the NSPS
would cover many of the concerns about degradation,
he said:

> ". . . I don't know if (nondegradation) means
> that you can't put coal-fired power plants
> anywhere where there is any antidegradation
> standard or if antidegradation standards simply
> mean you have to use the best available control
> technology currently available to the industry .
> . . If it means the latter then it still doesn't
> mean that you are not going to degrade the air
> in some way, because you are.[106]

The discussion between Senator Eagleton and
Administrator Ruckelshaus continued through another
day of hearings with little change in the statements
or the position of either party. If anything, the
second day of hearings was more acrimonious than the
first day. In keeping with the partisan tone of the
hearing, however, Republican Senators Dole and Baker
appeared to defend Ruckelshaus, who continued to
maintain that 1) he did not know what
"nondegradation" meant, and

2) whatever it meant, the Clean Air Act did not
require it.

In the course of this second day of hearings,
Senator Baker offered a thoughtful observation. In
the debate over the 1970 Amendments, Baker had
favored an emissions standards system as opposed to
one based on air quality criteria and standards, and
was trying to get such an approach adopted in the
pending Clean Water Act. In his remarks, Baker took
advantage of the non-degradation debate to observe
that the Congress had created the problem by
adopting an ambient standard approach to the Clean
Air Act.

> Senator Baker: It is my view we ought not to
> legalize and mandate that if you have clean air
> you are entitled to pollute it until it gets
> dirty enough to make somebody stop you. That is
> the theory of the criteria system . . . but it
> doesn't have anything to say about non-
> degradation . . . there is no corresponding
> requirement for non-degradation unless we change
> the Act and supply the language that is not now
> in it that says you do not have the right to
> pollute up to a particular level just because
> your air is pure.
>
> Whether I like it or not, the law is
> contrarily stated and there is no nondegradation
> requirement other than Section 101(a)(1) in
> title I of the Air Act.
>
> Senator Eagleton: I disagree . . .
>
> Senator Baker: They [the air and water bills]
> are 180 degrees over from each other and the
> water bill is better in approach and technique
> than the air bill and you can't make the air
> bill better by just arguing about it. We have
> to change it.[107]

In the face of this opposition, Eagleton made
one final effort to get Dr. Middleton to endorse his
view on nondegradation as required by Section

101(b)(1), thus placing Dr. Middleton in a very
awkward position. Following this, the matter was
dropped.[108]
    Disagreement has persisted about why Ruckelshaus
modified the language of the Part 51 regulations on
significant deterioration.[109] In fact, why he
changed them is only of limited importance.
Certainly, the EPA's lawyers had a long-standing
concern about the requirement, and their increased
importance in the new EPA gave them ample
opportunity to press their views. Ruckelshaus was a
lawyer and was likely to be responsive to any
argument which said the Act did not require him to
do something in the face of all the things it _did_
require. Moreover, Ruckelshaus was known to have,
and has since expressed, policy reservations about a
requirement which, in his words, "protects prairie
dogs and not people."[110] Ruckelshaus was also not
impressed with Middleton's obvious advocacy of a
nondegradation standard.[111]
    Yet the acrimony of the debate between Senator
Eagleton and Administrator Ruckelshaus over
significant deterioration obscured some important
points which were raised publicly for the first time
in the Senate hearing. One was simply the vagueness
of the concept itself. The attempt to put some
language incorporating this requirement into legally
enforceable regulations forced EPA to realize, as
Ruckelshaus put it, that "no one knew what it
meant." Neither EPA nor NAPCA before it had ever
had to think about what the phrase meant because no
concrete action had ever flowed from it. In this
respect, the OGC opinion was correct. The 1969
"Guideline" language on significant deterioration
(which was repeated in Veneman's testimony and
largely copied in the Senate report) represented a
statement of hopes and aspirations, but could not be
said to be a "policy" in any meaningful way. This
is reflected in the nature of the arguments about
non-degradation at this time. Almost all of them--
both those of EPA and its opponents--focused on the
narrow legal question of whether the Act _required_
the prevention of significant deterioration. No one
except Senator Baker asked the fundamental question

of whether, as public policy, non-degradation was a
good idea. The arguments were over the significance
of words and phrases rather than the importance of
non-degradation as public policy.

While the OGC attorneys had the better of the
argument on this point and must have influenced
Ruckelshaus' thinking, they underestimated both the
symbolic appeal of non-degradation and the real
problems which resulted from the ambient standard
approach taken in the Clean Air Act. On the one
hand, nondegradation represented an important
statement of principle for environmental groups that
in addition to cleaning up existing air pollution
problems, new ones should not be allowed to occur.
This was a simple concept which was easy enough, in
principle, for the average citizen (or Congressman)
to understand and endorse. Yet, as Senator Baker
pointed out, the ambient standards approach implied
that new air pollution should be allowed to occur
without restraint until such time as the ambient
standards were violated. The response that the
ambient standards would "protect against all known
or anticipated efforts of air pollution," even if
technically correct, was not very satisfying since
it still implied a "right to pollute" up to that
level. Ruckelshaus did note that new source
performance standards (NSPS) would prevent some
deterioration by requiring the use of best control
technology on new sources, but this point was not
strongly emphasized in his testimony.
Interestingly, NSPS had this effect precisely
because they were inconsistent with the ambient
standards philosophy of the rest of the Act.

The February, 1972 hearings showed that the
repetition of the phrase "significant deterioration"
in a variety of contexts had the effect which its
proponents wanted: it had gained a sort of
legitimacy as an "official" policy, OGC's objections
notwithstanding. It enabled Senator Eagleton, the
Senate committee staff and the environmental groups
to make a credible argument that EPA had changed a
past policy, authorized by an unchanged section of
the 1967 Air Quality Act, and attack Ruckelshaus'
response that the Act did not allow him to impose a

non-degradation requirement. While this line of
argument had little effect on Ruckelshaus, it would
have more impact in the courts.

**Sierra Club vs. Ruckelshaus: Access Through The
Courts**

     Nondegradation advocates could not have been
pleased with events in the winter of 1971-72.
Ruckelshaus' action in dropping "significant
deterioration" from the Part 51 regulations had
reversed a pattern of including this language in
such policy documents as the NAPCA "Guidelines,"
Secretary Finch's testimony, the Senate Committee
report on the 1970 Amendments, and the NAAQS
regulations. Ruckelshaus' clear intention <u>not</u> to
continue this practice forced the advocates of
nondegradation to take a different approach.
     As noted earlier, §304 of the 1970 Amendments
included a provision which authorized any citizen to
bring suit against EPA for failure to perform any
duty under the Act which was not discretionary with
the Administrator. Having failed to convince
Ruckelshaus to change his mind through comments on
the proposed Part 51 regulations or political
pressure during the House and Senate hearings, a
court suit under this section appeared to be the
next logical step.
     However, it was not until May 24, 1972--a mere
seven days before EPA was scheduled to announce
which State implementation plans would be approved--
that the Sierra Club filed suit in the U. S.
District Court for the District of Columbia,
charging that EPA's failure to disapprove
implementation plans which allowed significant
deterioration was a violation of a nondiscretionary
duty under the Act and should be enjoined. Two
reasons why this took so long have been suggested.
The first is that there was an uncertainty among the

environmental groups as to whether a suit should be
filed in this case at all. There was some fear
among some of the groups that, should they win the
case, it could prove to be so far-reaching that it
would create a backlash which would threaten the
gains made in the 1970 Act. Another practical
matter also caused delay; this was only the second
citizen suit filed under §304, and it took time to
determine just what needed to be done in the absence
of clear precedents on how to proceed in such a
case.[112] As it was, only the Sierra Club litigated
the case, though they were ultimately joined by 20
State attorneys general acting as intervenors.[113]

The Sierra Club did not ask the court to
overturn EPA's Part 51 regulations as being not in
conformance with the Act. Presumably this would
have been very difficult to do since the section of
the regulations at issue repeated, word for word,
the language of the statute. Instead, the Club
focused on EPA's action in approving implementation
plans, arguing that this action would violate
statutory intent. The Club's request, therefore,
was for a temporary restraining order (TRO) to
preclude EPA from approving any plans. Because it
focused on individual plans, it was entered in the
D.C. District Court rather than in the D.C. Circuit
Court of Appeals where challenges to generally
applicable EPA rules would ordinarily have been
filed, and kept the Club from having to give the
required sixty day notice for rule challenges under
§307.

The judge in the case, John H. Pratt, reportedly
intended to grant the request for a TRO when it was
brought to him on May 24th. He was dissuaded from
doing so by the government's arguments that the case
deserved a fuller hearing, and that no
implementation plans would be approved before May
31st in any event. He therefore denied the request
for a TRO, but scheduled a hearing for May 30th on a
motion for a preliminary injunction.[114]

At the May 30th hearing, EPA attorneys were
disappointed at both the weakness with which they
felt their arguments were made by the Department of
Justice (which represents EPA in court), and by the

appearance, to them, that Judge Pratt had already
made up his mind in the case prior to oral
argument.[115] For whatever reason, at the conclusion
of the oral hearing, Judge Pratt announced a
decision which represented a clear victory for the
environmental groups. He issued the preliminary
injunction, in handwritten form, ordering EPA not to
approve any implementation plan except with the
proviso that it was subject to subsequent review by
EPA "to insure that it does not permit significant
deterioration of existing air quality in any portion
of any state where the existing air quality is
better than one or more of the secondary standards
promulgated by the Administrator." EPA was given
four months to conduct this review and six months to
propose regulations for any state implementation
plan found deficient in this respect.[116]

In a memorandum opinion issued three days later,
Judge Pratt formally stated the reasons for his
decision. In every respect, he endorsed the legal
arguments of the environmental groups over those of
EPA. None of these arguments were new; they were
the same ones which had been made previously before
the Senate Committee. However, Judge Pratt accepted
without question the fundamental argument that
Ruckelshaus had changed a pre-established policy of
non-degradation without examining at all what the
content of that so-called "policy" had been. Thus,
the three main sections of the opinion agreed that
section 101(b)(1) required the prevention of
significant deterioration; the NAPCA Guidelines,
Veneman testimony and Senate report language had all
established a legislative history which supported
the policy of preventing significant deterioration;
and the NAPCA Guidelines and the "significant
deterioration" phrase meant that EPA was being
contradictory in now failing to prevent significant
deterioration.

The extended discussions of each of these
documents in this chapter suggest that none of these
assumptions stand up under scrutiny. All of the
bits of "history" cited in the opinion were of
dubious value in establishing whether any true
policy had ever been established to "prevent

significant deterioration of air quality." Yet it
was upon these slender reeds that the court based
its decision.[117] While Judge Pratt reportedly
thought that in fact a policy of non-degradation was
not altogether wise, he clearly believed that
Congress had intended it even if not everyone fully
understood it.[118]

Such a conclusion requires a leap of faith which
is difficult to make. What appears more likely is
that, over a period of years, a coalition of
environmental activists, sympathetic agency
officials and friendly Senate committee staff had
cooperated to build de facto legislative and policy
support for a doctrine of non-degradation without
attracting real attention. The motives behind these
actions were varied, ranging from concerns about the
impact of growth and development on air quality to a
desire by Democrats in Congress to appear strong on
environmental protection and embarrass the Nixon
Administration. This coalition was not successful
in building an administrative record which would tie
the hands of Executive Branch officials who focused
attention on just what "significant deterioration"
might mean. It was enough, though, to satisfy one
judge in one court. It would turn out that the
opinion of this single judge was enough to tip the
scales in favor of those who supported the concept
of nondegradation and against those who opposed it.
In this sense, Sierra Club vs. Ruckelshaus was truly
a landmark decision.

Whether it was in accord with the principles of
"juridical democracy" is another question. Even if
one agrees that a nondegradation provision was
incorporated in the preamble to the Clean Air Act,
this requirement was extremely vague. A court which
behaved in accordance with the principles of
juridical democracy, rather than directing an agency
to develop a program to carry out such a vague
requirement, would more properly have thrown out the
case with the instruction to Congress that if it
wanted to prevent significant deterioration of air
quality, it should lay out more clearly what it
expected the agency to do. By failing to take this
approach, the initial decision in Sierra Club vs.

<u>Ruckelshaus</u>, though ostensibly the judicial
enforcement of an Agency-forcing statute, did little
to advance the rule of law that Lowi would have
advocated. In fact it did precisely the opposite by
effectively delegating broad responsibility to the
EPA.

While the environmental groups had won the first
round battle of textual analysis in support of their
contention of what the Clean Air Act required, it
remained to be seen whether a substantive program
which would satisfy the environmental groups could
be wrung from a reluctant EPA by using the courts as
a lever. For while he upheld the Sierra Club's
request, Judge Pratt gave no more guidance than had
any earlier policymakers as to exactly what EPA was
supposed to do to "prevent significant
deterioration." EPA had to do something, but it was
not at all clear just what kind of "something" was
needed to satisfy this court. The next chapter will
explore how EPA began to adapt to this challenge.

NOTES

1. While it is not my purpose to engage in an
    extended discussion of the historical or
    philosophical roots of this belief, it is a
    pervasive theme in air pollution control. Hans
    Morgenthau's assertion that the distinguishing
    characteristic of the modern age is that
    "whatever different philosophic, economic, and
    political beliefs people may hold, the are
    united in the conviction that science is able,
    at least potentially, to solve all the problems
    of man" can be identified often in the public
    rhetoric of air pollution control. (<u>Scientific
    Man vs. Power Politics</u> (Chicago: University of
    Chicago Press, 1946), p. 4.) The air pollution
    debate has generally turned on the rate at which
    technology can produce progress, and the cost of
    achieving it, rather than on whether progress
    can be achieved. To use Rick Freeman's terms,
    what <u>ought</u> to be done (a political choice) is
    assumed to be constrained by what <u>can</u> be done
    (an economic choice) only in an instrumental and
    not an ultimate sense. A. Myrick Freeman, "Air
    and Water Pollution Policy," in Paul M. Portnoy,
    ed. <u>Current Issues in U.S. Environmental Policy</u>
    (Baltimore: Johns Hopkins University Press,
    1978), pp. 18-19.

2. U.S. Senate, <u>Air Quality Act of 1967</u>, S. Rpt.
    403 to Accompany S.780, 90th Congress, 1st
    sess., 1967. The account which follows draws
    heavily on John C. Esposito, et al., <u>Vanishing
    Air: The Ralph Nader Study Group Report On Air
    Pollution</u> (New York: Gossimer Publishers,
    1970), pp. 270-76, though its outlines were
    confirmed to me in interviews. One need not
    subscribe to the Nader group's interpretation of
    these events to agree that they described them
    accurately.

3. U. S. Department of Health, Education and
    Welfare: Public Health Service. <u>Proceedings:
    The Third National Conference on Air Pollution,</u>

Washington, D. C. December 12-14, 1966
(Washington: Government Printing Office, n.d.),
p. 597.

4.   Ibid., pp. 597-98.

5.   Zuckerman, Elias, "Senator Muskie and the 1970
      Amendments to the Clean Air Act," Kennedy
      School of Government Case Study C94-76-140,
      1976, p. 18. Muskie's opposition can be seen in
      U. S. Congress, Senate, Committee on Public
      Works, Hearings Before the Subcommittee on Air
      and Water Pollution of the Committee on Public
      Works, 90th Congress, 1st sess., May 15, 16, 17,
      and 18th, 1967.

6.   Esposito, Vanishing Air, pp. 273-278. See also
      J. Clarence Davies and Barbara S. Davies, The
      Politics of Pollution, 2nd ed. (Indianapolis:
      Bobbs-Merrill, 1975), pp. 49-52.

7.   Interview data.

8.   Vanishing Air, pp. 154-158, 275-278; Clean Air
      Act as amended by the Air Quality Act of 1907
      (Public Law 90-148), reprinted in U. S.
      Congress, Senate, Committee on Public Works, A
      Legislative History of the Clean Air Amendments
      of 1970, 93rd Congress, 2nd sess., Volume 2, pp.
      1543-1573, (hereafter cited as 1970 CAA
      Legislative History).

9.   See both the Senate and House Reports on the
      1967 Act. Neither report gives any discussion
      of precise reasons for the addition of language
      to the purpose clause. U.S. Congress, Senate,
      Air Quality Act of 1967, S. Rpt. 403 to
      Accompany S.780, 90th Congress, 1st sess., p.
      40; U.S. House of Representatives, Air Quality
      Act of 1967, H. Rpt. 728 to Accompany S.780,
      90th Congress, 1st Session, p. 30. (Hereafter
      cited as 1967 Senate Report and 1967 House
      Report).

10. 1967 Senate Report, p. 4.

11. Walter Rosenbaum, The Politics of Environmental
     Concern (New York: Praeger, 1973), pp. 154-156,
     and Charles O. Jones, Clean Air: The Policies
     and Politics of Pollution Control (Pittsburgh:
     University of Pittsburgh Press, 1975), pp. 122-
     132, contain discussions on this point.
     Esposito, Vanishing Air, contains a rather more
     polemical discussion, particularly in Chapter 7
     but also scattered in other places throughout
     the book.

12. Davies and Davies, The Politics of Pollution, p.
     53; Jones, Clean Air, pp. 176-78.

13. Interview data.

14. Air Quality Act of 1967, §107.

15. Esposito, Vanishing Air, p. 280.

16. Ibid., pp. 286-282. Richard K. Vietor,
     Environmental Politics and the Coal Coalition
     (College Station, Texas: Texas A&M University
     Press, 1980), pp. 142-150, reaches a similar
     conclusion to the Nader task force on how and
     why these criteria were altered.

17. Air Quality Act of 1967, §108(c)(1).

18. 1967 Senate Report, p. 26.

19. Ibid., pp. 28-29.

20. Air Quality Act of 1967, §108(c)(1).

21. Jones, Clean Air, p. 123.

22. Paul Sabatier, "Social Movements and Regulatory
     Agencies: Toward a More Adequate--and Less
     Pessimistic--Theory of Clientele Capture,"
     Policy Sciences 6 (1975): 311; following
     Theodore Lowi, "American Business, Public

Policy, Case Studies, and Political Theory,"
<u>World Politics</u> 16 (July, 1964): 677715.

23. Sabatier, "Social Movements and Regulatory
    Agencies," p. 312; Esposito, <u>Vanishing Air</u>, pp.
    141-2; Interview data.

24. Interview data.

25. Ibid.

26. The Nader report observed that the drafting of
    the 1967 Air Quality Act forced NAPCA to
    interpret the phrase "air quality standards" in
    the Act to mean "ambient air standards and
    implementation plans," while the phrase
    "standards of air quality" referred to ambient
    standards only. Apart from its merits, the
    "enforceable guidelines" approach was apparently
    on shaky legal ground. One law review article
    cited in the Nader report observed that the Air
    Quality Act left "the fundamental questions of
    whether, and when, effective emissions standards
    applicable to individual industrial plants may
    be promulgated by the Secretary [of HEW]" in "a
    state of utter confusion." Esposito, <u>Vanishing
    Air</u>, p. 171.

27. Interview data; also Sabatier, "Social Movements
    and Regulatory Agencies," pp. 311-313. Sabatier
    observes that even this approach was
    controversial within NAPCA; he states that
    "Public Health Service professionals who had
    long dominated NAPCA" would have favored the
    "safe and traditional" course of "bargaining
    with state officials in the hopes of obtaining
    as stringent a program as possible without
    resorting to overt conflict and coercion." The
    public education strategy, according to
    Sabatier, reflected NAPCA's attempt to improve
    its base of support by mobilizing a specific
    constituency which favored programs to control
    air pollution.

28. U.S. Department of Health, Education and
    Welfare, Public Health Service, "Guidelines For
    the Development of Air Quality Standards and
    Implementation Plans", May, 1969, pp. 1-15.
    (Hereafter cited as 1969 NAPCA Guideline.)

29. Several of my interviewees disparaged this
    aspect of the "Guidelines" and criticized the
    lack of legal rigor on the part of those who
    prepared them.

30. 1969 NAPCA Guidelines, pp. 11-12. Sabatier,
    "Social Movements and Regulatory Agencies," p.
    313, describes the public hearings aspect of the
    adopting of air quality standards as "immensely
    successful." A detailed case study of the
    Pittsburgh experience in this area can be found
    in Jones, Clean Air, pp. 146-152.

31. 1969 NAPCA Guidelines, p. 7.

32. See Esposito, Vanishing Air, pp. 172-174, for a
    case study of New York's behavior on this point.

33. See especially Jones, Clean Air, chapter 7; and
    Zuckerman, "Senator Muskie and the 1970
    Amendments."

34. I have not been able to find anyone in my
    interviews who believes that either Congress as
    a whole, its committees with jurisdiction over
    the 1970 amendments, or even the committee staff
    gave any serious thought to what implications a
    "significant deterioration" policy might have.
    Later, after the decision in Sierra Club vs
    Ruckelshaus, both Senator Muskie and his chief
    aide, Leon Billings, made statements to the
    effect that "of course, this was what we
    intended in 1970." Yet the officials I
    interviewed, with the one exception discussed in
    the text, regard this assertion as revisionist
    history. If this was "intended", it was not
    widely advertised.

35. A transcript of this hearing (hereafter cited as
     "March 17th Hearing") is reprinted in U. S.
     Senate, <u>1970 CAA Legislative History</u>, pp. 965-
     1050.

36. Statement of John Veneman, ibid., pp. 971-974;
     also provision of S.3466, reprinted in ibid.,
     1474-1494, especially section 7.

37. Veneman statement, pp 971, 974-976; S.3466,
     section 8.

38. Ibid., pp. 972-973.

39. Ibid., p. 983.

40. Interviews with then HEW officials.
     Undersecretary Veneman's testimony the previous
     day before the House Subcommittee on Public
     Health and Welfare of the Interstate and Foreign
     Commerce Committee contains identical language.
     As the following discussion shows, this part of
     the statement did not get a lot of attention in
     the Senate; it got even less in the House. See
     <u>1970 CAA Legislative History</u>, pp. 1361-1413
     (reprint of March 16, 1970 Subcommittee hearing
     which includes Veneman's testimony). The
     "significant deterioration" passage is on p.
     1365.

41. March 17th Senate Hearing, pp. 991-993.

42. Ibid., pp. 995-996.

43. Ibid., pp. 998-999.

44. Ibid., p. 1004.

45. Transcript of May 27th hearing in <u>1970 CAA
     Legislative History</u>, pp. 1182-1183.

46. Jones, <u>Clean Air</u>, pp. 194-205.

47. Interview data.

48.   May 27th hearing, pp.1184-1188.

49.   Ibid., pp. 1188-1189.

50.   Ibid., pp. 1189-1190. The "other topics" also
      included the issue of a date certain by which
      the ambient standards were to be attained. The
      committee was successful in getting Dr.
      Middleton to say that "1975 may be a reasonable
      target date." (p. 1196) What is fascinating
      about this is the follow up discussion by
      Senator Eagleton, where he proposed that this
      occur by January 1, 1972 or 1973. Eagleton
      justified his belief that such a standard could
      be met by saying he wanted "a reasonable period
      of time in which industry ought to quit injuring
      our health." (p. 1197)
          A somewhat more level-headed version of this
      same discussion recurs on pp. 1206-1207. In
      this version Dr. Middleton says he would
      "seriously doubt that the oxidant and carbon
      monoxide standards would be met in all places by
      1975,"...."and that in general, States are not
      going to be able to attain (the standards) any
      sooner than the fuels and controls needed become
      available." Senator Eagleton then questioned
      whether "a national standard, unless you set
      specific target dates, is really helping to
      achieve anything beyond what you are presently
      doing [with regional standards]."

51.   Ibid., pp. 1200-1201.

52.   Ibid., pp. 1203-1204.

53.   Ibid., pp. 1211-1212.

54.   Ibid.

55.   Ibid., p. 1212.

56.   See, for example, the discussion in Sabatier,
      "Social Movements and Regulatory Agencies", p.
      313, and Jones, Clean Air, pp.156-174, on the

effect of local groups on ambient standard
setting. Both Jones and Sabatier note that it
was difficult to translate public pressure into
"tough" implementation plans. See Sabatier, pp.
313-315, and Jones, pp.214-238.

57. U. S. Congress, Senate, <u>National Air Quality
<u>Standards Act of 1970</u>, Report of the Committee
on Public Works to Accompany S. 4358, 91st
Congress, 2nd sess., 1970 (hereafter referred to
as <u>1970 Senate Report</u>). Reprinted in <u>1970 CAA
Legislative</u> <u>History</u>, p. 403. Further references
to the Senate report are numbered as they appear
in the <u>1970</u> <u>Legislative History</u>.

58. S.4358, Section 111(a)(2)(A); <u>1970 Senate
Report</u>, p. 412.

59. Ibid.

60. Ibid., p. 487.

61. Ibid., p. 410. The report and amended bill
called for two types of standards, one to
protect strictly against health effects, the
other to protect "the public health and welfare
from any known or anticipated adverse effects
associated with the presence of such air
pollution agent or combination of such agents in
the ambient air." These were later to be
distinguished as the "primary" and "secondary"
ambient standards.

62. S.3458 uses the words "goals" and "standards"
interchangeably. This reflects the same kind of
ambiguous drafting which, in the 1967 Air
Quality Act, forced NAPCA to interpret "air
quality standards" as meaning both ambient air
quality standards and implementation plans.

63. <u>1970 Senate Report</u>, p. 411

64. Interview data.

65. Interview data. This second interpretation is much more speculative than the first; if this kind of arrangement existed between Senate committee staff and NAPCA officials, it was either based on such a "mutual understanding" that it was almost unspoken, or it was a closely kept secret. However, in light of both the sweeping nature of the 1970 Amendments and the intensity of the later debate over significant deterioration, this interpretation does have a certain plausibility.

66. Senate debate on S. 4358, September 21, 1970, reprinted in 1970 CAA Legislative History, p. 267 (all subsequent references are numbered as in the Legislative History.)

67. Ibid., p. 289.

68. Ibid., p. 270.

69. See Zuckerman, "Senator Muskie and the 1970 Amendments," and "Epilogue."

70. See, among many examples, Environment Reporter, June 12, 1973; U.S. Congress, Senate, Committee on Public Works, Nondegradation Policy of the Clean Air Act, Hearings before the Subcommittee on Air and Water Pollution of the Committee on Public Works, 93rd Congress, 1st session, July 24, 1973, p. 1 (hereafter cited as 1973 Senate Nondegradation Hearings); Joshua Gotbaum, "Nondegradation, the Courts, and the Clean Air Act," Kennedy School Case Program, No. C95-77-164, 1976.

71. The best description of this conference is in Zuckerman, "Senator Muskie and the 1970 Amendments."

72. For discussions of how and why EPA was created, see Alfred Marcus, Promise and Performance: Choosing and Implementing An Environmental Policy (Greenwood Press: Westport, Conn.,

1980), chapter 1. One of the advantages of
proposing EPA's creation through a
reorganization plan was that it did not require
affirmative action by the Congress, only a
failure to object within sixty days. See also
Peggy Wiehl, "William D. Ruckelshaus and the
Environmental Protection Agency," Kennedy School
of Government Case Progress, No. C1674-027,
1974.

73.   President's Remarks, December 31, 1970.
Reprinted in 1970 Legislative History, pp. 105-
106.

74.   The following citations are from Section 4 of
the Clean Air Amendments of 1970, P.L. 91-604.

75.   Wiehl, "William D. Ruckelshaus", pp. 10-12.

76.   Ibid., p. 12.

77.   This distinction is elaborated on in Francis
Rourke, Bureaucracy, Politics and Public Policy,
2nd ed. (Boston, Little Brown: 1976), chapter 3.

78.   Wiehl, "William D. Ruckelshaus," pp. 9-12;
Marcus, Promise and Performance, pp. 86-94 and
102-106; Melnick, Regulation and the Courts, pp.
40-41.

79.   Interview data; Melnick, Regulation and the
Courts, p.41. While individuals in each group
often had great respect for each other, both
groups tended to see each other as caricatures--
the traditional, old line bureaucrats versus the
aggressive, domineering, impractical lawyers.
This was exacerbated by the physical separation
of the two groups, with most of the lawyers in
Washington and most of the program staff in
Durham, North Carolina.

80.   See Jeff Berry, Lobbying for the People
(Princeton: Princeton University Press, 1977),

chapter 2; Melnick, <u>Regulation and the Courts</u>, p. 37.

81. Clean Air Amendments of 1970, §307; Melnick, pp. 5556; interview data.

82. Wiehl, "William D. Ruckelshaus," pp. 11-12; Marcus, <u>Promise and Performance</u>, pp. 90-91; interview data.

83. See EPA's Response to Questions in U.S. Congress, Senate, Committee on Public Works, <u>A Hearing Before the Subcommittee on Air and Water Pollution of the Committee on Public Works</u>, 92nd Congress, 2nd session, February 16-18, 23, 1972, pp. 313-14 (hereafter cited as <u>1972 Senate Implementation Hearings</u>).

84. Melnick, <u>Regulation and the Courts</u>, p. 79.

85. 36 <u>Federal Register</u> 8186; 40 CFR 50.2(c).

86. 36 <u>Federal Register</u> 8186.

87. "Appendix D, Preparation, Adoption, and Submittal of Implementation Plans: Summary of Comments on, and Revisions of, Proposed Regulations." Reprinted in <u>1972 Senate Implementation Hearings</u>, p. 59

88. John T. Middleton to the Administrator, June 28, 1971, reprinted in <u>1972 Senate Implementation Hearings</u>, pp. 47-48.

89. John T. Middleton to the Administrator, August 3, 1971, reprinted in <u>1972 Senate Implementation Hearings</u>, p. 49.

90. See Richard Ayres testimony, <u>1972 Senate Implementation Hearings</u>, pp. 3-24. This testimony will be discussed in more detail below.

Given Senator Muskie's past aversion to national emission standards, his reaction to the

controversy over Appendix B is interesting. On
May 4, 1971, Muskie wrote to Ruckelshaus
expressing precisely this concern. However,
Muskie did not attend the hearing in February,
1972 on this question--presumably his campaign
for the Presidency gave him more pressing things
to do--and there is no record of his further
comment on this subject. See <u>1972 Senate
Implementation Hearings</u>, pp. 232-234.

91. U.S. Congress, House, Committee on Interstate
and Foreign Commerce, <u>Clean Air Act Oversight:
Hearings Before the Subcommittee on Public
Health and the Environment of the Committee on
Interstate and Foreign Commerce</u>, 92nd Congress,
2nd sess., 1972, pp. 530-31.

92. See <u>New York Times</u>, January 29, 1972,

93. See <u>New York Times</u>, February 17,1972; <u>Washington
Post</u>, February 17, 1972.

94. Reprinted in <u>1972 Senate Implementation
Hearings</u>, pp. 307-310.

95. Testimony of Richard Ayres, February 16, 1972,
<u>1972 Senate Implementation Hearings</u>, pp. 4-6.

96. Written statement of Richard Ayres, <u>1972 Senate
Implementation Hearings</u>, pp. 37-38.

97. <u>1972 Senate Implementation Hearings</u>, pp. 12-13.

98. <u>1972 Senate Implementation Hearings</u>, pp. 14-15.
Senator Eagleton had been the most vocal speaker
on this point in the hearings on the 1970
Amendments (though he had also exhibited a
failure to understand some of the key principles
in the debate). Mr. Ayres and the
environmentalists were, of course, delighted to
have Senator Eagleton make their case for them.
However, interviews which I conducted suggest
there was considerable anxiety among the
environmentalists about what they regarded as

Mr. Ayres' _faux_ _pas_ of implying that
nondegradation was not required by the Clean Air
Act. This was one factor cited in why, when a
suit was ultimately brought against EPA, NRDC
was not a party to it.

99.   Ibid., p. 178. Wake's fundamental argument was
      with the overall philosophy of the ambient
      standards approach. He observed:

> "The philosophy of the ambient air quality
> approach---if the standards set are more
> dirty than the actual ambient air quality---
> will encourage a systematic, and legal,
> deterioration of air quality that is better
> than the standards. Using ambient air
> quality standards as the determining factor
> in whether or not control devices will be
> employed is to guarantee the deterioration
> of air quality in these areas where air
> quality is better than the standards.
>   The thrust of this whole philosophy is
> that the Nation must become uniformly dirty
> . . ." (_1972 Senate Implementation Hearings_,
> p. 178).

Wake's specific problem was with copper smelters
in Montana which were strongly resisting State
efforts to impose controls. Wake wanted a
stronger statement by EPA on the need for
specific emissions limits at the smelters which
would require continuous emissions reductions,
so that smelters would not be allowed simply to
meet the ambient standards by curtailing
operations at times when the weather was bad.

100. Ibid., pp. 205-222. (Quote is on p. 219.)

101. Interview data.

102. Testimony of William D. Ruckelshaus, _1972 Senate
      Implementation Hearings_, pp. 231-232.

103. Ibid., p. 246.

96   **Protect and Enhance**

104.   Ibid., p. 246-247. Senator Eagleton quoted
       language in the <u>1969 NAPCA Guideline</u> to
       Ruckelshaus and asked if he thought that defined
       a requirement which was in the 1970 law, and
       should apply to implementation plans.
       Ruckelshaus replied by pointing out that the
       1970 Act required the secondary NAAQS to protect
       against all known or anticipated adverse effect
       from air pollution, and that he felt the
       requirements of the 1970 Act and the purpose
       clause of Section 101(b)(1) were satisfied by
       these provisions.

105.   Ibid., p. 248.

106.   Ibid., p. 249.

107.   Ibid., p. 275.

108.   Ibid., p. 276. EPA was asked at the hearing to
       provide, at a later date, a written response to
       the staff paper. Ruckelshaus provided the
       response on March 15, 1972, attaching a memo
       from the Office of General Counsel dated
       February 23, 1972. The OGC response reiterates
       Ruckelshaus' answers to the Committee and
       amplifies them. It flatly states that "there is
       no legal authority in the Clean Air Act
       authorizing the Administrator to require States
       to achieve air of better quality than that
       required by the national primary and secondary
       standards," and that a non-degradation
       requirement "could not" be legally supported
       solely by the statement of purpose carried over
       without comment from the 1967 Act. This was
       despite "some indication by program personnel,
       <u>without the clearance of the Office of General
       Counsel</u>, that the language of §101 (b)(1) . . .
       was a nondegradation requirement" [emphasis
       added]. The 1969 HEW "Guidelines" were
       dismissed as mere "suggestions and statements of
       policy," rather than legally enforceable
       regulations like the Part 51 requirements. One
       can hear the echoes of the NAPCA-HEW General

Counsel conflict in these statements. (<u>1972</u>
<u>Senate Implementation Hearings</u>, pp. 313-314.)

109.   For example, compare Melnick, <u>Regulation and the</u>
       <u>Courts</u>, pp. 78-79, with Mark Bremer Mihaly, "The
       Clean Air Act and the Concept of Non-
       Degradation," <u>Ecology Law Quarterly</u> 2:82930.
       See also Vietor, <u>Environmental Politics and the</u>
       <u>Coal Coalition</u>, pp. 173-78; 203.

110.   Melnick, <u>Regulation and the Courts</u>, p. 79;
       interview data.

111.   Interview data.

112.   Interview data.

113.   See note 98 above on why the NRDC was not a
       party to this case. The motives of the
       attorneys general appear to have been tied to a
       desire on the part of the intervening States to
       prevent rural areas from adopting lenient
       emissions control requirements to attract
       industry. (See Melnick, <u>Regulation and the</u>
       <u>Courts</u>, p. 82.) Melnick notes that very few of
       these attorneys general consulted with the air
       pollution control officials in their State
       before deciding to intervene in the case.

114.   Joshua Gotbaum, "Non-Degradation, the Courts,
       and the Clean Air Act," Kennedy School Case
       Program, Case # C9577164, 1977, p. 11.

115.   Interview data. There was also, among some
       interviewees, a sense that EPA staff did not
       take the court case seriously at first, and
       therefore lost the opportunity to put its
       strongest case forward early.

116.   Preliminary Injunction, filed May 30, 1972 in
       Civil Action 1031-72, <u>Sierra Club et al., v.</u>
       <u>Ruckelshaus</u>, in the U. S. District Court for the
       District of Columbia. 34 F. Supp. 253 (1972).

117.   344 F. Supp. 253 (1972). A more extensive legal
       critique of Judge Pratt's decision can be found
       in an article by Richard Stewart, "Judicial
       Review of EPA Decisions," 62 Iowa Law Review
       (1977): 741-50. I do not wish to attempt to
       critique the decision as law here, but simply to
       point out that all of the documents and
       statements the decision relied on were, in fact,
       a very weak basis for support for anything and
       that this was well known to the "insiders" who
       had developed them or knew their details.

118.   Gotbaum, "Nondegradation", p. 18.

CHAPTER III

EPA RESPONDS TO THE COURTS

Judge Pratt's order may have forced EPA to begin define just what PSD meant, but it was not sufficient by itself to compel the Agency to respond with a full-blown program. In fact, all the reasons which had led EPA--and particularly Administrator Ruckelshaus--to resist the nondegradation concept were as present after the court order as before. EPA still officially regarded PSD as questionable on both legal and public policy grounds, and its management appears to have felt that the court decision would be overturned on appeal. While the decision was regarded as disturbing, it was not viewed as cause for alarm.

This chapter will trace EPA's initial reaction to the district court decision, and how further developments in the courts increased the pressure on the Agency to abandon its passive stance and begin developing a Federal PSD program. It traces the early history of thinking within the Agency on PSD rules and how this thinking became the basis for EPA's first set of formal PSD proposals in July, 1973. The chapter will also describe the technical concerns which went into these proposals, and how technical judgments necessarily incorporated policy choices about the tradeoffs between environmental quality and economic growth and development.

Initial EPA Reaction to the Sierra Club Decision

The decision by Judge Pratt in <u>Sierra Club vs.</u>
<u>Ruckelshaus</u> had little immediate effect on the
officials within EPA responsible for implementing
the Court's decision. Judge Pratt's order had
called for EPA to review all State Implementation
Plans (SIP's) by September 30, 1972 and disapprove
any portion which failed to effectively prevent the
significant deterioration of air quality in any
portion of any State.[1] However, EPA's Office of Air
Quality Planning and Standards (OAQPS), which was
NAPCA's successor in the new EPA structure and was
primarily staffed with former NAPCA officials, did
not actually initiate this review until September
7th.[2] At the same time, EPA filed papers with the
court requesting an extension of the September 30th
deadline on the grounds that any action EPA could
take would be "simplistic" and "would not have been
adequately considered at any governmental level."[3]
OAQPS officials also expressed the view that the
significant deterioration issue could not be
successfully addressed except in a much larger
political context, saying that:

> "Non-degradation is essentially a long-range
> problem extending over a period of many years
> with potentially significant socio-economic
> impacts, and it requires the time to do a
> comprehensive analysis and arrive at the best
> possible solution."[4]

While this concern for the potential long-range
impact of PSD policy was genuine, it was not the
sole EPA consideration which argued for delay in
carrying out the Court order. In fact, EPA
officials appear to have been convinced, on advice
from attorneys within the Agency, that Judge Pratt's
ruling would be overturned on appeal. This
conviction made it easy for EPA officials to place a

lower priority on actions to comply with the
District Court's ruling. This was true not only for
that portion of the ruling which required the review
of State SIP's within four months, but also for the
requirement that EPA prepare and publish proposed
regulations on PSD, and promulgate them, within six
months, or by November 30, 1972.[5]

While this was going on, EPA and the Justice
Department were preparing their appeal of the Sierra
Club decision to the D.C. Circuit Court of Appeals.
Oral arguments before the Court were heard on
October 27, 1972, and on November 1, 1972, the Court
of Appeals unanimously affirmed Judge Pratt's
decision.[6]

Most treatments of the Court of Appeals decision
have passed over it lightly, as only one stop on the
way to the Supreme Court review which Sierra Club
vs. Ruckelshaus ultimately received.[7] However, this
understates the effect of the Appeals Court decision
on EPA. For one thing, this decision made it clear
to EPA's attorneys that while the result in the
Sierra Club case was based on the opinion of a
single judge, that opinion could very well continue
to stand up legally given a spirited defense of it
by the Sierra Club.[8] Moreover, while the Agency's
attorneys and the Justice Department apparently
still felt confident that they could win on appeal
to the Supreme Court, the quick timing and summary
nature of the Appeals Court decision created doubt
in the minds of both the attorneys and OAQPS staff
that the Agency's position with respect to
significant deterioration would in fact be
sustained.[9]

Administrator Ruckelshaus appears to have
contributed personally to this "consciousness-
raising" within EPA. One EPA official recalled a
meeting with the Administrator immediately following
the Appeals Court decision, in which the
Administrator expressed two concerns: a desire to
avoid being cited for contempt of court, which
Ruckelshaus clearly wanted to avoid as a stain on
his professional legal reputation; and a displeasure
that despite having been aware of the District Court
decision and accompanying court order for five

months, virtually nothing had been done by EPA to
develop regulations to satisfy the court order.
That order required the <u>promulgation</u> (not merely the
proposal) of regulations by November 30th.[10]
Ruckelshaus may not have changed his views on the
value of PSD as a national policy, but he seems to
have been clearly aware that despite the legal
assurances of his attorneys--and perhaps despite
what he himself felt the law did or did not say--the
Agency was in danger of losing on this case and he
needed to be prepared for it. Moreover, Ruckelshaus
had staked much of his and the Agency's credibility
on meeting deadlines--even unreasonable ones.[11]

As a result, the first signs of organized
thinking in EPA about PSD began to appear in
November, 1972. Massive levels of effort were not
devoted to this project--most of the initial work
was assigned to two staff members in EPA's Office of
Air Quality Planning and Standards (OAQPS).
However, this work was given some urgency because of
the Administrator's expressed concern, the pending
November 30th court deadline, uncertainty about
whether the Supreme Court would in fact agree to
take the case, and the previous lack of organized
thinking by either the courts or anyone in EPA about
just what "significant deterioration" meant.

The first written products to emerge from this
effort were a series of rough handwritten outlines
from staff in OAQPS of just what a PSD regulation
might look like. In light of what later became of
the various plans for PSD, it is worth looking at
this initial proposal to see how it attempted to
give meaning to the "significant deterioration"
concept.[12]

This proposal described six possible options.
The four principal ones are described below.

1) <u>Maximum technology plus impact statement</u>.
Under this proposal, all new plants in clean air
areas would be required to install the best control
technology available to the plant in its particular
location. In addition, the plant would have to
submit for public review a statement of their
expected emissions rates, types of controls, and
ambient impact of source emissions.

2) <u>Emissions ceilings</u>. An emissions ceiling
approach would have put a cap upon allowable
increases in emissions over some unit of area (e.g.,
100 tons per year per square mile). The ceiling
could be based on either a percentage increase over
the existing emissions density in a given area, or
it could be a uniform national allowable increase,
based on existing emission densities in relatively
clean areas.

3) <u>Sierra Club Proposal</u>. The Sierra Club had
developed a proposal for what it thought
"significant deterioration meant. The first written
evidence of this proposal is contained in a November
20, 1972 letter from Bruce Terris, the principal
attorney for the Sierra Club in the case, to John
Quarles, then EPA's Assistant Administrator for
Enforcement and General Counsel. The Sierra Club
plan would have set up two possible types of
definitions for "significant deterioration." Both
definitions involved a change in the concentration
of pollutants in ambient air-following the approach
of the ambient air quality standards. However, the
two definitions differed with respect to how these
concentrations would be measured. The first
alternative called for concentrations to be measured
"over that volume of air within one kilometer of the
source;" the second alternative would use
concentrations "measured at ground level within one
kilometer of the source." Both alternatives would
be applied as a test for any new or modified source
locating in a clean air area, with the more
restrictive one governing whether a source would be
allowed to build and operate. The Sierra Club plan
also provided for an EPA permit system,
demonstration by the source of its impact on air
quality, monitoring of air quality by industry, and
the use by industry of "the best available
demonstrated [control] technology."[13]

4) <u>Ambient Air Quality Ceiling</u>. The fourth plan
would have specified allowable increases in ambient
air quality, though in this case the concentrations
would be measured at ground level and would be
averaged over a year's time. Two conceptual
alternatives were presented: one in which the

allowable increase in concentration would be a 20%
increase over existing air quality, and another in
which EPA would set a fixed ceiling, expressed in
the proposal as "X micrograms per cubic meter
(ug/m^3)", which would apply nationwide.

Two other alternatives were discussed more
briefly in the initial options outline. The first
would have keyed emissions density or air quality
ceilings to intended land use. However, the outline
indicates that "no analysis" was to be presented on
this option because of "time, data, technique
constraints." A second option, emission charges,
was similarly not to be pursued "due to radical
departure from present regulatory methods."

EPA did not have to rush to judgment on these
options because the Supreme Court agreed to hear an
appeal to overturn the D.C. Circuit Court's ruling.[14]
This was fortunate for EPA, since despite EPA's
assurances to the contrary, it is apparent that EPA
could not have met the court order. If the Supreme
Court had refused to take the case, EPA would have
had to obtain an extension based on a hurried
proposal or some other evidence that the Agency was
proceeding in good faith. The nature of the courts
as reactive institutions is apparent in this
instance. While they could command EPA to do
something and set time limits, it was not within
their power to actually do the Agency's work.[15]

Nonetheless, the use of the courts by
environmental interest groups to escalate their
attack on EPA's policy had already had an effect.
Real resources in EPA were now being applied to
examine just what significant deterioration meant
and how it might be implemented. One consequence of
this was the creation within EPA of a group of staff
who had a stake in making PSD work. Moreover, the
Agency's top officials had been forced to pay
attention to PSD, and these officials were having to
begin thinking about the possibility that their
original policy position would not be sustained.
From an organizational standpoint, these
developments constituted a major victory for the
environmental groups and a significant shift in the

level and kinds of organized attention which EPA was
giving to PSD.

Despite this, the Sierra Club was not impressed
with either its success to date or EPA's
responsiveness to its policy concerns. Following
the Appeals Court ruling, Assistant Administrator
Quarles wrote to the Sierra Club asking it to
suggest means to carry out Judge Pratt's order. In
response, the Sierra Club protested "the
unreasonable manner in which the Environmental
Protection Agency has treated the plaintiffs
throughout this litigation . . ." The Club
criticized EPA for having "flagrantly violated" the
District Court order, and charged EPA with ignoring
the Sierra Club's offers to work with EPA "except
for a single preliminary meeting held at our request
on August 30, 1972." Even the November 13th letter
was attacked as not "in good faith" because "instead
of offering to meet and discuss this extremely
important and complicated matter, you simply request
that we put our position in writing . . . in a
period of 6 days . . ."[16]

EPA's legal battle with the Sierra Club
continued through the winter and spring of 1973.
Briefs for the Supreme Court were prepared by both
the Sierra Club and the Justice Department, which
represented EPA, and oral arguments were presented
on April 18, 1973.[17]

The substance of these legal arguments has been
amply analyzed elsewhere.[18] For our purposes, it is
more important that the delays caused by the legal
process afforded EPA's technical staff an
opportunity to think about what they would do if EPA
lost the suit and had to propose a PSD regulation.

The Evolution of EPA's Proposals

During the winter/spring of 1973, OAQPS staff
began to flesh out the ideas which had been

hurriedly identified in November, 1972 when it
appeared that a court order might force a very rapid
proposal. At that time, OAQPS staff had been
prepared to argue that the only practicable
alternative was one which imposed a maximum
technology plus analysis of impact requirement or
sources. OAQPS favored this approach despite
concerns that such a plan would not meet the court's
requirement because it would impose no theoretical
upper bound on emissions increases and air quality
deterioration in an area (though it would presumably
slow the rate at which such increase/deterioration
would occur).

While the technology approach continued to be
viewed favorably in OAQPS, the additional time
allowed for some further analysis of other options.
Although these other options appear to have been
developed with little outside input, some of their
core assumptions were to change very little over
time and form the basis of ideas which were
eventually codified in legislation in 1977. The
options developed in OAQPS in late 1972 and early
1973 also share one other characteristic of later
discussions of PSD. Despite the effect which PSD
was expected to have on growth, land use, and
development, most of the decisions about the rules
turned on relatively arcane technical and
engineering judgments whose importance was
appreciated only by a very small group of "insider"
experts.

PROPOSALS IN THE WINTER/SPRING OF 1973

As noted above, had EPA been required to propose
regulations in compliance with the court-ordered
deadline of November 30, 1972, OAQPS' preferred
approach would have been a plan which emphasized
technological controls. The plan would have called
for the application of "best practical control
techniques" on sources in clean air areas, combined
with a requirement that a source notify the public

of the expected effect of the source on the area's
air quality. This approach would have essentially
defined "significant deterioration" as "unnecessary
deterioration," imposing technology-based
restrictions on what a source could emit without
attempting to otherwise influence where a source
should locate or how much development an area could
allow (unless the attainment or maintenance of any
national ambient air quality standard were
threatened). The vehicle for imposing this
requirement would have been a review, prior to
construction, of any proposed new or modified source
to ensure that the source would be equipped with
"best practicable control technology" (BPCT).[19]
      From the standpoint of the <u>Sierra Club</u> decision,
this plan had one obvious flaw. Though the plan
called for the use of BPCT, it imposed no
theoretical upper bound on how high emissions could
ultimately go or how much air quality could
deteriorate. Hypothetically, at least, either a
concentration of well-controlled sources (e.g.,
significant growth in an area) or a large "well--
controlled" single source such as a large power
plant could cause an area's air quality to decline
substantially. The only effective limits to this in
principle were the ambient air quality standards,
and the court in upholding the Sierra Club's
position had implied that an approach which
permitted degradation up to these standards would
not be allowed. Moreover, the courts had rejected
EPA's contention that New Source Performance
Standards (NSPS)--a set of technology-based
standards--would be sufficient to prevent
significant deterioration.
      Faced with this dilemma, OAQPS staff began to
examine the other alternatives to prevent
significant deterioration in more detail--especially
those which contained some actual upper limit on
emissions increases or air quality degradation. In
doing so, the OAQPS staff quickly identified, at
least in rudimentary form, all of the major issues
which have continued to trouble PSD ever since. In
effect, any proposal to prevent significant

deterioration was forced to provide answers to five
basic questions.
1)   What pollutants would be covered?
2)   What types of control equipment would be
      required on which sources of pollution?
3)   Would the proposal focus on emissions or
      air quality?
4)   What upper limits on growth would exist?
5)   What role would State and local governments
      have in determining "significant
      deterioration"?
The following sections discuss each of these
questions briefly.
    1) <u>What Pollutants Would Be Covered?</u>--Judge
Pratt's order did not mention any specific
pollutants.[20]   The only mention of specific
pollutants anywhere in the litigation history of
<u>Sierra Club vs. Ruckelshaus</u> occurs in the briefs
filed by the Sierra Club, where it was stated that
all of the six pollutants for which national ambient
standards had been set (the so-called "criteria
pollutants") should fall under the scope of
significant deterioration rulings.[21]   Consistent with
that position, the earliest EPA proposals envisioned
that at least five of the six criteria pollutants
would be covered under PSD rules, with photochemical
oxidants left out because they were not emitted
directly from sources but rather were byproducts of
emissions of other pollutants, notably hydrocarbons
and nitrogen oxides.[22]   However, carbon monoxide,
hydrocarbons, and nitrogen oxide emissions
predominantly came from <u>mobile</u> sources (e.g., cars
and trucks) rather than the stationary sources
which, in EPA's eyes at least, were the main focus
of efforts to prevent significant deterioration.
Expansion of the PSD concept to cover the "mobile
source pollutants" would be very controversial
because 1) the 1970 Clean Air Amendments already
required a 90% reduction in the emissions of these
pollutants from new cars by 1975, and 2) further
requirements to prevent mobile source emissions from
degrading air quality would have gotten very quickly
into detailed local issues of land use patterns and
growth.[23]

2) What Types of Control Equipment Would Be Required?--The term "best practicable control techniques" obscured major disagreements about the sources which would be subject to such controls under a PSD program. Two possible candidates existed. The first was to apply this requirement only to those sources which were eventually going to be subject to NSPS anyway. In this case, PSD would amount to little more than an acceleration of the NSPS program (with one important exception, discussed below).

The other alternative was to set, in advance, an emissions threshold so that any plant with projected emissions above the threshold would have to meet the BPCT requirement, regardless of whether EPA expected to promulgate an NSPS for that source or not. Under this approach, the scope of the significant deterioration program would be dramatically affected by whether this threshold was set at a relatively high or low level: the lower the level, the more sources which would be subject to significant deterioration control requirements. Moreover, another important definitional question had to be settled: would the emissions of plants which were potentially subject to PSD regulations be measured before or after any control equipment was otherwise put on by the source? This would also affect the coverage of the PSD regulations, though the degree of this effect was initially unknown.

There was one type of source where "BPCT" had the potential to be quite different from NSPS: coal-fired power plants burning low-sulfur Western coal. In 1971, EPA had promulgated an NSPS for coal-fired power plants which would require the use of "scrubbers", expensive, complicated (and at that time, relatively unproven) devices for removing sulfur dioxide from the exhaust gases of power plants burning high-sulfur coal. These standards, however, could be met without using scrubbers by power plants which burned relatively low-sulfur Western coal.[24] Requiring the use of such "scrubbers" as BPCT on power plants burning low sulfur coal under a BPCT requirement would be a major policy shift for EPA.

3) <u>Would the Proposal Focus on Emissions or Air Quality?</u>--As noted above, EPA staff initially proposed two different ways of establishing a theoretical upper limit on the amount of pollution which could be added to a given area. The first variation focused on emissions, by allowing a certain percentage increase in emissions (with a fixed maximum absolute increase) in any given area. The second variation also proposed to allow increased emissions, but the basis for the allowable increase was to be the effect of these emissions on the surrounding ambient air quality.

This was a critical distinction which hearkened back to the air quality standards/emissions standards debate of the mid-1960's. The choice of one approach or the other was a key decision for PSD policy for two reasons. First, the two programs have somewhat different objectives. Second, the implementation of the programs would differ substantially.

A program based upon permissible emissions increases would limit total emissions loadings into the atmosphere. Such an approach would be implemented through an engineering estimation, prior to the construction of a proposed source of pollution, of the expected emissions which the source would produce. These expected emissions would then be compared to the allowed extra amount of emissions which an area could have, and this relatively straightforward accounting calculation would determine whether the source could be constructed in a given area. The principal drawback of this approach from an air pollution point of view was that the same amount of emissions could have quite different effects on the surrounding ambient air depending on the geography and meteorology of the area in which the emissions were released and the method of their release (e.g., as ground level fugitives, through a tall smokestack, and so on).

The air quality approach would also require an estimation of emissions, but would go an extra step in taking into account the effect of the projected emissions on the surrounding air quality. This effect would have to be modeled, using computer

simulations. The modeling exercise would estimate
the expected additional effect, or increment of
deterioration, which would be caused by the
emissions from the proposed new source on the air
quality of the surrounding area. The modeling used
for these projections would require information on a
variety of factors specific to the location of a
source, including the type of terrain surrounding
it, the meteorology of the area, and the
characteristics of the pollution stream emitted by
the source.[25]

4) <u>What Upper Limits On Development Would
Exist?</u>--For either the emission or air quality
approach, some basis would have to be found for
determining just how much "extra" pollution could be
allowed without having allowed "significant"
deterioration. Obviously, the answer to this
question was tantamount to defining what
"significant" meant. There were two possible ways
of making such a definition: either constructing a
more or less arbitrary absolute value, measured as
emission units per square mile, or (for the ambient
approach) as concentrations of pollution per volume
of air; or defining "significant" in relation to
existing air quality as some more or less arbitrary
percentage of what was already there.

5) <u>What Role Would State and Local Governments
Have in Determining "Significant Deterioration"?</u>--No
matter which approach was taken to designing a PSD
program, it would involve a number of technical and
policy judgments about which there could be
substantial disagreement. Yet these judgments could
have a profound effect on the economic future of an
area--or so it was thought at the time by both
supporters and opponents of PSD.[26] If this was the
case, who would be responsible for making these
judgments? What would the respective role of
Federal, State, and local governments be?

This was an important issue to EPA officials for
a variety of reasons. First, the Nixon
Administration espoused a strong belief in the
philosophy of the "New Federalism," designed to
strengthen the roles and responsibilities of State
governments. Secondly (and somewhat to the

contrary), the 1970 Amendments and the creation of
EPA had forced a massive rearrangement of the
traditional patterns of Federal-State relations
which had been established with NAPCA prior to 1970;
these new relations were still being worked out and
sensitivities were high on all sides. Finally, and
perhaps most importantly, the issue of land-use
planning was forcefully raised by the significant
deterioration issue. This is one of the most
sensitive areas of government for State and local
authorities.[27]

MOVING AWAY FROM "BEST PRACTICAL CONTROL TECHNOLOGY"

     OAQPS staff, following internal discussions, met
with Administrator Ruckelshaus in November, 1972,
with a variation on the emission density plan which
they had developed. It appears that this proposal
was suggested by OAQPS staff in response to their
feeling that "Headquarters wasn't happy with
anything else we had given them." At the conclusion
of the meeting, Ruckelshaus announced that he had
decided to take the Sierra Club case to the Supreme
Court rather than adopt any particular PSD proposal
at that time. Ruckelshaus also repeated the policy
objections which he felt made PSD a bad policy idea
in the first place. He believed that it would
encourage the concentration of industry in urbanized
areas which were already suffering from pollution
worse than the health standards. From an
administrative standpoint, he argued that PSD would
force him to spend scarce EPA manpower addressing
areas which, in his judgment, were not as important
a national priority as the control of urban air
pollution.[28]
     With the delay resulting from the acceptance of
the case by the Supreme Court and accompanying stay
of Judge Pratt's ruling, OAQPS staff continued to
examine how the various possible plans might work.
The most definitive statement of OAQPS thinking
during the period between December 1972 and June of

1973 was contained in reports prepared by Robert
Coleman, an engineer on the staff of the Strategies
and Air Standards Division. Two drafts of this
paper were in the files: one, which was described
as a "second draft" dated April 16, 1973, and a
second dated May 24th.[29]
    Both drafts set out three basic alternatives:
the Best Practicable Control Technology alternative,
an ambient concentration alternative, and an
emissions increase alternative, and analyze the
likely effects of each one. While the reports do
not use the analytic framework of the five questions
laid out in the preceding section, they do provide a
set of answers to them.

Best Practicable Control Technology Plan

    Both drafts describe this alternative in terms
similar to those identified in the earliest OAQPS
thinking in November, 1972. With respect to
pollutant coverage, however, while the April draft
addressed all five criteria pollutants, the May
draft only discussed particulate matter and sulfur
oxides. Moreover, while the April draft contained a
list of 24 source categories which would be covered
under PSD, the May draft listed only 16 such
categories.[30] The reason for these discrepancies was
not stated in the report; however, it appears that
they reflected changes in thinking within OAQPS over
the expected scope and coverage of the NSPS which
would be the basis for the sources to be regulated
under PSD.
    Coleman's reports indicate that the BPCT plan
would have little effect on emissions over and above
NSPS. The April report stated that once NSPS were
promulgated, plants covered by them "would have the
emissions shown under BPCT." This reflected an
assumption that the NSPS would equal BPCT.[31]
However, in the May report, a qualifier has been
added which notes that BPCT "would have a significant impact on emissions if additional NSPS are
not promulgated."[32]

In a memo dated April 16, 1973, Coleman shed
some additional light on the kinds of discussion
which were going on in OAQPS about the BPCT option
at this time. He wrote:

> "I really do not agree with Dr. Steigerwald [by
> then the OAQPS Director, John Middleton having
> resigned] that NSPS and BPCT are different for
> SO_2 as our regulation is now written. It seems
> to me that what we are in fact requiring is flue
> gas desulfurization and not low sulfur fuel.
> The actual emissions from the plan will remain
> the same. There is a possibility that power
> plants in the western United States where the
> low sulfur fuel supply is adequate will emit
> less but this seems small reason to call our
> plan BPCT.
>
> My own inclination is to drop the title [of
> BPCT] and build up public involvement . . . I
> feel our preamble should stress even stronger
> than it does now that we feel that "significant
> deterioration" is not a nationally definable
> term but will vary from location to location
> depending on the desires of the local population
> for a balance between the high degree of air
> quality and industrial or urban expansion."

The emphasis on local definition in this
discussion highlights the feature of the BPCT plan
which was most attractive to OAQPS officials--it
preserved local decision-making authority over
matters which OAQPS staff regarded as primarily
local in character. This approach is consistent
with a view that the goals of air pollution control
could be advanced through essentially technological
means, and without the use of extensive Federal
involvement in local land use planning activities.
OAQPS's views were in striking contrast to the ones
articulated by the Sierra Club and other
environmental groups, who regarded land use as the
key to achieving air quality as well as other
environmental goals.   This perspective was to

persist throughout the discussions on PSD and helps
to explain many of OAQPS' judgment calls.[31]

The April draft of the report summarizes the
assessment of the BPCT plan by saying that "in
general, this plan does not directly address itself
to improving air quality or preventing significant
deterioration of air quality . . . The quantifiable
features of this plan indicate that it does nothing
more or faster than EPA is planning on doing now."[34]
This language was toned down somewhat in the May
version, which also noted that "the main advantage
of this type of this approach is . . . that a review
procedure involving a decision on the local level is
set up.[35] In both reports, however, there is a clear
skepticism about whether a BPCT approach alone would
be capable of meeting the basic test imposed on EPA
by the court decision.

Air Quality Limit Plan

Both drafts noted that under an air quality
limit plan, "significant deterioration means an
increase in the concentration of any pollutant for
which there is a national standard up to some level
below the standard." They observed that "the level
is entirely arbitrary as there are not known adverse
effects on public health or welfare below the
standard."[36] There were two ways to calculate such
levels--as a percentage increase in ambient
concentrations or an absolute allowance, both of
which depended on meteorological diffusion modeling.

In his drafts, Coleman attempted to predict the
likely impact of certain types of new sources on
surrounding air quality. He noted that "estimates
obtained in this manner should only be used as gross
indicators since the meteorological and
topographical characteristics [which affect air
quality in] any specific area are sometimes of great
importance in determining ground level
concentrations." He also noted that "models are
generally available to predict SO_2 [sulfur dioxide]
and TSP [total suspended particulates]
concentrations only."[37]

The remainder of Coleman's analysis of this
option was therefore limited to these two
pollutants. Most of his analysis was restricted to
SO_2 emissions from coal-fired power plants, for
these reasons:
1)   A "large" power plant controlled to BPCT "puts
     out five times as much SO_2 as the next largest
     source;"
2)   At this time, it was projected that "about three
     times as many power plants as all other major
     SO_2 sources will be built;" and
3)   "Costs of flue gas cleaning devices for SO_2 from
     power plants far overshadow control costs for
     any other industry."[38]
Coleman's analysis presented the results of
modeled SO_2 impacts of power plants using different
assumptions about size and stack parameters, as well
as some modeling of other sources. He concluded
that power plants "as expected" have the greatest
short-term impact on air quality, though petroleum
refineries may have a larger long-term impact, and
that both terrain and stack height have a
significant effect on short term ground
concentrations.[39]

Coleman's report criticized the Sierra Club's
proposed variation on the ambient impact plan.[40] It
described the concentration increase proposed by the
Sierra Club, 4 ug/m^3, as "totally restrictive in
terms of growth for all time periods except the
annual [average]." Even when the short term (3 hour
and 24 hour) averages were adjusted to reflect the
same relative stringency as the annual averages,
only 3 of 14 modeled power plants "could possibly be
built," and since even these were assumed to be
"located in areas of very good dispersion[,] if
dispersion were even somewhat limited, it is
doubtful that [even] these plants could be built."
The report noted that the Sierra Club plan "could be
less severe in areas which already had moderate SO_2
concentration (e.g., areas at the fringes of cities)
where SO_2 reductions were expected as a "fallout"
from SO_2 control action in urban areas."[41]

Having discussed the consequences of the Sierra
Club plan, the report proposed an alternative: "a

[percentage] increase [above existing air quality]
or allowance which will not have such a severe
impact." The report suggested the use of "numbers
which will permit the construction of new sources--
especially power plants." It observed:

> If this reasoning behind the selection of a
> percentage and allowance is correct, the
> question arises as to the necessity for the
> percent portion of the plan. If the allowance
> is enough to provide growth in all areas the
> percent increase only acts to give areas with
> high concentrations more allowance. It does not
> appear that the percent increase plays any
> constructive role in the plan.[42]

The report then described a possible allowance,
designed to "give all areas sufficient allowance to
develop to some degree," though it recognized that
the allowance would force the use of tall stacks on
power plants, prevent "clustering of point sources,
and inhibit location of sources in" certain
locations (such as a valley with unsuitable
meteorological conditions). The values estimated in
the report were:

Averaging Time	SO_2 Increase	TSP Increase
3 hours	300 ug/m^3	----
24 hours	100 ug/m^3	30 ug/m^3
Annual	15 ug/m^3	10 ug/m^3

These values were selected to allow the
"typical" 1000 megawatt power plant to be
constructed without violating the selected ambient
increment values.[43] However, the report noted that
"in the long term, this option has a significant
impact on national growth patterns by imposing a
lower ceiling on ambient concentrations than
presently exists. The time when this impact will be
felt will vary from place to place . . . "[44]

Coleman's report summarized its analysis of the air quality limits plan by concluding that while the Sierra Club plan could cause "significant disruption" in development patterns, a plan "similar to the Sierra Club plan" which permitted "an absolute increase in concentration" could be implemented without "as severe an impact." The report recognized that the modeled estimates were just estimates and that "it would be preferable" if they would be "verified by observation," but that such verification was "impossible" because of limited data. The models therefore represented "the best means presently available to estimate the impact of sources on ambient air quality."[45]

A variation of the air quality limits plan was ultimately adopted as a regulation by EPA. In light of this, it is interesting to note that Coleman's report raises almost all of the objections and problems which have accompanied this plan, including modeling uncertainty, accommodation of growth, assumptions about terrain and meteorology, and assumptions about emissions. The role of States in allocating growth is not discussed, nor is there much discussion of how this plan might be implemented. The unspoken assumption underlying this plan appears to be that implementation would take care of itself once the ground rules were laid out.

Emissions Limitations Plan

The third alternative discussed in the Coleman report was a plan based on limiting new emissions in an area. As noted above, the outline for this plan was first developed in November, 1972, in the wake of the Appeals Court decision, as EPA staff cast about for a plan that would satisfy the court order. The Coleman report now tried to work out this plan in more detail.

Under this plan, "significant deterioration" meant an "increase in the level of emissions from a given area over those emissions levels which existed in some baseline year." The selection of values for

the allowed increase was "a wholly arbitrary
decision." According to the report, the emission
limitations plan had two advantages over the air
quality limit plan: it was easier to measure or
calculate emission changes than air quality changes,
and it gave an area more flexibility in locating
sites than the air quality plan by defining away the
problem of localized degradation of air quality
because of poor terrain or meteorology. However,
the report noted that "by limiting total emissions
we have little knowledge of the effect on air
quality."[46] It is interesting to note that the two
advantages of the emissions limitations plan were
both implementation advantages.

There were three different ways of calculating
how much of an emissions increase would be allowable
as "non-significant." The first would allow a
percent increase over existing emissions, measured
in tons per year (TPY) in an area at a given time.
The second would have allowed a specified percent
increase in emissions density (e.g., TPY per square
mile). The third would allow no net increase in
emissions (e.g., any new increased emissions would
have to be offset by a decline in emissions
somewhere else). Again, only SO_2 and TSP were
considered in this option, the reason being that
large future HC/CO emissions decreases were assumed
nationwide because of controls on cars, and NO_x
emissions were not well understood at that time.[47]

The analysis of the effects which such emissions
control schemes would have on new power plant
siting, however, showed a number of difficulties.
With regard to the first such approach, the report
noted that "even with a 40% increase in existing
emissions 85% of all [clean air areas] could not
support a 1000 megawatt power plant or any
combination of plants equalling 1000 megawatts."
Even worse, 74% of such areas could not support even
a 500 megawatt power plant. This was because clean
areas generally had few existing emissions sources--
40% of a low figure was still low. Even smaller
allowed increases (10%, 20%) would of course create
greater problems.[48]

In discussing the emission density plan, Coleman's analysis came face to face with the conflicting philosophies of air quality control and emissions control. In trying to develop a reasonable rationale for an emissions density increment, the report attempted to define a relationship between emission density and air quality. Although such a relationship "seemed obvious," the analysis showed "there is little direct relationship between emission density and air quality on a national scale. This is only to be expected because of great variations in meteorology and source characteristics from region to region." Therefore Coleman in his report "arbitrarily" chose densities of 3 TPY/mi^2 for SO_2 and 1 TPY/mi^2 for TSP for his analysis, since these "corresponded" to ambient levels significantly below the ambient standards.[49]

However, Coleman found that this approach was not much more useful. As compared to the plan just described, "the restriction on the location of new power plants is lessened but is still severe for plants greater than 500 MW." Moreover, the third approach--no net increase in emissions--was even worse, since many clean areas had essentially no emissions to "net out." Finally, the report identified no way to resolve the still difficult problem of the relationship between emissions and air quality without getting into the same kind of area by area modeling calculations which it was the object of the emissions limit plan to avoid. In short, while the emissions density approach appeared easier to implement than the air quality limit plan, it would, using Coleman's assumptions, place "significant restrictions on the potential locations of large sources."[50]

Summary of the Options as of June, 1973

Coleman's report avoided recommendations on the grounds that "they really went beyond the quantifiable scope of the report."[51] However, the report assessed the options in summary form against five criteria: impact of the plan, data required, data reliability, feasibility of implementation, and major problems. The summary indicated general support for an emissions increase plan, on the grounds that its feasibility of implementation was greater than the ambient increment plan, and that the BPCT plan, which was rated as most practical, might not be acceptable to the Sierra Club or the court. However, the summary noted that there was no certainty concerning the impact of an emissions increase plan, and that for all the plans other than BPCT, the chief problem was availability of data. Data reliability was "poor" for the ambient air quality plan because of the limitations inherent in modeling.[52]

Shep Melnick has suggested that OAQPS engineers favored the emissions density plan for two reasons: it avoided the uncertainties associated with the ambient air quality approach; and it posed far fewer administrative and technical problems than the ambient increment approach, especially in the area of data needs and availability.[53] Coleman's report bears out this conclusion, though it is important to remember that the emissions increase plan was itself a fallback from the initial "favorite" in OAQPS--the BPCT plan--as it became apparent that BPCT would not meet a key perceived need of EPA's legal officials in presenting a plan which they felt would satisfy the court. Moreover, the potential effects of an emission density plan in restricting power plant siting were a source of concern in OAQPS.

However, even in developing the emissions increase plan, Coleman's report reached some very important conclusions which affected the way issue would be framed from that point on. Returning to

the original five questions raised earlier in this
chapter, several had been answered.

1) <u>What Pollutants Would Be Covered?</u>--Both the
air quality and emissions increase plan would
effectively limit PSD to two pollutants, SO_2 and
TSP, for technical reasons of feasibility and
because mobile source controls were expected to
prevent deterioration and even cause improvements
for the others.

2) <u>What Types Of Control Would Be Required?</u>--All
of the plans envisioned BPCT as a baseline. The
only serious debate about what this meant concerned
whether new Western power plants would have to use
"scrubbers."

3) <u>Would PSD Focus On Emissions Or Air Quality?</u>
--The strength of each plan was the weakness of the
other. The basic approach of the air quality
increment plan gave at least the <u>appearance</u> of being
able to meet the critical legal test--preventing
significant deterioration of <u>air quality</u>--but it
could do so only by relying on a technique, air
quality modeling, which was very sensitive to
assumptions and produced results with a high degree
of uncertainty. Using an emissions approach would
increase certainty and be easier to administer, but
whether that "certainty" would allow a lot or little
deterioration of air quality was difficult to say.

4) <u>What Upper Limits On Development Would</u>
<u>Exist?</u>--These values were calculated differently for
the air quality and emission limit plans.
Ironically in each case, the values were derived
using the opposite approach. The air quality limits
were based on projections of the impact from a 1000
megawatt power plant, while the emission density
limits were based on working backwards from air
quality values. More important than the actual
values or their method of computation, however, was
the acknowledgement that in both cases, the values
selected <u>were essentially arbitrary</u>. OAQPS
engineers knew no better than the court how to
define "significant." In fact, to return to a point
Coleman made in this report, OAQPS did not <u>want</u> the
responsibility for making this decision, but felt
this definition should "vary" from location to

location depending on the desires of the local
population for a balance between the high degree of
air quality and industrial or urban expansion."[54]
    5) <u>What Discretion Would States Have Vs. Federal
Control</u>--Clearly the OAQPS, while preferring to
grant maximum discretion to State and local
officials, believed that if the court decision was
to mean anything some Federal restrictions would
have to be placed on the upper allowable limits of
air quality deterioration. However, OAQPS officials
were reluctant to engage in debates over "growth"
issues that seemed to be larger social questions
which were properly the province of State and local
government officials and should not be driven by
Federal decisions about air quality levels.[55]

The Supreme Court Decision of June 11, 1973

    Between December and June, 1973, EPA and the
Sierra Club were continuing the legal battle over
significant deterioration. The Supreme Court had
stayed Judge Pratt's decision on December 11, 1972,
thereby relieving EPA of the immediate
responsibility of promulgating regulations, and
granted certiorari on January 15, 1972. Both sides
then presented written briefs to the court, and oral
arguments were heard on April 18, 1973. The Sierra
Club was joined in its suit by several parties who
submitted <u>amici</u> <u>curiae</u> briefs, while EPA was
supported as well by <u>amici</u> briefs, mostly by
industry. The most notable <u>amicus</u> brief filed in
support of the Sierra Club was one filed by 22 State
attorneys general in support of the Sierra Club's
interpretation of the statute.
    As noted above, the merits of the legal
arguments presented by both sides have been
adequately discussed elsewhere.[56] Both sides clearly
hoped that the Supreme Court would not only decide
in their favor, but adopt their policy rationale for

124 **Protect and Enhance**

significant deterioration. However, on June 11th,
1973, the Court ruled that in the case "the judgment
is affirmed by an equally divided Court." The Court
split four to four, and as a result, Judge Pratt's
decision became the sole guidance on the "official"
legal meaning of the "protect and enhance" language
of Section 101(b).[57]

Reaction to the Court decision was swift. Carl
Bagge, president of the National Coal Association,
said that the Court's decision "makes the energy
crisis far worse. It will stop the construction of
any new fossil fuel power plants in the United
States." He called upon Congress to amend the Clean
Air Act "to give America's need for heat, light, and
energy equal standing with its need for clean air."
Similar if less dramatic public statements were made
by heads of the Edison Electric Institute (a trade
association for the utilities) and the U.S. Chamber
of Commerce.[58]

The Sierra Club, on the other hand, hailed the
Court's decision as a dramatic vindication of its
position. Bruce Terris, counsel for the Club in the
case, said that the Club believed that the decision
put the burden on EPA to define what "significant
deterioration" meant, but stated that in any event
EPA could not "satisfy the Act by imposing some
other requirement such as 'best practical
technology.'"[59] Terris' sentiments were backed up by
an unidentified spokesman for the staff of the
Senate Public Works Committee, who declared the
Court's interpretation "totally consistent with the
[Senate committee] staff's interpretation of the
Act." Senator Muskie also issued a statement saying
that the Court had preserved "a critical element of
the Clean Air Amendments of 1970," which would
provide "a means to require the best emission
control technology available and then take another
look to assure that available technology will not
result in significant deterioration."[60]

For its part, EPA reacted cautiously. Bob Baum,
EPA's associate general counsel for air, promised
that the Agency would propose PSD regulations
"within the next ten days," but noted the absence of
any guidance on significant deterioration. He

referred specifically to the problem of "trying to
decide whether to use an ambient air approach or a
technology approach," and observed that "it is
inevitable that there will be litigation over the
regulations as they finally are promulgated."
However, Baum also said that EPA did not intend to
ask Congress to amend the Clean Air Act and
recommended that EPA's proposed regulations be
reviewed before deciding whether such amendments
were needed.[61]

While EPA did not quite meet this ten day
timetable, it did move relatively swiftly to propose
regulations. However, rather than settle the issue
within the Agency about whether to propose a BPCT,
air quality limit, or emission limit approach, EPA
took an unusual step. In its proposed regulation,
published in the Federal Register on July 16, 1973,
EPA described all three approaches and asked for
public comment on them, stating that a PSD policy
raised issues which were "potentially so far
reaching that the question of how such a policy
should be defined and implemented cannot properly be
addressed, much less decided, on narrow legal
grounds. Rather, it is a question that must be
discussed, debated, and decided as a public policy
issue, with full consideration of its economic and
social implications . . ."[62] This open airing of the
policy questions surrounding PSD stands in marked
contrast to the approach used by NAPCA officials in
the 1968-70 period, as well as the debate within EPA
on PSD policy in 1971, where the discussion was
largely confined to agency officials and staff.
This reflects another
effect of court intervention in Agency rulemaking--
the forcing of internal debate into the open.

THE JULY 16TH PROPOSAL AND THE COLEMAN REPORT

In a statement announcing the proposed
regulations, Acting EPA Administrator Robert Fri
recited the judicial history of PSD, and went on to

describe the "long lasting impact" of the policy "on
the nature, extent, and location and future
industrial, commercial, and residential development
throughout the United States." It could, he stated,
"affect the utilization of the nation's mineral
resources, the availability of employment and
housing in many areas, and the costs of producing
and transporting electricity and manufacturing
goods."[63]

Fri stated that the broad impact of the
regulations justified the unusual "four
alternatives" approach in the proposal. All four
alternatives, in his view, were aimed at the same
two objectives: "minimizing emissions from new
sources of air pollution," and "determining where to
build these sources--in other words, how to control
land use." Fri's statement highlighted one common
thread in all four proposals--the requirement of
BPCT--though now the terminology had changed to
"best available control technology" (emphasis
added).[64] Another common element among the four
proposals is that their increment or emissions
density features covered SO_2 and TSP only, though
best available control technology would be required
for all pollutants.[65] In Fri's judgement, "the main
difference among the alternatives is how land use
decisions would be made."

The July 16th proposal contained essentially the
same options set forth in the Coleman paper, with
one major exception. The July 16th notice proposed
four rather than three alternatives.

I. Air Quality Increment Plan (AQIP)--This is
the same as Coleman's air quality approach, and used
the same set of air quality increments. The
rationale set forth in the Federal Register for
these numbers was that they "represented the
Administrator's best judgment of increments which
would prevent significant deterioration of air
quality in currently clean areas, and yet not
totally prevent the economic development of selected
areas if that development were in the public
interest." To support this, the notice cited power
plant air quality impacts similar to the ones in the

Coleman report, as well as other types of
development modeled in analyzing this option.[66]

II. Emission Limitation Plan--This proposal,
too, reflected the one contained in Coleman's paper,
even down to its initial specification of air
quality control regions as the appropriate areas
(though the notice observed that, if adopted,
provisions to use different areas would be
included). One interesting difference from the
Coleman plan does appear in the proposal: instead
of Coleman's densities of 3 TPY/mi^2 for SO_2 and 1
TPY/mi^2 for TSP, these values were tripled, to 10
TPY/mi^2 for SO_2 and 3 TPY/mi^2 for TSP. Presumably,
someone in EPA had concluded that the original
values were too restrictive and had picked a
different set of "arbitrary" numbers. The basis
used in the July 16th notice to justify the new
numbers was that no air quality control region with
SO_2 densities below these values had air quality
worse than the secondary ambient standards.[67]

III. The Local Definition Plan--This was the
BPCT plan, "dressed up" as Coleman's April 16th memo
had recommended. EPA stated that the approach's
"major advantage" was "that the governmental units
and citizens most affected by decisions on
maintenance of air quality would make these
decisions . . . thereby ensuring that local
requirements and preferences with regard to such
matters as land use, economic development, and use
of natural resources are taken into consideration."
However, EPA's discussion on the alternative also
notes "justifiable concern that States and local
agencies could be subjected to undue pressure by
industries . . . that . . . could cause definitions
of 'significant' which were not in the best long
range interests of these populations." Moreover,
"there is no control over the ultimate level of
deterioration, which could progress . . . up to the
level of the secondary standards."[68]

IV. Area Classification Plan--This alternative
was new, not having been discussed in the Coleman
paper. However, it was a variation on Alternative
I, the increment plan, in that it too relied on
ambient increments of deterioration. The difference

was that <u>two</u> sets of such increments would be
established under this plan. One set (Zone II)
would be the same as those set up under Alternative
I. However, the second set (Zone I) would be much
more restrictive; the increments proposed for Zone I
would be:

Averaging Time	SO$_2$ Increase	TSP Increase
3 hours	25 ug/m^3	----
24 hours	5 ug/m^3	15 ug/m^3
Annual	2 ug/m^3	5 ug/m^3

The intent of Zone I would be to prohibit the
introduction of almost any medium scale residential
or commercial development. As a practical matter,
new sources of any size could be introduced into an
area only if any existing emissions were reduced or
an extremely effective control technology were used.
EPA "anticipated that Zone I would normally be
applied to these ultra-clean areas such as national
and state forests or parks, and other recreational
areas in which it is desired to maintain essentially
no deterioration of air quality."[69]
Under this proposal States were to be
responsible for classifying their land as either
Zone I or Zone II by submitting a "zoning plan"
within six months after the date of promulgation of
the regulations. Zone II would be assumed to be the
norm, with the State required to conduct public
hearings before designating any area as Zone I. A
variance from either the Zone I or Zone II
increments could be obtained "in special
circumstances" after a public hearing and approval
by EPA; however, EPA would normally have no
authority to approve a State's zoning. EPA
acknowledged that the Area Classification Plan
suffered from the same kinds of data availability
problems as the AQIP, but nevertheless felt that
this plan, more than the others, would "ensure that
future developmental patterns can be based on
rational planning . . ." and would require that

"States establish long range growth patterns and
goals." There were other problems: States would
have to "make very difficult and comprehensive
decisions impacting on land use, in a tight time
frame," and States would have to use care in
establishing Zone boundaries "so that the effect of
a source in Zone II does not cause the air quality
in a Zone I to increase [get worse] more than
allowed." Still, with all this, EPA suggested that
the area classification plan "appears to be superior
in many, if not all respects."[70]

This conclusion appears to have been based on
the belief that it was desireable to afford extra
protection to areas such as parks, and that
Alternative IV gave States a means to be more
protective if they so chose. However, the area
classification plan had all of the disadvantages of
the single increment plan and a number of new ones
(e.g., how would you draw a boundary between one
zone and another?). The variance provisions could
provide greater "flexibility," but there was no
reason why such variances could not be provided in a
single increment plan, and without the restrictive
Zone I they would not be needed as much. The Area
Classification Plan was not based on any additional
technical data--in fact, the increments for Zone I
were even more arbitrary than those for Zone II.[71]
Even if it did give States which wished to restrict
development a new air quality tool with which to do
that, there was no reason under existing law that
States could not already do so if they so chose by
imposing more stringent secondary ambient
standards.[72]

It appears from the July 16th proposal that
despite its description as providing "flexibility,"
the only reason for Alternative IV was to respond to
certain other values which the three other proposals
did not address, or at least to combine the values
embodied in the Coleman paper proposals in different
ways. In some ways the area classification plan
borrows from all three of the other proposals: a
strong emphasis on public hearings from Alternative
III; highly restrictive de facto limits on emissions
(in Zone I areas) from Alternative II; and, of

course, the increments from Alternative I. The only
new element was the six month requirement for a
State to submit a "plan" which "puts emphasis on
longer range strategic planning as opposed to short
range case by case decisions." It is this explicit
emphasis on the need for "long range planning" which
most distinguishes Alternative IV.

Alternative IV does not appear to have
originated in OAQPS. Rather, this was added to the
proposal during its review by other Headquarters
offices at EPA. There, a coalition of Agency
officials interested in stimulating national land
use planning were able to successfully argue on
behalf of the creation of the new Alternative IV and
insert it into the regulatory proposal. A similar
alternative could have (theoretically) been
constructed using emission densities as well; the
reason it was not appears to have been the
insistence of EPA's Office of General Counsel that
an air quality increment approach "would stand a
better chance of surviving judicial review" than
would an emissions increment plan.[73]

EPA had thus completed a major step in defining,
under the pressure of court action, just what the
concept of "significant deterioration" meant. The
Agency had narrowed this sweeping concept down to
one which--the rhetoric of the proposal
notwithstanding--essentially had the effect of
identifying certain constraints on land use in
general and on power plant siting in particular.
Yet one can see in the July proposal the seeds--some
new, some of long standing--of a more expanded view
of PSD which some Agency officials felt would
stimulate State thinking about "long range growth
patterns and goals."[74]

Some EPA officials were uneasy about the 1973
proposal, sensing that the Agency's reach was
exceeding its grasp. This feeling is reflected in
the length of the July preamble where EPA attempts
to discuss the significance of PSD for land use
planning, while at the same time insisting that EPA
wanted to maximize State flexibility.[75] The further
development of the tensions between the different
groups in EPA and their different visions of PSD

will be traced in the next chapter, which reviews
EPA's further efforts to develop final PSD
regulations.

The July proposal began the formal regulatory
history of PSD. In many ways it reflected the
dilemma in which the Agency found itself. In the
absence of any clear guidance, yet with a demand
that it do "something," the Agency was forced to
rely on its own judgment about what approach to
take. Yet even as the process of defining PSD
began, it became clear very early to EPA staff that
technical and policy judgments about PSD could not
be readily separated. The subsequent development of
PSD was to highlight this even more, as EPA,
interest groups, other Federal agencies, and the
Congress struggled to affect major national
development and growth policies through the
technical mechanisms of PSD.

NOTES

1. Preliminary Injunction, D. C. District Court, Civil Action 1031-72, <u>Sierra Club, et al. versus Ruckelshaus</u>, filed May 30, 1972. 34 F. Supp. 253 (1972).

2. Bernard J. Steigerwald to Regional Air Division Directors, September 7, 1972.

3. Deposition by Bernard J. Steigerwald to the D.C. Circuit Court, August 24, 1972.

4. Ibid. In part, Pratt denied EPA's application to stay his original order, which forced EPA's Regional office to accelerate their review of State SIP's. Even this acceleration was insufficient to meet the September 30th deadline, however, and according to one official, the Sierra Club then informed the Administrator that he was in danger of being cited for contempt of court. Upon assurances by EPA that it required only a few more days to complete the necessary review of State plans, the Sierra Club wrote to Judge Pratt and asked him to withhold the contempt citation. In the event, <u>all</u> State plans were disapproved in that they all failed to provide for prevention of significant deterioration. Marc Bremer Mihaly, "The Clean Air Act and the Concept of Non-Degradation: Sierra Club vs. Ruckelshaus," <u>Ecology Law Quarterly</u> 2:801; 37 <u>Federal Register</u> 23836. See also footnote 9 below on this point.

5. Interviews with EPA officials. The deadlines of four and six months were evidently taken from Section 110 of the Clean Air Act, and reflect the agency-forcing character of the Act. In Section 110, these time periods constitute strict deadlines by which EPA had to approve initial State SIP submittals or promulgate its own regulations to replace them if a State failed to submit a satisfactory SIP. Interestingly, the original six months deadline

appears to have been based on a reading of
Section 110 which presumed that States were
"required" in their original SIP submissions to
have prevented significant deterioration, though
as noted above, EPA had said earlier in its
regulations governing SIP's that this was not
necessary except as needed to protect the
ambient standards. (Clean Air Act 110(c)(1)).

6. Sierra Club vs. Ruckelshaus, 4 ERC 1815 (D. C.
    Circuit, November 1, 1972). EPA officials were
    not pleased at the conduct of the oral hearing.
    One official noted that the judges asked the
    Justice Department attorney in the case whether
    it wasn't easier to prevent pollution in the
    first place than to clean it up later. The
    Justice attorney answered "yes," rather than
    make the point that the issue was the
    requirement of the Clean Air Act rather than the
    desirability of PSD as a public policy.

7. Mihaly, op. cit., p. 808; W. Stanley Blackburn,
    William H. Roj, and Ralph A. Taylor, Jr.,
    "Review of EPA's Significant Deterioration
    Regulations: An Example of the Difficulties of
    the Agency-Court Partnerships in Environmental
    Law," Virginia Law Review 61:112 (1975); R. Shep
    Melnick, Regulation and the Courts, p. 74.

8. Interviews with EPA officials. There is some
    conflict over just how "surprised" EPA officials
    were when the Supreme Court ultimately upheld
    the District Court ruling: accounts differ on
    this and are necessarily somewhat clouded by the
    passage of time. As will be seen below,
    however, organized work within EPA to translate
    significant deterioration into an operational
    construct dates from the time of the Appeals
    Court decision. Moreover, as one official put
    it, "Any time a Court of Appeals rules
    unanimously against you, you can't be confident
    about the Supreme Court."

9.   It is noteworthy in this respect that formal
notice disapproving all SIPs "to the extent that
they do not contain provisions which will
effectively prevent 'significant deterioration'
of air quality" was not published in the Federal
Register until November 9, 1972--a week after
the Appeals Court decision. The notice stated
that while many States endorsed a general policy
of nondegradation, "no State included detailed
provisions in its enforcement procedures or
regulations for implementing such a policy." In
a reflection of the continuing uncertainty
surrounding PSD, however, the notice also said
that "some of the State plans . . . may in fact
fulfill the requirements of the court order as
that order is finally implemented." See 37
Federal Register 23836-7 (November 9, 1972).

10.   Interview with EPA official. EPA's notice on
the deficiencies of all State SIP's with respect
to PSD included a promise that EPA expected "to
publish, as soon as possible, proposed
regulations setting forth appropriate
requirements for modifications of State
implementation plans." 37 Federal Register
23836 (November 9, 1972). In fact, not only was
it impossible to meet the court's schedule given
the time required between proposal and
promulgation for public comment, EPA as an
organization had absolutely no idea at that time
what it would propose as a regulation.

11.   See "William D. Ruckelshaus and the
Environmental Protection Agency," Case # C16-74-
027 prepared for the John F. Kennedy School of
Government, Harvard University, pp. 11-12.

12.   The following discussion of the six plans draws
largely on handwritten notes found in the OAQPS
files and dating from November 1972. Also found
in Washington files was a package described as
"the Court's Sierra Club package." This
document appears to have originated at about the
same time--e.g., when EPA was under pressure to

meet the District Court order--but contains only
two alternatives: the "best demonstrated
control" approach and the "emission
ceiling/density approach." Interestingly
enough, the ambient air quality increment
approach which ultimately became the basis for
the PSD regulations is not among the
alternatives listed here.

13. Letter, Bruce J. Terris to John Quarles,
     November 20, 1972.

14. EPA petitioned the Supreme Court for a writ of
     certiorari on December 5, 1972. The Court
     stayed the effect of the District Court's order
     to EPA to promulgate regulations on December 11,
     1972, and then actually granted certiorari on
     January 15, 1973. The attempt to have the case
     reviewed by the Supreme Court was opposed by the
     Sierra Club. See Mihaly, op. cit., p. 808-809.
     See also the Sierra Club's brief to the Supreme
     Court opposing certiorari, which is reprinted in
     U. S. Congress, Senate, Committee on Public
     Works, A Hearing Before the Subcommittee on Air
     and Water Pollution of the Committee on Public
     Works, 93rd Congress, 1st session, July 24,
     1973, pp. 239-258 (hereafter cited as 1973
     Senate Nondegradation Hearings).

15. Joseph Padgett to Mr. B. J. Steigerwald, p. 6 on
     "No Significant Degradation Plan," November 7,
     1972. Padgett discusses what could be done in
     response to the court order, and lays out a
     schedule which does not show EPA promulgation of
     State regulations until 2/30/74. Padgett's memo
     reflects a completely different process for
     ensuring such regulations, however, than the one
     envisioned by the court. Under this process,
     EPA would have just issued "Guideline to States"
     on how to prepare SIP revisions for PSD, and EPA
     would have had to receive these SIP and decide
     whether to approve or disapprove them before
     promulgating regulations of its own. The exact
     regulatory status of the "Guidelines," which EPA

was to issue by January 31, 1973, is unclear--a
situation which parallels the problem with the
1969 NAPCA "Guidelines on the Development of Air
Quality Standards and Implementation Plans"
described in Chapter 2. Padgett observed, "I
believe plans developed in response to these
Guidelines would be feasible and responsive to
the Court order with the exception of the
11/30/72 deadline. Although plan development
and submittal would not be complete until August
30, 1973, the 'baseline' still could be
11/30/72. Thus the sense of the Court ruling---
i.e., to prevent significant deterioration as of
now--would be met . . . It seems to me a plan
such as this is the minimum action we could take
to respond to the sense of the Court ruling . .
. "

16. Terris to Quarles, op. cit., November 20, 1972.

17. The briefs for both parties are reprinted in
     1973 Senate Nondegradation Hearings, pp. 259-
     417.

18. See Mihaly, op. cit., especially pp. 809-818;
     Hines, "A Decade of Non-Degradation Policy in
     Congress and the Courts: The Erratic Pursuit of
     Clean Air and Water," Iowa Law Quarterly, 62:
     643 (1977); Richard Stewart, "Judicial Review of
     EPA Decisions," Iowa Law Quarterly, 62: 740-750
     (1977).

19. In addition to the documents cited in note 12
     above, additional documents bearing out this
     conclusion are in the OAQPS files. See
     specifically "EPA Regulations For Disapproved
     State Implementation Plans: Significant
     Deterioration of Air Quality" dated "P.J.B.
     11/6/72" with the penciled notation "by
     Bierbaum;" also see a draft of "Subpart A, Part
     52, Chapter I, Title 40, Code of Federal
     Regulations," proposed amendment to §52.21(b)
     which lays out regulatory language for this
     alternative.

20. 344 F. Supp. 253 (1972).

21. See, for example, the Sierra Club brief to the Supreme Court, reprinted in <u>1973 Senate Nondegradation Hearings</u>, pp.323-324.

22. Draft 40 CFR 52.21(b) cited above, note 19.

23. The effect of the 1970 Clean Air Amendments on automobiles is described, among other places, in Jones, <u>Clean Air</u>, chapter 7; two case studies for the Kennedy School of Government: "Senator Muskie and the 1970 Amendments to the Clean Air Act" (C94-76-140), and "Senator Muskie and the 1970 Amendments to the Clean Air Act: Epilogue (C94-76-140S); Henry D. Jacoby, John D. Steinbruner, <u>et al.</u>, <u>Clearing the Air: Federal Policy on Automotive Emission Control</u> (Cambridge, Mass.: Ballenger), 1973; and Alfred Marcus, <u>Promise and Performance: Choosing and Implementing An Environmental Policy</u> (Westport, Conn.: Greenwood Press), 1980.

24. Again, the story of EPA and scrubbers is a separate tale which is already well documented elsewhere. See in particular Bruce Ackerman and William Hassler, "Beyond the New Deal: Coal and the Clean Air Act," <u>Yale Law Journal</u>, 89 (1980) 1466-1571. Though it is a somewhat different story, PSD and the NSPS for coal-fired power plants are linked throughout this period.

25. More technical information on modeling can be found in U.S. EPA, Office of Air Quality Planning and Standards, "Guideline on Air Quality Models", June, 1978 (and updated several times since).

26. See, for example, the statements of Lawrence Moss, president of the Sierra Club, and Carl Bagge, president of the National Coal Association in the <u>1973 Senate Non-degradation Hearings</u>.

27. See Jones, <u>Clean Air</u>, especially pp. 226-240, 249253, 276-292. Though he particularly focuses on the effects of changing roles and responsibilities in one area (Pittsburgh), similar crises and confrontations were going on throughout the country at this time.

28. Interviews with EPA officials. A similar statement is cited in Melnick, <u>Regulation and the Courts</u>, p. 79

29. Only the May 24th version of this report has a title, "Impact of Selected Alternative Plans to Prevent Significant Deterioration of Air Quality (A Quantitative Assessment)." The OAQPS files contained an April 16th, May 24th, and "June 19th" drafts, the last of which appears to be a copy of the April document. There are some significant differences between the April/June version and the May 24th draft. The April/June version will be cited as <u>Coleman Report A</u>; the May 24th draft will be cited as <u>Coleman Report B</u>. It is worth devoting some space to this report because it is a relatively full statement of the options which EPA eventually translated into regulatory choices. Moreover, Coleman was highly regarded by other OAQPS staff; one official referred to Coleman as "the father of PSD."

30. <u>Coleman Report A</u>, Tables A-1 and A-2; <u>Coleman Report B</u>, Tables A-1 and A-2.

31. <u>Coleman Report A</u>, Section A, IV, A.

32. <u>Coleman Report B</u>, Section A. IV. A.

33. Interviews with EPA officials.

34. <u>Coleman Report A</u>, Section A. IV. C. and A. Summary.

35. <u>Coleman Report B</u>, Section A. IV.

36. Coleman Reports A and B, Section B. I.

37. Ibid., Section B. II. B. Coleman states three
     reasons why models are not available for
     nitrogen oxides, oxidants, or carbon monoxide;
     the historical fact that SO_2/TSP models were
     worked on first; the difficulties involved in
     predicting NO_x/oxidant concentrations in the
     atmosphere because of the reactive qualities of
     these gases; and because stationary sources are
     relatively insignificant contributors of CO when
     compared to mobile sources.

38. Ibid., Section B. II. C.

39. Ibid.

40. The Coleman report does not consider the
     "volumetric averaging" provision of the Sierra
     Club's plan, which would have been even more
     restrictive of development.

41. Ibid., section B. III. A. 1.

42. Ibid., section B. III. A. 2.

43. Ibid., section B. III. A. 2., Table B-8. The
     figures which Coleman devised for the "standard"
     1000 megawatt power plant, using two 450 foot
     stacks and 0.7% sulfur coal without scrubbers,
     showed a maximum 3 hour concentration of 273
     ug/m3 (see Table B-3). The 3 hour SO_2 increment
     was always assumed to be the most restrictive
     one because of the inherent statistical
     instability of the model in predicting short
     term averages. The 1000 megawatt basis for
     selecting the increment values was confirmed by
     interviews with EPA officials. The rationale
     for a 1000 megawatt size was EPA's belief at
     that time that most planned power plants would
     be of that size or smaller.

44. Ibid.

45. Ibid., Section B. Summary.

46. Ibid., Section C. I. and II.

47. Ibid., Section C. III.

48. Ibid., Section C. III. A.

49. Ibid., Section C. III. B.

50. Ibid., Sections C. III., IV., V. Curiously, Coleman does not discuss explicitly any plan of how a fixed emission density could be quite permissive of growth if the area involved was sufficiently large. In part this was because Coleman used air quality control regions (AQCR'S) as assumed areas. However, it would appear by simple arithmetic that if the impact of emissions from (say) a power plant could be spread over a large(r) area, then it could be more easily permitted--especially since large power plants are not "ordinary" projects. On the other hand, this observation is made with 1980's hindsight; growth in needed electrical generating capacity was expected to be much larger in the early 1970's than turned out to actually be the case.

51. Coleman to Padgett, op. cit., April 16, 1973.

52. Coleman Report, Section D., especially Table D-2.

53. Melnick, Regulation and the Courts, pp. 89-91.

54. Coleman to Padgett, op. cit., April 16, 1973. The principle of leaving such choices to state and local governments was such a constant theme among the OAQPS officials whom I interviewed that it may fairly be said to be a part of their organizational culture. OAQPS officials were particularly critical of other parts of EPA which, they felt, were more interested in

"maintaining Washington control over land use
decisions."

55. This same reluctance was to characterize OAQPS
     attitudes about some of the other ambitious
     schemes to use the Clean Air Act to engineer
     large scale social changes. See Melnick,
     Regulation and the Courts, chapter 9 on OAQPS'
     attitude toward transportation control planning.

56. See note 7 above.

57. Fri vs. Sierra Club, 412 U. S. 541 (1973),
     reprinted in 1973 Senate Nondegradation
     Hearings, p. 418. I have been unable to find
     any record of which judges voted which way on
     the case or why. Mr. Justice Powell took no
     part in the decision of the case, thus allowing
     the tie to occur.

58. 4 Environmental Reporter 212 (June, 1973)

59. Ibid.

60. Ibid., pp. 212-213.

61. Ibid., p. 213.

62. 38 Federal Register 18986 (July 16, 1973).

63. "Statement by Robert W. Fri, News Conference on
     Proposed 'Significant Deterioration'
     Regulations, July 13, 1973." Fri was the Acting
     EPA Administrator at that time by virtue of the
     appointment of Mr. Ruckelshaus to be Acting
     Director of the FBI in April, 1973, following
     the L. Patrick Gray scandal. From there, of
     course, Ruckelshaus was appointed Deputy
     Attorney General, and was subsequently fired by
     President Nixon during the famous "Saturday
     Night Massacre" in October 1973 because of his
     refusal to follow the President's order to fire
     Watergate special prosecutor Archibald Cox.

64. Ibid., pp. 2-3. Who was responsible for this change or what it was felt to mean in practical terms is unclear.

65. "Questions and Answers," attached to the Fri statement cited in note 63 above. These questions and answers, prepared as backup material for the press conference, cite three reasons for this: the application of best available control technology would be required for all criteria pollutants; Federal emissions controls on cars would significantly reduce HC, CO, and NO_x emissions already; and the absence of any ability to model HC and NO_x emissions from sources--the same reasons cited in the Coleman report.

66. 38 <u>Federal Register</u> 18990. For example, the values cited in the notice for SO_2 increases from an apartment complex in New York are directly from table B-5 of the Coleman report.

67. Compare Section C. II. B. of the Coleman report to 38 <u>Federal Register</u> 18991.

68. 38 <u>Federal Register</u> 18992.

69. 38 <u>Federal Register</u> 18993.

70. Ibid. The July 16, 1973 notice also discusses two other proposed plans: the Sierra Club's plan, and one based on emissions charges (e.g., an assessed charge per pound of pollutant emitted). They are not discussed further here because neither was seriously considered.

71. Interviews with EPA officials suggest that they did not care just what these increment values actually were. As the intent was to prohibit development, the exact numbers did not matter so long as development was effectively restricted. Also, the technical support document for the July 16, 1973 proposal consists entirely of data taken from the Coleman report. No additional

information to support the Zone 1/long range
plan alternative is presented.

     See U. S. EPA, "Technical Data In Support
of Significant Deterioration," referenced at 38
Federal Register 18985.

72.   See §116 of the Clean Air Act on the retention
of State standard-setting authority, not to
mention the other land-use planning tools at
state disposal.

73.   Melnick, Regulation and the Courts, p. 90. My
independent interview data support this
interpretation.

74.   38 Federal Register 18993.

75.   This results in some wonderfully contorted
preamble language, such as the following:
"Areas assigned to Zone I could retain an option
for significant growth capability. The very
stringent air quality criteria requires only
that any growth be restricted to a form which
has a low air pollution potential. Use of the
land is the prerogative of the State and local
population, and hence complete flexibility is
provided, consistent with prevention of
significant deterioration as appropriate for
each zone." 38 Federal Register 18993. The
preamble was obviously written by a committee.

CHAPTER IV

SHAPING THE 1974 REGULATIONS

EPA's original work plan called for promulgating a final set of PSD regulations by December 22, 1973, six months after the Supreme Court ruling.[1] The six months' timetable was a product of the original ruling by Judge Pratt. However, final EPA rules were not to be published until almost a full year later, and only after a major confrontation had occurred within the Executive Branch over these rules.

This chapter will trace the development of the PSD rules between the July, 1973 proposal and the December, 1974 final rulemaking. Of particular interest is how the struggle among different parts of the Executive Branch--EPA, OMB, the Commerce Department, the Federal Energy Administration, and the White House--affected the behavior of the EPA staff and officials who were involved in drawing up and analyzing these rules. Congressional committees and their staff also played a role, though their effect was more on the overall climate within which EPA functioned and less on PSD specifically than in either the earlier or later periods. Within EPA, the most striking difference at this time is the degree of both management and analytic attention which focused on PSD, as if to compensate for the earlier neglect.

The Context of EPA Action

Before describing the events of 1973-74, it is worth exploring some of the factors which lay behind the further development of the PSD rules. These included the energy crisis, other air pollution control requirements, the activities of environmental groups, EPA's leadership, and the bureaucratic actors within EPA.

EPA AND THE ENERGY CRISIS

The 1972-1973 period witnessed a growing public awareness of what would become known as "the energy crisis." This was most immediately apparent to the general public in the form of gradually increasing prices for gasoline and home heating oil. However, this crisis had a strong effect on pollution control strategies.

Many states, especially in the Northeast, had encouraged industries and utilities to switch from burning coal and begin burning oil or natural gas in the late 1960's and early 1970's as a means for reducing air pollution. The reason for this was that both oil and gas could be burned more cleanly than coal without the use of expensive pollution control equipment. This strategy worked well as long as oil and gas were abundant at low cost. However, it quickly became clear to EPA that individual "clean fuels" requirements by States in their implementation plans had produced a nationwide demand for these fuels which exceeded the available supply. By mid-1973, only a year after approving State implementation plans with restrictive emissions limits, EPA had already announced a "Clean Fuels Policy." Its intent was to encourage some States to relax their emissions limits to "reduce the demand for low-sulfur fuels and control

equipment in some locations, thereby increasing
their availability in others where severe
environmental problems require their use."[2]
President Nixon had even endorsed the idea of
imposing a tax on sulfur emissions as an
economically sound means of allocating scarce low-
sulfur fuels and stimulating the development of
reliable sulfur dioxide control equipment.[3]

Seen in this light, the 1973 oil embargo only
exacerbated trends that were already developing.
However, this probably understates its effect on the
early discussion of PSD. The charges made by Carl
Bagge of the National Coal Association after the
1973 Supreme Court decision, that the uncertainty
created by a nondegradation policy would "be
crippling to expanding coal production capacity" and
might "preclude the establishment of a synthetic
fuel industry based on coal" took on new weight
in the face of widespread expectations that coal
would be America's energy "ace in the hole".[4] The
degree to which the pressure of the oil embargo
affected even the most ardent environmental
supporters can be seen in a November 12, 1973
hearing of the Senate Subcommittee on Air and Water
Pollution on a bill sponsored by Senator Muskie to
allow temporary variances from Clean Air Act
requirements. Muskie, acknowledging that "clean air
advocates and environmental regulators must accept
the interim disruption of compliance schedules in
order to assure the long-term goal of clean air,"
stated that "we can no longer rely on fuel switching
as a clean air alternative." However, he held out
the hope of a technological fix, saying that
"continuous emission controls through the
application of technology must be the means we
adopt."[5]

Others both inside and outside government were
less reluctant to use the energy crisis as an
opportunity to attack the requirements of the Clean
Air Act in general and the PSD decision in
particular. The immediate focus of these attacks
was to urge the conversion of existing oil-burning
power plants to coal and the "temporary" relaxation
of low-sulfur fuel requirements.[6] In particular,

Administration officials outside of EPA joined with private sector interests to call for the relaxation of "unnecessarily stringent" air quality regulations.[7]

OTHER AIR POLLUTION CONTROL CONTROVERSIES

Significant deterioration was not the only target of a concerted attack by industry, and by industry's client organizations within the Administration, on those provisions of EPA's regulations under the Clean Air Act which limited the use of "dirty" fuels, especially high sulfur coal. The most important of these provisions, other than significant deterioration, were national ambient standards for sulfur oxides, stack heights and the use of intermittent control systems. Controversies were ongoing in all three of these areas in the fall of 1973 when EPA rulemaking began on significant deterioration. While an in-depth review of all of these controversies is unnecessary here, a brief discussion of each is required because of their relationship to significant deterioration.

The Sulfur Dioxide Ambient Standard

The health criteria used to set the sulfur dioxide ambient standard had been controversial since the mid-1960's.[8] In 1972, the Kennecott Copper Corporation filed suit against EPA to overturn the secondary SO_2 ambient standard. As a result of the suit, EPA's original secondary SO_2 standard was repealed (though later replaced by one with a different averaging time).[9] This was only the opening round, however, in a concerted attack upon the health basis for the primary SO_2 standard. Coal interests succeeded in getting the Senate Subcommittee on Air and Water Pollution to direct the National Academy of Sciences to review and

critique the data base for the ambient standards,
with the hope that they would be found too
stringent. This resolution passed the Senate on
August 2, 1973, and an Academy panel began work that
fall.[10] In the meantime, EPA had already agreed to
postpone fixing any specific time by which secondary
standards would have to be met, and President Nixon
had announced this as an element of his energy
policy.[11]

Tall Stacks and Intermittent Controls

   While attacking the scientific basis for the
ambient standards, industrial interests were also
challenging the feasibility of controlling SO_2
emissions to attain the standards by the Clean Air
Act deadlines. The principal argument was over the
availability of control devices, known as
"scrubbers," which removed SO_2 from combustion
exhaust gases before the gases were vented to the
atmosphere. EPA had first joined this argument in
1971, when it issued a New Source Performance
Standard for new large coal-fired boilers (including
electric utility boilers) which found that scrubbers
were "adequately demonstrated."[12] This controversy
spread to existing coal-fired power plants, where
scrubbers were proposed as a means for eastern and
midwestern utilities to meet the SO_2 ambient
standards.
   In opposing the use of scrubbers, electric
utilities argued that: 1) scrubbers were very
expensive and unreliable; 2) dispersion of SO_2
through the use of tall smokestacks was a better way
to reduce ambient concentrations of SO_2; and 3) any
remaining problems in meeting ambient SO_2 standards
could be best addressed by using "intermittent
control systems." Intermittent controls, as the
name implies, were techniques for reducing emissions
which did not have to be used all the time. They
took advantage of the fact that concentrations of
SO_2 in excess of ambient standards generally
occurred only under unfavorable weather conditions
(e.g., an inversion which trapped air in a basin

around a power plant.) Using intermittent controls
meant that when these unfavorable conditions
occurred or were expected to occur, the power plant
would switch fuels or curtail operations to reduce
its emissions, then return to the higher emissions
rate when the weather improved.[13]

Faced with these arguments, EPA struggled to
maintain its position that, with a few exceptions,
continuous controls were required on sources subject
to implementation plan limits. EPA did agree to a
limited exception to allow sources in isolated areas
to use intermittent controls, and had proposed
regulations in September, 1973 to determine when
these exceptions would be permitted.[14] However, the
oil embargo and its repercussions increased the
pressure on EPA to allow a larger universe of
sources to use intermittent controls. This argument
was in full swing in the fall and winter of 1973-
1974, and was an important part of the context in
which significant deterioration was considered.

Linked to the debate on intermittent controls
was the debate over stack heights. EPA, in
approving the original 1972 implementation plans,
had approved provisions which allowed unrestricted
increases in stack heights as a means of achieving
the ambient standards by dispersing pollution more
widely. The Agency was sued on this point by the
Natural Resources Defense Council, and the case had
been argued in the Fifth Circuit on May 9, 1973.[15]
This decision was still pending in the fall of 1973.
NRDC's argument was essentially that the Clean Air
Act did not authorize the use of dispersion to
achieve the ambient standards and that dispersion as
a policy was intrinsically bad. Both the ICS and
the stack heights issues had their roots in the same
tension in the Clean Air Act between limiting
emissions and limiting ambient concentrations which
lay behind the nondegradation controversy.
Industrial firms, of course, recognized that a
dispersion approach to air pollution control would
be far less costly and difficult than the
installation of emissions controls, and they brought
great pressure to bear on EPA and Congress to
accommodate the dispersion philosophy. On the other

hand, environmental groups such as the NRDC and the
Sierra Club argued that dispersion was an
illegitimate means of pollution control under the
Act, and pursued their position forcefully both in
litigation and in testimony before Congress. EPA
for its part struggled in 1973 to maintain a middle
position between these two perspectives.[16]

EPA AND THE ENVIRONMENTALISTS

     EPA's relationship with environmental activist
groups was mixed. On the one hand, the groups
provided a core base of support for EPA's
fundamental goals and a counterweight to industrial
interests which might otherwise have found EPA
easier to capture. As the Sierra Club case amply
demonstrated, the citizen suit provision of the
Clean Air Act and its use by the environmental
groups gave them a powerful tool with which to
influence events. On the other hand, these groups
tended to strongly resist accommodation with the
Agency. The continued aggressive posture of the
environmental groups, particularly the NRDC and the
Sierra Club, is striking in view of the tenor of the
times. These groups did not back off from their
positions in the face of the energy crisis, but
persevered in arguing against any major revisions to
the Clean Air Act in the face of strong attacks by
industry, the Administration, and some Congressmen
looking for scapegoats on whom to blame the energy
crisis. The strength of the environmental groups in
the face of these attacks rested on three things:
their continued ability to use the courts to put
pressure on EPA through the courts; sympathetic
chairmen and staff on the key Congressional
committees; and, even in the face of the energy
crisis, a latent public support which made members
of Congress fearful of being tagged as a supporter
of "gutting" the Clean Air Act.
     In 1973 and 1974, PSD emerged as a key issue for
environmental groups intent on protecting the gains

which they believed had been made in the early
1970's. For example, Lawrence Moss, president of
the Sierra Club, attacked EPA's July 16, 1973
proposal on PSD as "one more example of the lawless
activity which seems so prevalent these days, of the
determination of the Executive Branch to ignore the
will of Congress and the orders of the courts."[17]
Moss and his successor, Richard Jahn, along with
Dick Ayres and David Hawkins of the NRDC, were to
appear at almost every Congressional hearing on
bills to weaken the Clean Air Act in response to the
energy crisis. They defended the Act's provisions
and their actions in filing suits to enforce them,
and urged that any amendments to the act contain
"safeguards to insure that relaxation of clean air
standards is truly necessary."[18]

THE LEADERSHIP OF EPA

      The final important "context" was a change in
the leadership of EPA. The Watergate scandal began
to have an effect on the Agency, as William
Ruckelshaus was asked by President Nixon to become
Acting Director of the FBI in April, 1973 after L.
Patrick Grey's resignation. After a period of
several months in which there were two acting
administrators, Russell Train, the Chairman of the
Council on Environmental Quality, was nominated as
the new Administrator in the summer of 1973.
      In Train, EPA was led by an individual who was
more sympathetic to the overall goals of preventing
significant deterioration of air quality than
Ruckelshaus had been, although he was less likely
than Ruckelshaus to get into the details of what the
program meant. Officials who worked for Train
report that he had considerable sympathy for what
one might call the "environmental planning" school,
to which PSD appeared as a real opportunity.
Moreover, Train already had considerable independent
environmental prestige as a result of his service at
CEQ. Perhaps more than it realized, the White House

had selected someone who was an even stronger
environmental advocate than Ruckelshaus had been.

BUREAUCRATIC ACTORS AT EPA

By the summer of 1973, EPA had overcome some of
its birth pains and settled into more established
patterns of operation. In particular, EPA's
organization and internal decision-making processes
reflected conscious decisions by the Agency's senior
executives about the kinds of perspectives they
wanted to affect national regulations.[19] Four
principal offices within EPA were concerned with the
further development of the PSD regulations. Each of
these offices brought a different perspective to
these regulations and sought to ensure that they
incorporated somewhat different values. The lack of
specificity of the court order and the inconclusive
legislative history of the statute provided little
guidance to the regulation writers, as EPA was fond
of repeating whenever it was asked how it intended
to proceed with the regulations. However, this lack
of guidance gave somewhat more freedom to EPA
officials to pursue their own policy objectives--an
ironic outcome of a statute designed to be action-
forcing and to limit discretionary agency authority.
    The four principal offices were:
    (1) The Office of Air Quality Planning and
Standards (OAQPS). This office had the lead
responsibility for actually drafting the regulations
and the preamble language that would accompany and
explain them. OAQPS was primarily composed of air
pollution control professionals, many of whom were
engineers who had transferred into EPA from NAPCA
when EPA was formed. OAQPS staff were most
conscious of the tension in the Act between an
emissions standards approach and the air quality
basis of much of the Act, and were cautious about
the limits of technical capability in moving from
one to the other. As noted in Chapter 3, this
skepticism, combined with the professional

propensity of engineers to prefer technological
solutions, had led OAQPS to originally support a
best technology approach to preventing significant
deterioration. Moreover, senior OAQPS officials,
particularly Director Bernard J. Steigerwald, were
concerned about the exaggerated claims being made
for PSD's likely effect on larger issues of long-
term community land use planning. Steigerwald
believed that an attempt to compel such planning
through an air quality mechanism reflected a
disproportion between societal means and ends which
would ultimately threaten the credibility of the air
pollution control program.[20]

(2) The Office of General Counsel (OGC). OGC
had, prior to the Supreme Court decision, been the
chief opponent of PSD within EPA. In the face of
the Supreme Court's failure to overturn Sierra Club
vs. Ruckelshaus, however, the view of the OGC began
to change. The Federal Register notice in July,
1973 still contains the diffident opinion that
"there has been no definitive judicial resolution of
the issue whether the Clean Air Act requires
prevention of significant deterioration of air
quality."[21] However, this argument was soon to
disappear from OGC's language. It was replaced by a
strong concern for making the PSD program developed
by EPA defensible in court when, as was inevitably
expected, the new regulations were litigated. OGC's
influence on PSD stemmed from this anticipation of
judicial review; OGC was the authoritative Agency
voice on what was or was not likely to pass judicial
muster.

As Shep Melnick has noted, this concern with
making the regulations legally defensible had two
implications for OGC's substantive position on the
regulations. First, it led OGC to favor an approach
to PSD which relied on ambient air quality
increments, despite the concerns raised by the OAQPS
technical experts about the ability to measure or
model these increments. However, OGC argued that
since Judge Pratt had focused on degradation in the
ambient air, an air quality increment approach stood
on sounder legal ground. Secondly, OGC insisted--in
striking contrast to OAQPS--that some limit on

state-allowed deterioration had to be a part of any
PSD regulations. Any plan which allowed the
unlimited increase in pollution levels up to the
ambient standards would, in OGC's view, run a
substantial risk of being successfully challenged by
the Sierra Club. As noted above, the Club had
already indicated its dissatisfaction with the path
EPA had started down in complying with Judge Pratt's
order.[22]

(3) The Office of Planning and Evaluation (OPE).
OPE was an EPA creation which had no precedent in
any of the organizations which were merged to form
the new Agency. It was established by Administrator
Ruckelshaus for two purposes: to improve the
Agency's ability to analyze the prospective impacts
of its regulations on society; and to provide a
mechanism for regulatory review which responded
solely to the Administrator's perceived needs as
compared to those of the more "institutionalized"
program offices. This latter function had two
sides: to satisfy some of the demands being made of
EPA by the White House, OMB, and other Executive
branch critics; and to provide EPA's leaders with
arguments they could use to refute charges by the
White House and other critics of EPA that the Agency
was insensitive to the costs of its regulations.
OPE staff tended to be young, with strong
backgrounds in economics and public policy analysis,
and with a preference for quantitative studies of
the costs, benefits and other effects of EPA
regulations.[23]

OPE was also the custodian of the "Steering
Committee" process by which proposed regulations
were reviewed within EPA prior to their signature by
the Administrator. Under this process,
representatives of the major components of EPA--
program officers, the enforcement office, research
and development, and OGC as well as OPE would all
review, comment and agree on proposed regulations
before they could be seen or signed by the
Administrator. The idea was that such forced
consensus would improve the quality of the Agency's
regulatory actions.

Control of this process gave OPE considerable
leverage over the content of regulations as well.
An OPE "non-concurrence on a regulation was a
serious bureaucratic matter, as it could provoke a
high level confrontation between political
appointees within the Agency and delay any program's
attempt to get its regulations approved.
Consequently, program staff had significant
incentives to avoid this kind of open conflict, and
accommodate OPE objections or persuade OPE staff
that their objections were not well founded. Not
surprisingly, most programs attempted to deal with
this potential stumbling block by involving OPE
staff early in the development of proposed
regulations, in the hope that consensus at the staff
level would avoid confrontations among the Agency's
principal officials.

This kind of accommodation often took place, but
not always. When it failed to occur, one reason was
conflict between OPE's role in representing an
Executive Branch position (e.g., making regulations
less costly) and the program offices' role in
carrying out Congressional mandates in the law. In
this respect, EPA's organization reflected the
separation of powers and system of checks and
balances in the Federal Government.[24] Such
conflicts, when they occurred, tended to reinforce
the authority and influence of the OGC as the "third
branch" which could conclusively say what the law
was and anticipate the judgments of the judicial
"third branch".

(4) Office of Enforcement (OE). The Office of
Enforcement did not play as large a role in the
development of the PSD regulations as the three
offices described above. However, it did review
them from the standpoint of whether or not they
would be readily enforceable. This perspective
argued especially in favor of an emissions control
approach to PSD, given the difficulties of
"enforcing" air quality increments in any meaningful
sense. (This was the same concern behind OE's
adamant opposition to intermittent control systems.)
In addition, as Melnick has noted, enforcement
officials were aggressive advocates of tough,

inflexible regulations to prevent the problems of
inconsistency which inevitably occurred when the
regulations left room for enforcement discretion.[25]
    With this background, we may now turn to the
creation of EPA's PSD program.

Opening Developments: August 1973-January 1974

    The public comment period for the July 16, 1973
proposal closed on October 16th. During the public
comment period, a working group within EPA was
formed to put together a final regulatory package.
While OAQPS had the lead responsibility for the
group, OE, OGC, and OPE staff were represented on it
along with staff from the Office of Research and
Development (ORD) and an official from the Office of
Federal Activities (OFA), whose primary concern was
the effect of PSD regulations on Indian lands.
Significantly, one of the early decisions was that
OPE would hire a contractor to do an analysis of the
economic impacts of each of the four regulatory
alternatives described in the July notice.[26]
    The work group had the task of more carefully
defining EPA's answers to the five basic questions
described in Chapter 3:
    o   What pollutants would be covered?
    o   Would PSD focus on emissions or air quality?
    o   What upper limits on development would exist?
    o   What types of control would be required?
    o   What discretion would States have in carrying
         out these Federal requirements?
These same questions were of concern to a larger
audience as well, as evidenced by a memo sent to the
White House Domestic Council in early September
which lays them out as subjects on which Agency
decisions would be required.[27]
    Answering these questions turned out to be a
very difficult task for the working group during the
months between August and December, 1973. One thing

became immediately clear: EPA would not meet its
original December timetable for the final
rulemaking.

What Pollutants Would Be Covered?--EPA in July
had proposed to apply best control technology
requirements to sources of all pollutants, but had
proposed to apply further restrictions only to
sulfur oxides (SO_x) and particulates (TSP). There
was a proposal made by OAQPS staff--presumably in
response to pressure from the Sierra Club--to create
either an air quality or an emissions increment for
carbon monoxide, hydrocarbons and nitrogen oxides.[28]
However, this proposal does not appear to have been
taken very seriously, and its origin in OAQPS is
somewhat odd. Increments for CO, HC and NO_x would
have made PSD much more of a true land use planning
program because these pollutants are much more
directly associated with vehicles, residences, and
other characteristics of economic growth in an area.
While the land use planning advocates within the
Agency--and especially OPE--might have been expected
to seize upon this fact and advocate $HC/CO/NO_x$
increments as a means of advancing these objectives,
one would not have expected OAQPS to propose such a
thing. Moreover, the planners within OPE could
foresee the enormous practical difficulties of such
a suggestion--especially given the furor which
accompanied EPA's earlier proposals to require
transportation controls to meet ambient standards,
let alone prevent significant deterioration.[29] As a
result, the proposal to expand increments beyond TSP
and SO_2 died a quiet bureaucratic death.

Would PSD Focus on Emissions or Air Quality?--
The working group appears to have settled very
quickly on the notion of zones, as discussed in
Alternative IV of the July proposal. The zone
concept appealed to several representatives of the
working group, although for differing reasons. To
OPE, it offered "increased flexibility and
consistency with a reasoned approach to land use
planning."[30] OAQPS staff saw the zones as a way to
respond to widely divergent public comments in
support of "both very stringent and very lenient
criteria--both opposing viewpoints seem to be

justified, and yet are irreconcilable within a
single increment."[31] Moreover, the zones allowed
differential determinations of what kind of
deterioration was "significant" by basing this
determination on the characteristics of the land in
question. Thus "significant" could be very small in
areas such as the Grand Canyon, yet larger in other,
less pristine but still clean areas. The zone
concept solved a major problem for OAQPS by allowing
both very stringent and relatively lenient standards
to be incorporated under nationwide criteria.

Whether these zones would be zones of emission
densities or incremental increases in ambient air
quality, however, remained a subject of dispute for
a time. The work group members were fully aware of
the difficulties inherent in using either air
quality monitoring or modeling in determining
whether the increments were being met. The ORD
representative, for example, submitted a paper to
the work group which stated that a key assumption of
the air quality increment scheme was "untenable"--
that modeling or monitoring could establish a
"baseline" of existing air quality to which an
increment could be added to establish a new allowed
level of air quality.[32] Yet emission densities had
their own problems, the most severe of which was
that the permissible growth in an area could depend
on how the size of the area was calculated, with
smaller geographic areas being at a disadvantage.
Moreover, emission inventories--a key variable in
density plans--offered few technical advantages to
air quality modeling. One OAQPS official noted that
errors in the inventories "may be 30-40-50%," that
they "generally run several years behind time," and
that "the emission levels must be arbitrary and not
very well related to air quality."[33]

Faced with a lack of any solid technical answer
as to how to carry out the zoning concept, the
working group eventually settled on the air quality
increment zones as the lesser of the evils and the
more potentially workable despite the problems with
monitoring and modeling. An air quality based
scheme, of course, was suggested by OGC as most
consistent with the concerns in Judge Pratt's

order.[34] Moreover, the economic analysis and impact
study conducted by OPE reached the conclusion that
an emission density plan would be more restrictive
of growth and development in most cases than an air
quality increment plan. OPE also concluded that
since the overriding objective of PSD was to protect
air quality, it seemed "silly" to use an indirect
emissions scheme to do so.[35]

However, in the course of developing consensus
around an air quality increment scheme, two
important changes were made in the approach outlined
in the July 16 proposal. The first, obvious change
was that a third zone was incorporated into the
thinking about Alternative IV. This third zone was
to represent "large resource development areas or
growth in areas (generally around cities) developing
in industry and population," and reflected a
recognition of the limits to growth which Zone II
could create under certain circumstances.[36] Given
the earlier objection by the OGC attorneys to the
Local Definition Plan (Option 3) as being in
violation of the court order because it potentially
could allow deterioration up to the ambient
standards, it is surprising just how quickly the
Zone III concept was incorporated into the Area
Classification Plan. In this instance, however, the
attorneys appear to have refrained from actively
attacking the OPE proposal.

The second important shift in the air quality
increment scheme had to do with the way in which
compliance with the increments would be determined.
The members of the work group generally agreed that
if an air quality increment scheme was to be used,
air quality modeling rather than monitoring would
have to be the basis for determining whether the
ambient increments had been consumed in an area.
Modeling, in contrast to monitoring, offered a
"consistent, reproducible way to estimate
'hypothetical' air quality increments" for SO_2 and
TSP. (The inability to use models to predict
concentrations of other pollutants accurately
mitigated even further against their inclusion in
air increment scheme.) However, the Agency's
modeling experts warned that the ability to predict

how much SO_2 or TSP increment a given source would
consume was estimated to be accurate at best "to
within a factor of two," and that "even in the best
case the possible errors in the modeling process due
to for example, uncertainties in meteorological
parameters may overwhelm the air quality increment
under consideration."[37]

Thus, even as the logic of their evolving
program forced the work group to rely heavily on air
quality modelling, it also forced them to deal with
a series of questions about just how these models
would be used to enforce the air quality increments
in the proposed plan. This practical concern was
initially and most forcefully raised by the Office
of Enforcement. OE's principal concern was with the
specific legal mechanisms which EPA or States would
use to prohibit construction of a new source which
would threaten these increments, and with the
establishment of a specified emissions limit on a
source subject to PSD which could be directly
enforced in the event of failure by the source to
comply. The absence of such a directly enforceable
emissions limit would, in OE's view, render PSD
almost meaningless since it would be impossible to
claim that a single source had caused a violation of
an increment level after the fact except in very
rare cases.[38]

OPE picked up on these concerns and agreed with
them in its own proposal. Specifically, OPE agreed
that a necessary complement to an air quality
increment scheme would be "a permit system" which
"should specify tons of emissions, stack height,
emissions rate, etc., used in modelling. The plant
would then be in violation only if those specific
controllable details were violated, not on the basis
of ambient air quality" [emphasis added].[39] Thus OPE
proposed to relieve the tension between ambient air
quality increments and the need for enforceable
emissions limits on sources through the use of a
permit system which would require preconstruction
approval by the Federal government of the conditions
under which a source which threatened to cause
"significant deterioration" could operate. While
the preconstruction review of sources which might

cause significant deterioration was a part of all
proposals or PSD, it is worth noting that a detailed
permit system, specifying enforceable conditions of
source operation, was an inevitable outgrowth of the
decision to go with ambient air quality increments.
Since the increments themselves could never be
directly checked and enforced, only surrogate
measures--the permit's terms and conditions--could
give any guarantee that the objectives of PSD were
being met.

The permit system was the key element of an
agreement that a workable ambient air quality
increment system could be devised. Its proposal and
gradual acceptance by the work group was a big step
in the development of the increment system.
However, while the ambient increment/zone system
appeared to solve many of EPA's problems with PSD,
the Director of OAQPS, Bernard Steigerwald,
continued to be skeptical about its value.

Back in October, Steigerwald had met with a
group of seven State air pollution control directors
to solicit their opinion about which PSD alternative
EPA should choose to satisfy the court order. The
results of this meeting were striking in several
respects. One was the lack of support by these
State air directors for the position taken by the
State attorneys general in their amicus curiae
brief in Sierra Club vs. Ruckelshaus. In
Steigerwald's words,

> All the States except Oregon feel very
> strongly that a way should be found to allow the
> States to decide on prevention of significant
> deterioration. There is little concern over
> 'economic blackmail.' Most felt that the State
> support of the Sierra Club position in the
> lawsuit was not the official State position,
> only that of the Attorney General . . . .[40]

The States represented at this meeting also
indicated that they were not especially pleased
with the direction EPA appeared to be going in
with respect to PSD. About half the States felt
EPA should ask for a change in the law to allow

us to limit our concern to maintenance of the
secondary standards.
     All feel that we will not get firm land use
decisions from the States using air quality
alone as leverage . . .
     No one, except possibly Oregon, feels that
rational decisions on siting can be made against
a small air quality increment . . . .[41]

In general, the States present at this meeting
endorsed Alternative 3, the local definition plan,
as "the only plan considered acceptable," even if
this required a change in the Clean Air Act.
According to Robert Coleman's notes of the meeting,
there was "consensus except for Oregon that no
scheme which involved increases in emissions or
increases in concentration was viable--nationally."[42]
Steigerwald observed that if EPA felt it necessary
to go beyond Alternative 3, a compromise might be
possible, but only if States were given up to two
years to "add land use guidance (i.e., define zones)
to the case by case review procedures." He noted in
closing that "this sort of a plan is not a strong
response to the court order, but at this time I
think EPA should promulgate a sensible, workable
system and let the court or Congress support or
overturn us."[43] Steigerwald's interest in State
opinions on PSD issues was not shared, however, by
either the Office of Enforcement or the Office of
General Counsel, both of which seemed more concerned
with making sure that EPA would have sufficient
authority to overrule "incorrect" State decisions.[44]
     What Upper Limits on Development Would Exist?--
The major change in this area which the working
group developed--the addition of a "Zone 3" in which
air quality would be allowed to deteriorate up to
the secondary standards--has already been discussed.
The work group originally proposed that all areas be
initially designated as Zone 2; a conscious State
decision would be required for an area to move to
either Zone 1 or Zone 3. The land use planning
interest in PSD is evident here as the zones were
defined "in terms of allowable economic growth."
Zone 1 areas were to remain pristine, "with

standards set to allow little or no growth." Zone 2
areas "should be limited to isolated industrial
sites rather than broad development or co-location
of industry." Zone 3 "should be reserved for large
resource development areas or growth in areas
(generally around cities) developing in industry and
population."[45]

In light of later arguments about the precise
air quality increments to be associated with the
Zones, it is interesting that only OPE proposed an
alternative set of zone numbers during the staff
discussions in the fall of 1973. OPE's suggestions
were based on the results of its impact study and
used the same kind of approach adopted by OAQPS to
determine what kind of plant would "fit" in a given
increment. However, the calculations performed by
OPE's contractor yielded different results from the
calculations used by OAQPS in setting the original
numbers. As a result, OPE recommended raising the
annual Zone 2 TSP increment from 10 ug/m^3 to 15
ug/m^3, and doubling the 24 hour increment from 30
ug/m^3 to 60 ug/m^3. When coupled with allowing
sources to use tall stacks, this would enable the
model 1000 MW power plant, a medium-size copper
smelter or a cement plant to be located in a Zone 2
area.[46]

In a related issue, OAQPS had proposed to deal
with the problem of uncertainty in monitoring and
modeling by allowing sources to obtain variances
from the Zone 1 and 2 increments if a source
prepared an environmental impact statement and the
State held a public hearing on the exceedance.
OPE's proposal recommended against allowing
variances for Zone 1--essentially making them no-
growth areas--and stricter conditions for variances
from Zone 2, expecting that serious Zone 2 problems
would be handled by reclassification to Zone 3.[47]
OAQPS also wished to leave the question of
desireable growth limits up to the States by
remaining purposely vague on what a State would have
to do to reclassify an area from one zone to
another. OPE, however, argued that "States must be
given specific criteria for what should be

classified Zone 1 and what <u>can</u> be classified Zone 3."[48]

What Types of Control Would Be Required?--This was one of the most difficult issues faced by the task force, because it had a direct bearing on the question of how much growth would be allowed under the increments for each zone and because it related directly to the scrubbers/tall stacks/ICS controversy.

OAQPS' initial position had hardened since the spring of 1973 in favor of requiring BACT for sources subject to PSD. The universe of sources remained the same as in the July proposal--the sixteen which were subject or were soon expected to be subject to NSPS, plus any other source with a "total annual potential emissions rate equal to or greater than 4000 tons" of PM, SO_2, NO_x, HC, or CO.[49] The principal issue with BACT remained whether SO_2 scrubbers would be required on Western power plants using low sulfur coal which would otherwise comply with the power plant NSPS which EPA had set in 1971.[50]

OPE attacked this position, arguing that requiring scrubbers on Western power plants should be a State rather than a Federal decision. The essential choice, in OPE's view, was whether a State wanted to control emissions more tightly and thereby preserve the SO_2 increment for future growth, or whether it wanted to forego scrubbers but place greater limits on growth. OPE also pointed out that Western coal, when shipped East, could be burned without scrubbers in power plants which met NSPS.[51]

OPE also adopted a position in favor of allowing tall stacks. OPE's technical analysis had shown that tall stacks would allow facilities such as power plants, copper smelters, and cement plants to be accommodated under the proposed Zone 2 increments, while disallowing tall stacks appeared likely to forbid such sources. Moreover, OPE argued that the increased emissions loadings which tall stacks would create would be an acceptable tradeoff for protecting local air quality--a view consistent with OPE's opposition to scrubbers. OPE also argued that the Zone 2 increments would have to be increased if tall stacks were not allowed.[52]

OAQPS initially opposed the OPE position on both scrubbers and the use of tall stacks. While OAQPS won some support from ORD on tall stacks, there was little support from OGC in the fall of 1973. However, on the scrubbing issue, OAQPS found itself in an internal debate as the year progressed. One memo, prepared by an OAQPS special assistant, argued that the special requirement for power plants was "inappropriate." The memo continued, "If the special application is desirable and equitable, it should be used to modify NSPS. It unnecessarily complicates the significant deterioration issue, and is of much broader scope."[53] Thus, while the BACT issue remained unresolved through the fall, its resolution appeared to be moving away from the original position taken by OAQPS in favor of establishing scrubbers as BACT.

What Discretion Would States Have in Carrying Out These Federal Requirements?--The preceding discussion shows that this issue, rather than being decided in the abstract, found expression in the answers given by different EPA offices to the other four questions. Moreover, no office had a fully consistent position on this issue. OAQPS, for example, generally wished to defer most to State judgments on air quality increments and zoning, but was less willing to allow discretion on the use of tall stacks or (at least initially) scrubbers on Western power plants. OPE, in contrast, was willing to fall back on State discretion on control technologies and stack heights, but felt that EPA had to provide "guidelines" on classifying land use areas and should act more aggressively to limit State freedom to endorse actions which might affect "pristine" regions. The Office of Enforcement wanted to ensure that EPA had the "last word" on permit reviews and that source emission limits could be directly enforced by the Federal government without waiting for States to act. OGC, to the extent it concerned itself about the States, worried mainly about any provision which appeared to give the States unlimited discretion to allow deterioration up to ambient standards and threatened EPA's legal position.

All of the EPA offices involved envisioned some role for State governments in implementing PSD. However, no one--with the exception of the Director of OAQPS--was willing to endorse the approach which State air pollution control directors held was most desirable--the local definition plan, coupled with a BACT requirement. Once this alternative was rejected, the question of Federal preemption of State discretion became one not of whether, but of how much.

PSD Evolves From January to August, 1974

By the end of 1973, the main elements of an EPA program to prevent significant deterioration were beginning to emerge from the intra-agency debates. However, EPA was not to issue a new public version of its regulations until August 27, 1974--and this, rather than being a final set of regulations, was yet another proposal, albeit a more focused and detailed one than the July 1973 version. Moreover, between January and August of 1974, PSD was to become a key element in a major dispute between EPA and other parts of the Executive Branch.

That a dispute would come was evident early on. The reaction to the Sierra Club suit made it clear that significant deterioration would be watched closely by these who were concerned that EPA's balancing of values weighed environmental concerns too heavily. Outside industrial groups, especially the "coal coalition," had vigorously opposed the concept of significant deterioration since before the 1970 Amendments.[54] In the context of an energy crisis which was perceived as severe and growing, they turned to sympathetic ears within the Nixon (and later, Ford) Administration to do battle with EPA over the PSD regulations.

However, this dispute proceeded at two levels:
one a high stakes political drama; and the other a
more routine form of what might be called
bureaucratic guerilla warfare. The high-status
drama appears to have had the effect of hardening
EPA's position against any attempt to seek
legislative relief from Congress on PSD. On a lower
level, however, intervention by other Executive
Branch agencies reinforced offices within EPA who
were pressing for changes in the proposed
regulations.

INTERNAL AND EXTERNAL PRESSURES AT EPA

As 1973 drew to a close, EPA was under pressure
to publish final PSD regulations. For one thing,
the Sierra Club was getting restless with EPA's
failure to meet the six month deadline for
promulgating regulations specified in the original
court order. Moreover, in the Club's discussions
with EPA, it was apparent that the Agency would not
adopt the PSD plan recommended by the Club. An
internal EPA analysis of the Sierra Club plan
summarized the agency's reaction to it by describing
its assumptions as "unrealistic," with "a very
substantial impact on the power and oil industries"
and requiring types of monitoring analysis which
were "not presently possible to perform."[55] Meetings
between Club representatives and EPA officials
indicated that while the Club might be willing to
accept something less stringent than their original
proposal, they nonetheless found the approach being
pursued by EPA unacceptable and expected to engage
in further litigation.[56]
Moreover, another more subtle factor began to
increase the pressure for action on the PSD
regulations. Russell Train had been confirmed as
Administrator on September 10, 1973. By December,
the initial "shakedown period of the new team which
Train brought in was largely completed. The last
major relevant player in this team appeared in

January, 1974, when Roger Strelow replaced Robert
Sansom as Assistant Administrator for Air Programs.
Strelow had close personal ties to Train, and while
his appearance had little immediate effect on the
content of the PSD package, Strelow did take a more
active interest in the details of the proposed
regulations than Sansom had. These developments,
combined with the gradual progress of the work
group, meant that the subsequent consideration of
PSD issues focused on those areas where major
disputes persisted. In contrast to the months of
August-December, 1973, this consideration often
involved high level officials within the Agency.[57]

THE DECISION ABOUT WHETHER TO APPROACH CONGRESS

In early January, 1974, there appears to have
been an attempt to re-raise fundamental questions
about EPA's approach to PSD to the attention of
senior EPA officials. Bernard Steigerwald's
skepticism about the value of the air quality
increment plan--which was by then accepted as the
preferred alternative although key details remained
to be worked out--has already been noted. In
January, support for this skepticism appeared from
an unexpected source: OPE.
A meeting had been arranged for January 11,
1974, in which Administrator Train was to meet with
the Governors of several States to discuss the
current EPA working proposal for PSD (i.e., the air
quality increment plan). In anticipation of this
meeting, OPE staff prepared a memo for Alvin Alm,
Assistant Administrator for Planning and Management,
which argued that notwithstanding all of the effort
which OPE had put into the zone system, it ought to
be abandoned. While not going so far as to endorse
an amendment deleting nondegradation from the Clean
Air Act, the memo argued that EPA should limit what
it was trying to do in PSD to protect only those
areas (i.e., large national parks) where very clean
air was desired, rather than trying to impose a

classification/ planning scheme on the whole
country. The memo's author, Roy Gamse of the
Economic Analysis Division, argued:

> I personally favor a policy of protecting the
> pristine areas only. I think we have shown that
> it is possible to create a structure which
> limits degradation without crippling the economy
> for a 10-15 year period and which would have
> favorable aspects related to environmental and
> land use planning. But I am afraid that in
> doing so we have created an administrative
> nightmare. I think that on balance the country
> would be better off setting up stringent
> limitations to the areas that most need
> protecting and attacking the rest of the problem
> with legislation on power plant siting and land
> use planning.

Gamse noted that while this approach would "probably
require Clean Air Act amendments, . . the same may
be true of the proposal we have developed."[58]

Train, however, chose not to take this course of
action. At the meeting with the governors, he
stated that EPA was exploring options which would
not require direct legislation, though he indicated
that EPA would consult with Congress in developing
the PSD regulations. Some of the governors present,
including Governor Dan Evans of Washington,
indicated their support for Congressional relief
from PSD, and expressed concern that PSD might
restrict desirable economic growth.[59]

Train attempted to deal with these concerns by
pointing out the classification procedures of EPA's
plan, emphasizing the view that while the Federal
government should ensure that the States have a good
process for making land use decisions which
considered air quality, the substantive decisions
about what to allow or not allow were a State and
local responsibility. Train said that a principal
thrust of PSD was "to encourage more effective land
use planning on the part of the States, with air
quality consideration becoming one component [of]
the overall land use decision-making process." This

belief extended to the questions of whether a State
would be allowed to rezone all of its area as Zone 3
(pollution up to secondary standards); in an answer
that must have given OGC an anxiety attack, Train
and the other EPA officials at the meeting indicated
that "most likely" they would not prohibit this
result if adequate public notice and comment on such
a decision occurred. Considerable stress in this
meeting was laid on the ability of States to
reclassify to Zone 3 if a source which wanted to
locate in a Zone 2 area would exceed the allowable
Zone 2 increments.[60]

CONFRONTATION WITH THE WHITE HOUSE

     Train's decision not to seek legislative
clarification from Congress on significant
deterioration heightened a conflict which had
already developed between EPA and the White House
over amendments to the Clean Air Act which were part
of emergency energy legislation in response to the
energy crisis. A first version of such a bill was
passed by both Houses in early 1974, but the
Democratic Congress changed it so much from what the
Administration originally wanted that President
Nixon vetoed it on March 6, 1974.[61] A chief subject
of dispute in the vetoed legislation had been
whether to explicitly allow sources unrestricted use
of intermittent controls (ICS) to comply with air
quality standards. The Senate Environment and
Public Works Committee had fought off an attempt to
incorporate such a provision, which EPA had long
opposed, in the emergency energy legislation.[62]
     The renewed effort to get emergency energy
legislation through Congress resulted in heavy
Administration pressure on EPA to endorse a package
of amendments to the Clean Air Act. This pressure
reached a climax in the first week in March 1974--
just as the first Energy Emergency Bill was being
vetoed--when a pitched battle was fought in White

House meetings between Train and representatives of
OMB, the Domestic Council, and the Federal Energy
Office.[63]
   Most reports of this battle have focused on
Train's refusal to accede to President Nixon's
request to support the Energy Office's proposed
amendments on ICS.[64] This was indeed a critical
conflict and one on which Train refused to yield.
However, the second element of Train's dispute with
the White House was the significant deterioration
issue. The Federal Energy Office, responding to
industry demands in the wake of the Supreme Court
decision in Sierra Club vs. Ruckelshaus, took the
energy emergency as an opportunity to advocate an
amendment to §101 (b) (1) which would have negated
the decision. The proposed amendment read:

> Section 101 (b) (1) of the Clean Air Act is
> amended to read as follows:
> "(1) to protect and enhance the quality of the
> Nation's air resources by establishing,
> achieving and maintaining national ambient air
> quality standards, standards of performance for
> new stationary sources, and national emissions
> standards for hazardous air pollutants so as to
> promote the public health and welfare and the
> productive capacity of the Nation, but nothing
> in this act is intended to require or authorize
> the establishment by the Administrator of
> standards more stringent than primary or
> secondary ambient air quality standards;
> (changes from 1967/1970 version of §101 (b) (1)
> are underlined.)[65]

In the wake of the Nixon veto of the Energy
Emergency Act, the White House decided that EPA
should transmit proposed Clean Air Act Amendments to
Congress as part of a new attempt at energy
legislation. In a letter transmitting the
Administration amendments, however, Train continued
to refuse to endorse the amendment on significant
deterioration. Instead, his letter said that "EPA
believes that meaningful steps can be taken to
protect areas with already high air quality" through

the three zone classification system the Agency was
then developing. Train went on to assert that "no
hard air quality or emissions increments would be
promulgated by EPA as limiting factors," and that
this failure made it likely that the Agency's
regulations would be challenged in court. He then
concluded:

> Because of the potential for further litigation,
> the importance of this issue to our
> environmental and energy problems and the
> potential impact of EPA's regulations on State
> and local land use responsibilities, EPA
> believes that Congress should explore all
> alternatives for dealing with the significant
> deterioration issue in testimony and debate.[66]

The White House reaction to this opposition by
Administrator of EPA can only be imagined. This
kind of outright defiance by an Administration
official is highly unusual. That Train was not
asked to resign in this case can be attributed to
two things. First, Train was very careful not to
offer to resign. He agreed to transmit the proposed
amendments to Congress, but did not agree to support
them. This made open and explicit the kind of
debate which often goes on behind the scenes in the
Federal government. To make such a strong public
statement, yet not offer to resign, was a remarkable
move.
     But the ultimate success of Train's move has to
be attributed in large part to the second factor:
the Watergate Scandal. By March, 1974, the Nixon
Administration was in the final agonies of
Watergate. Seven Nixon associates had just been
indicted on criminal charges by a grand jury; the
battle over the Nixon tapes was in full swing; and
the House Judiciary Committee was pursuing
investigations prior to hearings on impeachment
charges. Moreover, and importantly, the "Saturday
Night Massacre" was still vivid in the public mind.
It was ironic that William Ruckelshaus, EPA's former
Administrator, was one of the victims of the
massacre. In this climate, there is no reason to

question Shep Melnick's conclusion that Nixon simply
could not afford to fire Train for his actions, even
if he had wanted to.[67] Thus, at this crucial moment,
the weakness of the presidency enabled EPA
to establish a public position on PSD which was at
variance with that pressed upon it by an
Administration which was otherwise very sympathetic
to the case against PSD presented by coal company,
utility, and other industrial executives.[68]

Melnick has also argued that the OGC attorneys
played a large role in determining both the ultimate
shape of the PSD program adopted by EPA, and the
tactics followed by EPA in pursuing it. While much
of this argument is true, it is important to note
that whatever Train's reason for opposing the
Administration amendment on PSD, these reasons were
not based on the arguments of his legal staff.
Staff attorneys in OGC, like the OPE staff, favored
the "go back to Congress approach," primarily
because the uncertainties of any PSD program adopted
by EPA seemed so forbidding. The only outcome OGC
could see of an EPA regulation was protracted
litigation in which, no matter what EPA did, it was
likely to lose. In early 1974, OGC's view was that
"it would be preferable to obtain legislation
authorizing or directing" any PSD approach to be
used by the Agency. OGC noted that "Congress, at
least in theory, is the most appropriate institution
to make the necessary decisions. Furthermore, the
legislative process, as opposed to simply keeping
the Muskie committee informed, is probably a better
way to advise Congress of the complex problems in
this area that EPA is attempting to deal with."[69]
While Train's did agree to seek guidance from
Congress, he also made it clear that he thought EPA
was quite capable of writing PSD regulations--an
approach that flew in the face of this legal advice
from his attorneys.

PROGRESS ON PSD REGULATIONS

While this political firestorm was building, the
Agency's regulation writers were pinning down
specific details of the Area Classification Plan.
Press reports on the Agency's progress accurately
described the three-zone scheme and portrayed it as
one which left more discretion to States to control
development than had been previously thought. The
lead of a Wall Street Journal article reflected this
perspective: "The Environmental Protection Agency,
after proposing to advance boldly into land use
planning with the aim of preserving pristine air
quality, is on the verge of leaving most of the task
to individual States." The article also predicted
conflicts with environmentalists over charges that
"the agency had allowed itself to be swayed by the
nation's energy development needs."[70]
Such reports saw EPA's new proposals as "leaving
most of the task to States" only in comparison to
earlier, industry-exaggerated fears of an EPA-
dominated program. In fact, the question of EPA's
proper role was a major concern in the next round of
internal debates over PSD.
The action-forcing event for this round was a
draft regulatory package which OAQPS distributed for
working group review on February 15, 1974. The
draft package advocated promulgating final
regulations, noting that "returning the initiative
to Congress would be viewed in many sectors as a
sell-out of the environment," but made a striking
description of the zones as "flexible air quality
guidelines rather than inviolable increments."[71] In
fact, an element of the "local decision" thinking in
original Alternative 3 had entered into at least the
language OAQPS wanted to use to describe the
proposed PSD regulations to the Administrator. In
cases where increments would be exceeded, a State
would have to hold a public hearing and submit
information to the Administrator showing that the
deterioration was insignificant relative to the
social and economic benefits of the project. The
Administrator could disapprove a State's approval,

but could do so "only upon procedural or technical grounds"--a phrase which obscured the provision in the regulation which required prior EPA approval of procedures employed by the State in making a determination of approval or disapproval.[72] Still, the thrust of the proposed regulations was to compel sources which would threaten the increment values to do so in a public manner, either through a public hearing on a variance, or through a redesignation to Zone 3, or "Class 3" as it was referred to in the package.[73]

On other key issues, the package reflected the following proposals:

o   The Class I and Class II increments were the same as in the July, 1973 proposal.

o   All areas were to be initially designated Class II; redesignation could occur at any time, and EPA could not disapprove it except on "procedural grounds."

o   Where a State and a Federal agency or Indian Governing body disagreed on the designation of Federal or Indian land, OMB was to be the arbiter.

o   Nineteen source categories--those covered or expected to be covered by NSPS--were subject to the regulations. No sources other than the 19 were to be subject to PSD (i.e., there was no general requirement for sources greater than some fixed emissions potential to be subject to PSD). Mandated coal conversions (a big issue because of the Administration's energy proposals) were exempted from PSD.

o   "Best available control technology (BACT) was to be required on the 19 sources where an increment would be exceeded." However, <u>reasonably</u> available control technology (RACT), a less stringent requirement, could be used if it did not result in an increment's exceedance.

o   Tall stacks (i.e., those in excess of "good engineering practice") generally were prohibited in lieu of better controls as a measure to avoid exceeding the deterioration increment. However, if the increment would be exceeded even <u>after</u>

the application of BACT, then "the regulations
require[d] consideration of increased stack
height as a means for minimizing the impact on
air quality."

o   Where BACT was required, it was assumed to be
     equal to NSPS <u>except</u> for power plants larger
     than 1,000 MMBtu/hour heat input (roughly 300
     MW), where "individual analysis . . . may result
     in additional controls for individual plants."

o   No further consideration was given to controls
     of HC, CO, or NO_x; the regulation applied solely
     to SO_2 and TSP.

o   Assessment of increment consumption was based on
     modeling; any monitoring requirements were
     dropped as "of little justification."[74]

All in all, while the regulations were more
complex than perhaps Mr. Steigerwald would have
wanted, they gave considerable discretion to the
States, and were felt by OAQPS to satisfy the
criteria of "a workable system." One phrase in the
draft preamble, however, is particularly striking.
In response to industry comments that EPA should
seek legislative relief from the Congress, the
preamble states:

     . . .The Administrator recognizes that the
     intent of the Clean Air Act was to prevent
     significant deterioration, and he believes that
     the regulations promulgated herein will
     effectively accomplish that goal in a manner
     which is in the best interests of the public.[75]

This is a fascinating statement when compared to the
words of the July, 1973 proposal ("No definitive
judicial resolution of the issue . . ."). It is
hard to imagine William Ruckelshaus endorsing such a
statement in a regulatory package on PSD, and it
reflects just how far the Agency's official thinking
had shifted since July.
     Other EPA offices, however, were not content
with several provisions of the OAQPS proposal.
Almost all of these objections had the effect of
reducing State authority and discretion in the

implementation of PSD. ORD, for example, wanted
more specific guidance to States on what kinds of
modeling techniques would be acceptable, as well as
a more restrictive definition of "baseline date"
which would have reduced the increment available to
new sources over that proposed by OAQPS.[76] The
Office of Enforcement objected to the removal of the
requirement that sources not on the list of 19, but
with greater potential emissions than 4000 tons per
year be reviewed under PSD. OE also argued that the
regulations should be written as a responsibility of
the Administrator, which could then be delegated to
States if EPA saw fit. This notion in some ways
turned OAQPS' conception of PSD on its head.
Moreover, OE argued further that EPA, not States,
must issue PSD permits to Federal facilities (i.e.,
military bases). Finally, OE pressed and won
"tentative agreement" from OAQPS "that EPA retain a
veto power on all State approvals of significant new
and modified sources" [emphasis added].[77]
     The Office of Federal Activities, in their
comments on the draft proposal, also pushed for the
clarification and expansion of Federal authority.
OFA argued in favor of Federal procedures, to run
concurrent with any State review, for assessing
whether sources on Federal or Indian lands should be
authorized to construct under PSD. OFA also argued
in favor of provisions to allow Indian land managers
or Federal land managers for parks, national
forests, and other federal lands to initiate
redesignations in a State.[78]
     OPE's comments also followed this trend. OPE
maintained its previous position on allowing tall
stacks and not requiring any control on Western
power plants beyond NSPS. However, on issues
affecting the classification of areas, OPE continued
to argue in favor of procedures which would restrict
State authority. Two points in particular were key.
First, OPE argued that Class I area increments
should be inviolable standards, and prohibit new
growth unless an explicit reclassification was made.
Secondly, OPE argued that "a procedural requirement
be imposed on the States to hold hearings to
consider Class I designation of pristine areas."

Some OPE staff also argued for provisions in the
regulations which would allow the States to consider
"only designated areas for Class III status."   These
comments give evidence that land use planning
thinking had certainly not been dismissed from OPE's
perspective on PSD.[79]

There were two OPE comments which would not
normally have been expected from a group whose chief
focus and concern was on the cost of clean air
controls. The first comment was that OPE, in
contrast to OAQPS engineers, argued that all PSD
sources should have to apply BACT, not just those
which would otherwise violate an increment.[80] One
reason for this was a concern that increment
consumption would proceed more rapidly, and thus
constrain growth, if sources were allowed to use
less effective controls. The second comment--an
ironic one in view of the pressure from the White
House to promote coal conversions--was against
allowing an automatic exemption for such
conversions. OPE recommended that "only temporary
changes be excluded" from increment consumption,
while permanent changes should be accounted for.[81]
Obviously the part of EPA which was supposed to be
most responsive to the Executive Branch had not
completely gotten the message--or else was receiving
a strongly contradictory one from the Administrator.

Further Development of the Regulations

These issues and conflicts were discussed at a
February 22nd meeting. OPE received support from
OGC for its notion of an inviolable Class I area,
with the OGC representative asserting that "a
proposal of this type might go a long way to
satisfying [the] Sierra Club." Other offices
objected that such stiff requirements on Class I
areas might prevent the designation of any Class I
areas. OPE, with support from OGC, nonetheless
continued to press the view that States should be
required to consider certain types of areas for
Class I, the argument being that the public pressure
generated by such a requirement "would serve to give

the Sierra Club and others a foot in the door to act."[82] OPE staff were less successful in pressing their tall stack views, which were unanimously opposed by other offices (especially OGC) on the grounds that they would compromise the agency's hard-line position on ICS/SCS for existing sources in non-attainment areas.[83]

Based on these reactions from the other EPA offices, OAQPS prepared another draft of the preamble to the regulations. The effect of the other offices' comments can be seen in the language changes in this new version. New sentences were added to respond to the comments, especially those made by OE and OPE.

The most striking change concerned EPA's authority over State decisions. Whereas the earlier action memorandum had said that there were no provisions for EPA to overrule a State's judgment on what was "significant deterioration" if correct procedures were followed, the new memorandum (in direct contradiction of Train's answer to the Governors) said that while "consideration was given to allowing States complete control over their own land use decisions, . . . it is believed necessary to retain EPA control over redesignation of areas to Class III in order to prevent a State from in effect, voiding these regulations by redesignating its entire area to Class III." Moreover, a provision was inserted to "prevent State avoidance of this requirement by means of a Class I or II designation by authorizing an excessive number of sources to exceed the increment." Such a provision would force a State to consider redesignating an area as Class III. If a State refused, "then EPA may require that no further authorization be given to exceed the increment." The following assurance that only "arbitrary and capricious" State actions would be subject to such scrutiny does nothing to lessen the impact of this change in philosophy.[84]

Nor was this the only change. Federal facility reviews were clearly placed under EPA control. State administration of the PSD requirements was made contingent upon acceptance by the State of delegation from EPA, on EPA's terms. The delegation was to be subject to withdrawal by EPA; and 30 EPA work years were projected as needed to review State PSD activities (as compared to 60 State work years to actually do the work). If a State did not accept delegation, EPA itself would do the work of reviewing proposed new sources. This last point had always been assumed, but the revised action memo brought it out with greater force. Finally, additional control was given to Federal land managers and Indian governing bodies over what classification their lands would have.[85]

OAQPS did not agree with all the suggested changes by other offices. OPE's recommendations on inviolable Class I areas were rejected, as well as procedures for forcing States to consider classifying areas as Class I. The use of tall stacks to meet increments was also rejected. However, while OAQPS did not give up on requiring Western power plants to put on scrubbers, it did redefine RACT as "generally that technology capable of meeting New Source Performance Standards." Since BACT was defined the same way except for power plants, the difference between the controls required of sources (other than Western power plants) which would exceed increments and all other sources was narrowed considerably.[86]

There was to be one more round of revisions to the PSD action memorandum prior to its transmission to EPA's political executive, however. These revisions occurred between March 25th and April 1, and they are revealing.

First, they show a continuation of the push to expand EPA authority at the expense of the States. Page 2 of the final version of the revised action memorandum contains an additional phrase assuring that "although decisions are intended to be made at the State and local level, the Administrator retains approval authority over all major decisions." For example, a Federal disapproval of a State decision to allow a source to exceed an increment "would normally be based upon procedural or technical grounds, <u>but could be based upon the State's failure to adequately consider relevant environment, social and economic factors</u>" [emphasis indicates new

language].[87] This was a far cry from the original
OAQPS assertion that disapprovals could be based
only on procedural or technical grounds.   An
alternative, new to this package, of having EPA
review every State substantive decision was of
course rejected as in "conflict with the basic
philosophy of the regulations," but this seems
insignificant in light of the expansion of the
Administrator's authority envisioned by the revised
package.[88]

Second, an entirely new classification scheme
was discussed, to initially classify all areas as
Class 1 instead of Class 2, in order to (1)
initially establish a nationwide "minimal growth"
policy, (2) force States to accept delegation of
authority in order to permit moderate growth, and
(3) provide conservationist elements with a strong
initial legal advantage over growth-oriented
elements.[89]   It is not clear who made this
suggestion, though the most likely candidate is OGC,
which had met with Sierra Club attorneys just prior
to the preparation of this last revision.   Although
this particular option was rejected as "not in the
public interest and likely to provoke unfavorable
public reaction, the action memo discussed the
advantages of EPA designating some areas as Class 1.

Finally, earlier versions of the memo had
contained a statement saying that a major
alternative to promulgating the regulations was to
request Congressional action to clarify EPA's
intended role in PSD.   The statement went on to
express the view, contained in a formal OGC
memorandum,[90] that "from a purely legal standpoint,
[returning to Congress] is likely the preferable
alternative."   This statement was struck from the
final version; instead, a return to Congress was
characterized merely as an "attractive
alternative."[91]

These changes reflected a hardening of EPA's
position on asking Congress to address PSD in the
wake of the political position staked out by Train
and his senior advisers.   They also reflected
pressure from the Sierra Club.   In a meeting with
EPA officials on March 25, 1974, Sierra Club

representatives condemned EPA's plan as so "weak"
that "the threat of Congressional action to remove
EPA's authority" to promulgate PSD regulations "did
not represent a sufficient deterrent to further
litigation on this point." The Sierra Club lawyer
stated that "We are losing in the regulatory process
what we won in court."[92] Certainly any attempt by
EPA to co-opt the Sierra Club on PSD had been
unsuccessful.

Consideration of PSD by EPA Political Executives

     Under normal circumstances, one might expect the
senior political executives of a conservative
Republican Administration, espousing a "New
Federalism" philosophy, to temper staff desires to
expand Federal authority at the expense of States.
However, instead of advocating restraint, in this
case EPA's political executives initially encouraged
the expansion of the Federal role over the
objections of the staff in OAQPS.
     This trend was apparent in a memorandum sent by
Roger Strelow, who had recently become Assistant
Administrator for Air and Waste Management.
Strelow's rise to this position appears to have
coincided with a pronounced shift of the initiative
in PSD decision-making from OAQPS to the immediate
office of the Assistant Administrator in Washington.
The general effect of this shift was to further
increase the influence of those seeking to use PSD
to promote land use planning and reduce State
flexibility and discretion in favor of Federal
authority and control.[93]
     Strelow's memo directed OAQPS to make changes to
the regulations in five key areas, based on
"extensive discussions" with the Assistant
Administrators for Enforcement and General Counsel,
Research and Development, and Planning and
Management. The five changes were:
     (1) Instead of the original plan of zoning
everything as Class 2, States were to be required to
take affirmative action within 18 months to
designate areas as Class 1, 2, or 3. Areas not

explicitly classified by that time would revert to
Class 1. The intent of this provision was "to force
states to make explicit zoning decisions with regard
to clean air areas and in order to put the burden on
the States to justify any substantial increases in
air pollution levels . . ."

(2) In a sharp break from OAQPS' previous
approach, the Class 1 and 2 increments were to be
treated as firm air quality ceilings, with no
variances. While OPE had supported such a provision
for Class 1, this new policy took the OPE position
to its logical conclusion, arguing that any
exceedance of an increment should require the area
to go through reclassification proceedings.

(3) Previous drafts of the PSD regulation had
ignored emissions for PSD purposes resulting from
any but the 19 source categories. Strelow argued
that emissions from other source categories should
not be "arbitrarily excluded," though how he
proposed to include them was unclear. Moreover,
while endorsing the OAQPS view of modeling vs.
monitoring, he discussed the increments as if they
were real, measurable air quality units rather than
the modeling constructs established by the staff
working group.

(4) Strelow did make one important change which
no doubt pleased OAQPS. Though he acknowledged that
"I may not fully understand the ramifications of the
EPA delegation approach which apparently has been
adopted in the latest draft," he argued that EPA's
authority to review State or local decisions "should
be strictly limited," and that any regulation which
failed to do this "would be quite unacceptable to
the Administrator, to the States, and probably to
Congress." However, for his "limits," Strelow held
that either procedural flaws or arbitrary and
capricious disregard of relevant economic, social
and environmental factors would be grounds for EPA
review. This was a step back from the most recent
staff version ("failure to adequately consider" such
factors), but not as far back as OAQPS' original
proposal (procedural violations only were grounds
for review).

(5)   Finally, Strelow appeared to support the reinstatement of some form of ambient monitoring requirement on sources. This is hard to explain since it is unclear that any of the groups in EPA supported it.[94]

Much of Strelow's memo reflected positions which OPE had been advocating for some time. Yet there were still some key differences, and OPE staff continued to push them. For one thing, OPE felt that in disallowing variances in Class 2 areas, the Assistant Administrators had gone overboard in a way that would "unduly constrain growth over much of the country." OPE also continued to oppose requiring new Western power plants to use scrubbers and argued against imposing any monitoring requirement on sources. OPE's opposition on this point led it to ask OGC for a formal ruling that such a requirement would be illegal. However, OPE does appear to have dropped its previous advocacy of tall stacks; one assumes that this had been rejected in light of the Fifth Circuit Court decision in February, 1974 in the NRDC vs. EPA case on stack heights.[95]

At about this time, a Washington staff created by Strelow which shared OPE's land use planning perspective began to aggressively press its views. For example, additional language was added to the regulations stressing PSD's links with other governmental planning processes (e.g., §208 of the Clean Water Act relating to water quality planning, OMB Circular A-95 relating to intergovernmental coordination, etc.). Strelow's endorsement was sought for regulatory language which said that an option to the administration of PSD by a State air pollution control agency was its administration by "a State land use planning and/or regulatory agency." Finally, this group again raised the idea of including oxidants as a concern in PSD, which OAQPS staff had rejected long before. Strelow's memo was moderate on this point, primarily suggesting the expansion of BACT to include control of major hydrocarbon sources. However, planning-minded air staff in Washington saw this as an argument for an "explicit State option" to set up oxidant increments which could force "recreational

areas, large new communities or housing
developments" to be subject to PSD review.[96] These
positions reflected an eleventh hour effort by EPA
land use planning advocates to "improve" the PSD
regulations to expand their scope and effect.

PSD and the June Senate Hearings

     EPA's thinking at this time is reflected in the
testimony which Train gave to the Muskie
Subcommittee on June 23, 1974. Train spoke directly
to the March 22nd package of proposed Clean Air Act
Amendments, noting that "other Federal agencies
think an amendment is needed that would add language
to the act providing that it is not to be construed
as requiring the prevention of significant
deterioration . . . EPA believes, unlike some
agencies, that the Federal Government has a
responsibility of providing guidance to the States
in preventing significant deterioration."[97] In
outlining the EPA regulation, which he promised
would be proposed "in the near future," Train
reinforced the need to consider "economic and social
considerations" as well as air quality in
determining what deterioration was "significant,"
and described the zone system as reflecting this.
He repeated his argument to the Governors (referred
to in the April 5th Strelow letter) that judgments
about how to balance such considerations "should be
made by the States, not by EPA." Train continued to
refer to procedural oversight as EPA's role, limited
to ensuring that States would "produce factually
based decisions with full public participation."
However, States were to be forced to be rational
planners; Train endorsed the two year Class 2
provision with subsequent reversion to Class 1 to
"put pressure on the States to make them designate
zones . . ."[98]
     Senators at the hearing did raise some questions
about PSD. Senator Domenici asked whether the
Sierra Club was happy with a proposal which involved
"States settling this for themselves;" Train and
Roger Strelow both responded that the Club "was not

entirely happy about it."[99]   Both Senator Domenici
and Senator Buckley questioned the two year zoning
provision, with Senator Buckley suggesting that its
practical effect would be to get EPA in the business
of making zoning decisions for the States.   Buckley
was also the only Senator to suggest that PSD, with
its land use implications, "may possibly have gone
beyond what the Congress wanted in enacting the
legislation."[100]   However, what is striking about
these hearings is that despite a concerted effort by
industry to condemn PSD and push for an amendment to
explicitly remove the requirement, Train was
subjected to almost no hostile questioning on the
issue.   Moreover, no Senator challenged Train's
position of disagreeing with the rest of the
Executive Branch on submitting a legislative
amendment.   This remarkable behavior, in the face of
the "energy crisis," can only be ascribed to the
continued weakness of the White House at this time
in dealing with Congress.   However, it was an
important precedent for EPA.   By confirming the
alliance between the Agency and the Committee, it
reinforced EPA's willingness to take a hard line in
the interagency review of the PSD regulations, which
was going on at that time.

It will be recalled that in 1971, "interagency
review" had been a factor in the controversy over
the deletion of the "significant deterioration"
language from the original 40 CFR 51 regulation.[101]
Once again, interagency review would have a
restraining effort upon EPA.   In this case, however,
it would bring the regulations closer to how OAQPS
had originally intended them to look.

PSD AND INTERAGENCY REVIEW

EPA officials recognized that the PSD
regulations would face a hostile audience in
interagency review.   In the winter of 1973-74, the
Environmental Quality Subcommittee of the White
House Domestic Council had formed an interagency

Task Force at the staff level to examine the PSD
regulations as they were being developed. EPA
officials who chaired the Task Force tried to
restrict its scope to "technical issues" and avoid
using the Task Force as a platform for philosophical
debates about the virtues (or lack thereof) of PSD.
Indeed, the Commerce Department had generated some
data about the possible impacts of PSD which seemed
to confirm the earlier OPE work.[102] However, the
formation of the Task Force was an indication of the
concern which other agencies had about PSD, and this
concern did not lessen over the months in which the
regulations were drafted.

   An interagency meeting on PSD was held on May
20, 1974, and comments followed shortly thereafter.
Several agencies (TVA, Interior, Commerce, Federal
Energy Office (FEO)) all argued against any
automatic reversion to Class I after 24 months on
planning grounds, asserting that it would increase
uncertainty and thereby hinder good planning. The
same agencies also objected to any specification of
BACT as more stringent than NSPS, and to the
provision that ICS and tall stacks would not be
allowed for compliance with increments.[103]

   In addition, FEO, Commerce, and OMB raised
several other issues which would have substantially
weakened EPA's proposal. One basis for the
FEO/Commerce/OMB objection to PSD was the passage of
the second Nixon energy bill--the Energy Supply and
Environmental Coordination Act (ESECA)--in June,
1974. Commerce and FEO both argued that the new
Section 4 of ESECA overruled the Sierra Club vs.
Ruckelshaus decision, enabling EPA to weaken the PSD
regulations or make them optional for States. The
Commerce Department further argued that instead of
promulgating regulations which would be directly
incorporated into State implementation plans ("Part
52 regulations"), EPA should only promulgate
guidelines ("Part 51 regulations") for States to
submit their own implementation plans--a distinction
which though it seemed small, would result in years
of delay in implementing any PSD program. Finally,
Jim Tozzi of OMB recommended that the Class 2

increments be doubled to allow additional growth in
Class 2 areas.[104]

EPA staff refused to yield to these objections,
and a "principals only" meeting was set up between
Train, Frank Zarb, the new head of the Federal
Energy Administration (the renamed FEO), and Rogers
Morton, the Secretary of the Interior. In the face
of this opposition from other agencies, EPA staff
united to prepare arguments for Train to use at this
meeting. OGC sent forward a brief but strongly
worded memo opposing the use of tall stacks and ICS
in PSD, arguing that such a decision would undermine
EPA's overall legal position on both tall stacks and
ICS. One EPA air attorney went to far as to say
that "if we concede unrestricted [tall stacks/ICS]
in the non-significant deterioration regulations, I
think we've conceded the principle altogether."[105]
OPE officials prepared materials supporting
reclassification to Class I after 24 months;
applying ESECA to _existing_ rather than new plants;
the existing Class II increments; and retention of
the Agency's position on ICS/tall stacks. (However,
OPE's argument on this last point was half-hearted.
Their memo states that "the case against SCS
[supplementary control systems, which here included
tall stacks] in general is stronger than it is
here.")[106]

EPA's views were summed up in a July 12th
memorandum from Roger Strelow to Administrator
Train.[107] In brief, they were:
(1) The court order required EPA to promulgate "Part
    52" regulations, rather than "Part 51"
    guidelines.
(2) ESECA applied only to _existing_ facilities, not
    new ones. For support, Strelow noted that the
    ESECA conference report contained a paragraph
    which read, in part, "the conferees wish to
    emphasize, however, that many important
    legislative issues pertaining to the Clean Air
    Act have yet to be resolved. Among these are
    the issues relating to the prevention of
    significant deterioration."[108] Strelow also
    observed that on both this and the preceding

issue, the Justice Department sided with the
Agency against FEA, Commerce, and OMB.
(3) The PSD increments should not be increased.
Strelow argued that the existing increments
would be adequate to allow for growth.
Moreover, he adopted the argument that "if we
double the increment, the court is likely to
reject the approach since the increments would
be half the ambient standards."
(4) EPA should hold firm on ICS/tall stacks and try
to defer this controversy.
Strelow's memo did recommend that Train concede
on two issues. On the issue of automatic Class I
zoning after 24 months, Strelow told Train that
"although there is a strong consensus among the AA's
within the Agency that the current proposal is
preferable, I don't feel it would be calamitous if
you obliged on this point." His reasoning is
interesting in light of the earlier debate over
variances: "I don't believe the Sierra Club would
be as upset about a reversal on this point as they
would about another one which was never raised in
our interagency discussions, namely, the current
provision that no plant by plant variances will be
given unless this can be accomplished by a selective
Zone redesignation."[109] Even this concession to
OMB/FEA/Commerce/Interior shows how far PSD had come
from OAQPS' original concept of the increments as
targets which could be exceeded with a relatively
straightforward showing by the State. It also shows
the influence of the Sierra Club's arguments on
EPA's political executives as compared to their
relatively unsympathetic treatment by OAQPS
engineers. While the numbers of the increments had
not changed, the concept of what the numbers meant
was drastically different and much closer to the
Sierra Club's notion that changes in air quality
would determine growth patterns and power plant
construction. The second concession which Strelow
recommended to Train also showed the lack of OAQPS
influence. Strelow agreed with the other Federal
agencies, and with OPE, that the independent BACT
requirement should be eliminated. This meant that
Western power plants which could meet the SO_2

increments and NSPS without scrubbers would have no
independent requirement in PSD to install them.
While Strelow had argued in discussing SCS that
scrubbers on large Western power plants were "the
gut issue with Sierra Club," and used the point to
justify not accepting SCS in the PSD regulations, he
nevertheless recommended that Train not push the
issue of minimizing new emissions through the use of
best technology. This reinforced the ambient rather
than an emissions focus of PSD.[110]

The principals' meeting on July 15th initially
appeared to be a victory for EPA. While "giving up"
the requirement for BACT on Western power plants and
the automatic redesignation to Class I, EPA staff
reported after the meeting that the "prohibition" on
ICS and tall stacks as means of preventing increment
consumption "had been maintained." Perhaps more
importantly, they believed that "it was generally
agreed "that §4 of ESECA does not affect the
significant deterioration concept."[111]

This "agreement," however, was not as conclusive
as it appeared. While the scope of the argument
that §4 of ESECA overturned the Sierra Club decision
became somewhat narrower, the "general" agreement
did not stop attorneys from the Department of
Commerce and the Federal Energy Administration from
lobbying the Justice Department to overturn
fundamental elements of EPA's proposal.

One example was the "regulations vs. guidelines"
issue. EPA staff believed after the July 15th
meeting that they had solid Justice Department
support, that OMB would treat this issue as "moot"
given the need to get something out quickly, and
that any EPA promulgation would "have virtually the
same substantive effect." Still, Commerce did
manage to keep the issue alive by getting an
extension of time to submit formal legal views to
the Justice Department.[112]

A second example was FEA's argument that §4 of
ESECA would allow States "the option of deciding
whether fuel burning stationary sources should be
subject to the [PSD] regulations." This option
which would have exempted power plants--the sources
of greatest concern--from PSD.[113] EPA attorneys

continued to oppose these views, ostensibly on
purely legal grounds.[114] Again, however, these legal
arguments were buttressed by the conviction of
senior EPA political officials that they had the
critical support of the Justice Department in the
battle of legal interpretations.[115]

A final aspect of the July 15th meeting was more
difficult for EPA to deal with. The other agencies
succeeded in getting a commitment from Administrator
Train to develop a brief paper on the issue of
doubling the values of the particulate matter and
SO_2 Class II increments.[116] As discussed above, EPA
staff (especially OGC) had argued that such a
doubling was unnecessary and would threaten judicial
acceptance of EPA's approach in court. OGC staff
were already unhappy at the prospect of defending
regulations which in theory would allow degradation
up to the secondary standards (through
reclassification of an area to Class III).
Therefore, when it became clear that the idea of
doubling the Class II increments was still alive,
OGC responded with additional defenses of the
current figures. In addition to the "it makes it
even harder to defend" argument, OGC also objected
that no one had raised the doubling suggestion
during the public comment period on the regulations.

The reasoning behind this argument is worth
citing as an example of the way in which the
increment numbers had taken on a life of their own.

. . . Critics of the alternatives involving air
quality increments disliked the whole approach,
not the specific increments. I recognize that
the increments in the July, 1973 proposal were
necessarily rather subjective. However, we did
publish those increments and any change from
those levels would have to be justified at least
by cogent reasoning and preferably should be
based on the record developed from responses to
the July, 1973 proposal.[117]

OGC did propose one possible means of dealing
with this conflict. Richard Denny of OGC suggested
that "if the Agency is encountering strong

opposition on this point, I suggest our fallback
position be that we keep the present Class II
increment in the proposed regulations and state in
the preamble that we would like comments on the
adequacy of the present increment."[118] This
concession became important soon thereafter.

In the meantime, EPA continued to push these
issues to closure. The Agency was aided in this
effort by the Sierra Club. On July 25th, the Club
filed an action with Judge Pratt to compel EPA to
issue the PSD regulations.

This suit clearly served the Agency's purposes.
On July 26th, Roger Strelow wrote to Jim Tozzi at
OMB stating EPA"s intent to propose the regulations
by August 12th. Strelow cited the Sierra Club suit
as underlining "the urgency of this prompt action."
The memo indicated (1) that Train and Zarb had
reached a basic understanding and agreement; (2)
that the Justice Department had supported EPA on the
legal issues of SIP regulations and the effect of
ESECA on PSD; and (3) that EPA did not intend to
yield on the ICS/SCS issue or the doubling of the
increments. The letter concluded coldly, "we are
moving forward to propose regs in accordance with
the above points. Please advise me of any points
you wish to discuss further."[119]

EPA was not the only group writing to Tozzi.
The Department of Commerce sent a letter arguing in
favor of doubling the annual SO_2 increment from 15
ug/m^3 to 30 ug/m^3. The letter focused almost
entirely on power plants and attacked both EPA's
analysis and the rigidity with which EPA defended
numbers originally described as subjective. It
concluded that "not only is the use of the
originally proposed increment as the Class II area
increment an illogical misapplication, but the
present magnitude of the increment is unjustifiably
restrictive and is not defensible. To EPA's
response that any areas needing a larger increment
could reclassify to Class III, Commerce argued that
this would "unnecessarily" open up larger areas to
"Class III degradation"--a disingenuous argument at
best given Commerce's constant opposition to PSD in
any form.[120] FEA also continued to support this

position in correspondence to Strelow. Though it
used milder language, the essential point was the
same--that the benefits of doubling the increments
far outweighed the "relatively insignificant"
environmental costs.[121]

Faced with this continuing controversy, EPA's
senior political managers decided in early August to
make a partial accommodation. An August 11th
"action memorandum" records EPA's decision to (1)
accept OGC's proposal to solicit "comments on the
desirability of increasing the level of the Class II
increments proposed herein," and, more importantly,
(2) to make "a change in the 3-hour SO_2 value [from
300 ug/m^3 to 700 ug/m^3] to make it compatible with
the 3-hour value under most meteorological
conditions."[122] EPA asserted in the regulation's
preamble that this was just a technical change "to
ensure that it is no more stringent than the 24 hour
increment for large point sources . . ."[123]

Given the intensity with which EPA had defended
the 300 ug/m^3 figure only four weeks earlier, this
reasoning seems incomplete. One possible
explanation is that EPA compromised with OMB and the
Commerce/FEA/OMB coalition on the single most
critical increment value for power plants, while
preserving the appearance (and satisfying EPA's
attorneys) that an overall "tough" set of increments
had been maintained. The evidence is not altogether
clear on this point, however, as OAQPS technical
staff had last-minute second thoughts. An August
12, 1974, internal memorandum from OAQPS' modelers,
in striking contrast to EPA's longstanding assertion
that a 1000 MW power plant would not cause increased
three hour concentrations over 300 ug/m^3 under
normal terrain conditions, reported that for such a
plant "an allowable increment of 750 ug/m^3 was more
appropriate." It seems likely that this technical
flip-flop was communicated up the line prior to the
date of this memorandum and would have weakened the
desire of EPA's political officials to stick with
the lower increment value.[124] This last-minute
technical shift allowed EPA to avoid confrontation
with the other departments, though it obscured a
significant and important policy choice about how

difficult it should be to construct a new, large coal-fired power plant.[125]

One other area was affected by the continued pressure of the Commerce Department. While EPA maintained its position that the terms of the court order required it to issue regulations, the Agency bent from its original position by agreeing that "guidelines" would be issued "in the near future" under 40 CFR Part 51. In contrast to the regulations issued under 40 CFR Part 52, which were uniform nationwide, the "Part 51" guidelines would allow States to develop their own more flexible plans to prevent significant deterioration. How similar or different such plans had to be from EPA's own regulations was an open question. EPA commented only that "the State plans need not be identical to the regulations proposed herein, but should be developed to accommodate more appropriately individual conditions and procedures unique to specific State and local areas." Once such a plan was developed and approved as a revision to a State's official implementation plan, EPA would withdraw its own Part 52 regulations from that area.[126] One can see the spirit of the local option plan behind this proposal. Not surprisingly, a conflict was to develop later within EPA over just how much flexibility the Part 51 "guidelines" would allow States to have.[127]

In all other respects save one, this final draft of the proposal incorporated the agreements which had been hammered out within EPA, and between EPA and the other Federal agencies over the preceding several months. All areas were to be initially classified as Class II; there were to be no reversions to Class I after two years. In a return to the original OAQPS approach, the PSD regulations applied only to nineteen specific categories of major stationary sources of air pollution; all other sources were exempt. While the preamble asserted that the impact of minor source growth would be assessed by review at the time any major source was considered, this was clearly expected to be a rare concern. The preamble--responding to OAQPS' technical concerns in preference to those who saw

PSD as creating a budget of actual air quality--
noted that because "modelling results will be used
to keep track of the available (or "unused")
increment . . . an accurately measured baseline is
not an essential consideration in implementing these
regulations."[128] The concept of "best available
control technology was defined very narrowly--it
applied only to emissions of particulate matter and
SO_2, and was defined as equal to NSPS where these
standards existed. Since all nineteen categories of
sources either were covered or were soon to be
covered by NSPS, this essentially eliminated the
application of BACT as a separate control concept in
PSD. The notion of using PSD to require scrubbers
on Western power plants was dropped.[129] Finally,
State classification decisions could be overturned
by EPA only if "the State has arbitrarily and
capriciously disregarded relevant environmental,
social or economic consideration in any
redesignation."[130]

     The proposed regulations also revealed that EPA
stood its ground in the face of heavy pressure from
the FEA about the treatment of coal conversions and
increment consumption. EPA's position was subtle
but significant. While agreeing that coal
conversions at existing plants should not be
required to go through PSD review--and would thus
escape being subject to the 1.2 lb/mm Btu SO_2
emission standard--EPA contended that emissions from
switches to higher sulfur fuel should be counted in
computer modeling of how much of a area's available
air quality increment had been used up. This led to
the paradoxical situation, described by EPA in the
regulatory preamble, that a power plant not subject
to PSD could switch fuel and "use up the entire
available deterioration increment, and in some cases
exceed the increment, thereby precluding the
introduction of other major sources in the area
unless the area is reclassified."[131] The FEA had
maintained, on the other hand, that such conversions
should be included in "baseline" air quality and not
constrain future growth by limiting the available
increment.[132] EPA, however, argued successfully that
State flexibility to inhibit or prevent fuel

switching, or reclassify to a higher classification, dealt adequately with this concern.[133]

There was one final last-minute relaxation in the PSD regulations on monitoring requirements. However, this change was not forced upon EPA from outside, but rather came from within.

It will be recalled that the monitoring requirements had been a source of dispute between professional engineers in OAQPS and those who saw monitoring data as a guarantee that the increments would not be violated. In the winter of 1973-74, OAQPS staff had successfully argued that this requirement should be deleted. However, in the course of review by other EPA offices in the spring and early summer of 1974, the requirement was reinserted on the grounds that other desirable uses for the monitoring data existed even if the data would not be useful for determining PSD increment consumption.[134]

OPE attacked this reinstated requirement. Their weapon was to ask for a formal legal opinion, as they were told informally by OGC staff that "the requirement may not have a firm legal footing."[135] This approach produced quick results: two weeks later OGC issued a formal opinion that the monitoring requirements "were of doubtful legal validity."[136] In the face of sustained opposition from OPE, OGC and OAQPS, the advocates of the monitoring requirements were forced to back down, and it was deleted from the regulations in late July.[137]

EPA ANNOUNCES ITS PROPOSAL

EPA and OMB reached final agreement on the proposed regulation during the first week in August, at a time when the government was effectively paralyzed by the events surrounding the resignation of Richard Nixon. A revised _Federal Register_ notice was sent to the various offices for concurrence on August 11, and on the 16th EPA Deputy Administrator

John Quarles announced the proposal of the
regulations at a press conference. The reason for
the date of the announcement was that the Justice
Department, in response to the Sierra Club suit on
July 25th, had told the court that EPA would
repropose the regulations by the 16th.[138] Only one
day was allowed by this schedule for review of the
proposed regulations by the Deputy Administrator,
though of course the major issues had been discussed
with him earlier. Administrator Russell Train was
absent from the press conference announcing the
proposal.

In his prepared statement, Quarles alluded to
the vagueness of the court order and the
"extraordinary effort" by EPA to obtain comments on
and discuss the regulations within potentially
affected parties. He justified the issuance of a
reproposal as necessary "to focus more clearly on
procedural and technical issues." After outlining
the regulations, Quarles responded to charges that
PSD would stifle development or "result in a policy
of no growth" by asserting that the proposal would
"also encourage well planned and adequately
controlled growth." He cited it, along with other
air quality planning requirements, as "additional
tools which state and local governments can utilize
to develop effective and comprehensive land use
programs that will serve a variety of economic and
environmental needs."[139]

Quarles' statement on the proposed regulations
contained references to the ideals of planned growth
and land use and development control mechanisms
which were held in high esteem by PSD's strongest
proponents both inside and outside the Agency. Yet
this bold rhetoric should not obscure the degree to
which the PSD program which EPA proposed in 1974 was
a far cry not only from the one envisioned by the
Sierra Club, but from earlier PSD proposals
developed within EPA. The final proposal covered
only 19 specific categories of sources and only 2
pollutants--SO_2 and particulate matter. It did not
require controls tighter than New Source Performance
Standard requirements. While it did create air
quality increments and ceilings, these were to be

calculated by mathematical modeling and were not
expected to be measurable through air quality
monitoring. Reclassification was left largely to
the discretion of the States, with EPA able to
intervene only in the case of "arbitrary and
capricious" State behavior. Deterioration was to be
permitted up to the secondary amount air quality
standards in Class III areas, and the most
restrictive Class II increment had been doubled. In
short, while EPA had adopted the air quality plan
with all of its attendant difficulties as the basis
for its proposal, intra- and inter-agency review had
eliminated some of the more burdensome features of
the air quality plan in the interest of making the
program easier and less costly to implement.

Developments Between Proposal and Promulgation

The proposed regulations were immediately
attacked. Industry, especially coal producers and
electric utilities, criticized the proposed
regulations on the grounds that they would
unnecessarily restrict growth. However, without
abandoning the bureaucratic arena, industry seems to
have turned its attention primarily toward lobbying
Congress to amend §101(b) of the Act to overturn
Sierra Club vs. Ruckelshaus and to preparing for the
litigation which would follow EPA's final rules.
The Sierra Club responded to the proposed
regulation in a press conference on August 19. The
Club claimed that the Agency's rules showed contempt
for the court order, and especially attacked the
provisions for allowing Class III areas to
deteriorate up to the national standards and for
allowing new power plants using low-sulfur coal to
operate without scrubbers. Bruce Terris, the Club's
attorney who had originally sued EPA, announced that
the Club would "promptly challenge" EPA's regulation
court once they were finalized.[140]

The Club wasted little time in continuing its efforts to force final Agency action and return the issue to the courts, where the Club believed it had a comparative advantage. Under the terms of the D.C. Circuit's July 25th order, EPA was supposed to promulgate final PSD regulations no later than 90 days following their proposal. On September 19, the Sierra Club obtained a subsequent court order from Judge Pratt which specified November 25, 1974, as the date by which final regulations were to be issued.[141] Though perhaps not intended by the Sierra Club, this time pressure gave a distinct advantage to those who wished to preserve the proposed PSD regulations as written. It also made it much easier for EPA to fend off any attempt by OMB, the Commerce Department, or FEA to undo the agreements reached prior to the proposal of the regulation.

Not surprisingly, therefore, very few changes were made in the final regulations based on the public comments following the August proposal. In the final rulemaking, announced on November 27 and published on December 5, EPA rejected the Sierra Club's protest that the proposal permitted deterioration up to the air quality standards, again saying that this did not make the regulations inconsistent with the court's ruling. EPA also reaffirmed its philosophical position that a balancing between air quality and economic considerations was relevant to the determination of when deterioration was "significant," and that its increment classification approach was an appropriate vehicle for this balancing to take place.[142]

In the August 27th proposal, EPA had specifically solicited comment on whether the Class II increments should be increased.[143] (In light of the increase prior to proposal from 300 ug/m^3 to 700 ug/m^3 for the 3 hour SO_2 increment, some would have argued that the debate was over redoubling the increments). Utilities pushed for an expansion, but the final rules promulgated by EPA rejected any further changes in the Class II increments. Instead, EPA argued that areas where it was feared that "development" (read power plants) would threaten the increment levels should go through the

process of redesignating to Class III. This was
important, because EPA also retained the initial
designation of the entire country as Class II. No
one knew exactly how a redesignation process would
work, or exactly what criteria EPA would apply in
approving one, and the utilities argued hard for an
expansion of the Class II increments or, failing
that, an initial designation of all areas as Class
III. Environmentalists, in contrast, had argued for
an initial designation of all areas as Class I. EPA
rejected both arguments, restating its opinion that
(1) an initial designation of all areas as Class II
was a "reasonable compromise," and (2) that "a Class
II increment should be compatible with moderate,
well-controlled development in a nationwide context,
and that large-scale development should be permitted
only in conjunction with a conscious decision to
redesignate the area as Class III."[144]
     The relatively small changes EPA made to the
final regulations suggest that the utilities'
concerns were not unfounded. The most substantive
of these changes dealt with the procedures and
considerations EPA would use in reviewing requests
for redesignation, and seemed to indicate that EPA
land-use planning advocates were able to exercise
some influence over the final regulations. One
change specified that EPA would publish a notice of
all proposed redesignation in the <u>Federal Register</u>,
and allow at least 30 days for public comment.
Another change--one which would later become
controversial--gave Federal Land Managers the
authority to subject Federal lands to a more
stringent designation than the State would otherwise
assign to them. This was a significant shift from
the proposal, which had given the States the ability
to elevate such disputes to the Executive Office of
the President. This dispute resolution provision
was deleted from the final regulations.[145]
     EPA also formalized the information a State had
to submit for a redesignation to be approvable by
EPA. It did so by adding requirements that such
information be part of a State's "hearing record"
and that it show "consideration of (1) growth
anticipated in the area, (2) the social, environ-

mental and economic effects of such redesignation
upon the area being proposed for redesignation and
upon other areas and States, and (3) any impacts of
such proposed redesignation upon regional or
national interests."[146] Finally, EPA indicated that
if another State or an Indian Governing Body
protested a redesignation to EPA, then the Agency
would "take an expanded role of review in which [the
Administrator] would balance the competing interests
involved."[147] These changes signified that the
concept of redesignation had shifted yet again from
a relatively simple tool which State and local
governments would have available, to a complex
procedure which would carry with it a significant
Federal role.

    Two other noteworthy changes relate to BACT.
The first specified that BACT requirements would
apply to sources in Class III areas well; this was a
change from the August proposal, which had limited
this requirement to sources in Class I and II areas
only. In contrast to the land use planning emphasis
of the redesignation requirements, this change aimed
directly at reinforcing PSD's role in limiting total
emissions loadings. EPA justified this change by
referring to the potential impact of sources in
Class III areas on Class I and II areas, but also
noted ". . . the necessity to minimize emissions as
much as possible in all areas. . ."[148] Finally, EPA
required that for sources subject to review under
PSD, "an emissions limitation be established as a
condition to approval." This provision indicated
how far EPA had come from 1972 when Administrator
Ruckelshaus and Senator Eagleton had debated about
whether SIP's required "emissions limits"! By 1974,
EPA was quite specific on this point. The Agency
did leave itself a technical out, allowing for a
design or equipment standard to be specified if an
emissions limit could not be specified because of
technological or economic limitations on measurement
methodology, but this was only for cases where an
emissions limit could not be practically
established.[149]

    If anything, these changes represented a
marginal tightening of the rule between August and

November. The basic structure of the rule, however, did <u>not</u> change. The increment system remained intact, with three classes at the levels of the proposal; BACT was still required on affected sources (though power plants could still use low-sulfur coal <u>if</u> they did not violate the increments); only a limited number of sources listed in the regulations were to be subject to review; deterioration up to the level of the secondary standards was still allowed in Class III areas; and no program was established for pollutants other than SO_2 and particulate matter (though the final notice did ask for comment on how a program for other pollutants might be implemented). The continued court pressure by the Sierra Club left little time for further rethinking of the rules after the August proposal. With the December promulgations, the arena for the debate over PSD was to return to Congress and the courts.

In announcing the final rules, Administrator Train noted that the Agency would "continue to solicit further Congressional guidance." He also conceded that there was a "fair amount of disagreement" within the Executive Branch over the regulations, and that he continued to expect other Federal agencies to support amendments to the Clean Air Act which would overturn the <u>Sierra Club vs. Ruckelshaus</u> decision.[150] Train was correct on this last point. A day before EPA announced the final PSD regulations, a memorandum from the Federal Energy Administration to OMB indicated that FEA still felt as strongly on this point as ever.[151] The stage was set for the next round in Congress in the battle over PSD.

EPA and the 1974 Regulations

The 1974 regulations marked the culmination of more than two years of EPA work following the decision by Judge Pratt in <u>Sierra Club vs. Ruckelshaus</u>. In that time, the Agency's posture had changed from skepticism about whether PSD was a wise public policy to advocacy of rules which expanded the Federal role in key decisions about industrial plant siting, air pollution control requirements and economic growth. EPA's shifting position on PSD amounted to a statement of belief that the ambient standards approach of the Clean Air Act of 1970 did not capture all of the Agency's environmental concerns about air pollution. Moreover, upon recognizing the potential effect of PSD on growth and land use, some EPA officials made a conscious effort to use PSD to expand EPA's ability to influence such decisions. While not all such ideas developed by EPA staff were incorporated in the final regulations, the principle that allowable increases in air pollution should depend on the planned land use in a given area was at the very heart of the PSD increment system which EPA developed.

The preceding discussion shows that several factors contributed to this change. The most important appears to have been the different approach of EPA's political leadership in the 1973-74 period. William Ruckelshaus may have been willing to do what was necessary to comply with a court order on PSD, but Russell Train and his senior advisers seem to have embraced PSD as an opportunity. It is remarkable that these leaders, despite an Administration whose principal actors lined up almost solidly against them, persisted and were successful in maintaining the position that a PSD program should be established. The <u>Sierra Club</u> case provided the reason why some form of PSD program <u>had</u> to be developed, but the effort EPA devoted to developing and defending its program

shows that more than reluctant compliance was at
work.

Having said this, it is important not to
overlook one key reason why Administrator Train was
successful in maintaining a position in favor of
PSD. Train skillfully took advantage of the
relative weakness of Presidential authority in the
1973-74 period to maintain an independent position
on PSD. In doing so, Train was assisted by the
tradition established by Ruckelshaus of an
independent EPA which characterized itself to the
public as a representative of a general public
interest. Though EPA was still a young Agency, this
tradition assisted Train and his senior associates
as they attempted to maintain their independence
from the pressure exerted by the Administration.

However, while EPA's top officials sought to
position the Agency as a spokesman for the general
public, the differences within the Agency about
PSD's objectives and how they should be served
reflected both the differing professional norms of
internal groups and the constituencies to which they
responded. For example, OAQPS, which was composed
primarily of air pollution control engineers,
focused on how PSD would affect the technological
requirements for emissions control on new sources,
and whether or not the various goals embodied in the
PSD proposals could be technically carried out. The
Office of Enforcement's lawyers worried about how
these requirements would be made legally binding on
pollution sources and enforceable by the Federal
government. OGC's attorneys, with their orientation
toward the Justice Department and the courts,
worried about how various proposals would be
received by the judiciary and whether the Sierra
Club's objections were sufficiently met so that the
Agency's regulations could be successfully defended
in subsequent litigation. OPE's planners were
interested in PSD's value as a land use tool, while
its economists worried about the relative costs of
PSD-imposed scrubbers and tall stacks.

Just as no single group within the Agency
accomplished all of its objectives in the December,
1974 rulemaking, neither industry nor the

environmentalists were very satisfied with the
rules. The Sierra Club's displeasure can be readily
understood; the rules were a far cry from the plan
favored by the Club, and a determined source could,
at least in theory, use reclassification to ensure
that it would not be subject to any additional
control requirements than would otherwise have been
the case under NSPS and the ambient standards. This
could hardly have constituted "preventing
deterioration" to the Club.

Industry's continued violent opposition to PSD
is a little more difficult to understand. EPA's
rules did impose additional procedural requirements
on large new facilities, and while these may not
have been costly, they could be burdensome, time-
consuming and a source of uncertainty in project
planning which no industrial interest would welcome.
Beyond this, however, there seems to have been
little industrial willingness to deal with the PSD
provisions at all on their merits. This may perhaps
have been because, given EPA's political/cultural
orientation, industrial groups thought their chances
were better in Congress. Industry may also have
seen a "window of opportunity" opening up as a
result of the energy crisis that would enable them
to roll back some of the dramatic gains made by
environmental groups in the 1970 Clean Air Act.
However, it is hard not to agree with Richard
Vietor's observation that beyond their opposition to
PSD as a particular policy, industrial interests
opposed it because it represented a "limits to
growth" viewpoint which was anathema to American
industrial society.[152] The financial interests at
stake in PSD for industry were significant--
especially for the energy industry, where the
country looked to coal to rescue the nation from the
energy crisis. The vehemence of industry's
challenge, however, goes beyond its mere financial
stake and suggests that industry saw in PSD an arena
in which two incompatible views of the world were in
conflict.

This struggle over the symbols which PSD
represented had, by the end of 1974, obscured the
fact that on balance, the regulations established by

EPA were relatively modest and represented only an
incremental change from the status quo prior to the
Sierra Club suit. The intra- and interagency review
process had in this respect done its job. While EPA
had stood its ground on the threshold question of
whether PSD should exist at all, the most extreme
proposals had been winnowed out. EPA's program
covered only two pollutants, was limited in scope to
only the largest industries, required no controls
beyond NSPS, preserved the ability to pollute up to
the secondary ambient standards through
reclassification, and had a key increment changed to
allow greater flexibility. This hardly represented
"limits to growth" regulation. The one area in
which real change did occur was in the notion that
the Federal government had an oversight role in new
land-use and industrial siting decisions because of
the air pollution consequences of these decisions.
EPA's PSD regulations opened this door to a greater
extent than had been the case previously. However,
they did so in a tentative, incremental way, using
the tools of procedure rather than substance. Not
all of this caution was to be preserved, however, in
the subsequent rounds of reconsideration of PSD by
the Congress, the Agency and the courts.

NOTES

1. Joseph Padgett to Working Group Members,
    "Preliminary Schedule for Action on Prevention
    of Significant Air Quality Deterioration,"
    September 5, 1973.
        I am especially indebted to Cheryl Wasserman,
    a member of the original EPA work group, for
    documentation of this period. Cheryl very
    carefully saved a record of the work group's
    deliberations, thus allowing an unusually full
    reconstruction of them. Without her gracious
    assistance, the story in this chapter could not
    have been put together. The interpretations,
    however, are strictly my own responsibility.

2. U.S. EPA, State Air Pollution Implementation
    Plan Progress Report, April 1974, pp. 17-18
    (reprinted in U.S. Congress, Senate, Committee
    on Public Works, Clean Air Act Oversight,
    Hearings Before the Subcommittee on Environment
    Pollution of the Senate Committee on Public
    Works, 93 Cong., 2nd sess., 1974, pp. 1209-1320.
    (Hereafter cited as 1974 Senate Oversight
    Hearings.) Also see Allen V. Kneese and Charles
    L. Schultze, Pollution, Prices, and Public
    Policy (Washington: Brookings, 1975), p. 67.

3. A. Myrick Freeman, "Air and Water Pollution
    Policy," in Paul R. Portney, ed., U.S.
    Environmental Policy (Baltimore: Johns Hopkins
    University Press), p. 45.

4. 1973 Senate Nondegradation Hearings, p. 73.

5. U.S. Congress, Senate, Committee on Public
    Works, The Fuel Shortage and the Clean Air Act,
    Hearing before the Subcommittee on Air and Water
    Pollution of the Committee on Public Works, 93rd
    Cong., 1st sess., 1973, p. 2. (Hereafter cited
    as 1973 Senate Fuel Shortage Hearing.)

6. See, for example, the testimony of the National
    Coal Association in ibid., pp. 77-97, and Fred

Hart, New York City Commissioner of Air
Resources, pp. 97-109. Of course, the Coal
Association did not hesitate to identify the
"short term" needs, calling (for example) for
allowing variances by NSPS plants from the 1.2
lb/mm Btu limit if adequate low sulfur coal was
not available (p. 89).

7. See, for instance, the statements by Dr. Betsy
Ancker-Johnson, Assistant Secretary of Commerce
for Science and Technology, and John Love, the
Nixon Administrations's (first) "energy czar,"
cited in Richard H. K. Vietor, Environmental
Politics and the Coal Coalition (College
Station, Texas: Texas A.& M. University Press,
1980), p. 207.

8. See the summary in Vietor, Environmental
Politics and the Coal Coalition, pp. 137-54, and
Esposito, Vanishing Air, pp. 286-87.

9. Kennecott Copper Corp. vs. EPA, 462 F.2d 846
(D.C. Cir.1972).

10. Congressional Research Service, Environmental
Protection Affairs of the Ninety-Third
Congress, (Washington: U.S. Government Printing
Office, 1975), p. 16.

11. "Special Message to the Congress on Energy
Policy, April 18, 1973," Public Papers of the
Presidents: Richard Nixon (Washington: U.S.
Government Printing Office, 1975), pp. 308-9.

12. 36 Federal Register 24876.

13. The utilities' position is repeated again and
again in testimony before Senator Muskie's
subcommittee. See 1974 Senate Oversight
Hearings, esp. pp. 3-184. Environmentalists, of
course, opposed the use of intermittent controls
and derided them as the "rhythm method of
pollution control."

14. 38 <u>Federal Register</u> 25697.

15. <u>NRDC vs. EPA</u>, 489 F.2d 390.

16. The best summary of the ICS/stack heights controversies is in Melnick, <u>Regulation and the Courts</u>, chapter 5.

17. "Sierra Club Calls Plan By EPA on Air Pollution Short of Legal Rulings," <u>Wall Street Journal</u>, July 17, 1973.

18. Testimony of Laurence I. Moss in <u>1973 Senate Fuel Shortage Hearing</u>, p. 43. See also the associated statement of Dick Ayres and David Hawkins.

19. For a fuller discussion on this point, see Marcus, <u>Promise and Performance</u>, chapter 4, and Melnick, <u>Regulation and the Courts</u>, pp. 38-43.

20. Interview information.

21. 38 <u>Federal Register</u> 18986.

22. Melnick, <u>Regulation and the Courts</u>, p. 87.

23. <u>Ibid.</u>, p. 41. On the origins of OPE, see also Marcus, <u>Promise and Performance</u>, pp. 96-97, and Wiehl, "William D. Ruckelshaus and the Environmental Protection Agency," pp. 11-12.

24. See Marcus, <u>Promise and Performance</u>, pp. 97-99.

25. Melnick, <u>Regulation and the Courts</u>, pp. 40-41.

26. Joseph Padgett to Addressees, "Working Group Meeting on August 23, 1973," September 5, 1973.

27. Joseph Padgett to Working Group on Non-Degradation, "Analytical Studies and Questions of Interests in Regard to Prevention of Significant Deterioration," September 11, 1973.

28. Draft "Proposed Alternative Plan to Prevent
     Significant Deterioration," November 8, 1973.
     This draft was prepared by Robert Coleman.

29. Melnick, <u>Regulation and the Courts</u>, chapter 9,
     tells the story of the fate of transportation
     control planning at EPA. He also cites the
     large secondary literature on this topic.
         An anecdote told by an EPA official sheds an
     interesting light on this subject. The official
     recalls standing in the ninth floor office of
     Robert Sansom, who was then EPA Assistant
     Administrator for Air and Water Programs.
     Sansom, looking out at a typical evening
     Washington traffic jam, turned to the official
     and remarked that "the Clean Air Act gives me
     the power to change all that." The official
     remarked that he was skeptical about the
     difference between the <u>authority</u> to require such
     changes in transportation patterns and the
     <u>ability</u> to bring them about.

30. Roy Gamse to Joseph Padgett, "OPE Status Report
     and Comments," October 17, 1973.

31. Richard G. Rhoads to Joseph Padgett, "Survey of
     Views on Significant Deterioration," October 25,
     1973.

32. Steve Reznek to Joseph Padgett, "Review Papers
     on Measurement, Modeling and Effects," October
     16, 1973.

33. Robert Coleman to Working Group Members," Non-
     Degradation Plan," October 23, 1973.

34. Melnick places great stress on this point in his
     interpretation of this part of the story. See
     <u>Regulation and the Courts</u>, pp. 90-91.

35. Gamse to Padgett, "OPE Status Report," October
     17, 1973.

36. Roy Gamse to Joseph Padgett, "OPE Proposal for Non-Degradation," October 26, 1973.

37. Unpublished ORD paper, "Scientific Facts Bearing on Regulatory Policies to Assure Non-Degradation of Air Quality" (undated but found with other papers dated December 1973).

38. Dick Wilson to Chief, Program Development Staff, DSSE, "Significant Deterioration Regulations," September 18, 1973, and Wilson to Working Group, "Proposed Non-Deterioration Regulations," October 16, 1973.

39. Gamse to Padgett, "OPE Proposal," op. cit.

40. B. J. Steigerwald to The Record, "Meeting with State People on Significant Deterioration," October 15, 1973.

41. Ibid.

42. Robert Coleman to Joseph Padgett, "Chicago Non-Degradation meeting," October 12, 1973.

43. Steigerwald to the Record, op. cit.

44. See, for example, Wilson to Working Group. op. cit.
       "In general, the following contingencies should be provided for no matter which alternative is selected.
   (a)   A procedure to reconcile a state determination to EPA's determination when EPA does not concur in the State's determination.
   (b)   A procedure to implement EPA's determination when a state fails to make a determination...."
Interestingly, the Office of Enforcement endorsed Option 3 on the grounds that it came closest to establishing enforceable emissions limitations--the traditional enforcement concern. However, it did note that Option 3

"allows the State to determine what constitutes
significant deterioration of air quality. This
decision would be final and not subject to
reversal by the Administrator."

45. Gamse to Padgett, "OPE Proposal," op. cit. See
    also Cheryl Wasserman and Bud Ehler, "Criteria
    for the Designation of Zones," n.d. but
    apparently from the end of October 1973.

46. Ibid.

47. Ibid.

48. Ibid.

49. 38 Federal Register 18999, July 16, 1973.

50. See the discussion at 38 Federal Register 18989.

51. Gamse to Padgett, "OPE Position," op. cit.

52. Ibid.

53. Richard G. Rhoads to Joseph Padgett, "Summary of
    Views on Significant Deterioration," October 25,
    1973.

54. In addition to chapter 2, supra, see Vietor,
    Environmental Politics and the Coal Coalitions,
    pp. 194-208. Vietor describes the coal
    coalition's origin, tactics, and means by which
    they obtain access to sympathetic government
    organizations such as the Department of Commerce
    in considerable detail in chapter 2.

55. "Sierra Club Proposal," analysis by OAQPS staff,
    dated November 8, 1973.

56. Deputy Assistant Administrator for General
    Enforcement to the Administrator, "Meeting with
    Sierra Club--Information Memorandum," January
    21, 1974.

214   **Protect and Enhance**

57. Interview data.

58. Roy Gamse to Alvin L. Alm, "Nondegradation
    Status and Issues," January 7, 1974.

59. "Summary of January 11, 1974, Meeting with
    Governors," internal OAQPS document, n.d. I
    have also relied in part on handwritten notes of
    this meeting found in the OAQPS file, which I
    believe to be those of Jean Schueneman, Director
    at that time of the Control Programs Development
    Division in OAQPS.

    The attendance list for this meeting shows
    Governors from the following States: Arizona,
    Colorado, Rhode Island, Washington, Wisconsin,
    and Wyoming, along with lesser representatives
    from ten other States. Also present were
    representatives from the White House, OMB, the
    Departments of Commerce and Housing and Urban
    Development, and House and Senate Committee
    staff.

60. Ibid.

61. Council on Environmental Quality, <u>Environmental
    Quality 1974: The Fifth Annual Report of the
    Council on Environmental Quality</u> (Washington:
    Government Printing Office, 1974), pp. 98-100

62. Melnick, <u>Regulation and the Courts</u>, pp. 127-28.

63. Ibid., pp. 128-29.

64. See, for example, "White House Challenged By
    Environmental Chief," <u>New York Times</u>, March 11,
    1974. This story also reports that the White
    House pressured EPA to endorse amendments which
    would include taking cost-benefit considerations
    into account in setting national ambient air
    quality standards. This would have been
    considered the ultimate heresy, both at EPA and,
    perhaps more importantly, at the Muskie

Committee. It was not pressed further by the
Federal Energy Office or the White House.

65. Attachment B, "Legislative Language That Would
    Implement the Views of Other Agencies on the
    Issue of Significant Deterioration," contained
    in Russell Train to the Honorable Gerald R.
    Ford, President of the Senate ("Dear Mr.
    President"), March 22, 1974.

66. Ibid.

67. Melnick, Regulation and the Courts, p. 129.

68. These first-round industrial arguments against
    PSD are collected in the 1974 Senate Oversight
    Hearings, pp. 186277 and 624-763.

69. Richard J. Denney to Joseph Padgett,
    "Significant Deterioration--Legal Strategy
    Paper," January 18, 1974.

70. "EPA Is on the Verge of Leaving to States Most
    of Task of Preserving Air Quality," Wall Street
    Journal, February 14, 1974, p. 4. A similar
    article had appeared in Business Week in January
    ("The EPA Compromises on Clean Air Rules,"
    Business Week, January 26, 1974, pp. 21-22.)
    The Sierra Club's Laurence Moss announced in
    this article that the Club, to no one's
    surprise, would reopen litigation if the Agency
    proceeded with the three zone plan.

71. Draft, Assistant Administrator for Air and Water
    Programs to the Administrator, "Regulations to
    Prevent Significant Deterioration of Air
    Quality--Action Memorandum"; attachment to
    Joseph Padgett to Working Group Members, "Draft
    Action Memo on 'Non-Degradation,'" February 15,
    1974.

72. Ibid.

73. At this time, the word "class" replaced the word "zone," the ostensible reason being that confusion had "resulted from the term 'zoning'. . . . because conventional zoning considers very small areas (city blocks or districts), whereas air quality 'zoning' would encompass much larger areas." Although unstated as a reason, this change also lessened the land-use planning jargon of PSD. Ibid., transmittal memo, p. 9.

74. Ibid., pp. 16-22.

75. Ibid., Draft preamble, p. 19.

76. Tom Bath to Director, Strategies and Air Standards Division, "Draft 'Non-Degradation' Regulatory Package--ORD Comments," February 22, 1974. ORD also objected to the notion that returning to Congress was a "sell-out" and recommended this language be dropped.

77. Draft, R. D. Wilson to Joseph Padgett, "'Non-Degradation' Draft Regulations," n.d. but circa February 20, 1973.

78. Rebecca Hanmer to Joseph Padgett, "OFA Comments on draft memorandum, preamble and regulations for preventing significant deterioration of air quality," February 21, 1974.

79. Roy N. Gamse to Joseph Padgett, "Significant Deterioration Regulations," February 21, 1974.

80. Ibid.

81. Ibid.

82. Bob Coleman to Joseph Padgett, "February 22nd Meeting with NSD Working Group," March 5, 1974.

83. Ibid.

84. Joseph Padgett to Working Group Members, "Draft Action Memo on Non-Degradation," February 28, 1974, p. 14.

85. Ibid.

86. Ibid.

87. Acting Assistant Administrator for Air and Water Programs to the Administrator, (draft) "Regulations to Prevent Significant Deterioration of Air Quality--Action Memorandum," n.d., pp. 2, 9.

88. Ibid., p. 15.

89. Ibid., p. 16.

90. See note 69 above.

91. Compare p. 6 of Padgett to Working Group, February 28, 1974, op. cit., with p. 6 of the final version.

92. Dave Morrell to Roger Strelow, "Significant Deterioration--Meeting with Sierra Club," April 4, 1974.

93. PSD was not the only program where such a shift in influence to Washington occurred during Strelow's tenure. For example, Strelow created the Office of Transportation and Land Use Planning (OTLUP) as a staff office to the Assistant Administrator, in the face of OAQPS' refusal to support the elaborate plans of transportation and land use planning advocates within EPA. Indirect source review (ISR) of air quality, the control of pollution resulting from cars going to shopping malls, stadiums, or other large developments, was one of the stillborn initiatives of this office. Not surprisingly, OTLUP and other planning-minded staff within EPA saw links between ISR and other programs such as air quality maintenance planning and PSD, and

218   **Protect and Enhance**

kept trying to include these links in the PSD
regulations over the objections of OAQPS.

The bureaucratic history of transportation
control plans is a fascinating story of its own
which shows many common threads with PSD. It is
told best in Melnick, <u>Regulation and the Courts</u>,
chapter 9.

94. Roger Strelow to Bernard J. Steigerwald,
     "Nondeterioration Regulations," April 12, 1974.

95. Roy Gamse and Cheryl Wasserman to Alvin L. Alm,
     "Final Nondegradation Package," April 29, 1974;
     also Roy Gamse and Cheryl Wasserman to Alvin L.
     Alm, "Nondegradation Revisited," April 22, 1974.
     In an internal OPE dispute, Gamse and Wasserman
     disagreed about the variances in Class II areas
     issue; Gamse was concerned that the absence of
     Class II variances would restrict growth, while
     Wasserman agreed with the deletion of the
     variances.

     On the NRDC decision (<u>NRDC vs. EPA</u>, 529 F.2d
     755; reprinted in <u>1974 Senate Oversight
     Hearings</u>, pp. 361-402) see Melnick, <u>Regulation
     and the Courts</u>, pp. 130-36. On OPE's tactics to
     oppose a monitoring requirement, see Alvin L.
     Alm to Alan Kirk, "Nondegradation Monitoring
     Requirement," June 24, 1974.

6.   See Roger Strelow to Mr. Bern Steigerwald and
     Mr. Dave Morrell, "May 3 Briefing of House and
     Senate Staff on Significant Deterioration
     Regulations," May 8, 1974, and Dave Morrell to
     Bernard Steigerwald, "Significant Deterioration:
     Response to Mr. Strelow's Memo of May 8 and
     Related Comments," May 16, 1974. Morrell was
     one of the chief advocates of land use planning
     approaches in the Washington air office.

97. <u>1974 Senate Oversight Hearings</u>, p. 1093.

98. Ibid., pp. 1092-93.

99. Ibid., pp. 1103-1104.

100. Ibid., pp. 1112-13.

101. See chapter 2 above.

102. "Report of the Interagency Task Force."

103. See "Roy N. Gamse to Alvin L. Alm, "Nondegradation Meeting at OMB with Crabhill on July 3, 1974," July 3, 1974. Also see letter, with attachments, of Peter A. Krenkel (TVA) to Mr. Alvin Alm, June 10, 1974. Also see Richard Denney to Roger Strelow, "No Significant Deterioration Regulations," June 28, 1974 (response to legal questions raised by the Commerce Department).

104. Roy N. Gamse to Alvin L. Alm, "Nondegradation Meeting at OMB with Crabhill on July 3, 1974," July 3, 1974.

105. Richard J. Denney to Roger Strelow, "Non-Significant Deterioration Regulations," July 8, 1974.

106. Alvin L. Alm to Roger Strelow, "Briefing Memo for the Administrator on Nondegradation," n.d.

107. The following points are all taken from this same memo, Roger Strelow to the Administrator, "July 15 Meeting on Significant Deterioration Regulations--Briefing Memo," July 12, 1974.

108. For more on the inconclusiveness of ESECA, see Melnick, Regulation and the Courts, pp. 127-28, 178-80, and William F. Pedersen, "Coal Conversion and Air Pollution: What the Energy Supply and Environmental Coordination Act of 1974 Provides," 4 Environmental Law Reporter 50101 (1974). Melnick's point about how Senator Muskie and his staff consciously worked to limit ESECA's effect on the ICS/SCS/tall stacks controversies applies with equal force to significant deterioration.

109. Strelow to the Administrator, July 12, 1974.

110. Ibid.

111. Richard G. Rhoads to Joe Padgett, "Changes to Significant Deterioration Package," July 16, 1974.

112. Roger Strelow to Richard Denney, "Significant Deterioration Regulations," July 15, 1974.

113. Robert Montgomery, Jr., Acting General Counsel, FEA, to Wallace H. Johnson, Jr., Assistant Attorney General, Land and Natural Resources Division, Department of Justice, "Proposed EPA Regulations to Prevent Significant Deterioration of Air Quality," July 25, 1974. It should be noted that the record shows that while the Commerce Department was the chief force behind the continuation of this legal dispute, they worked in close cooperation with OMB in doing so. See, e.g., Karl E. Bakke, General Counsel, Department of Commerce to Donald Crabhill, Deputy Associate Director for Natural Resources, OMB, n.d. (presented at 7/15/74 meeting of Agency heads), and Karl E. Bakke to Hon. Roy L. Ash, Director, OMB, n.d. (focusing mostly on the regulations vs. guidelines issue. Also see Denney to Strelow, 6/28/74 and 7/9/74.

114. See Alan G. Kirk II to Roger Strelow, "No Significant Deterioration Regulations," July 24, 1974.

115. Strelow to Denney, July 15, 1974.

116. Rhoads to Padgett, 7/16/74, op. cit., and Strelow to Roger Sant (FEA) and Stan Doremus (Department of the Interior), "Follow-up on Significant Deterioration Meeting," July 15, 1974.

117. Denney to Strelow, "No Significant Deterioration
     Regulations," July 17, 1974. This response is
     full of legalistic analysis.

118. Ibid.

119. Letter, Strelow to Jim J. Tozzi, July 26, 1974.

120. William C. Roundtree, Assistant General Counsel
     for Legislation, Department of Commerce to
     Tozzi, August 5, 1974. Curiously, the Commerce
     letter makes no mention of the short-term (3
     hour) SO_2 increment of 300 ug/m^3, which EPA's
     analysts had always regarded as the most
     stringent increment due to the high
     concentration which can result from short
     periods of adverse weather and variations in
     short-term SO_2 emissions rates.

121. Roger Sant to Roger Strelow, "Doubling of Class
     II Ambient Air Quality Deterioration Limits,"
     August 8, 1974.

122. Richard G. Rhoads to Addressees, "Final Review
     of Significant Deterioration Regulations,"
     August 11, 1974. The quote on soliciting
     comments is from the proposed regulation as
     published; see 39 Federal Register 31002.

123. 39 Federal Register 31002.

124. Joseph A. Tikvart to Richard G. Rhoads,
     "Nondegradation and Power Plant Size," August
     12, 1974.

125. In the preamble to the proposed regulations, EPA
     inserted an explicit reference to 1000 megawatts
     as the size power plant which could be
     accommodated by the Class II increment. As
     noted in the text, this was the same size power
     plant which EPA's earlier technical analyses had
     said could be accommodated by a 300 ug/m^3 3-hour
     increment.

126. 39 _Federal Register_ 31000.

127. EPA's lack of enthusiasm for the guidelines
approach was further demonstrated by the fate of
this commitment. OAQPS staff proceeded to begin
developing these guidelines, but their efforts
were abruptly halted in October, 1975 when the
guidelines were sacrificed as part of an effort
to cut Federal "regulatory red tape." See 6
Environment Reporter 1206-7. Part 51 guidelines
were not published until after the passage of
the 1977 Amendments--and then under very
different circumstances.

128. 39 _Federal Register_ 31005.

129. Ibid. See also Strelow to Tozzi, July 26, 1974,
op. cit.

130. 39 _Federal Register_ 31004-5, 31008.

131. 39 _Federal Register_ 31004.

132. See Robert Montgomery, FEA to Wallace Johnson,
Dept. of Justice, July 25, 1974, _op. cit_. FEA
found that once a locality discovered that an
ESECA-mandated coal conversion could restrict
its future growth, it would oppose the
conversion on these grounds, "seriously impede
the program and frustrate Congressional intent."

133. 39 _Federal Register_ 31004.

134. Richard G. Rhoads to Roger Strelow, "Deletion of
Ambient Monitoring Requirement from the
Significant Deterioration Regulations," July 26,
1974. Such "other uses" included (1) possible
use by States "in some cases . . . to determine
whether other sources could locate in the area,"
(2) model validation, and (3) determination of
background levels of air pollution in "clean"
areas.

135. Alvin L. Alm to Alan Kirk, "Nondegradation Monitoring Requirement," June 24, 1974.

136. Alan G. Kirk to Alvin L. Alm, "No Significant Deterioration Regulations--Monitoring Requirements," July 5, 1974.

137. Rhoads to Strelow, July 26, 1974, op. cit.

138. Ibid.

139. "Remarks by John R. Quarles, Jr., Deputy Administrator, Environmental Protection Agency, at a Press Conference on 'Significant Deterioration' of Air Quality, Friday, August 16, 1974."

140. 5 Environment Reporter 508 (August 23, 1974)

141. W. Stanley Blackburn, William H. Roj, and Ralph A. Taylor, Jr., "Review of EPA'S Significant Deterioration Regulations: An Example of the Difficulties of the Agency-Court Partnership in Environmental Law," Virginia Law Review, Vol. 61 (1975), p. 1123.

142. 39 Federal Register 42510.

143. 39 Federal Register 31002.

144. 39 Federal Register 42510, 42512.

145. Compare §52.21(c)(3) of 39 Federal Register 4251516 with §52.21(c)(3) of 39 Federal Register 31007-8.

146. Ibid. See also 39 Federal Register 42513.

147. 39 Federal Register 42513-14.

148. 39 Federal Register 42513.

149. 39 Federal Register 42514. EPA appears to have reflected in this passage some of the difficulty

it was having on enforcing work practice
standards for its asbestos NESHAP regulation.
See Melnick, <u>Regulation and the Courts</u>, pp. 208-
9.

   This provision has particular importance in
that EPA clarified in the December final
regulations that all emissions points from
sources listed in the regulation would have to
be taken into account in review source impacts
on an area, and had to apply BACT, not just
those emissions points regulated under NSPS. In
other words, all facilities (emissions points)
within a source (a collection of one or more
such facilities) had to be regulated. The
definition of "source" and "facility" were to
become enormously more complicated following
passage of the 1977 Clean Air Act amendments.

150. 5 <u>Environment Reporter</u> 1235 (December 6, 1974)

151. Roger Sant to Jim Tozzi, "Proposed Amendments to
the Clean Air Act," November 26, 1984.

152. Vietor, <u>Environmental Politics and the Coal
Coalition</u>, pp. 194-197, 205-208.

CHAPTER V

CONGRESS REWRITES PSD

Senator Edmund S. Muskie opened the 1975
oversight hearings of the Subcommittee on
Environmental Pollution with the solemn declaration
that "the more we learn about air pollution, the
more extensive the problem appears to be."[1]
However, Senator Muskie's views were not universally
shared. What was clear by 1975 was that the
ambitious goals of the Clean Air Amendments of 1970
were not going to be met. In addition, the painful
experiences of oil shortages and rising energy costs
had raised new questions about the appropriateness
of these goals, the timetables for achieving them
even if they were appropriate, and their costs to
national energy policy.

PSD was to become a focus for these concerns.
Major American industrial groups saw the non-
degradation concept as threatening U.S. economy
health and energy independence. As an oil industry
representative put it, "unless this issue is quickly
and intelligently resolved, efforts to strengthen
our economy and develop a stronger domestic energy
base will be stymied."[2] An "intelligent"
resolution, in his view, was to amend the Act to
eliminate any requirement for air pollution control
which went beyond the attainment and maintenance of
the national ambient standards.

Industry was not alone in its push for the
legislative elimination of the PSD requirements.

225

While FEA, the Department of Commerce and OMB had
succeeded in modifying EPA's 1974 PSD rules, the
leaders of these organizations remained convinced
that PSD posed a significant threat to the nation's
economic health. Special concern existed about the
effect of PSD on the Administration's energy
independence initiatives, all of which called for
increased use of coal. Conflicts between the use of
coal and environmental quality had already appeared
in the controversy over the use of scrubbers, tall
stacks and intermittent control strategies for
attainment of the health-based standards in the
vicinity of existing power plants. Given the
assumption that new coal-fired power plants would be
needed to supply a growing percentage of a growing
national energy demand, the idea that such plants
would have to meet even stricter air pollution tests
was anathema to those agencies charged with
promoting a national energy policy. Thus, both
Rogers Morton, the Secretary of Interior, and Frank
Zarb, the FEA Administrator, agreed that the
significant deterioration requirement should be
eliminated. To use Zarb's words, "FEA does not
believe the potential benefits from the significant
deterioration program justify the potential cost of
constraining the development of domestic energy
resources."[3]
    With this as background, one might have expected
that at least a significant weakening of EPA's PSD
rules would have occurred as a result of
Congressional amendments to the Act. Yet when the
Clean Air Act Amendments of 1977 were signed by
President Jimmy Carter, the provisions of PSD had
been made more restrictive in almost every respect.
    To understand the reasons for this remarkable
outcome, this chapter will take a close look at the
way in which Congress considered the 1977 amendments
to the Clean Air Act and how it treated those
amendments relating to PSD. It will attempt to show
that the fundamental explanation for why PSD evolved
the way it did is that the two principal responsible
committees--the Subcommittee on Environmental
Pollution in the Senate (the "Muskie committee") and
the Subcommittee on Health and Environment of the

House Committee on Interstate and Foreign Commerce
(the "Rogers Committee") began by developing very
stringent versions of PSD and relaxed only narrow,
specific provisions when faced with competing
interests which could not be ignored. The net
effect of this approach was that the amendments,
when finally passed, represented a collection of
compromises and conflicting language whose
particulars, while almost painfully specific, were
probably not understood in full by anyone--an
outcome which may have been an inevitable
consequence of Congress' attempt to legislate in
such fine detail on a highly complex issue. This
chapter will also examine EPA's role in these
developments and how the Agency affected the
environment in which the House and Senate
deliberations took place. The answer to questions
such as these speaks to the fundamental assumption
that highly specific laws passed by Congress will
best serve the public interest. The experience of
the 1977 Clean Air Act Amendments suggests that this
assumption can only be maintained by ignoring the
realities of the interests and behavior of
Congressional committees and their staff.

Major Issues Facing the Congress

     The promulgation of PSD rules by EPA had
resolved for the moment the question of whether
there would be a PSD program. To be sure, both
industry and environmental groups immediately filed
lawsuits challenging EPA's action. Industry, in
addition to charging that EPA's regulations were far
too restrictive, reopened the argument about whether
Congress had in fact written PSD into the 1970 Act.
Environmentalists, on the other hand, countered that
any scheme which in principle allowed degradation up
to the secondary standards obviously could not
prevent significant deterioration and was

inconsistent with the decision in the <u>Sierra Club</u>
case.[4] Nonetheless, the rules stood, and EPA
indicated that while it would welcome "early
consideration" of PSD by Congress, the Agency also
believed that the approach taken by the 1974
regulation was "reasonable" and would be carried
out.[5]

The first question facing the Congress, then,
was whether PSD should exist at all. On this point,
there is no evidence that either Senator Muskie or
Representative Rogers, the two Congressional leaders
on the Clean Air Act, ever seriously considered
accepting the argument that PSD was not, in some
sense, "worth it." Both had publicly stated early
in the history of the <u>Sierra Club</u> litigation that
they believed the "significant deterioration"
principle to be incorporated in the Act, and neither
gave any indication of retreating from this view.
However, accepting this principle raised other long-
standing questions about PSD.

o   How much deterioration was environmentally
     "significant"? What kind of balancing of other
     concerns (energy, cost, technology constraints)
     should be taken into account in determining
     "significant"?

o   Who should decide how this balance was to be
     struck? In particular, what was the respective
     role of Federal and State governments?

o   To what extent should PSD rules serve the
     interests of interstate "equity" by creating
     environmental rules for clean-air areas similar
     to those for "dirty" areas?

While numerous other rationales for PSD were
discussed and considered, these were the key policy
calls which faced the Congressional committees as
they began to mark up possible Act amendments on
PSD.[6]

The 1975 Senate and House Hearings

Both the House and Senate subcommittees began hearings early in 1975 on the Clean Air Act. PSD, of course, was not the only Clean Air Act issue under review. Congress' most immediate need was to deal with the claims of automobile manufacturers that they could not meet the emissions control requirements for cars, raising the possibility that automakers would be faced with a choice between selling 1978 model cars illegally or shutting down all production of such vehicles. Other pressing issues concerned the failure of numerous areas to meet the 1975 deadlines in the law for attaining the national air quality standards; protests over EPA's policies concerning transportation control plans and indirect source review; and the use of continuous emissions limits and stack gas scrubbers versus tall stacks and intermittent controls on large power plants.[7]

Nonetheless, PSD was quite high on the list of concerns of both the committees and those who wished to amend the Act. Statement after statement by industrial representatives in both the Senate and House hearings urged Congress to reverse Sierra Club vs. Ruckelshaus and adopt the amendment proposed by the Ford Administration to §101(b) of the Act. Utility representatives presented themselves as in support of clean air as reflected by the national ambient air quality standards and challenged whether anything more would provide any benefit to the public despite imposing enormous costs.[8] Coal mining interests took up the same theme,[9] as did representatives from the oil,[10] iron and steel,[11] and general manufacturing industries.[12] Generally, utilities led the attack on PSD, an attack which was not limited to simple protests about PSD's costs. Sixty-five utilities joined together to form a group called the "Electric Utility Industry Clean Air Coordinating Committee," and in this form sponsored studies on the projected air quality impact of various emission strategies, the effect of these

230   **Protect and Enhance**

strategies on costs and fuel supplies, and the
quality of the scientific data relating to the
health effects of ambient sulfate concentrations.[13]
Millions of dollars were spent on these studies, the
purpose of which was to challenge data supplied by
EPA and other sources to the committees. Ironically,
EPA was trying to get similar information,
especially on utility costs; the two sets of studies
proceeded somewhat in parallel. Each needed the
other: EPA needed the utilities to get otherwise
unavailable data, while the utilities needed EPA
research data on sulfates so it could be critiqued,
and generally wanted EPA to support the utility
assumptions as much as possible to give the studies
added credibility.[14]

     This testimony represented a major push by
almost all segments of American industry to use
concerns about the energy crisis and the then-
current recession to overturn the PSD requirements.
Given this push, two things are striking. The first
is that the circumstances of recession and energy
crisis had no apparent effect on the position taken
by the environmental groups whose lawsuits had been
responsible for PSD in the first place. Far from
being defensive about PSD's possible effects on
national energy supplies, the Sierra Club at the
hearings criticized EPA's regulations for covering
only SO_2 and particulate matter and for allowing in
principle deterioration up to the level of the
ambient standards.[15] In the ensuing discussion,
however, it was apparent that the Sierra Club's
principal concern was with the construction of new
coal-fired power plants in the West. Richard Lahn,
the Club's president, and Bruce Terris, the attorney
who filed the <u>Sierra Club</u> case, argued that 1) EPA's
Class II increments would allow significant growth;
2) neither the ambient standards nor the NSPS truly
required the "best technology" which was needed to
protect against the ill effects of air pollution in
the West; and 3) that if forced to by tough non-
degradation rules, industry would be able to
identify ways to have needed power plants and reduce
air pollution simultaneously.[16]

The second remarkable element of the opening hearings and debate over PSD was the position taken by EPA and its Administrator, Russell Train. In the March 13, 1975 House hearing, while ostensibly endorsing the position that Congress should give "early consideration" to significant deterioration, Train made it clear where his sympathies lay, stating that through the PSD program "we are better able to protect the environment and to foster better air pollution control planning."[17] Upon further questioning he was even more forthcoming, acknowledging his differences with the rest of the Administration and stating that "the regulatory approach which we have taken while probably not perfect represents a very positive and effective way of getting at the problem."[18] Train testified again before the House Subcommittee on March 26; at that time Chairman Rogers specifically asked Train for a legislative recommendation. Train continued to make it clear he supported PSD, but maintained that the Administration's official position was that Congress should clarify its intent in legislation while considering "both options." EPA did submit proposed language, but it was a one sentence amendment to §110(a)(2) that required State implementation plans to contain "adequate provisions, consistent with rules promulgated by the Administrator, for preventing significant deterioration of existing air resources in areas that are cleaner than that required by the national ambient air quality standards."[19] Train's testimony before the Senate subcommittee on this subject, while not as detailed, made the same points.[20]

EPA's continued resistance to the rest of the Administration on PSD policy was significant for the Congressional debate for four reasons. First, it helped to further legitimize the concept of PSD. For the Sierra Club to advocate PSD was one thing. For EPA to do so was quite another, even if the PSD program it favored was not all the environmentalists wanted. Secondly, EPA kept the Administration from being able to lead a unified attack on PSD. This meant that PSD's advocates were able to attack the credibility of PSD's industrial opponents, while

industry was left in the position of having to make
its own case without unified Administration support.
The fact that Russell Train was willing to take such
a stand is testimony to the remarkable degree of
independence which EPA had established in the last
months of the Nixon Administration--an independence
that carried over under President Ford. Moreover,
it is also an interesting reflection of Train's
personal philosophy of environmental protection.
Based on his earlier actions, William Ruckelshaus
would have taken a very different course on PSD.[21]

Third, EPA's endorsement of the validity of its
own regulations reinforced the ability of the
Congressional committees to use EPA's rules as a
starting point to develop a program of their own.
This would have been much more difficult to do had
EPA adopted the stance that its rules were forced
upon it, necessary but onerous. As it was, the
Congress could always fall back upon the rules
deemed to be acceptable to EPA in structuring its
own program. The very existence of the rules aided
PSD advocates in that a "default" existed if
Congress took no action. Since EPA opposed any
further administrative changes to PSD, its opponents
had to go the legislative route, thus giving PSD
advocates leverage which they would not have
otherwise enjoyed.[22]

Finally, EPA's stance enhanced its ability to
serve as a "disinterested" source of technical
information, and as an evaluator of information
supplied by others. Given the highly technical
nature of PSD, this role was to prove to be crucial
in the Congressional debate. It assumed even more
importance as industry unfolded its strategy of
attacking PSD by projecting dire consequences from
the proposals which the committees were to develop.
Without EPA as an arbiter, the contest would have
been between the competing technical analyses of
industry and environmental groups. With EPA as a
participant, these debates took on a much different
tone.[23]

Senate-House Markups--1975

The March-May hearings laid out the lines of
confrontation and dispute over PSD. However, the
real action was to come in the committee markups.
These began in May in the House and June in the
Senate, and were to last the rest of the year.
Two things distinguished the markup experience
in 1975 from that of 1970. The first is that the
markup sessions were open, and were followed avidly
by environmental and industry interest groups. This
resulted in what one Congressional staffer called
"the most overwhelming lobbying campaign I've seen
in the ten years I've worked on Capitol Hill."[24]
Industry had learned its lessons from the 1970
amendments and the Sierra Club case, and was
determined not to let new air pollution control
legislation pass unchallenged.
The second big difference was the role played by
the House. In 1970 the Senate, and specifically the
Muskie Committee, had been the dominant
Congressional force in the passage of amendments.
By 1975, however, Chairman Rogers had built up his
subcommittee and hired additional staff to the point
where it could now compete effectively in technical
competence with Muskie. Moreover, Rogers had staked
out a personal leadership role on the air pollution
issue to a far greater degree than any House member
did in 1970, and had gained the expertise needed to
become a respected and effective spokesman. Neither
he nor his staff were inclined simply to accompany
Muskie's solo.[25] Finally, the scope of the 1970
Amendments and the more sophisticated approach taken
to lobbying on clean air issues meant that House
members were increasingly contacted by local groups
(such as auto dealers or shopping center developers)
who were affected by the Act and who learned how to
vocalize these concerns in ways that got their
Representatives' attention. This development is
perhaps one of the truest measures that the 1970
amendments really did have a significant impact on
American life.

SENATE SUBCOMMITTEE ACTION

The Muskie subcommittee began active discussion
on PSD provisions on June 17, 1975. Muskie
expressed the desire to get a bill to the floor by
mid-July with passage before Labor Day.[26] This
turned out to be wildly optimistic. By August 1,
the committee was not even close to completing its
work, in part because of protracted debate about the
appropriate level for the nitrogen oxide emission
standard for cars, and in part because of delays
induced by Senate preoccupation with other issues.
However, in late July the subcommittee did begin
to stake out a position on PSD. Not surprisingly
given Muskie's statements with regard to the Sierra
Club case, the subcommittee endorsed the principle
of PSD. Predictably, the proposals were based on
EPA's regulations. However, there were a number of
modifications, many made at the initiative of
Senator Pete Domenici (R-New Mexico). (In the
Senate oversight hearings, a State air quality
official from New Mexico had been one of the most
vocal advocates of a tougher PSD policy than that
adopted by EPA; New Mexico's attorney general had
also been the organizer for the amicus brief filed
by twenty State attorneys general in support of the
Sierra Club's position in the court case.[28])
The most important modification, and one which
must have pleased the Sierra Club, was the
elimination of the Class III increment, the option
of allowing deterioration up to the secondary
standards. The committee even defeated a proposal
by Senator James Buckley to allow variances from
Class II increments under "extraordinary"
circumstances. The committee staff defended this
decision by saying that it would simultaneously
allow moderate growth, protect clean air areas, and
"provide a 'strong incentive' for industry" to
develop better control technology. However, an
unnamed industry spokesman reacted by charging that

the decisions would mean "no growth" for substantial areas of the country.[29]

Other subcommittee actions also evidenced a strong interest in the wilderness preservation aspects of PSD which were of concern to the Sierra Club. The subcommittee designated national parks, wilderness areas, wildlife refuge areas and international parks as automatic Class I areas. A second set of areas, including national monuments, seashores, recreation areas and wild and scenic rivers were also to be designated Class I initially, though they could be redesignated to Class II with the concurrence of the Federal Land Manager (FLM). Moreover, all other Federal lands, including the very large land holdings in the West, could be unilaterally designated Class I by the FLM.[30] In this respect, the subcommittee was following the path taken by EPA between the August and December, 1974 regulations.[31] EPA's regulations had come under attack by Western political interests; these attacks, however, do not appear to have had much effect on the Senate subcommittee at this time.[32]

Finally, the subcommittee addressed the issue of pollutants other than PM and SO_2 which EPA had not covered in its regulations. These pollutants, according to the proposal, were to be studied for inclusion in air increment schemes. In the meantime, large new sources were to be subject to best available control technology (BACT) for hydrocarbons (HC) and nitrogen oxides (NO_x). "Automobile-related" pollutants were "not to be covered" under PSD, but regulated under different sections of the Act. These two contradictory statements are probably best explained by recalling that about half of all HC and NO_x emissions come from automobiles and that the subcommittee intended that BACT be used on large new <u>stationary</u> sources of HC and NO_x without having to meet an increment test.[33]

Outside reaction to the Senate proposals was swift. The National Association of Manufacturers sent a letter in late August to its environmental quality committee members which charged that not only would EPA's regulations preclude growth in vast

areas of the country, but that the Senate proposals
were "tougher than the regulations." Included with
this letter were maps which NAM had prepared showing
areas where development would be precluded. By
using the assumption that a 50-mile distance would
be needed to prevent significant impact on a Class I
area, NAM charged that only limited parts of 15
States could allow further development. Labelling
EPA's regulations (and by inference, the Senate
bill) as "no-growth," NAM suggested that plant
manager communication to their respective
Congressmen would be "especially effective."[34]

   This prompted what one EPA staff member aptly
called "the war of the maps."[35] Industrial opponents
used these maps to launch a grass-roots public
relations campaign aimed at creating the perception
that PSD would halt economic growth in most of the
United States. These groups were not shy. The
American Paper Institute, for example, sponsored a
study purporting to show the effects of PSD in areas
with hilly terrain, and ambushed Muskie at a union
meeting in Augusta, Maine with a 50 page study of
the proposed Senate approach's effect on Maine.[36]
Even EPA got into the act, criticizing the dropping
of Class III from the subcommittee's proposal.[37]

   These criticisms had little effect on the subcommittee's actions. The subcommittee staff took
the principles decided upon in late July and
prepared a staff working paper which codified them
into statutory language. This working paper
remained the basis for subcommittee agreement
through protracted markups, as Muskie had difficulty
maintaining a voting quorum of subcommittee
members.[38] When the subcommittee finally reported
its bill to the full committee on November 3, the
vote at the end of July remained the only
substantive direction from the subcommittee
principals to the staff--and one of only two votes
taken on the package at all.[39]

   The staff paper did go through several drafts
during this time. While the major elements of the
EPA framework remained intact, the version current
at the time the subcommittee reported to the full
Public Works Committee had several interesting

features which hearkened back to the debate at EPA
prior to the promulgation of the 1974 regulations.
For example, the Senate proposal expanded the scope
of EPA's program by applying it to the construction
of any "major emitting facility." A "major emitting
facility" was any facility which "emits, or has the
potential to emit, 100 tons per year or more of any
air pollutant" and was in one of 28 specified
industrial categories. EPA's rule had limited PSD's
application to 19 specified categories of sources.
The Senate proposal also reflected a more
comprehensive view of the analyses which any
proposed PSD source would have to perform. Not only
was the air quality in the area to be examined, but
also "climate and meteorology, soils and vegetation
and visibility." In another change, EPA's final
regulations had indicated that the reviewing agency
was responsible for determining what the source's
impact on air quality would be: in practice, this
was a question of who would perform the necessary
modeling. The Senate staff paper placed this
responsibility clearly on the industry which wanted
to build. Finally, while EPA had defined best
available control technology (BACT) to mean NSPS
except in cases where one had not been set, the
subcommittee staff paper defined BACT in such a way
that NSPS was a minimum requirement, leaving it open
for requirements more stringent than NSPS to be
placed on sources independent of whether these
emissions were projected to cause exceedances of the
increment ceilings.[40]

The net effect of the subcommittee review and
staff paper was the development of a PSD program
which tightened EPA's rules and increased the
Federal role in every key area. In its scope of
sources covered, in its identification of additional
non-air criteria for source review, in its
application of BACT, in its view of redesignation
responsibilities, and in its elimination of Class
III, the Senate bill came down on the side of
Federal authority in the critical question of whose
responsibility it was to strike the balance between
economic and environmental concerns. The Senate
staff did accept EPA's definition of "significant"

in that the PM and SO_2 concentrations established
for Classes I and II were incorporated directly as
they appeared in EPA's regulations.[41] This saved the
Senate staff from having to justify these levels all
over again, and allowed the Senate advocates of PSD
to adopt all of EPA's arguments about just how much
growth these increments could really accommodate.
All of these Senate subcommittee changes however,
had the effect of making PSD more stringent than
EPA's program.

HOUSE SUBCOMMITTEE CONSIDERATION

    The House Subcommittee on Public Health and
Environment seemed to proceed along the same lines
as the Senate by taking EPA's rules as a starting
point for modification. However, it became clear
very early that the House discussions were going to
take a rather different tack than those in the
Senate. For one thing, PSD was much more
controversial. A number of key votes on PSD were
sharply contested, and subcommittee Chairman Rogers
was able to maintain his approach to the bill only
with some difficulty. The Administration proposal
to delete PSD even came to a vote (it lost, 10-5);
such a development would have been unthinkable in
the Muskie subcommittee.[42] Perhaps more importantly,
however, the House staff showed more inclination
than the Senate staff to tinker with EPA's increment
scheme. In contrast to the Senate, the House staff
tried to write into the law a concept of PSD as a
set of <u>tertiary</u> air quality standards, one which
assumed that ambient increments could be measured
reliably by ambient air quality <u>monitors</u> (as opposed
to models). This concept was to lead to
considerable difficulties later on.[43]
    The Rogers subcommittee got off to a slower
start than the Muskie subcommittee. After approving
a very general set of staff instructions in early
May, there was little action until after the Muskie
committee had voted on PSD proposals in late June.

However, Rogers quickly began to make up for lost time, and on September 4, as industry began gearing up to attack the Senate proposals, the House subcommittee voted on its first set of PSD requirements.

These requirements broke with both the EPA and the Senate proposals in several key respects. The most obvious was the increment system. While the subcommittee retained three "classes," nothing else about the scheme was consistent with the EPA/Senate approach. The increments were to be set for all pollutants, not just SO_2 and particulates. Moreover, instead of being based on their ability to accommodate sources such as power plants, the increments were to be set as percentages of the national ambient standards. Finally, in addition to the increment itself, each PSD area was to have a ceiling of 75% of the existing ambient standard, a ceiling which would function as a true "tertiary" standard.[44]

This approach was more stringent than that of either EPA or the Senate. Table 1 compares the proposed increments and gives some idea of the direction of the House proposal.[45] The table shows that the three hour House SO_2 increment, at 325 ug/m^3, is less than half of the EPA-Senate proposal. This, of course, was precisely the increment value which was increased at the last minute prior to EPA's August 16, 1974 proposal, after OMB and other agencies challenged the figure and EPA's modelers changed their minds about the ability of a 1000 megawatt power plant to meet that value.[46] Other elements of the House proposal which imposed greater stringency than the Senate version included the designation of more areas as mandatory Class I; the application of a permit requirement to any major stationary source "which emits, or has the design capacity to emit, one hundred tons per year or more of any air pollutant" regulated by an ambient standard; and inclusion of a provision that "the Administrator shall require up to one year of continuous air quality monitoring preceding the

TABLE 1

TABLE 1: ALLOWABLE AIR QUALITY INCREMENTS UNDER ALTERNATIVE SIGNIFICANT
DETERIORATION PROPOSALS
(ug/m^3)

Pollutant Standard	CLASS I			CLASS II			CLASS III		
	EPA Regs.	Senate Proposal	House Proposal1/	EPA Regs.	Senate Proposal	House Proposal1/	EPA Regs2/	Senate Proposal	House Proposal
Sulfur Dioxide									
Annual	2	2	1.6	15	15	20	80	No Class III	40
24-hour	5	5	7.3	100	100	91	365		183
3-hour	25	25	26	700	700	325	1300		650
Total Suspended Particulates									
Annual	5	5	7.5	10	10	19	75	No Class III	38
24-hour	10	10	15	30	30	38	150		75

1/ The increments for the House proposal are based on limitations of 2% of NAAQS for Class I,
25% for Class II, and 50% for Class III, except that the limit for total suspended particulates in Class I is 10% of NAAQS. In addition, the House proposal stipulates that the concentration of all pollutants cannot exceed 75% of the national ambient air quality standards
in any of the classes.

2/ EPA's Class III allows degradation up to the NAAQS:

Sulfur Dioxide		TSP	
Annual	80 (primary)	75 (primary)	
24-hour*	365 (primary)	150*(secondary)	
3-hour*	1300 (secondary)		

* The 24-hour and 3-hour standards are not to be exceeded more than once per year. There
are no primary 3-hour standards for sulfur dioxide and particulates, nor is there a 24-hour
primary standard for particulates.

Source: EPA-FEA Report

application for a construction permit in order to establish air quality baselines."[47]

On the other hand, there was one important provision of the EPA-Senate approach which the House strongly rejected: the authority of Federal Land Managers to classify Federal lands over the objections of the State in which these lands were located. The House staff draft stated clearly that designation or redesignation was to be carried out "by State or local government," and "with approval by State legislature and by local governmental units representing a majority of people in the area affected . . ."[48] Rogers was fundamentally suspicious of the way in which EPA's regulations gave authority to the Federal Land Managers, and consequently was open to the argument that these regulations interfered with the proper role of State and local governments in deciding land-use questions.[49]

Even with this provision, the September 5 House staff draft was significantly tighter than its Senate counterpart at the same time. Moreover, its fundamental approach differed from the Senate bill. While the Senate's chief concern seemed to be with the protection of visibility and other environmental values in national parks and wilderness areas in the face of proposals to construct large new Western coal-fired power plants, the House staff seemed to have a more comprehensive vision in mind. This vision encompassed power plants and park/wilderness protection, but by establishing PSD limits to apply to all pollutants, imposing ceilings on all pollutants regardless of increment allowances, and requiring extensive ambient air monitoring as a condition for growth, the House staff paper turned PSD from a program aimed primarily at power plant control to one which would become a driving force for land use and air quality management throughout the country.[50]

It is likely that the original House staff draft was deliberately set up as a strong "straw man" in anticipation that compromises would have to be made in dealing with more conservative House members.[51] Whether this was its intent or not, Rogers quickly

242   **Protect and Enhance**

made concessions on the House package even before it
could get out of subcommittee. In forestalling
an attempt by subcommittee Republicans to eliminate
PSD altogether, Rogers offered amendments which
loosened some of the bill's more restrictive
elements. For example, the new amendments increased
the minimum size of mandatory Class I areas from
1,000 to 10,000 acres, and dropped all but national
parks and natural wilderness areas from the list.
This had the effect of reducing the number of such
areas from 460 to 116. Rogers also offered
amendments prohibiting EPA from requiring "buffer
zones" around classified areas, and added provisions
which would "grandfather" sources which commenced
construction before the passage of Act amendments.[52]
With these changes, the subcommittee was able to
complete its markup and report the bill to the full
subcommittee on October 8.[53]

It is worth a moment to analyze why Rogers
offered these weakening amendments at the very end
of the subcommittee's markup. A substantial part of
the impetus came from a joint study which EPA and
FEA staff released in early October. The study
analyzed the relative impact of the Senate and House
provisions, and displayed maps which graphically
portrayed the results. While industry groups were
already using such maps to make their points about
PSD's potential impact, this was the first such
analysis which had EPA's imprimatur on it.
Moreover, it was the first analysis to show the
effects of the specific House proposals of early
September. Interestingly enough, the impetus for
this study came not from EPA's air office, but from
the economic analysts in the Office of Planning and
Evaluation, who collaborated with their FEA
counterparts in producing the study. Administrator
Train did not approve the report before its results
were released.[54]

The analysis looked at the impact of the various
proposals on the siting of a 1000 MW power plant.
Stripped of the accompanying caveats, the report
concluded that 85% of the analyzed electric
generating capacity might be affected by the House
proposal, assuming that power plants only had to

meet the then-existing new source performance
standard of 1.2 lbs. SO_2/million BTU heat input,
that both mandatory and discretionary areas were
classified as Class I, and that a 60 mile "buffer
zone" around a power plant meeting NSPS would be
needed to ensure that such plants would not violate
the Class I increments. The map reflecting these
assumptions appears to show that few such plants
could be located anywhere in the United States.[55]
While the Senate proposals were analyzed in a
similar manner, the results were not as alarming due
to 1) the Senate provision for BACT, which could
reduce emissions below NSPS levels and thereby
reduce projected ambient impacts; 2) the smaller
number of mandatory Class I areas in the Senate
proposal; and 3) the larger short-term SO_2 increment
in the Senate's Class II.[56]

Still, even the possible impacts of the Senate
proposal were enough to alarm the average
Congressman. Environmentalists recognized this, and
saw the potential damage that a report with EPA's
blessing could do to them. They wasted no time in
attacking it. Richard Ayres described it in a
letter to Train as presenting "a thoroughly biased
picture which suggests a massive conflict between
environmental and energy goals that does not
exist."[57] A "'pro-environment' Congressional
staffer" charged that FEA had "'railroaded' the
report through to Congress," a charge which EPA
staff denied.[58]

This was the context in which Rogers had to face
the challenge over the House PSD provisions. It
seems reasonable to conclude that he accepted
changes in order to appear reasonably willing to
respond to some of the perceived excesses of the
House staff proposals. What is interesting,
however, is what did <u>not</u> change: the PSD increments
and ceilings themselves were left alone. Moreover,
the amendment prohibiting the use of buffer zones
reflects how poorly the subcommittee members
understood just what they were doing. "Buffer
zones" simply reflect the fact that emissions of air
pollution from a smokestack do not disperse
immediately in the atmosphere. As a result, models

which predict how this dispersion will occur show
that increases in ambient air pollution equal or
greater than the level of the Class I increments can
still occur at considerable distances from the
source of the emissions. As long as it was still
intended to prevent increases in <u>ambient</u>
concentrations in Class I areas, then "buffer zones"
would exist whether they were legislatively
prohibited or not. The House subcommittee staff was
aware of this at the time this amendment was
considered. However, in light of the outcry
prompted by the "buffer zones" in the EPA-FEA and
Chamber of Commerce maps, the subcommittee staff
chose to put forward an amendment on buffer zones
which looked like a concession in principle but was
meaningless in practice without calling the entire
increment system--and PSD itself--into question.[59]

One final element accompanied the package which
Rogers' subcommittee reported to the full Commerce
Committee. The EPA-FEA Report made it clear that
the effect of PSD would be less if more stringent
controls were required on new power plants. Yet the
House bill contained no provision comparable to the
Senate bill requiring larger new sources in PSD
areas to use "best available control technology."
The House subcommittee dealt with this problem not
directly, but through a special modification to the
language of §111 dealing with New Source Performance
Standards. Buried in the language of the
subcommittee bill was an amendment which would
require NSPS for power plants to be based on "the
degree of emission reduction achievable through the
application of the best technological system of
continuous emission reduction the Administrator
determines has been adequately demonstrated."[60] This
was to ultimately turn into the forced scrubbing or
"percent reduction" amendment for new power plants.
Bruce Ackerman and William Hassler have argued that
this amendment was originally conceived as an
environmentalist backstop in case significant
deterioration provisions failed to pass the House.
While this may be true, it is also important to note
that forcing new Western utilities burning low
sulfur coal to scrub their emissions would also have

the effect of shrinking the wide impact circles
associated with the small increments and large Class
I areas of the House PSD proposal without opening up
the BACT debate across the board in the House.
Evidently the subcommittee's NSPS amendment had more
than one use.[61]

Markups By The Full Congressional Committees

The emergence of the subcommittee proposals in
both houses of Congress intensified the lobbying
battle between industry and environmental groups.
The U.S. Chamber of Commerce denounced both the
House and Senate bills as "the most insidiously
deceiving federal land use control bill[s]
imaginable," and said they threatened "economic
development, national energy goals and
employment."[62] The National Clean Air Coalition, on
the other hand, defended the concept of PSD but
criticized the House subcommittee for failing to
provide sufficient protection for parks and
wilderness areas, and the Senate for not developing
increments for nitrogen oxides.[63] Responding for
EPA, Air Assistant Administrator Roger Strelow
issued a statement suggesting that the original EPA-
FEA study tended to "overestimate" the impact of the
original House staff proposal, and that the modified
House proposal would have "considerably less"
impact. Administrator Train said that "the facts
simply don't support" the "no growth" claims of
industry critics of EPA's regulations.[64] However,
utilities and other industrial groups continued to
issue periodic attacks on the proposals.[65]

PSD in the Senate Public Works Committee

The full Senate Committee on Public Works met on
November 18 to begin considering the amendments.

The "full" committee differed from the subcommittee only by the addition of three Senators, but two were important: Randolph of West Virginia, the committee chairman, and Baker of Tennessee.[66] Auto emission standards came first, and it was 1976 before the committee took up the PSD provisions again. By then, EPA, FEA and industry had all come up with new analyses of the cost and impact of the various proposals. EPA used "new assumptions" to reduce the expected impact of the Senate requirements on new power plant siting.[67] FEA estimated the significant deterioration provisions would cause scrubbers to be required on an additional 95,000 megawatts of generating capacity at a capital cost of $11.5 billion and increased operating costs over 15 years of $16.5 billion.[68] The industry estimates were somewhat higher, with capital cost increases estimated at between $6.9 and $18.6 billion (depending on BACT assumptions), and annual cost increases of $15.7 to $61.9 billion.[69]

These concerns had some effect on the Public Works committee, though not as much as industry had hoped. The committee staff proposed a series of revisions to the subcommittee's proposals which moved in the same direction as the weakening changes approved earlier in the House. These revisions included: an increase in the minimum size for automatic Class I areas from 1000 to 5000 acres; transfer of national wildlife refuges to Class II; an increase in minimum size to 10,000 acres for national monuments and recreation areas which would be Class I unless the State and the Federal Land Manager agreed that Class II was sufficient; and a set of procedures which gave States a greater opportunity to demonstrate that new sources would not have an adverse impact on the "air quality related values" of a Federal Class I area even if compliance with the Class I increments could not be demonstrated. These last two provisions appear to have been crafted to allow the committee to claim it had made Class I increments "a flexible test" and eliminated "buffer zones." Also, in a provision aimed at relaxing any automatic scrubbing requirement, the committee also softened its BACT

language to direct that "economic, energy and
environmental costs" be considered in deciding what
BACT would be on a case by case basis. Pressure
from Senators Randolph and Baker contributed to
these changes from the earlier subcommittee
proposals.[70]

These relaxations were sufficient to withstand
any further challenges to PSD. The committee voted
to report S.3219 to the full Senate on February 5,
1976, by a 12-1 vote. Only Senator Gary Hart
dissented, on the grounds that the auto standards
were too lenient. This apparent show of unanimity,
however, masked continued concern about the bill, as
12 of the 13 Senators on the Committee submitted
individual views on the "committee" report. Five of
the twelve comments addressed PSD. Still, despite
the changes adopted by the Committee, the Senate
bill's provisions remained significantly more
restrictive than EPA's, while retaining the basic
framework of EPA's rules.[71]

House Commerce Committee Consideration

PSD's passage through the full House Commerce
Committee was not nearly so smooth. Despite the
objections of the Maguire-Waxman faction of the
committee, Rogers was forced to accept further
weakening amendments to the subcommittee proposal.
Two notable changes were an increase in the minimum
size for mandatory Class I areas from ten thousand
to twenty five thousand acres, and an increase in
the allowable air quality ceiling from 75% to 90% of
the ambient standards.[72] Rogers also had to accept
amendments lengthening the amount of time allowed to
States to submit PSD implementation plans, and
clarifying that areas which were above the new 90%
threshold, but below the ambient standards, would
not have to submit new plans to get below the 90%
level.[73]

It is the amendments governing how source
emissions were to be counted under PSD, however,
which display the most vivid evidence of both the
pressures on PSD and the different understandings of

just what the provisions meant.   In EPA's final
regulations, "baseline air quality concentration"
(above which increments were to be used up) had
referred to ambient levels of SO_2 and particulate
matter existing in 1974, along with the estimated
emissions from sources which had received approval
to construct under existing State new source review
procedures before January 1, 1975.[74]   The reference
to ambient levels in this definition was a remnant
of earlier efforts by the planning groups within EPA
to push PSD in their direction; in practice, EPA
expected modeling of large point source emissions to
be the principal tool in tracking PSD.   However, EPA
did envision that such large point sources would
have to track increment consumption by other,
smaller sources in the area.[75]

In contrast to EPA's approach, the Senate
committee bill had specified that only "major
emitting facilities" would consume increment and no
"baseline" would be calculated until the time of the
first application to construct by a prospective
major facility.   While the Senate bill protected
EPA's in-place regulations by specifying that
emissions from any major facility which "commenced
construction" after January 6, 1975 would consume
increment, this change raised the confusing prospect
that "baseline dates" could vary depending on the
date of the first application for a PSD permit.[76]
Taken literally, this meant baseline dates could
vary all across the country.

The House Committee added to the confusion in
this area.   The Rogers Committee, following EPA's
regulation, had initially specified that the
baseline would include only plants in operation and
those which had received State permits before
January 1, 1975.   However, the Committee amendments
allowed those sources which had filed for (but not
received) permits before January 1, 1975 to be
included in the "grandfathered" list as well.   In
addition, the Committee added a provision which
allowed sources not subject to SIP permit
requirements (but nevertheless subject to PSD) to
have their emissions grandfathered if they had
"reached a stage, on or before the date of enactment

of this section, comparable to the stage at which
permits are normally required . . ."[77] The effect of
this addition was not at all clear. The House bill
referred to the State plans which implemented
existing sections 110(a)(2)(D) and 110(a)(4) of the
Clean Air Act, but these were limited to sources
subject to NSPS and, by extension through EPA's
general new source review regulations, to ensuring
that new sources would not cause violations of the
ambient standards. Thus this last provision
appeared to extend the real effective date of PSD to
the time at which the statute passed Congress. The
House Committee also added provisions allowing
certain exemptions from increment consumption to
sources subject to coal conversions under ESECA or
fuel switching because of natural gas curtailment.[78]

Rogers accepted these amendments to the
subcommittee bill for the simple reason that they
were necessary to get the PSD provision through at
all. In this sense his efforts (and those of his
staff) in the full committee were a continuation of
the strategy at the subcommittee level: make
necessary tactical concessions in order to preserve
the main PSD provisions in the bill. This is not to
belittle the importance of the different concepts of
baseline; literally millions of dollars in costs for
individual plants would depend on whether their
emissions could be grandfathered in this way. It is
simply to recognize that, as in the case of "buffer
zones" earlier, Rogers and other advocates of PSD
were pragmatists in their efforts to get PSD
approved. "Technical" changes which gave the
appearance of reasonable accommodation without
undermining PSD's basic structure seemed, from this
perspective, a small price to pay. The full cost of
those accommodations would not be apparent until
later, when EPA would find itself struggling to
accommodate the many exceptions, loopholes and
inconsistencies which the law would contain as a
result of this process.

Unlike the Senate, which had distanced itself
from the Ford Administration, the House Committee
leadership did spend time in the winter of 1975-76
going over its positions with Administration

officials. Some of the weakening amendments
introduced by Rogers were consistent with those
outlined in a White House staff paper which appeared
in January, 1976, including the lifting of the PSD
ceiling to 90% of ambient standards and the
exemption of power plants making mandatory coal
conversions.[79] The paper noted that any compromise
by the House would require "a major modification" in
the Administration's position." The chief political
argument for a compromise was that the Senate
Committee bill was more stringent, that a House-
Administration coalition would be on stronger ground
in a conference proceeding, and that the
Administration's original position on PSD had little
chance of being sustained in Committee. Unstated
but running through the paper was the recognition
that a veto fight over the Clean Air Act in a
Presidential election year would be a severe
liability. More explicitly, the paper noted the
press of the automobile deadline and the need to do
something to forestall it.[80] While these discussions
continued and may have had some effect on which
provisions Rogers decided to accept, no major
official Administration position change emerged from
them. In fact, despite Rogers' amendments, action
on the House bill slowed as committee members
opposed to the bill adopted what Chairman Harley
Staggers referred to as "tactics to prolong" debate
which would presumably increase the likelihood of
success of an attempt to split the auto emissions
standards from the rest of the bill.[81]

These efforts were ultimately unsuccessful when,
on March 18, the Commerce Committee reported
H.R.10498 by a vote of 22 to 13.[82] In a statement
soon thereafter, Rogers defended the House bill as
one which reduced EPA's authority and gave States
increased responsibility for regulating air quality
over Federal lands. He criticized the attacks on
the bill by the Chamber of Commerce, noting that
only one percent of the Nation's land area would be
mandatory Class I under the House bill and saying
that "I don't see this as a no-growth bill."[83]

Thus, after protracted discussion in both the
House and Senate committees, March 1976 ended with

bills agreed to by both principal committees. On
the surface, both bills appeared to contain similar
provisions with respect to PSD. Both used the
increment system outlined by EPA; both expanded the
universe of sources to be regulated; and both
afforded special protection to parks and wilderness
areas through provisions for mandatory Class I
areas.

Yet beneath this surface agreement lay other
fundamental differences in the two approaches to
PSD. The Senate bill relied heavily on BACT. For
example, this provision was cited in the Senate
report as the reason why "growth options would be
enlarged" under the Senate bill despite the
elimination of EPA's Class III.[83] While repeating
assertions that "flexibility and State judgment are
the foundations of this policy," the Senate report
also went on to assert that "the Federal Land
Manager should assume an aggressive role in
protecting the air quality value of the land under
his jurisdiction." When in doubt, the land manager
was to "err on the side of protecting the air
quality related values for future generations."[85]
Moreover, from a philosophical point of view the
Senate report presented the bill as one which
"clarifies and details" a policy first written into
the 1967 Air Quality Act.[86] The form of the Senate
bill reflected this view; PSD was legally framed
only as a new subsection (g) of Section 110, which
dealt with the requirements for State implementation
plans.[87] The section of the Senate report dealing
with PSD was only nine pages long.

In contrast, the House report, when finally
issued on May 15, devoted sixty-nine pages to an
explanation and justification of the House proposal.
While agreeing with the Senate in asserting that PSD
was in fact a "nearly decade-old policy," a good
part of the report was spent outlining a detailed
justification for PSD in terms of health benefits
and avoidance of stratospheric and atmospheric
modification as well as the more conventional
rationales of preventing environmentally destructive
economic competition, protecting parks, and
preserving States' rights.[88] The "new" status of PSD

took legal form in the House bill through its
codification as a new Subtitle C in Title I.[89]
Moreover, as was discussed earlier, the House
subcommittee had started from several philosophical
assumptions which were at odds with those in the
Senate. States were to be given more leeway in the
final House version, both with respect to Federal
lands and reclassifications--a moot point in the
Senate bill due to the absence of Class III. Also
unlike the Senate, the House bill did not provide
for the application of BACT across the board (though
this was influenced by the proposed House amendment
to §111 requiring the "best technological systems of
continuous emissions reduction" on power plants).[90]
The House bill adopted fundamentally different
approaches to the question of what the increments
represented and how to "grandfather" sources.
Finally, in a provision which can best be explained
as an act of faith that scientists could treat
atmospheric air as a fixed, stable commodity, the
House added a costly set of monitoring requirements
to determine a "baseline" concentration and track
changes in air quality in a way which EPA had
earlier concluded could not be practically done.[91]

From a "broad" perspective these differences may
not have seemed significant. Yet these legislative
details were to be at the heart of PSD's subsequent
difficulties. It is important to recognize that
these differences were not inadvertent; each existed
for a reason. However, the sheer number of
sponsors, provisions and interests was bound to
produce confusion in the event that the time
available for the consideration and reconciliation
of each of these differences was compressed.
Unfortunately, this was precisely what happened
next.

Congress Takes Up PSD on the Floor

The next step in the consideration of amendments was for each respective House of Congress to take up the bills produced by their committees. However, in both the House and the Senate, months elapsed before Clean Air Act amendments could be brought to the floor. These delays reflected the controversial nature of PSD and the hopes of its opponents that through delay, the tough committee bills could be weakened or killed.

SENATE CONSIDERATION OF S.3219

When the Public Works Committee approved S.3219, Leon Billings had suggested that the bill might go to the Senate floor the first or second week in March, 1976.[92] However, as it happened, the bill was not called up until July 27th. The most important cause of this delay was a campaign by Senators Jake Garn and Frank Moss of Utah.[93]

Garn's objection to the bill was directly related to PSD. PSD posed a greater potential threat to the construction of new coal-fired power plants in Utah than in perhaps any other State. Utah contained substantial low sulfur coal reserves, and in light of the growing electricity needs of the Los Angeles area, Southern California Edison, along with San Diego and Arizona utility companies, had proposed to build a 3,000 megawatt, $4 billion power plant on the Kaiparowits plateau of southern Utah. However, the constraints of the Class I increments in both the Senate and House bills would have kept the plant from being built because of its impact on the nearby Capitol Reef National Park, a mandatory Class I area.

The Kaiparowits project had generated substantial opposition from environmental groups-- and in fact on April 14 (to Senator Garn's reported

surprise) the plant's sponsors announced that they
were abandoning the project. Utility executives
blamed environmentalists for "beating the project to
death," and its collapse seemed to symbolize the
ability of environmental requirements to inhibit
industrial development. Its demise also seemed to
threaten other proposed power plant projects in
Utah, and the fact that even more such projects
could be threatened by PSD made this a particularly
sore subject for Senators Garn and Moss.[94]

On April 13, Moss introduced an amendment to
S.3219 which would delete the PSD provisions
(section 6) and replace them with a requirement that
a proposed National Commission on Air Quality study
the potential impact of PSD and report back to the
Congress a year after the bill's passage.[95] This, of
course, would have weakened the position of PSD's
advocates enormously by detaching the PSD provisions
from other action-forcing portions of the bill--
especially the relaxation of the auto standards.
The Moss amendment was to be the major subject of
floor debate about S.3219.

This particular conflict dovetailed nicely with
the broader political needs of the Ford White House
to avoid having to deal with a potential veto of
Clean Air Act Amendments in a presidential election
year. In April, FEA prepared another staff paper
reviewing developments since February and outlining
two options. One was to back the Moss amendment
deferring legislation on PSD pending a study. The
second was to maintain the hard line of opposing PSD
altogether and advocate amending §101 of the Clean
Air Act to strike down the Supreme Court decision.
Any compromise with either the House or Senate
proposals was ruled out; the only "option" was
whether the President should meet with Senator Baker
before or after making a decision on how to
proceed.[96]

Muskie and the Senate committee were well aware
of these pressures. In the wake of the introduction
of the Moss amendment, a series of exchanges between
committee members and Moss commenced in the
Congressional Record, each an attempt to upstage and
refute the attacks of the other.[97] The most telling

broadsides came from Senators James Buckley, Gale
McGee and Howard Baker. In a piece entitled "The
Myth of Significant Deterioration," Buckley attacked
the U.S. Chamber of Commerce for "a spurious attack
on the Senate bill" and denounced the study on which
the Chamber's attack was based as having "no
relationship" to the bill's requirements.[98] On April
29, the five committee Republican Senators sent a
joint letter to other Senators endorsing the
committee bill and opposing the Moss Amendment.[99] On
May 4, Senator McGee of Wyoming, (who had previously
listed himself as a co-sponsor of the Moss
amendment) withdrew his support abruptly and
announced that he would "resist any proposal that
would delete or delay the implementation of
nondegradation."[100] Senator Baker, in a May 21
speech to the Aluminum Association, announced his
opposition to the Moss Amendment and compared the
Committee bill favorably to EPA's regulations.[101]
    These statements signified two important things.
The first was that Committee unanimity would hold in
the Senate in the face of White House pressure on
PSD. The rejection by these Senators of the intense
lobbying effort by the White House and industry
showed the effectiveness of Muskie's strategy
throughout the prolonged Subcommittee and Committee
markups on the bill.[102] The second significant point
about these statements was that they illustrated the
degree to which both industry and the Ford
Administration had lost technical credibility on
PSD. EPA's assistance to the Committee in the form
of "neutral" analysis had played a big role in this
(and must have been infuriating to the White House).
With no credible information base from which to
attack PSD, opponents were reduced to arguing that
more information was needed to assess its impacts--a
much weaker position than arguing that its effects
would be catastrophic.[103]
    The pressure from the Republican members of the
Senate committee perhaps reflected their concern
about the impact of a Presidential election-year
veto of a Clean Air Act. Behind the scenes, these
Senators had been urging President Ford to reach
some compromise on a set of amendments which would

have at least acknowledged the need for some limited
PSD protection of parks and wilderness areas.[104] The
President's response, however, was to send identical
letters to Senate Public Works Chairman Randolph and
to Chairman Harley Staggers of the House Energy and
Commerce Committee on May 28, covering both PSD and
auto emissions (where the President supported the
Dingell-Broyhill amendment postponing tighter
standards). On PSD, the letter cited the "economic
uncertainties" and "negative" energy impacts of the
House and Senate proposals, and asserted that "we do
not have the facts necessary to make proper
decisions." Ford asked that the Clean Air Act be
amended "to preclude application of all significant
deterioration provisions until sufficient
information concerning final impact can be
gathered."[105]

This letter produced an uproar in the Senate.
While Senator Moss was described by an aide as
"extremely pleased," the Republican members of the
Public Works Committee were distressed, and
announced through Senator Buckley that "none of us
can support the President's requests with respect to
the nondegradation provisions."[106] A subsequent
meeting on June 8 of the five Senators with the
President produced no immediate change in the
Administration's position, though it did highlight
once again the differences between the positions of
EPA and other Federal agencies.[107] Senator Muskie
responded to the Ford letter with a statement
entitled "President Ford Chooses Dirty Air," and
blasted the letter as an attempt "to use a phony
'job scare' approach to defeat the Senate bill."
Significantly, given EPA's role in providing the
information which Muskie used to challenge analyses
produced by PSD's opponents, one of Muskie's charges
against the President was that "his information is
wrong."[108]

This flurry of activity on PSD coincided with
the scheduled dates for the opening of full Senate
debate on the Clean Air Act Amendments. This date,
however, continued to slip. The debate, which Leon
Billings had at one time predicted would begin in
early March, was postponed until late March, then

May 4, then June 2, and finally June 10, when it was once again postponed. Each postponement had a rationale--Committee review of the report language in one instance, a filibuster in another, a request by Senator Garn for time to "study" the Committee report, an inflamed nerve which hospitalized Senator Muskie, and finally delays associated with the Democratic National Convention (which included the serious consideration of Senator Muskie as the Democratic candidate for Vice-President). The delays, however, worked in favor of PSD's opponents and increased the likelihood that the Congress would be unable to enact Clean Air Act amendments in 1976. The pressure for automotive standards revisions to force action was not proving to be enough to force rapid action on PSD. Leon Billings, in late June, cited the prospects for the passage of amendments in 1976 as only "fifty-fifty."[109]

Nevertheless, Muskie pressed on, and was finally able to bring the bill to the Senate floor on July 26. This development brought a reaction from the White House. In the wake of the June 8 meeting, discussions on "problem areas" and "grounds for potential agreement" had continued between the Administration and Senate committee members. EPA's regulations began to emerge from this discussion as a basis for a legislative compromise, though Administration officials also pushed for language which would explicitly exempt strip mines from PSD and delay the BACT requirement for power plants until 1985.[110]

This effort culminated in the presentation by the White House of a set of draft amendments to the Republican Senate Public Works Committee members on July 21. According to Senate staff members, these amendments would "fully resolve the problems the White House now sees regarding stationary source provisions of the Clean Air amendments."[111] In addition to the PSD provisions described above, the proposed amendments would have used EPA's increment values (including Class III, which was not part of the Senate bill), increased the minimum size for mandatory Class I areas to 25,000 acres (instead of 5,000), and specified that only sources which would actually emit (rather than have the <u>potential</u> to emit) more than 100 tons of a pollutant annually would be subject to PSD.[112]

To Senate Committee Republicans, this proposal represented success. Senator Howard Baker, in a statement prepared for insertion in the <u>Congressional Record</u>, said that it meant that the White House now supported the concept of no significant deterioration and thanked the President for "the care and understanding he has given to this question."[113] Baker's pleasure was short-lived, however. Only hours after the draft amendments were sent to the Committee Republicans, the White House withdrew them, claiming that they were only "discussion positions."[114] While White House staff blamed "confusion" on the Senate side for misunderstanding the status of the language, what appears to have occurred is that the opponents of PSD, once they became aware of the White House initiative, moved swiftly and forcefully to quash it. Congressman James Broyhill, point man for the Administration on the House side, criticized the proposals as "too environmentalist." The American Petroleum Institute and other industry groups met with White House officials to complain that they were not "consulted at all" on the proposed amendments, and that they represented "a complete capitulation to EPA" on significant deterioration.[115] In the face of this opposition, the White House position collapsed, and reverted to the official line articulated in the May 28 letter. This was the last Ford Administration opportunity to influence the details of the bill; its collapse polarized positions and left PSD's opponents with no option except to hope that the delaying tactics of the Moss amendment and debate postponement would succeed.

On the floor of the Senate, significant deterioration was debated more extensively than any other provision of the 1976 amendments. Proponents claimed that the Senate bill would allow States greater flexibility than EPA's regulations;[116] that it would prevent the nation from having uniformly dirty air;[117] that it responded(!) to industry's

demands for legislative action to promote certainty
in the law governing PSD;[118] that it would minimize
projected increases in national emissions of sulfur
and nitrogen oxides;[119] and that it would have little
impact on consumer costs.[120] These arguments were
used to counter the claims of PSD's opponents, led
by Senator Moss and Senator Scott of Virginia, that
PSD was unnecessary, expensive, unstudied, and
restrictive of economic growth.[121]

The debate quickly focused on Senator Moss'
amendment as compared to an amendment offered by
Senator Randolph. Randolph's amendment authorized a
study similar to Moss', but without deleting the PSD
requirements or postponing their implementation
until after the study was completed.[122] This was
obviously designed to provide Senators who believed
that PSD deserved more study with an alternative to
the Moss amendment. Moss and the other opponents of
PSD picked up on this immediately, and despite
Senator Muskie's innocent protests that "obviously
its effect is not to bypass the Moss amendment," a
filibuster began against the Senate bill which
lasted for three days. It ended only when Muskie
finally agreed in an elaborate unanimous consent
agreement to allow the Moss amendment to come up for
a vote prior to the Randolph amendment.[123]

After this long and sometimes bitter debate, the
Moss Amendment came to a vote on August 3, and was
defeated 31 to 63. Senator Muskie was reportedly
surprised at the margin of Moss' defeat;
environmentalists, despite their earlier criticism
of concessions in the committee deliberations on the
amendments, nonetheless regarded the Moss defeat as
the most significant environmental victory of the
94th Congress.[124]

It is probably futile to speculate on whatever
private reasons Senators may have had for supporting
Muskie and opposing Moss. However, it is worth
noting some of the reasons cited by Senators in
debate. These included: "eliminating the threat of
economic coercion" (Senator Domenici);[125] "my belief
that the Senate must resolve this issue, moving it
out of the hands of the courts and into the hands of
the States" (Senator Buckley);[126] "I am convinced

that Federal regulation is a good deal worse than
State regulation" (Senator Brooke);[127] "If [the Moss
amendment passes] . . . we would be left with the
EPA regulations which do not allow this increased
State participation" (Senator Nunn);[128] "I believe
some program is needed and that the Senate
committee's approach is superior to that of EPA"
(Senator Eagleton);[129] "Under this bill, business
will know the rules by which they can construct new
plants, rather than relying on regulations tied up
in the courts indefinitely" (Senator Taft).[130] These
comments, all of which reflect arguments made by
Muskie, say more about the effectiveness of the
Senate committee system and Senator Muskie's skill
at being able to call upon unified committee support
in defending his bill than they do about PSD.
Nonetheless, it seems reasonable in the face of such
statements to argue that those who supported Muskie
thought they were getting a PSD program with more
State flexibility, more certainty, and less
litigation than the one created by EPA's
regulations.

It is interesting to note the degree to which
Muskie and his supporters attacked EPA's regulations
as too rigid and inflexible. As Senator Moss noted,
this was an arguable point, especially given the
establishment of mandatory Class I areas and
elimination of Class III in the Senate bill.[131]
Other actors in the Ford Administration, once they
began to look past their previous implacable
opposition to PSD, also came to realize that
compared to either the House or Senate bills, EPA's
regulations offered considerably more flexibility.[132]
However, Muskie had repeated his assertion about the
relative stringency of the two proposals to the
point that opponents would have had to mount a major
attack on Muskie's data and his personal integrity
to affect this perception. Given this situation,
the news on August 2 that the D.C. Circuit Court of
Appeals had acted with surprising speed to uphold
EPA's PSD regulations in their entirety was a gift
which fell into Muskie's hands and which he did not
hesitate to use.[133] While it is too much to say that
this court decision tipped the balance against the

Moss amendment, it did send a clear signal that PSD
was not going away regardless of what Congress did.
This strengthened the hand of those who argued in
favor of affirmative Congressional action.[134]

One other aspect of the Senate's debate over PSD
is worth mentioning, since it reinforces the
importance of Muskie and his committee in gaining
Senate acceptance of PSD. The Moss amendment was
not the only one offered to the Committee's PSD
proposal. At the urging of environmental groups
which felt that Muskie had given up too much,
Senator Gary Hart offered an amendment which would
have included emissions from non-major sources, or
major sources not on the list of 28 categories
included in the Senate bill, in calculating
increment consumption. The committee's intent,
according to Hart, "was to simplify implementation
by limiting regulation to the largest potential
polluters."[135] However, Hart asserted that "sulfur
oxide is sulfur oxide--and it does not matter
whether it comes from one large source or from one
thousand small non-major sources."[136] He introduced
an EPA study to support his position, which stated
that 'facilities resulting from general area-wide
growth play a major role in determining overall air
quality." This study, interestingly enough, came
from the Office of Transportation and Land Use
Policy in EPA's Air Office, the group in the agency
which most strongly backed the use of both
transportation and land use planning as air
pollution control measures (in contrast to the more
conservative approach of the Office of Air Quality
Planning and Standards).[137]

However, despite Hart's assertion that his
amendment was "consistent with the intent and
purpose of the Clean Air Act," it was rejected by a
vote of 26-65. Only Senators Gravel and Culver from
the Environment and Public Works Committee voted
with Hart. It was the Committee Senators themselves
who led the attack on the Hart amendment. In so
doing, Senator McClure noted that the Committee's
provision was "not accidental." In fact, charging
only emissions from specified major sources against
the Class II increment was part of the

"administrative flexibility" to be included in Class II, to compensate for the elimination of Class III. Hart responded that "my recollection of the committee's deliberations was that we did not spend very much time on this . . . we just sort of slid over it . . . it is no scientific nightmare." McClure's immediate response was that Hart's proposal was "an administrative nightmare." Later on, however, McClure made a more telling point which showed the delicate nature of the compromises which Muskie had embodied in the Senate bill.

> What it boils down to is that really what the Senator desires is to tighten the increments. The increments are more generous than the Senator from Colorado would have permitted. This amendment has the effect of shrinking the size of the increments, which is not what the committee intended.[138]

The failure of the Hart amendment shows once again the critical role which the Muskie committee played in framing the issue of PSD for the Senate as a whole.[138] In the final analysis, while there were substantive reasons for supporting PSD, the key reason for PSD's success on the Senate floor was that Senators found themselves faced with a committee proposal which, notwithstanding heavy industry lobbying, had been successfully negotiated in committee with Senators from a wide range of backgrounds and beliefs. This process was a more important explanation of Senate action than any of the particular provisions of the proposal. In this respect, Muskie's strategy of discussion and conciliation in committee was highly successful. However, these developments point out just how crucial the Senate committee deliberations were, and how individual committee members and staff could wield enormous influence over the particular provisions of law and committee reports as long as they could maintain their credibility with the committee as a whole.

On August 5, 1976, the Senate approved the Clean Air Amendments of 1976 by a vote of 78-13. With

that vote, action on the 1976 amendments shifted
once again to the House of Representatives.

HOUSE CONSIDERATION OF THE 1976 AMENDMENTS

Chairman Rogers had as much difficulty as
Senator Muskie in bringing the 1976 amendments up
for floor action. Though reported on May 15 from
the full committee, it was July 27 before the Rules
Committee sent the bill, named H.R.10498, to the
floor.[140] Debate opened on August 4. The rule,
however, allowed for three hours of general debate,
and the House recessed for the Republican National
Convention with more than 40 minutes of this time
remaining, along with extensive amendments for
consideration. In particular, the automobile
companies had decided to make their major push for a
relaxation of the automobile emissions standards in
the House with the so-called "Dingell-Broyhill
amendment."[141]
The opening statements in the August 4 debate
had been enough to signal that the PSD provisions in
H.R. 10498 would be subject to the same kind of
debate which had occurred in the Senate.
Conservative House Republicans, led by Congressmen
James Broyhill, David Satterfield, and William
Chappell, recited the familiar litany of attacks
against PSD, and Rogers and his supporters responded
with the same arguments used in the Senate--that the
Committee bill would increase State control, provide
greater certainty through fewer lawsuits, and
clarify Congressional intent concerning a policy
which was already a part of the Clean Air Act. They
also noted the rejection of the Moss amendment in
the Senate the previous day and the decision of the
D.C. Circuit Court upholding EPA's regulations.[142]
Finally, liberal Democratic Congressmen Henry Waxman
and Andrew Maguire served notice that they would
attempt to amend the Committee bill to eliminate the
Class III provisions and strengthen the role of

Federal Land Managers in the classification of
Federal lands.[143]

When House debate finally resumed on September
8, speculation was widespread that legislation could
not be completed prior to Congressional adjournment
on October 2, and that even if Congress did succeed
in passing a bill, it would be either pocket-vetoed
or vetoed outright by President Ford.[144]
Nonetheless, Rogers and his supporters pressed ahead
for a vote. In doing so, they successfully defeated
the Waxman-Maguire amendment eliminating Class III
(107-247), and the Chappell amendment which, like
the Moss amendment in the Senate, would have
postponed the PSD requirements pending a study by a
National Commission on Air Quality. The vote on
this amendment was much closer than the vote on the
Moss amendment had been in the Senate--156 to 199
against--but it was enough.[145]

While Waxman-Maguire and Chappell were the
watershed amendments in the House, a number of other
amendments were offered on the floor by both PSD
supporters and opponents. These dealt mostly with
redesignation criteria and involvement of local
governments and Federal Land Managers in such
decisions. Though considerable time was spent
discussing these amendments, most were rejected on
the strength of Rogers' opposition to them.[146] Two,
however, did pass with Rogers' support and are worth
noting. The first, sponsored by Georgia's Elliott
Levitas, included clarifying amendments on both
redesignation procedures in States and exemptions
from the full one year monitoring requirements.[147]
It was noteworthy, however, because it also struck
from H.R.10498 the statement that one of PSD's
purposes was "to protect any State, region or area
of the country from the loss of jobs or tax revenues
to other States, regions or areas which, but for
this subtitle, would permit significant
deterioration of air quality."[148] Levitas observed,
"I do not consider that a fundamental purpose of the
Clean Air Act. This bill should be considered on
its merits as an environmental and health concern--
not as legislation which favors one area of the
country over another."[149]

Representative James Florio of New Jersey could not resist challenging this rather pious assertion, saying that "it would be naive not to reach the conclusion that many of the health decisions which are being made with regard to the Clean Air Act are . . . being made with an eye toward the economic impacts of these decisions."[150] Florio's point was not merely philosophical; as representative of a Northeast urban, industrialized, polluted State which feared the economic flight of industry to the Sunbelt, he spoke for a group of urban supporters of PSD who saw in the provisions a means to prevent the additional loss of jobs to rural, unpolluted areas. Florio's attempt to strike this portion of Levitas' amendment failed, however, by a 12-7 vote.[151] While this had no practical effect, the exchange represented an unusually candid moment in the House debate, and shows the degree to which in the House, as in the Senate, economic equity as much as air quality was at issue in the debate over PSD.

The second amendment accepted by Rogers was a harbinger of things to come, and again reflected his willingness to trade concessions on marginal points of principle if he felt it would help protect the overall integrity of the bill. It was offered by Congressman McKay, a Democrat from Utah. Unlike his colleagues in the Senate, McKay had voted against the amendment to delay the PSD provision pending the National Commission study. Given Rogers' narrow victory, it is likely that McKay's support for Rogers was tied to Rogers' acceptance of McKay's amendment. The amendment, which (as McKay noted) was very carefully worded in cooperation with Congressman Waxman, allowed for a variance from the Class I increments for sources whose emissions might affect a mandatory Class I area. This variance was not to exceed 3% of the days in the year. Before a Governor could grant it, he would have to determine that the source had met a number of very strict tests, and both EPA and the Federal Land Manager had to concur with this determination.[152] McKay noted the importance of such a variance to Utah due to its extensive mandatory Class I areas and its uneven terrain. The discussion which followed on this

amendment can best be described as confused, and
reflective of the complexity of PSD's increment
scheme and how it related to the ambient
standards.[153]

Congressmen Broyhill and Rogers, however, knew
exactly what it meant.

> Mr. Broyhill: I would like the attention of the
> gentlemen from Florida [Mr.
> Rogers], because I understood that
> the gentleman from Florida said
> that this amendment applies also to
> class II areas. Is that correct?

> Mr. Rogers: Only class I. Up to class II
> increments on 3 percent of the days
> of the year.

> Mr. Broyhill: This then only applies to class I
> areas . . . But there are a number
> of other areas of the country which
> are going to be classified as class
> II, and they are going to have a
> considerable problem. I would like
> to see this same principle adopted
> for these class II areas, as well.
> But I take it that the gentleman
> from Florida would not accept an
> amendment like that.

> Mr. McKay: He and perhaps some others.[154]

Congressman Howe from Utah went on to describe
the real purpose of the amendment: it would create
the necessary variance to allow the construction of
a large 3000 megawatt power plant in southern Utah.
The variance allowing this plant, which was to
become known as the Intermountain Power Project,
appears to have been the price for the successful
defeat of the Chappell amendment in the House.
However, unlike either the Moss or the Chappell
amendments, it attracted almost no attention.

With that, the House moved on to debate the
amendments relating to mobile sources, where (among

other things) it overrode Rogers and the committee
by accepting the Dingell-Broyhill amendment on
automobile emission standards.[155] With that, the
House finally concluded its consideration of
H.R.10498, passing it on September 15 by a vote of
324-68.[156]

The 1976 Conference

Operating under intense and increasing time
pressure because of the pending adjournment of
Congress on October 1, a conference committee was
immediately convened to attempt to reconcile the
differences in the bills passed by the two chambers.
Nor was time the only pressure on the conferees.
The White House assisted efforts to ensure that the
conference would not complete its work so that it
could avoid presenting President Ford with the
unpalatable choice of signing an unacceptable bill
or vetoing Clean Air Act amendments less than a
month before the election.[157]

Only at this late hour, and under these extreme
pressures, were the authors of the different Senate
and House approaches forced to come to grips with
the fact that the PSD provisions of the two bills,
while similar in their overall structure, each
incorporated many different assumptions which would
have to be reconciled. Now, with the end of the
session less than two weeks away, a select group of
Senators and Representatives was charged with the
unenviable task of trying to reconcile two years'
worth of debate into a single set of provisions
which was politically acceptable and logically
consistent.[158]

This would have been a formidable task if PSD
were the only item on the conferees' agenda, but
this was not the case. Auto standards, rules for
industrial expansion in non-attainment areas, and a
host of other changes to the Act had to be decided

as well. The committee staff in both branches of
Congress were thus given an enormous responsibility
for reconciling differences between the two bills in
a very short period of time.

The hectic circumstances surrounding the
conference negotiations explain some of the
bargaining which went on in the development of the
conference report, and some of the internal
inconsistencies which the final report contained.
This report was produced after the conference,
following long and protracted meetings and all-night
staff work, agreed on September 29 to a set of
proposed amendments.

Even though the conference report ultimately did
not pass in 1976, it is worth reviewing the
provisions of this hastily drafted bill with some
care. For one thing, they show how provisions which
otherwise make sense can be taken out of their
supporting context and given an altogether different
meaning in the rush to produce a last-minute bill.
Moreover, having gone through the agony of the
hurried conference once, the Senate and House
managers of the bills were understandably reluctant
in 1977 to reopen the compromises reached in 1976.
Thus, the failed 1976 conference report became the
basis for the 1977 Amendments. This meant,
unfortunately, that some of the flaws which resulted
from the hasty construction of the 1976 conference
report carried over into the new law.

The PSD section of the conference report
borrowed freely from both bills. The major areas of
compromise (and later controversy) are discussed
below.

1) Statement of Purpose--The Senate bill
contained no statement of purpose for PSD, on the
assumption that nondegradation policy, in the words
of the Senate report, "was incorporated into the
1967 Air Quality Act" and had been there ever
since.[159] The House bill, in contrast, contained an
elaborate statement of purpose which tied PSD to
health protection, national park preservation,
economic growth and public participation. The House
statement of purpose was added to the bill.

2) <u>Classes and Increment Values</u>--This was a particularly troublesome area. The greatest difficulty arose because from the beginning, the House and Senate bills treated the increments as fundamentally different things. The Senate bill followed EPA's lead in regarding the increments as modeling targets, and derived their values so that they could accommodate the modeled impacts of certain facilities, most notably 1000 megawatt power plants. The House bill, in contrast, treated the increments as if they were actual, measurable changes in air quality and derived their values from arbitrary percentages of the ambient standards. Rather than resolving this philosophical discrepancy, however, the conferees and their staff glossed over it by adopting proposals which borrowed bits and pieces from both bills with little regard for whether doing so made any sense.

For example, the conferees adopted a Class III, which enabled the House managers to claim a substantial victory. However, the increment values used to define the classes were mixed and matched in a classic example of Congressional horse trading, as can be seen in Table 2.[160]

The most apparent example of this trading occurred on the increment which was probably the single greatest source of concern to the utility industry--the three hour SO_2 Class II increment. This, of course, was the increment value which EPA changed at the last moment in August 1974, just prior to the proposal of its regulation, from 300 ug/m^3 to 700 ug/m^3. Because of its short term nature, it was likely to be the limiting increment of concern for power plants, especially in hilly terrain.

TABLE 2:   <u>Comparison of Increment Values in the
EPA Regulations and the Senate, House
and Conference Reports</u>

<u>Increment</u>	<u>EPA</u>	<u>Senate</u>	<u>House</u>	<u>Conference</u>
(All values in micrograms per cubic meter)				

<u>Class I</u>

<u>Particulate matter</u>
| Annual | 5 | 5 | 7.5 | 5 |
| 24-hour | 10 | 10 | 15 | 10 |

<u>Sulfur dioxide</u>
Annual	2	2	1.6	2
24-hour	5	5	7.3	5
3-hour	25	25	26	25

<u>Class II</u>

<u>Particulate matter</u>
| Annual | 10 | 10 | 19 | 19 |
| 24-hour | 30 | 30 | 37 | 37 |

<u>Sulfur dioxide</u>
Annual	15	15	20	20
24-hour	100	100	91	91
3-hour	700	700	325	512

<u>Class III</u>

<u>Particulate matter</u>
| Annual | 75* | No Class III | 37 | 37 |
| 24-hour | 150* | | 75 | 75 |

<u>Sulfur dioxide</u>
Annual	80*	No Class III	40	40
24-hour	365*		182	182
3-hour	1300*		650	700

*Rather than increments, these were the applicable
values for the National Ambient Air Quality
Standards

The conference report retained the 700 ug/m^3 figure, but only as the top increment in Class <u>III</u>. The figure of 512 ug/m^3 for the Class <u>II</u> 3-hour SO_2 increment represented neither a decision to adopt Class II increments which would accommodate power plants, nor a decision to set an effective tertiary air quality standard. Instead, the figure results from adding half the difference between the House and Senate Class II increments to the lower House increment. This process more nearly resembled traditional Congressional pork barrel legislation than an exercise in air quality management.[161] To add to the confusion, the conference also adopted the 90% ceiling requirement from the House bill, which appeared to be a tertiary standard but one which only applied to the longer averaging times where the increment values were of less concern.[162]

The conference report did adopt the Senate view of the nature of the Class I increments. However, it did so in a way which reinforced the perception of last-minute horse trading. Under the Senate bill, when a Federal Land Manager (FLM) identified a source that could cause a potential violation of an increment in a Class I area, this triggered a negotiation and discussion process between the Governor of the affected State and the Federal Land Manager, in which the Governor was afforded an opportunity to convince the FLM that the source should be allowed to construct, notwithstanding that Class I increments would be exceeded. The conference report, however, specified that such sources would have to meet the old House 3-hour SO_2 increment of 325 ug/m^3--a kind of "Class 1-1/2." The apparent reason for this is ironic; since the McKay variance had only provided for sources to go up to the <u>House</u> Class II increments, the conferees seem to have decided to build in this value in light of the relaxation of the general 3-hour Class II increment. The conference report did <u>not</u> include the House-passed McKay variance; however, the commentary (though not the bill) repeated the Senate language that disputes between the Federal Land Manager and a Governor would ultimately be resolved by the Administrator.[163]

3) <u>Applicability and Major Emitting Facilities</u>--
The conference settled the difference between the
Senate and House bills over which sources were
subject to regulation under the Act by including the
Senate list as sources which were to be subject if
they would emit, or have the potential to emit, one
hundred tons per year or more of any air pollutant.
However, they also adopted the more sweeping House
approach in specifying that any other source with
the design capacity to emit 250 tons per year would
also be considered a "major emitting facility"
subject to PSD.
   This had been a major issue, at least on the
Senate side. During the floor debate on the Senate
bill, Senator McClure commented that the
restrictions of PSD to specified sources categories
"assures that industrial plants of significant
impact are fully covered, yet also assures that
small activities are not subject to overzealous
regulation." He expressed concern that this was a
fine balance in which the committee had gone to
great pains to state "precisely what is included,
what is not, and what role the Administrator plays."
He buttressed his concern by entering in the record
a list of the kinds of facilities which could fall
under PSD if a definition like that in the House
bill was used.[165]   These same arguments had been used
by Senator McClure to bring about the defeat of the
Hart amendment on the Senate floor.
   Gauged by this standard, Senator McClure must
have been disappointed by the outcome of the
conference, which turned PSD in the direction of the
more comprehensive program envisioned by the House.
However, the definition of who was subject to PSD
was to open up an avenue which would ultimately
allow a less comprehensive program than might
otherwise have been the case. Following the
conferees' general pattern of working from the
Senate bill, the conference report used the term
"major emitting facility" to define the units
subject to PSD. The House bill had used "major
stationary source." While the conference report
appeared to treat the two terms interchangeably (and
even seemed to define them as identical in §302(a),

the difference between a "source" and a "facility"
would result in an extended legal debate in PSD's
subsequent implementation.[166] Moreover, the
conference report failed, as had the Senate and
House bills, to signify whether the term "potential
to emit" within the definition of major emitting
facility referred to expected emissions <u>before</u> or
<u>after</u> air pollution controls were applied. The
confusion this led to will be discussed in the next
chapter.

4) <u>Baseline Concentration and Ambient
Monitoring</u>--A final set of compromises which would
prove troublesome had to do with the definition of
"baseline concentration" and the ambient monitoring
requirements specified in the House bill. The
conference report adopted the definition of baseline
concentration contained in the Senate bill. This
Senate definition was designed for use with the
limited universe of "major emitting facilities"
contained in that bill, and did <u>not</u> envision
extensive new requirements for ambient monitoring
(though it gave States the option to require such
monitoring if necessary). The Senate definition of
baseline was tied to an application by one of the
listed sources for a permit to construct. The House
definition, by contrast, used January 1, 1975 as a
uniform national date for determining baseline air
quality levels, with adjustments which allowed
certain sources to be "grandfathered" under PSD.[167]

These different "baseline" provisions made some
sense within the pollution accounting schemes used
in each bill, though as noted earlier the House bill
suffered from the misconception that increments and
baselines could be readily added and subtracted as
if they were accounts in a ledger. However, the
combination of the definition of baseline from the
Senate bill with the expanded definition of major
emitting facility from the House bill caused a great
increase in the difficulty of implementing PSD. The
combined provisions made it possible in theory for
literally hundreds of areas to exist with their own
separate baseline dates, spread out across the
country like a patchwork quilt. While the text of
the Senate report called upon States to "avoid

allowing emissions from non-major emitters to use up
the safety margin between the increment and the
ambient air quality standards,"[169] the McClure-Hart
exchange had made the Senate committee's intent
clear that only major emitting facilities would
consume increments. Divorced from its logical tie
to the limited list of major facilities, however,
the Senate baseline definition would become a
troublesome theoretical concept.

The Senate report on establishing baseline
levels went on to describe how the baseline in each
area should be determined.

> The purpose is to use actual air quality data to
> establish the baseline. Where sufficient actual
> data are not available, the State may require
> the applicant to perform whatever monitoring the
> State believes is necessary to provide that
> information. This may involve modeling for 12
> months or more to establish an annual
> average.[169] (Emphasis added)

The House, as noted earlier, had taken a very
different approach to the baseline and increment
consumption. The "allowable increments" were "the
increases in pollution which will be allowed above
the baseline pollution level"--there was no
restriction on the source from which the increased
pollution might come. The "baseline," therefore,
was "the level of pollution calculated to exist."
How this was to be done was not specified; one House
staffer present has suggested that this issue was
not very clearly understood at the time.[170] Perhaps
this explains an unwritten assumption in the House
report that the baseline could be measured by
monitoring, though it was recognized that modeling
adjustments to the baseline would be required to
account for grandfathered sources.

The House report reflects a skepticism about
models which was not found in the Senate report.
This skepticism led the House to include a provision
(which the conference committee adopted) calling for
EPA to convene a national conference on air quality
modeling and to publish regulations specifying

acceptable models for use in PSD source evaluation.[171] It was also central to the House argument for the requirement that sources conduct up to a year's worth of pre-construction monitoring of ambient air quality. While there was little explicit discussion in the House about just how the monitoring requirements would work, there were several attacks on the quality of the models used to make PSD divisions.[172] The House members and staff succeeded in having conference adopt the House monitoring provisions, although with one change to make it easier for industry by providing that monitoring data was not to be required until the time of the public hearing on the permit application rather than at the time of the application itself.[173]

   5) <u>Permit Requirements</u>--Finally, the conference, in a major development, accepted the Senate language governing the basic conditions which a prospective new source would have to meet.[174] The most important result of the conferees' acceptance of the Senate language was that all new major emitting facilities would have to apply BACT. Together with the expanded definition of major emitting facilities, this was a very important outcome. It gave PSD the basic character of a technology-based program with a broader scope than either EPA or the Senate bill had envisioned. EPA analyses of the impact of PSD had noted that a BACT requirement would reduce the importance of the ambient increments as constraints on power plant growth,[175] and the rationale for the Senate bill had cited increment and growth protection as part of the rationale for BACT.[176] The conference agreement allowed the technology requirement to become the very heart of the PSD program, though given the extent of the discussion over increment values, variances and monitoring requirements, this does not appear to have been fully recognized at the time. This was even more true because BACT was to apply not just to particulate matter and SO_2, but to "each pollutant subject to regulation under this Act." It is hard to avoid the conclusion that the significance of this change, occurring as it did in the middle of a

PSD section whose complexity continued to increase, was perhaps less appreciated than it would have been had such a change been proposed in a more visible way.

In drafting the provisions for permit requirements, however, the conference ran into a problem: when would the new requirements take effect? This question raised several sticky questions. How would sources which received permits under EPA's old regulations--now to be superseded-- be handled? If the old requirements were less stringent, how was the Agency to handle applicants who rushed to get projects started to "beat the gun?" What would constitute fair notice to sources of new requirements without allowing new plants to use technical loopholes to evade the intent of the law?

This question had come up before when EPA was trying to decide who would be subject to its PSD regulations. The Agency had based its policy on the date that a source had "commenced construction," the idea being that it was unfair to retroactively impose PSD requirements on sources which had in good faith proceeded with projects prior to the promulgation of the PSD regulations. In addition, the 1974 regulations had allowed a grace period, until June 1, 1975, before sources would be subject to the PSD requirements. EPA did this "to avoid severe disruption of sources which are in the final planning and review process at the time of promulgation."[177] Further interpretations were issued by EPA to explain just what evidence a source had to give that it had indeed "commenced construction."[178]

The Senate report criticized EPA's definition and sought to tighten the "commence construction" language. Two methods were used to do this. The first was the addition of language in the Senate report specifying the committee's intent.[179] This language embellished a statutory definition of "commenced" which was written as §110(g)(6)(C) of the Senate bill.[180] Secondly, the Senate bill set June 1, 1975 as the date after which any major emitting facility that "commenced construction"

would be subject to PSD review.[181] However, in
§110(g)(6)(C), the Senate bill specified that the
review of any facility which commenced construction
between June 1, 1975 and the passage of the Act
would be conducted in accordance with EPA's 1974
regulations.[182] The bill went on in §110(g)(7) to
state that until State implementation plans were
revised, the 1974 regulations should continue to
provide the basis for PSD reviews, except where
those regulations were "inconsistent" with the new
bill. This last provision seemed to contain an
expectation that the new requirements would take
effect upon enactment. Indeed, §110(g)(7)
specifically cited increment values, Class I areas,
and BACT requirements for the 28 categories of major
emitting facilities as examples of inconsistencies
to be rectified.[183]

The House bill took a different approach to
making the new PSD rules effective. It will be
recalled from the discussion of the House committee
and floor debate that Chairman Rogers had accepted
numerous provisions designed to exempt certain
sources from increment consumption. Indeed, the
House report went so far as to state that "neither
construction nor generation of any of these existing
or proposed sources need be affected by the
provisions of the committee proposal."[184] These
exemptions were of two kinds: exemptions which were
written into the definition of "baseline
concentration" discussed above, and exemptions for
emissions increases which, though not part of the
"baseline," would also not be counted as consuming
the increment.[185] Their existence testified to the
importance of the increment accounting procedure in
the House bill.

The precise nature of the review which an
individual source would have to undergo was less
important under this scheme, however, than under the
Senate bill with its BACT and other review
requirements. Under the ambient-based scheme
incorporated in the House bill, what controls a
regulated source applied were of relatively less
importance as long as the source's emissions,
however much they were, could be properly counted

against increment consumption. Perhaps as a
consequence, the transition provisions concerning
the new rules were drafted with rather less care.
The House bill, like the Senate, assumed that PSD
would ultimately be applied through State by State
implementation plan revisions. However, rather than
specifying that EPA's regulations were to be
considered as amended upon passage of the bill
wherever the two conflicted, the House bill provided
only for the increment values and mandatory Class I
areas to be changed. More importantly, the House
bill specified that until an implementation plan
revision was prepared and approved by a State, EPA's
regulations would remain in effect. On its face,
this suggested that the requirement to review <u>all</u>
proposed major stationary sources with the design
capacity to emit greater than 100 tons per year of
pollution (as opposed to EPA's list of 19 source
categories) would not begin to apply for almost two
years after the passage of the bill.[186]
     Rather than resolve this inconsistency, however,
the conference only confused the issue by including
<u>both</u> the Senate provisions on permit review
(specifying immediate application of permit
requirements) <u>and</u> the House proviso that EPA's
regulations were to remain in effect until PSD SIP
revisions were approved.[187] It is clear that the
conference report was not fully cross-checked on
this point; one example is that the printed copy of
the conference report contains, in the section taken
from the House bill, a reference to a nonexistent
subsection.[188] There is no explanation in the
conference report about how the transition from the
old to the new requirements was to be handled. The
conference bill did require States to submit revised
SIP's within 9 months of the bill's passage which
would incorporate the PSD requirements, and it is
possible that the conferees assumed that this would
be a minor problem.[189] However, the confusion
resulting from the inclusion of both sets of
transition provisions in the conference bill would
create an issue where EPA and the courts would have
to sort out the effects of the conferees' hasty
work.

OUTCOME OF THE CONFERENCE NEGOTIATION

Even this extended discussion fails to capture
all of the choices and compromises made in the
development of the 1976 conference report just on
PSD, let alone the other provisions of the Act.
Given the magnitude of this task, it is hardly
surprising that confusing outcomes would result. It
is difficult to argue that such last minute, high
pressure lawmaking serves the public interest. Yet
in this two week period, the conferees and their
staff did nothing less than rewrite the PSD
provisions. The result was a program which was
unlike either the Senate or the House approach and
was in many ways more stringent than either one.
A legislative compromise is generally thought of
as one in which both sides "give" something in order
to arrive at a satisfactory middle position. In the
case of PSD, it appears that the work of the 1976
conferees can be more accurately described as an
effort in which the most stringent features of both
bills were combined--BACT from the Senate, lower
increments and monitoring requirements from the
House, more mandatory Class I areas from the Senate,
more covered sources from the House. To be sure,
both sides could claim they had made "concessions"--
the Senate on Class II and exemptions from increment
consumption, the House on 100 vs. 250 ton
applicability.[190] However, a close reading of these
"concessions" suggests that on the whole they did
not amount to much; Class "III" was no less
stringent than the Senate's Class II on the key
three-hour SO_2 increment; the Senate's 28 listed
categories were still kept at the 100 ton
applicability level; and the exemptions from
increment consumption did not provide (for example)
for coal conversions. The advocates of PSD, having
defeated the Moss/Chappell amendments, must have
been delighted with the stringency of the provisions
which emerged from the conference. Industry

representatives, once they got to see what the
conference had done, must have been aghast.

Perhaps this result was reached precisely
because the conferees recognized the likely sequence
of events which would follow the conference report.
Nevertheless, it is important to understand both the
process which produced the 1976 conference report
and the substance it contained because, just as
EPA's 1974 regulations had the effect of providing
PSD's advocates a framework from which adjustments
could then be made, the conference report provided
an environmental "high ground" from which to fend
off further attacks on PSD. The existence of such
an explicit bill, approved by a joint House-Senate
conference, made it difficult for anyone to argue
that PSD was all a mistake which Congress did not
really "intend" to create. Moreover, even if one
adopts the cynical argument that the 1976 conference
report was only a "straw man" designed for political
effect instead of as an actual program, its
existence lent an aura of credibility to PSD which
would have been hard to achieve otherwise. Finally,
the authors of the 1976 conference report must have
had some hope that their work would be enacted that
year. In the last days of a Congressional session,
strange things can happen. It was not unreasonable
to expect that the last-minute passage of the
conference report would be one of them. This would
have presented then-President Ford with a Democratic
dream and Republican nightmare--the difficult choice
of vetoing a clean air bill in the last month before
a close Presidential election in which the
environment was a salient issue.[191]

However, to the relief of the Ford White House,
this choice did not come to pass as time finally ran
out on the 1976 amendments. Senator Jake Garn of
Utah had warned all along that if the bill was not
"available far enough in advance that it could be
studied," that he would filibuster it.[192] The
conferees did not finish their session until
midnight on September 29; at that point the staff
proceeded to spend the next 20 hours recording just
what the conferees had done and putting a report
whose original was described as "a huge bill that

looks like chickens have scratched all over it."[193]
Senator Muskie succeeded in getting the bill called
to the Senate floor late on the night of the 30th,
but Senator Garn carried out his threat and
filibustered until the Senate's adjournment brought
an end to the Clean Air Amendments of 1976. While
Muskie blamed the automobile companies for the
bill's defeat, the object of Garn's attack was
PSD.[194]

The 1977 Amendments

In the wake of the conference report's defeat,
Muskie blasted the bill's opponents and, in a threat
aimed primarily at the automobile industry, said he
would provide "no quick fix" for them in the next
Congressional session.[195] However, this threat did
not last long. By mid-November, the Senate staff
was already looking at options for legislative
action on Act amendments.[196] One big difference, of
course, was that on November 2, 1976 Jimmy Carter
was elected President of the United States.
Carter's election was generally greeted with
pleasure by environmental groups and despair by
industry insofar as environmental issues were
concerned.[197] His election did mean that, for the
first time in many years, the Muskie and Rogers
committees would have overt political support from
the Administration as well as the tacit support
which they had received from the Train EPA. When
hearings on Act amendments were held in the spring
of 1977, new EPA Administrator Douglas Costle
delivered a statement which, in stark contrast to
the Ford Administration position, supported the
concept of specific legislative provisions for PSD
and, in particular, the increments and classes
contained in the conference report.[198] Both Muskie
and Rogers praised the Administration's stance on
the proposed amendments.

However, neither the Administration's support
nor the renewed opposition of industrial groups to
PSD in 1977 hearings on the amendments appeared to
have much effect on the Congressional committees.[199]
After introducing both the 1976 Senate bill and the
1976 conference report as prospective legislation in
early 1977, Senator Muskie proceeded to take the
1976 Senate bill once again as the vehicle for
committee markup. When the committee reported S.252
to the Senate in May, only a few changes had been
made to the PSD provisions which the Senate had
passed in August, 1976. Even the report language
was virtually a reprint of the 1976 version.[200] The
only changes to the PSD requirements were: 1) a
tightening provision to allow States to redesignate
Federal lands as Class I without having to get FLM
concurrence; 2) a provision that areas classified as
Class I before enactment would remain in that
category afterwards; 3) a change giving Indian
tribes greater authority in cases of disputes over
the effect of redesignating land adjacent to
reservations; and 4) an exemption from increment
consumption for modifications which, after applying
BACT, would emit less than fifty tons per year.[201]
The first point was billed as giving States
additional flexibility, but was aimed in part at
giving States a weapon to use against a development-
minded Federal Land Managers. Points 2 and 3 were
both aimed at a situation in Montana where the
Cheyenne Indian tribe was fighting the construction
of a large power plant. Point 4, however, touched
on an issue which would later become a major source
of controversy: did the term "major emitting
facility," which was defined as "any stationary
source of air pollutants which emits, or has the
potential to emit" 100 or 250 tons of air pollution
per year, refer to emissions <u>before</u> or <u>after</u>
controls? The exemption provision implied that the
term referred to the emissions <u>before</u> controls were
applied. Such a determination would greatly expand
the number of sources covered by PSD.

However, unlike 1976, the House preceded the
Senate in marking up a bill for action on the floor.
Rogers followed essentially the same strategy in the

House as Muskie in the Senate, reintroducing the
bill that passed in 1976. Unlike Muskie, however,
Rogers made a number of subtle changes in
reintroducing his bill. These changes: 1) excluded
nonprofit schools and hospitals from the definition
of major stationary sources (thus responding to 1976
floor criticism of the 100 ton definition of a major
source); 2) included natural monuments, primitive
areas, and recreation areas exceeding 100,000 acres
in size as mandatory Class I areas; 3) in a
significant philosophical shift, required
consultation with Federal Land Managers prior to
reclassifying Federal lands (ironic in light of the
Senate committee's deletion of the FLM consultation
requirement for Class I areas); and 4) most
importantly, deleted the McKay variance provision
from the bill.[202] In addition, the Rogers bill added
an entirely new section on visibility protection
which, though not technically a part of PSD, was
certainly related to it and reflected concerns which
PSD's supporters used as part of the rationale for
why PSD was needed.[203] The full committee made an
additional change, deleting the ceiling of 90% of
the primary standard from the subcommittee-approved
bill.[204]

Amid heated and bitter controversy over the auto
standards supported by Rogers and the Administration
versus those advocated by Dingell and Broyhill, the
bill, now titled H.R.6161, came to the floor for
debate on May 24. The PSD provisions were opened for
debate and amendment the next day, and at this time
the PSD supporters suffered their most significant
floor defeat.

It came in the form of an amendment offered by
John Breaux of Louisiana which was similar in some
respects to the McKay amendment approved the
previous year, but was broader in that it 1) applied
to both particulate matter and SO_2 and 2) allowed
variances for up to 5% of the time (18 days) for
sources affecting either Class I or Class II areas.
Breaux specifically cited the Intermountain Power
Project in Utah as a reason why his amendment was
needed. Rogers attempted to sidetrack Breaux's
amendment by getting Representative McKay to offer,

as a substitute, a slightly different version of his previous amendment authorizing a more restricted variance. Breaux and his supporters, however, denounced the "McKay substitute" as a "halfway measure" that would "not help anybody," and in a roll call vote successfully defeated the McKay substitute 170-235. The Breaux amendment then passed by the almost identical vote of 237-172.[205]

The House managers escaped without further amendments to the PSD provisions of the bill. In addition to losing on Breaux, however, they also lost by an even more overwhelming margin of 255-139 on Dingell-Broyhill. Thus, the bill which finally passed the House in 1977 appeared to justify the hopes of those who had held out against the conference report in 1976. Ironically, under the new "environmentalist" Administration, PSD's advocates had been less successful in gaining a legislative victory than they had been the previous year.[206]

Things would go somewhat differently in the Senate where debate on S.252 opened on June 8. Senator Muskie warned industry lobbyists against any attempts to separate the auto standards provisions from the rest of the bill, however, saying (again!) that "no more quick fixes would be forthcoming."[207] Although there was extensive debate about PSD, it seemed half-hearted compared to the passion of 1976, and the most heated debate was reserved for the question of automobile emissions standards. Only two points of debate about the PSD provisions had any significance: the Stevens amendment concerning variances, and the Jackson amendment on "commence construction."

The Stevens amendment would have allowed a 5% variance from the Class I and II short term (3-hour and 24-hour) increments, and was the same as the Breaux amendment adopted earlier in the House. Senator Muskie and the other committee Senators argued strongly against it as unnecessary, and with the assistance of strongly worded letters from President Carter and EPA Administrator Costle were able to defeat it by a vote of 61 to 33.[208] A later attempt by Senator Wallop to include a more limited

version of the same variance was also defeated,
prompting Senator Stevens of Alaska to threaten to
filibuster the conference report.[209]

Another proposed amendment to the PSD was
successful, however. This provision, offered by
Senator Jackson of Washington, was presented as a
"technical amendment" to the definition of "commence
construction." Though Senator Jackson's explanation
was oblique, the purpose of the amendment was to
assist the Montana Power Company in its attempt to
demonstrate that it had "commenced construction"
prior to the effective date of the PSD regulations
and would not need to undergo PSD review for a large
power plant at Colstrip, Montana. This was the same
power plant which the Cheyenne Indians were trying
to block by reclassifying their land as Class I.[210]
Muskie and Stafford, after a brief colloquy in the
middle of a discussion on the Metzenbaum amendment
of the use of local coal, accepted the amendment and
it was agreed to on a voice vote.[211] However, this
amendment did not escape the notice of Senator Hatch
of Utah, who challenged Muskie on why Senator
Jackson was able to get a "special consideration"
for _his_ plant (the Montana plant would provide
electricity to Washington State, among other
places), but the proposed Utah plants could not get
one. Trapped, Muskie tried to bluster his way out,
arguing that "as the Senator will learn when he has
been here long enough, there is no magic way to
write legislative language that is so precise that
it anticipates every potential inequity or every
potential unusual situation." Hatch persisted,
asking Muskie why _his_ special projects could not get
"consideration." The verbal duel ended with a final
sarcastic barb from Hatch, who questioned why "if .
. . significant deterioration does not constrain
development, then why did we need this significant
technical amendment which now opens up development
and significant deterioration for special interests
out in one area.[212]

With that, the Senate proceeded to pass the bill
on June 10, thus setting up a repeat performance of
the 1976 conference. It was a repeat in more ways
than one; the conferees were working against yet

another deadline of August 5 for adjournment. By
this time, the auto industry, which was poised to
begin its 1978 model run and needed the relief
granted by the amendments for the cars to be legal,
was threatening massive plant shutdowns and layoffs
if no bill was passed. Despite their personal
feelings toward the auto industry, neither Muskie
nor Rogers had any desire to appear responsible for
such a result, nor did Muskie wish to trigger a
repeat performance of the 1976 filibuster.
Nonetheless, despite these substantial pressures for
compromise, the conferees did not convene until July
18.[213] Once again, the key controversies were not
resolved until the last minute, as the conferees
agreed upon an eleventh hour compromise bill at 2:20
a.m. on August 3.[214]

The outlines of the 1977 conference report
remained the same as the 1976 conference report, and
much of the 1977 legislative and conference report
language was taken verbatim from 1976. Three
classes were once again adopted. The increments,
with the insignificant exception of a 1 ug/m^3
increase in the annual Class II particulate matter
increment, were identical. The Senate permit
requirements, including BACT, were accepted once
again, along with the House monitoring requirements
and the Senate description of procedures for
resolving disputes between States and Federal Land
Managers. The conference definitions of major
emitting facility, baseline, and BACT all remained
the same as in 1976.[215]

Nevertheless, there were a number of changes
from 1976 to 1977 which, though seemingly technical,
reflected a continuing desire to "fine-tune" the
statute to accommodate groups with particular
concerns about the bill. The Breaux amendment was
only the most visible of a number of such changes
made by the conferees the second time around.

o   While the conferees did not reject the Breaux
     amendment entirely, the Senate conferees were
     successful in restricting it substantially in
     several ways. First, they limited its
     application to Class I areas only. Second, the

variance was restricted to SO_2 only; no variance
was allowed for particulate matter. Third, the
conferees differentiated between the variance
allowed for "low-terrain" and "high-terrain"
areas. New 3-hour and 24-hour SO_2 increment
values were assigned for each of these cases;
the origin of these numbers is not clear.
Fourth, the variance could be applied only if a)
the Federal Land Manager agreed with the
recommendation, or b) if his disagreement was
overruled by the President. This precise form
of the variance provision was apparently the
subject of a great deal of last-minute decision-
making by the conferees, with the big issue
being whether a variance should be established
for the Class II increments. Thus, after more
than two years of Congressional consideration,
PSD's final shape was decided in a debate among
the House conferees over which Senate offer to
accept; one with the 1976 conference increments,
Class III and a Class I Breaux variance; or one
with only two classes, both with a variance.[216]

o   The conferees changed the effective date of the
     new conditions for permits from June 1, 1975 to
     the date of enactment of legislation.
     Interestingly, this change was not noted in the
     report language. However, it would later
     contribute to confusion over just what effective
     date the conference had intended, as the
     conference also retained, from the 1976
     conference and House bills, the sections which
     appeared to leave EPA's regulations in place
     until PSD SIP revisions were approved.[217]

o   The conferees adopted new language which tracked
     a Senate change concerning Indian lands. On its
     face, the provision appeared to give Indian
     tribes greater authority to redesignate their
     own lands, though a carefully worded proviso was
     added giving States the right to object and
     trigger a dispute resolution procedure that
     would ultimately wind up in the hands of the EPA
     Administrator. This proviso, along with the

special treatment of the Cheyenne Indian
reservation in Montana--the only area designated
Class I prior to enactment--seemed to favor
Indian interests. However, the conference bill
also included a modified form of the Senate's
Jackson amendment, thus trying to satisfy two
competing groups at the same time.[218]

o   Language added by the House which put additional
procedural requirements on States which
redesignated land over the objections of an FLM
was included by the conferees. This only added
to the net effect of a bill whose provisions
appeared to give less autonomy to the States
than the goals reflected in the language of both
the House and Senate report and articulated in
floor debate by both Senator Muskie and
Congressman Rogers.[219]

o   An additional exclusion in the House bill from
increment consumption for facilities located
outside the U.S. was also added. What made this
necessary was the continuing belief of the House
that the increments represented real, measurable
air quality changes and were not just modeling
exercises. Otherwise the amendment was
unnecessary, since this problem could be handled
simply by excluding such facilities from any
modeling. While understandable, the amendment
added complexity and another exception to the
PSD provisions.[220]

o   Finally, the conference added the House
provision on visibility with some
modifications.[221]

Exhausted from marathon late night negotiations,
Muskie and Rogers presented the new conference bill
to their respective Houses. To the end, PSD
remained the principal subject of debate.
Supporters in both Houses praised the conference
report, while opponents consoled themselves with the
addition of the partial Breaux amendment variance
and the retention of Class III from the 1976

conference bill. In the Senate, Senator Garn
pronounced that the bill was "as good a compromise
as we could hope to get under the circumstances,"
and while it remained "a bad bill, and one which I
think the country will live to regret," it was
nevertheless "considerably better" than earlier
versions.[222] In the House, PSD's opponents
emphasized the increase in the Class II increments
from the House to the conference bill, and commended
Congressman Breaux for his "effective"
presentation.[223] With that, the Clean Air Act
Amendments of 1977 were passed by both the House and
the Senate on voice votes, thus ending the two and a
half year struggle by Congress to, in the ironic
words of the Senate report, "clarify and resolve
this issue through legislation, rather than leave
this issue to the courts."[224] President Carter
signed H.R.6161 into law on August 7, 1977.[225]

PSD: Congressional Success or Failure?

The Congressional debate over PSD was certainly
the antithesis of traditional "New Deal"
legislating, where broad problems were identified
and remedies outlined which included substantial
grants of discretionary authority to the Executive
Branch. Indeed, while the rhetoric surrounding PSD
made it seem as if Congress meant to take
discretionary authority away from the Executive
Branch and grant it to State and local governments,
it appears from the behavior of key Congressional
leaders that they not only believed that PSD should
exist, but that it should exist in a particular form
whose most exacting details were to be decided by
the Congress.
Unfortunately, the two Houses of Congress did
not share the same view of what "the details" should
be. As a result, both the Senate and House
committees pursued their own particular versions of

PSD, versions which though superficially resembling
the regulations promulgated by EPA were in fact
wholly new programs. Nor were they simply
"different"; both of the proposals drafted by the
responsible House and Senate committees were more
stringent than the regulations promulgated by EPA in
almost every respect. In order to preserve this
stringency, both Muskie and Rogers adopted the
strategy of accepting minor amendments in order to
build alliances which would prove necessary in
defending the greater challenges to PSD's existence
mounted by those in the Congress and the
Administration who saw PSD as a threat to national
energy independence if not to the even more
fundamental value of economic growth.

The fact that the committee proposals were more
stringent than EPA's regulations meant that Muskie
and Rogers had to use this tactic frequently when
confronted with Congressmen who would take the time
to become educated on some aspect of PSD or who
learned of some particular impact of PSD on their
district. However, what is key for our purposes is
the specificity with which both the Muskie and
Rogers committees chose to frame these more
stringent proposals. Neither committee was content
to adopt the technical definitions developed by EPA
for such concepts as "major emitting facility",
"commence construction", "baseline air quality", or
"best available control technology", but instead
made revisions to these definitions the cornerstones
of their proposals.

A consequence of this approach was that it was
difficult to tell precisely what the committees had
done. This ambiguity worked to the advantage of the
Muskie and Rogers committees, in that it enabled
them to characterize changes proposed by themselves
or others as major or minor, desireable or
undesirable, with little fear of contradiction.
However, when the time came for the provisions in
the House and Senate bills to be reconciled in
conference, the specificity of the bills created
both problems and opportunities for policy
entrepreneurs when particular provisions, taken out
of the context in which they were created, had to be

blended with others to make a whole bill. The issue
of whether the requirements of the new Act were
effective immediately or only after States submitted
SIP revisions is one example of this. Perhaps the
most striking instance is the combination of the
House and Senate definitions of major emitting
facility and major stationary source to create a PSD
program which would apply BACT (a Senate concept) to
the larger universe of sources captured in the House
bill.

Another remarkable aspect of the House bill in
particular was the frequency with which it sought to
take on highly technical issues such as the
appropriate size of the increments and how increment
consumption was to be calculated. Where the Senate
had relied on EPA's estimates for appropriate
increment values for Class I and Class II, the House
committee chose to adopt a completely different
logic for calculating these numbers--a logic which
made little sense to air pollution professionals and
created increment values which were even more
arbitrary than EPA's in terms of their effect on
source construction. Despite this, Rogers was never
challenged on this point in the House, and many of
the House increments were incorporated in the final
amendments through compromises in the conference
with the Senate.

Another requirement added by the House which
made little sense to air pollution professionals was
the monitoring requirement. Such a requirement had
earlier been rejected by EPA's staff as unnecessary,
very expensive and unworkable, yet the House
included it because of a misconception of how
increment consumption could be calculated. Yet at
the same time that detailed requirements such as
these were being added to the bill, the committees
somehow managed to overlook the answers to such
basic questions as whether "potential to emit" (a
concept created by the Congress) referred to
emissions before or after the application of
pollution control equipment, thus leaving open a
dispute which would make an order of magnitude
difference in the number of sources to be regulated
under PSD.

A final area where Congressional intervention
had precisely the opposite effect from its stated
intentions was in the reclassification of areas by
States. After much internal debate, EPA had
established a reclassification system which, while
giving substantial authority to Federal Land
Managers for the classification of Federal lands,
was nevertheless relatively simple and allowed
States to make decisions about allowable air
pollution subject to only token procedural oversight
by the Federal government. Despite their rhetoric
about increased State flexibility, however, both the
Senate and the House created substantially higher
procedural hurdles for States which wanted to
reclassify their lands. These new hurdles ranged
from the designation of mandatory Class I and II
areas, to the requirement that EPA review the BACT
determinations for any area to be redesignated Class
III, to the additional consultation, analysis and
public hearing requirements in the new Section 164
which any redesignation request would have to
satisfy. Moreover, even having a Class III was a
hollow victory to those concerned about the effects
of PSD on electric utility construction, since the
key SO_2 increments in Class III were the old EPA
Class II increments which the Senate had adopted.
Finally, while narrow Class I and high terrain
variances did get adopted in the final bill, these
were special exemptions, the need for which would
have to be demonstrated in a long and complex
administrative process.

All in all, then, Congress ended up in 1977 with
something less than what might have been hoped for
when the legislative debate opened in 1975. PSD's
supporters, bolstered by the existence of EPA's
regulations and aided by technical support from EPA,
an overzealous industry lobbying campaign which
damaged the credibility of PSD's opponents, and
skilled Congressional advocates in Muskie and
Rogers, were able to make substantial additions to
PSD's scope and coverage. This was true especially
in conference, where advocates were able to combine
the most stringent features of both bills. However,
to do this these advocates had to accept seemingly

marginal changes and exceptions to preserve the
objective of a stringent statutorily mandated PSD
program. The price of accepting such changes was
that PSD became extremely complicated as PSD's
opponents, recognizing their inability to win a
direct confrontation, probed to see how far they
could go with "technical" changes to mitigate PSD's
effects in particular areas. Moreover, the growing
complexity of the program added to the influence of
the relatively few Congressmen and staff who truly
understood where the sensitive areas of the
legislation were. These were the real authors of
the PSD portion of the 1977 Amendments, and its
passage testifies to their skill and persistence.

However, if the objectives of PSD's advocates
included clarity, certainty, and a decline in the
amount of dispute over who had to do what to prevent
significant deterioration, these advocates were to
be sorely disappointed over the next three years.
PSD's legislative victory led to three more years of
EPA rulemaking, more courtroom litigation, and yet
another round of rulemaking. The 1977 Amendments
did not close the book on PSD, but merely set the
stage for the next round of disputes. These will be
described in the next chapter.

NOTES

1. U.S. Congress, Senate, Committee on Public Works, <u>Implementation of the Clean Air Act--1975, Hearings before the Subcommittee on Environmental Pollution of the Committee on Public Works</u>, 94th Cong., 1st sess., 1975, p. 132. (Hereafter cited as <u>1975 Senate Oversight Hearings</u>.)

2. Statement of C. Howard Hardesty, President, Eastern Hemisphere Petroleum Division, Continental Oil Co. and chairman of the American Petroleum Institute's Environmental Affairs Committee, <u>1975 Senate Oversight Hearings</u>, p. 867.

3. Prepared Statement of Frank Zarb, FEA Administrator, <u>1975 Senate Oversight Hearings</u>, p. 340. Zarb did not get to deliver this portion of the statement in his verbal testimony, because a major controversy erupted over a study which FEA had commissioned, independent of EPA, about the health basis of EPA's standards. Zarb was attacked by Senator Muskie and other committee members about this study, and spent a good bit of his time defending himself. In addition, Muskie pushed hard on Zarb to affirm that the EPA-FEA "compromise" on the "temporary" use of ICS for power plants would in fact envision the use of permanent controls on such plants after 1985. See <u>ibid</u>., pp. 285-313.

4. Fourteen suits against EPA's regulations were filed in six circuits following EPA's issuance of final regulations in December, 1974. In June, 1975 these suits were consolidated in the D.C. Circuit, where the litigation became known as the <u>Dayton Power and Light, et al., vs.EPA</u>. The consolidation of the suits in the D.C. Circuit was desired by both EPA and the Sierra Club; utilities had hoped that review could be conducted in other circuits which were

considered less sympathetic to the
environmentalists' arguments. 5 <u>Environment
Reporter</u> 358; on the D.C. Circuit, see Melnick,
<u>Regulation and the Courts</u>, pp. 362-65.

5.   Statement of Russell Train, <u>1975 Senate
Oversight Hearings</u>, p. 151.

6.   See Chapter 1 above; Melnick, <u>Regulation and the
Courts</u>, pp. 81-83; and U.S. Congress, House,
<u>Clean Air Act Amendments of 1977</u>, H.Rept. 95-294
to Accompany H.R.6161, 95th Congress, 1st sess.,
pp. 105-141, reprinted in U.S. Congress, Senate,
Committee on Environment and Public Works, <u>A
Legislative History of the Clean Air Act
Amendments of 1977</u>, Committee Print, 95th
Congress, 2nd sess., vol. 4. (Report hereafter
cited as <u>1977 House Report</u>; the Legislative
History will be cited as <u>1977 Legislative
History</u>.)

7.   For a summary of the issues of concern in the
Act amendments, see Robert E. Trumble et al., "A
Summary of Clean Air Act Oversight Hearings,"
reprinted in <u>1975 Senate Oversight Hearings</u>, pp.
1-130.

8.   See the statements and supplementary material of
William Lalor, Ben Fuqua, Thomas Steele,
Nathaniel Hughes, and Richard B. Waite, all
representing different groups of electric
utilities in U.S. Congress, House, Committee on
Interstate and Foreign Commerce, <u>Clean Air Act
Amendments--1975, Hearings Before the
Subcommittee on Health and the Environment of
the Committee on Interstate and Foreign
Commerce</u>, 94th Cong., 1st sess., pp. 744-822.
(Hereafter referred to as <u>1975 House Amendment
Hearings</u>.) These same sentiments were expressed
by utility groups in the <u>1975 Senate Oversight
Hearings</u>, for example in the statements of J. D.
Grist, pp. 862-66.

9.   Statements of David Swan, American Mining
     Congress and Robert Price, National Coal
     Association, 1975 House Amendment Hearings, pp.
     822-46; 887-93.

10. Statements of C. Howard Hardesty, Continental
     Oil Company (testifying for API), 1975 Senate
     Oversight Hearings, pp. 866-70; 1005-16;
     Statement of P. M. Gammelgard, American
     Petroleum Institute, 1975 House Amendment
     Hearings, pp. 638-39.

11. Statement for the Record, American Iron and
     Steel Institute, 1975 Senate Oversight Hearings,
     pp. 1631-36; Statements of Frederick G. Jaicks,
     Chairman, American Iron and Steel Institute,
     1975 House Amendment Hearings, pp. 678, 683-84.

12. See the statement of J. William Haun, National
     Association of Manufacturers, 1975 House
     Amendment Hearings, pp. 999-1001; 1007-8;
     Statement of Louis Welch, President, Houston
     Chamber of Commerce, speaking on behalf of the
     U.S. Chamber of Commerce; ibid., pp. 1022-23.
     Many other examples of such statements occur
     throughout the record of both the House and
     Senate 1975 hearings.

13. For a description of the utility studies, see
     1975 Senate Oversight Hearings, pp. 1445-58.
     EPA's information exchanges with industry are
     catalogued in pp. 1455-58 and 1469-80.

14. Ibid. Apparently considerable friction occurred
     in the review of EPA's research data regarding
     sulfates. The record contains an exchange of
     letters in which the industry consultants
     complain about EPA's lack of cooperation in
     providing requested data. This sparring
     foreshadowed a major and heated public attack on
     the integrity of some of this data and the EPA
     scientists who provided it in the spring of
     1976.

15. <u>1975 Senate Oversight Hearings</u>, pp. 853-54.

16. Ibid., pp. 886-96.

17. <u>1975 House Amendment Hearings</u>, p. 41.

18. Ibid., pp. 121-22.

19. Ibid., pp. 1181-82.

20. <u>1975 Senate Oversight Hearings</u>, pp. 151-52
     (prepared statement); p. 156 (verbal statement).
     The day after Train testified before the Senate
     subcommittee, he reappeared as part of a panel
     with FEA Administrator Frank Zarb and Interior
     Secretary Rogers Morton. Both Morton and Zarb's
     prepared testimony contained statements sharply
     critical of PSD, and this hearing could have
     provoked a major confrontation. However, Muskie
     deftly sidetracked the hearing by attacking Zarb
     for presenting an FEA report critical of EPA's
     data on the health effects of sulfates when EPA
     had not been given the report to review (see
     note 3 above). See ibid., pp. 285-304.
     The delicacy of the EPA-FEA sparring over PSD
     amendments and the "Administration's position
     can be seen in EPA's comment to FEA's
     Environmental Impact Statement on the 1975
     Energy Independence Act proposals." See ibid.,
     pp. 46567. Senator Muskie insisted that the
     Committee see <u>each agency's</u> views (meaning EPA's
     views) on this statement, as well as the
     completed product (ibid., pp. 283-84).

21. Ruckelshaus in fact spoke out during this debate
     on behalf of industrial interests, taping a
     television interview on the subject for the
     Chamber of Commerce. See 6 <u>Environment
     Reporter</u> 1210 (October 31, 1975).

22. See the discussion in Melnick, <u>Regulation and
     the Courts</u>, p. 98.

23. Ibid., pp. 99-100. According to one participant in these debates, Train recognized the importance of this role and actively "permitted a working environment to develop in which EPA staff could work with committee staff" on the analysis of different proposals (Interview data). The importance of EPA's role as an "objective" expert can be seen in the attempts of the utility industry to gain at least implicit endorsement of their analysis. See, for example, the very detailed descriptions of the Electric Utility Industry Clean Air Coordinating Committee's efforts to "include EPA at every step of the way during the performance of our studies" in their "Preliminary Report," reprinted in <u>1975 Senate Oversight Hearings</u>, pp. 1427-28, 1455-58.

24. Quoted in Vietor, <u>Environmental Politics and the Coal Coalition</u>, p. 218.

25. Interview data.

26. 6 <u>Environment Reporter</u> 218 (June 20, 1975).

27. Some of these "other issues" included the dispute over who won the 1974 Senate election in New Hampshire. However, Muskie decided to attack the auto standard question before proceeding to deal with significant deterioration. Bernard Asbell, <u>The Senate Nobody Knows</u> (Garden City, N.Y.: Doubleday, 1978), reports on Muskie's activities during this period and gives a good description of the other things that were occurring while Muskie was trying to move the subcommittee through markup.

28. See the testimony of Cubia Clayton, <u>1975 Senate Oversight Hearings</u>, pp. 855-62. The <u>amicus</u> brief can be found on pp. 991-1004. Ironically, one of its signers was Robert Morgan, who in 1972 was Attorney General of North Carolina, but in 1975 was a new U.S. Senator and member of

Muskie's Subcommittee. Morgan, however, became one of the committee's skeptics about PSD.

Part of New Mexico's concern about PSD stemmed from their experience with the opening of the Four Corners power plant, a large five unit power plant located in New Mexico but near its common border with Arizona, Colorado and Utah. In Mr. Clayton's words,

We in New Mexico remember that the startup of the Four Corners power plant during the 1960's hit New Mexico and the Nation with shattering impact. The dense plume, which even then was not unusual for many areas of the country, became a symbol of the environmental indifference which had become characteristic of too much of our own way of life.

Prior to this time such things as a visibility of 80 miles had been accepted, I suspect, as possessing the immutability of the law of gravity. . . Only when it was gone did we realize how priceless it was. . . We see NSD as a tool which can help us in that job.(ibid, pp. 856-57)

29. 6 <u>Environment Reporter</u> 548 (August 1, 1975).

30. Ibid.

31. See the discussion on this point in Chapter 4.

32. See, for example, the comments of E. Allen Hunter, President of Utah Power and Light Company, <u>1975 Senate Oversight Hearings</u>, p. 1985.

33. 6 <u>Environment Reporter</u> 548-49 (August 1, 1976). Some perspective on these early committee debates may be seen in Bernard Asbell's "outsider" description of them as a "brain-buster." To Asbell, who mainly focuses his book on the NO_x standard for autos, subcommittee members found themselves trying to "avoid" nondegradation discussions as much as decide

them (<u>The Senate Nobody Knows</u>, p. 217). This, of course, is another example of Melnick's point that the complexity of the PSD issue gave enormous leverage to "insider" committee staff who could take the time to understand PSD's intricacies (<u>Regulation and the Courts</u>, p.100).

34. 6 <u>Environment Reporter</u> 697-98 (August 29, 1975).

35. I am indebted to Cheryl Wasserman of EPA for this nicely turned phrase.

36. Asbell, <u>The Senate Nobody Knows</u>, pp. 302-14, continues a detailed account of this encounter. Muskie was especially sensitive about this, as he was up for re-election in 1976 and at that time appeared to be facing a strong challenge from then-Rep. (now Senator) William Cohen. See also 6 <u>Environment Reporter</u> 810-12 (September 12, 1975).

    This incident is also a revealing illustration of the politics of information. Muskie on September 30 sent the API study over to EPA for evaluation. EPA responded on October 3 in a letter from Russell Train, saying that the report appeared to include "several errors of analytic judgment and calculation." Based on this letter, Muskie released a public statement saying that the report was "riddled with inaccuracies" (6 <u>Environment Reporter</u> 1015 [October 17, 1975]).

37. 6 <u>Environment Reporter</u> 806 (September 12, 1975).

38. 6 <u>Environment Reporter</u> 1009 (October 17, 1975); Asbell, <u>The Senate Nobody Knows</u>, pp. 311-14; 333-38.

39. 6 <u>Environment Reporter</u> 1229 (November 7, 1975).

40. Ibid., pp. 1230-31.

41. Ibid., p. 1231. Earlier versions of the Senate proposal would not have even limited PSD to 28

source categories, but only cited them as
examples while using the 100 TPY figure as the
test. However, this proved objectionable to
some committee members (e.g. Senator McClure),
and the committee agreed to a narrower approach
which was ultimately included in S.3219. See
1977 Legislative History, pp. 5261-66 (statement
by Senator McClure during Senate debate).

42.   Vietor, pp. 214-15; 6 Environment Reporter, pp.
       978-79.

43.   See Melnick, Regulation and the Courts, pp. 107-
       8.

44.   6 Environment Reporter 819 (September 12, 1975).
       The final bill reported by the subcommittee did
       contain a provision which allowed a State, for
       pollutants other than TSP and SO_2, to submit a
       PSD plan which would carry out PSD's purposes as
       effectively as an area classification plan.
       Still, the increments for other pollutants were
       clearly meant to have a stringent, action-
       forcing effect. See 6 Environment Reporter
       1202-3 (October 31, 1975).

45.   Reprinted from Environmental Protection Agency
       and Federal Energy Administration, An Analysis
       of the Impact on the Electric Utility Industry
       of Alternative Approaches to Significant
       Deterioration, October, 1975, vol. 1, p. 5.
       (Hereafter referred to as EPA-FEA Report).

46.   See discussion in Chapter 4. I have no evidence
       to suggest that the closeness of the House
       figure of 325 ug/m^3 to EPA's original number of
       300 ug/m^3 is anything other than coincidental.

47.   EPA-FEA Report, Vol. 1, pp. 4-8; 6 Environment
       Reporter 819 (September 12, 1975); 1977
       Legislative History, p. 5789.

48.   6 Environment Reporter 819 (September 12, 1975).

49. Interview data.

50. Both Muskie and Rogers faced pressure within
their own committees from first-term members
elected in the Democratic Watergate landslide of
1974 whose general orientation was to support
environmentalist views. In Muskie's committee,
this pressure was applied primarily by Senator
Gary Hart. Muskie welcomed this pressure as a
useful countervailing force to his more
industry-minded colleagues; however, given the
culture of the Senate and especially the Public
Works Committee, these disputes were generally
muted and subtle (Asbell, The Senate Nobody
Knows, pp. 377-78, quoting Muskie). Rogers
faced a larger group of so-called "Watergate
babies," with Henry Waxman of California a
leading figure in this group. However, Rogers
also faced strong partisan objections from the
Republicans on his subcommittee, led by James
Broyhill of North Carolina, which Muskie did not
have. Given that, it is not surprising that the
House Committee's deliberations were much
stormier than those in the Senate (Interview
data).

51. See note 50 above. Apparently at least some of
industry (despite the ambush of Muskie) decided
early that the Senate committee was largely a
lost cause, and that other than getting on the
record, their main lobbying efforts should be
concentrated in the House. See Asbell, The
Senate Nobody Knows, p. 368.

52. 6 Environment Reporter 978-79 (October 10,
1975). The provision on "grandfathering"
sources was to later become the source of
tremendous confusion. See Chapter 6 below.

53. 6 Environment Reporter 1009 (October 17, 1975).

54. Ibid., p. 980; interview data.

55. EPA-FEA Report, pp. 18-22.

56. Ibid., pp. 18-25.

57. 6 <u>Environment Reporter</u> 982 (October 10, 1975).

58. Ibid., p. 980. I can find no support for this charge. However, there were disgruntled PSD advocates in EPA who were not happy with the study's appearance, and the analysts responsible for the study in EPA were more "pro-energy" than those in the air programs office might have been.

59. Interview data.

60. 6 <u>Environment Reporter</u> 1009 (October 17, 1975).

61. Ackerman and Hassler, "Beyond the New Deal", pp. 1493-95.

62. 6 <u>Environment Reporter</u> 1260 (November 14, 1975).

63. Ibid., pp. 1260-61.

64. Ibid., p. 1261 (Strelow) and 6 <u>Environment Reporter</u> 1424 (Train).

65. See, for example, 6 <u>Environment Reporter</u> 1356 (December 5, 1975); and 1382-83 (December 12, 1975).

66. The other was Quentin Burdick of North Dakota.

67. 6 <u>Environment Reporter</u> 1582-83 (January 16, 1976).

68. Ibid., pp. 1583-84. The analysis noted that if a BAT requirement was adopted in either the House or the Senate, it would have virtually the same effect on the utility industry as PSD.

69. 6 <u>Environment Reporter</u> 1382-86 (December 19, 1975). The utilities assumed a <u>smaller</u> estimate for megawatt capacity requiring scrubbers,

between 28,000 and 45,000 (as compared to FEA's 95,000).

70. 6 Environment Reporter 1689-90 (January 30, 1976). Senator Gravel of Alaska proposed an amendment at this time modifying PSD in the direction of the House proposal, with a tertiary standard cap. His proposal did not apparently include, however, the House Class I and II increments which were the most restrictive. Gravel's concern was that the Senate bill would preclude Alaskan development by classifying as much as 95 million acres--one-fourth of Alaska-- as Class I. On the "buffer zone" claim, see 1977 Legislative History, vol. 6, p. 4727.

71. The Committee Report can be found in 1977 Legislative History, pp. 4703-96. The individual views are contained in pp. 4797-4835. Senators Montoya, Gravel, Domenici, McClure, and Hart all comment on PSD in their views; Hart claimed it should be more stringent with respect to Federal lands, while the others all expressed some concern about its stringency and the need for a better balance between development and environmental quality.
     See also 6 Environment Reporter 1753 (February 13, 1976), and Asbell, The Senate Nobody Knows, pp. 392-95.

72. 6 Environment Reporter 1817 (February 27, 1976). Compare H.R.10498 as submitted by Chairman Rogers after subcommittee markup with H.R.10498 as reported by the Commerce Committee, 1977 Legislative History, p. 5782 and pp. 5784-85 vs. pp. 5937 and pp. 5940-44. In addition to the change for mandatory Class I areas, the Committee also increased the minimum size for areas which could be reclassified as Class I or II from 1000 to 10,000 acres.

73. H.R.10498 as reported by the House Committee on Interstate and Foreign Commerce, 1977 Legislative History, pp.5496-98.

74. 39 <u>Federal Register</u> 42514-15.

75. A close reading of the regulation shows some of
     the results of the tension described in Chapters
     3 and 4. The regulation states that an
     individual source, in addition to calculating
     its own input on increments, had to figure out
     the effects of all other sources increases and
     decreases, including "general commercial,
     residential, industrial and other sources of
     emissions growth not included in the definition
     of baseline air quality . . ." (36 <u>Federal
     Register</u> 42516). This provision in EPA's
     regulations was insignificant because EPA's
     regulations were limited to only 18 large source
     categories, dominated by power plants, and
     covered only two pollutants which were generally
     little affected by area source growth.

76. In this report, the Senate Committee rejected
     that portion of EPA's rules which would have
     attempted to make major sources calculate the
     impact on PSD of minor source growth. See the
     Senate Report on S.3219, <u>1977 Legislative
     History</u>, pp. 4781-82.

77. <u>1977 Legislative History</u>; compare H.R.10498 at
     p. 5783 with pp. 5938-39.

78. Ibid., pp. 5948-49.

79. "Federal Energy Administration Proposed Clean
     Air Act Position Paper Prepared for Energy
     Resource Council Meeting, January 21, 1976."
     Reprinted in 6 <u>Environment Reporter</u> 1713-15
     (January 30, 1976).

80. Ibid.

81. 6 <u>Environment Reporter</u> 1939 (March 19, 1976).

82. 6 <u>Environment Reporter</u> 1987 (March 26, 1976).

83. 6 <u>Environment Reporter</u> 2072 (April 9, 1976).

84. U.S. Congress, Senate, Committee on Public
     Works, <u>Clean Air Amendments of 1976</u>. Report of
     the Committee on Public Works, S.Rept. 94-717 to
     accompany S.3219, 94th Congress, 2nd session,
     pp. 22, 25. Reprinted in <u>1977 Legislative
     History</u>, pp. 4701-4928. (Hereafter referred to
     as <u>1976 Senate Report</u>).

85. Ibid., pp. 23, 27.

86. Ibid., p. 20.

87. U.S. Congress, Senate, A Bill to amend the Clean
     Air Act, as amended, S.3219, 94th Congress, 2nd
     sess., 1976, pp. 11-20.

88. U.S. House of Representatives, <u>Clean Air Act
     Amendments of 1976</u>, Report of the Committee on
     Interstate and Foreign Commerce to accompany
     H.R.10498, pp. 82-116. (Hereafter cited as <u>1976
     House Report</u>).

89. U.S. House of Representatives, <u>A Bill to amend
     the Clean Air Act, and for other purposes</u>,
     H.R.10498, 94th Congress, 2nd sess., 1976, pp.
     198-216.

90. See <u>1976 House Report</u>, pp. 137-39; 156-66. This
     point is fully discussed in Ackerman and
     Hassler, "Beyond the New Deal," pp. 1493-1502.

91. H.R.10498, p. 207. There is little evidence in
     the written record that the impracticality of
     this provision was brought up in any focused
     way. See the earlier discussion in Chapter 4 on
     this point. When asked about the reason for
     this requirement, one of the House staffers
     involved in the drafting of the provision said
     that it was generally put in to prod EPA to
     collect better ambient monitoring data than was
     then available. (Interview data)

92. Asbell, <u>The Senate Nobody Knows</u>, p. 395.

93. Ibid., pp. 398-99.

94. For a summary of the Kaiparowits story, see
    <u>ibid</u>., pp.398-99; Vietor, <u>Environmental
    Politics</u>, pp. 219-20, and 6 <u>Environment Reporter</u>
    2116 (April 16, 1976). For an example of some
    of the other utility developments being planned
    for Utah, see the statement of E. Allan Hunter,
    President of Utah Power and Light Company, <u>1975
    Senate Oversight Hearings</u>, pp. 1978-88. This
    subject was to be covered more fully in the 1977
    Senate hearings on the proposed amendments. See
    the statements of Mr. Hunter and Joseph Fackrell
    in U.S. Congress, Senate, Committee on
    Environment and Public Works, <u>Hearings Before
    the Subcommittee on Environmental Pollution of
    the Committee on Environment and Public Works</u>,
    95th Cong., 1st sess., 1977, pp. 36-43 and 334-
    410 (hereafter cited as <u>1977 Senate Hearings</u>).

95. <u>1977 Legislative History</u>, pp. 5639-59 (statement
    by Senator Moss and proposed amendments). It
    appears from the plain language of these
    amendments that they would <u>not</u> have had any
    effect on EPA's existing rules for PSD. See
    also 6 <u>Environment Reporter</u> 2109-10 (April 16,
    1973).

96. 6 <u>Environment Reporter</u> 2138-39 (April 23, 1976).
    EPA, reflecting its alignment with the Muskie
    Committee, recommended a meeting with Senator
    Baker prior to any decision.

97. These exchanges are described in Asbell, <u>The
    Senate Nobody Knows</u>, pp. 408-10, and can be
    found in <u>1977 Legislative History</u>, pp. 4519-39,
    4545-51; 4583-4601, 5639-44, 5675-66. One, on
    June 16 (pp. 4556-81), shows Senator Muskie's
    continuing concern about the attack by the
    American Paper Institute; it contains a study by
    EPA which purports to show that new pulp and
    paper mills would not be constrained by PSD.

98.   1977 Legislative History, pp. 4520-21.

99.   7 Environment Reporter 5-6 (May 7, 1976).

100. Ibid., p. 4533. Asbell, The Senate Nobody Knows, p. 409.

101. 1977 Legislative History, pp. 4536-38.

102. Vietor, Environmental Politics, p. 218.

103. In defending the Committee proposal, Muskie again and again cited EPA studies to refute the charge by Moss the PSD had not received sufficient review. See 1977 Legislative History, for example, pp. 4523, 4526-32, 4546-48, and repeatedly in Senator Muskie's comments during Senate debate.

104. Melnick, Regulation and the Courts, p. 99.

105. 1977 Legislative History, pp. 5701-2.

106. 7 Environment Reporter 195-96 (June 4, 1976).

107. 7 Environment Reporter 223-24 (June 11, 1976).

108. Ibid.

109. 7 Environment Reporter 387 (July 2, 1976).

110. 7 Environment Reporter 497 (July 23, 1976).

111. 7 Environment Reporter 532 (July 30, 1976).

112. Ibid., p. 533.

113. Ibid.

114. Ibid., pp. 532-33. Upon learning of this, Senator Baker reportedly withdrew the statement which he had already submitted to the Congressional Record.

115. Ibid.

116. See, for example, the comments of Senator Buckley in debate on July 26 (1977 Legislative History, pp. 4950-53).

117. Ibid, pp. 4970-71 (comments of Senator Gary Hart).

118. Ibid., pp. 4980-81 (comments of Senator Muskie).

119. Ibid., pp. 4978-79; 4983 (comments of Senator Muskie).

120. Ibid., p. 4987 (comments of Senator Muskie).

121. The vehemence of the debate and lobbying over PSD can be seen in an editorial published by the Wall Street Journal on July 26, the day the debate opened. The editorial, entitled "Senator Muskie's No-Growth Bill," derisively condemned PSD and urged the Senate to adopt the Moss Amendment or strike PSD altogether. It claimed that "whatever happens to the air, the Muskie proposal can certainly bring about 'a significant deterioration in local economies'" (reprinted in ibid., pp. 5070-71). Muskie attacked in turn by observing that "I have read in the public press and elsewhere more misinformation and more distortion of what the committee bill does on the question of nondegradation than on almost any other legislative issue I have ever been exposed to" (ibid., p. 5051).

122. Ibid., p. 5048.

123. Ibid., 5269. See also Asbell, The Senate Nobody Knows, pp. 424-25. Unanimous consent was important, of course, under Senate rules in order for an agreement to be reached to limit debate and allow the bill to come to a vote.

This was the reason why Moss' threat of
"extensive remarks" was so serious.

124.   Asbell, <u>The Senate Nobody Knows</u>, p. 427; Vietor,
       <u>Environment Politics</u>, p. 219. The Scott
       amendment, which was equivalent to the
       Administration's original proposal to delete PSD
       from the Act entirely, failed by an even more
       overwhelming vote of 17 to 74 (<u>1977 Legislative
       History</u>, p. 5328).

125.   <u>1977 Legislative History</u>, p. 5340.

126.   Ibid., p. 5336.

127.   Ibid., p. 5346.

128.   Ibid., p. 5361.

129.   Ibid., p. 5360.

130.   Ibid., p. 5362. What is perhaps most
       interesting about these comments is that so many
       of them were made by Eastern Senators. While it
       was not discussed very explicitly in the debate,
       it is reasonable to expect that while some of
       the Western supporters of PSD saw the program as
       a means of preserving scenic Western vistas,
       some of the Eastern supporters of PSD saw it as
       a means of requiring similar air pollution
       controls on new sources in Western clean air
       areas as would be required in Eastern "dirty
       air" areas. Seen in this light, Eastern
       Senators, even those normally skeptical of
       government intervention in business, could
       support PSD on the grounds of equity in matters
       pertaining to economic growth and the cost of
       required environmental controls. This helps to
       explain why Senators like Senator Taft of Ohio
       would support PSD. This argument about the
       relationship between pollution control, economic
       growth, and equity is a later echo of the
       earlier debate, discussed in Chapter 2, between

advocates of emissions standards and air quality standards approaches.

131. Ibid., p. 5333.

132. In addition to the earlier discussion on the abortive July White House initiative, see ibid., p. 5214 (May 3, 1976 letter from Interior Secretary Kleppe to Senator Moss, stating in part, "But we should be attuned to the need for adjustment and flexibility, and in this regard, I commend the EPA regulations, or something like them, to the Senate, as it prepares to pass a bill.")

133. Ibid., pp. 5230-32.

134. 7 Environment Reporter 572 (August 6, 1976). Some attorneys involved in the case speculated at the time of the decision that the delays in taking up PSD in Congress had stimulated the surprising action by the D.C. Circuit, which had been widely expected to withhold a decision in the case until after Congress had concluded its deliberations. One major blow to industry was that the court showed absolutely no willingness to review the correctness of Judge Pratt's original decision that significant deterioration was required in the 1970 Act. See also Asbell, The Senate Nobody Knows, p. 426.

   The Court's decision is reprinted in U.S. Senate, Committee on Environment and Public Works, Clean Air Act Amendments of 1977: Hearings Before the Subcommittee on Environmental Pollution of the Committee on Environment and Public Works on S.251, S.252, and S.253, 95th Congress, 1st sess., 1977, pp. 747-800.

   Shep Melnick reaches a similar conclusion about the effect of this decision. See Regulation and the Courts, pp. 96, 98.

135. 1977 Legislative History, p. 5405.

136. Ibid., p. 5406.

137. Ibid., p. 5407.

138. Ibid., pp. 5411-13. The roll call vote is on pp. 5428-29.

139. In another example, an amendment by Senator Hatfield to add certain national monuments to the list of mandatory Class I areas also failed by a vote of 35 to 56. Gary Hart was the lone committee supporter (ibid, pp. 5413-29).

140. 7 Environment Reporter 536 (July 30, 1976).

141. See 7 Environment Reporter 599-600 (August 13, 1976); also William Chapman's comments in Asbell, The Senate Nobody Knows, pp. 368, 429-30. Chapman was a GM lobbyist. Both supporters and opponents of the Committee-sponsored measure chafed at the delay, which one committee staffer attributed to a "completely unresponsive" House leadership.

142. 1977 Legislative History, pp. 6146, 6154-61, 6164-83, 6189-92.

143. Ibid., pp. 6197-98; 7141 (text of proposed Waxman-Maguire amendment).

144. 7 Environment Reporter 723 (September 10, 1976).

145. 1977 Legislative History, pp. 6268-6318 (debate on both Waxman-Maguire and Chappell amendments).

146. See ibid., pp. 6333-35 (Maguire amendment giving FLM's greater authority); pp. 6346-47 (Satterfield amendment giving redesignation authority solely to the Governor); pp. 6355-56 (Maguire amendment on Federal review of "arbitrary and capricious" redesignations); pp. 6356-60 (Broyhill amendment limiting PSD to only sulfur oxides and particulate matter); pp. 6356-60 (Broyhill amendment limiting PSD to only

sulfur oxides and particulate matter); and pp.
6366-70 (Carter amendment eliminating the 90% of
standards ceiling). Two minor amendments were
accepted, both by Congressman Broyhill. One
draft with the ceilings to be set for pollutants
other than SO_2 or particulate matter, the other
dealt with allowing one exceedance per year for
sources where the short-term average NAAQS was
the limiting concentration. This latter
amendment made the House bill consistent with
the practice used by EPA in defining when an
area had exceeded the short-term ambient
standards. The Broyhill "ceiling" amendment was
designed to protect against further ratcheting
down in the event EPA later made the ambient
standards more stringent. One can assume that
industry pushed for these amendments to provide
additional protection in the event the House
bill passed. Rogers' acceptance of them can be
seen as yet another example of his interest in
accommodating individual revisions while
preserving his bill's integrity.

Of course, the time involved in discussing
these points, whether intentionally or not,
certainly furthered the interest of those
seeking to delay action on this bill, all the
more so because opponents demanded roll call
votes on almost every issue.

147.   Ibid., p. 6328.

148.   Ibid., p. 5935.

149.   Ibid., p. 6330.

150.   Ibid., p. 6332.

151.   Ibid., p. 6333.

152.   Ibid., pp. 6360-61.

153.   Ibid., pp. 6363-64 (see comments of Mr. Carter,
Mrs. Fenwick, and Mr. McKay).

154. Ibid., p. 6364.

155. Ibid., p. 6454.

156. Ibid., p. 6537.

157. 7 Environment Reporter 893 (October 15, 1976);
     Asbell, The Senate Nobody Knows, pp. 431-32.

158. And public. The conference, as were the
     committee markups, was open to the public. The
     conference was so popular that large numbers of
     interested parties could not get into the room.
     See Asbell, The Senate Nobody Knows, pp. 431-39.

159. 1977 Legislative History, p. 4721.

160. Table values derived from H.R.10498, S.3271, and
     H.Rept.94-1742, Clean Air Act Amendments of
     1976, found in 1977 Legislative History, pp.
     5936-37, 4621-24, and 4326-28 respectively.

161. For more on the relative strength of the House 3
     hour SO_2 Class II increment, see the EPA-FEA
     Report, pp. 3, 6, 20.
         The reason is that the 90% limit applied only
     to the primary standards; deterioration up to
     the secondary standards was to be allowed.

162. The one exception to this overall point was the
     24 hour SO_2 primary standard of 365 ug/m^3. This
     later turned out to be an important exception,
     as the raising of the 3 hour SO_2 Class II
     increment had the effect of making the 24 hour
     increment the more constraining value in some
     circumstances.

163. 1977 Legislative History, pp. 4329-30; 4385-86,
     4720-21.

164. Ibid., p. 4332.

165. Ibid., pp. 5261-66.

166. Ibid., pp. 4332, 4354, 4686-87, 5945. In doubt about just what it had done, the conference bill required EPA to report in a year on "the consequences of that portion of the definition of 'major emitting facility'. . . which applies to facilities with the design capacity to emit 250 tons per year or more. Ibid., p. 4334. This requirement is not discussed in the conference report.

167. Compare ibid., pp. 4687-88 with 5937-39.

168. Ibid., p. 4782.

169. Ibid.

170. Interview data.

171. 1977 Legislative History, pp. 4331, 4334, 4388, 5946-47, 5951, 6686.

172. Ibid., pp. 6303-5 (comments of Congressmen Duncan and Hammerschmidt); 6311-13 (comments of Congressman Milford). Milford, a conservative Democrat from the Dallas-Fort Worth area, was a professional meteorologist and TV weatherman prior to his election to Congress.

173. Compare ibid., p. 4330 Conference Report, new §160(c)(1)(D)(ii) with ibid., p. 5943, H.R.10498, new §160(a)(4)(B).

174. Ibid., pp. 4328-31, 4388 (compare with S.3219 at 4622-25). The conferees did add language governing the ambient monitoring requirement discussed above, the buffer zone "prohibition," a requirement limiting the length of time allowed for permit review, and a requirement giving EPA additional responsibility for BACT review of sources in Class III areas. This last point was in neither previous bill.

175. See EPA-FEA Report, pp. 2, 6, 10, 16, 36-37.

176. 1977 Legislative History, pp. 22-23.

177. 39 Federal Register 31005-6.

178. Roger Strelow to Regional Administrators, "PSD
      Regulations--Interpretation of Commencement of
      Construction," December 18, 1975.
      It is important to remember the distinction
      between sources subject to PSD and sources whose
      emissions counted as part of increment
      consumption. Thus, for example, under EPA's
      1974 regulations, sources which increased
      particulate matter or SO_2 emissions after
      January 1, 1975 consumed increment regardless of
      whether they were subject to PSD.

179. 1977 Legislative History, pp. 4725-26.

180. Ibid., p. 4626.

181. Ibid., p. 4622.

182. Ibid., p. 4626.

183. Ibid., p. 4627. While the BACT requirement was
      significant in this respect, it must be recalled
      that the Senate bill did not contain Class III,
      and that its Class I and II increment values
      were the same as EPA's. Since no areas had been
      redesignated as Class III, the effect of this
      provision would have been limited to the new
      mandatory Class I areas.

184. Ibid., p. 6697.

185. See ibid., pp. 354-55 and 359 (§160(c)(2)(E) and
      §160(f)(1) of H.R.10498.

186. Ibid., p. 5950 (§160(h) of H.R.10498). The
      House bill did contain a specified schedule for
      submission, review and approval of PSD SIPs
      (§160 (e)).

187. Ibid., p. 4328 (§160(e) of the conference bill)
      and pp. 4333-34 (§160(j) of the conference
      bill). The 1976 conference report language
      contains a statement to the effect that EPA
      could not promulgate a PSD SIP, but it is
      unclear just which provision in the bill this
      refers to. This sentence was to be dropped from
      the conference report on the 1977 Amendments
      (see ibid., p. 533).

188. Ibid., p. 4334. There is no subsection
      160(e)(2)(C)(ii)(III) in the conference bill.
      The reference appears to be to
      160(e)(1)(C)(ii)(III), which deals with the FLM-
      Governor negotiation process over Class I areas.

189. Ibid., p. 4293 (conference bill §107(a)).

190. Senator Muskie in fact did so in the abortive
      Senate debate on the 1976 conference report
      (ibid., pp. 4433-34, 4444 (statement of Senator
      Baker)).

191. New York Times, editorial, October 19, 1976 ("On
      the range of environmental issues, . . . voters
      have an unusually clear and well-defined
      choice.") During the third Presidential debate,
      Carter labelled Ford's environmental record as
      "hopeless" and said that as President he "would
      do the opposite in every respect" (7 Environment
      Reporter 979 (November 5, 1976)). This is not
      to suggest that the 1976 election was by any
      means a referendum on the environment, but it
      seems fair to say that the environmental issue
      had some salience and was one in which the
      Democrats saw some advantage in attacking the
      incumbent Ford Administration.

192. 7 Environment Reporter 789 (October 1, 1976);
      the full text of Garn's letter to Muskie
      announcing his intention to filibuster is
      contained in 1977 Legislative History, p. 4448.

193. 1977 Legislative History, p. 4449.

194. Ibid., pp. 4411-4500 (Senate debate, September 30 October 1, 1976). At one point, Garn successfully requested that the Senate clerk read the 200 page conference report in its entirety, a tactic in addition to causing enormous delay would also have been an effective aid to sleep. See also Asbell, The Senate Nobody Knows, pp. 44347, and Vietor, Environmental Politics and the Coal Coalition, p. 220.

195. Ibid., pp. 4494-96. See also 7 Environment Reporter 835-36 (October 8, 1976--comments of Leon Billings).

196. 7 Environment Reporter 1131-32, 1156-57 (December 3, 1976), discussing scheduling memorandum from Leon Billings.

197. Cf. remarks of Congressman Louis Frey to the National Association of Manufacturers, "It's no longer a problem of getting a bill that's balanced. It's a matter of the Democrats sitting down and deciding what they want."

198. 1977 Legislative History, p. 3548 (statement of Douglas M. Costle to a hearing of the House Subcommittee on Health and the Environment, April 18, 1977. Interview data suggest that the Administration gave no serious consideration to taking any position on PSD other than supporting the Congressional committees. This is striking because at the same time that the Administration was supporting PSD revisions to the Act, it was also developing a new "National Energy Plan," which President Carter announced to the Nation in a "fireside chat" on April 20, 1977. While the developers of the energy plan (led by FEA, one of the chief past opponents) were clearly concerned about PSD's impact on the plan, EPA and other environmental advocates were successful in getting the Administration to take the position that energy development and PSD

need not conflict. For more on this point, see
7 Environment Reporter 1633-34 (February 25,
1977; 1977 Legislative History, pp. 3533-34
(statement of Douglas Costle before the Senate
Subcommittee on Energy Production and Supply of
the Committee on Energy and Natural Resources);
7 Environment Reporter 1934 (April 22, 1977).

199. An impressive array of industrial groups did
turn out to oppose PSD. Their testimony is
contained in U.S. Congress, Senate, Committee on
Environment and Public Works, Clean Air Act
Amendments of 1977, Hearings Before the
Subcommittee on Environmental Pollution of the
Committee on Environment and Public Works on
S.251, S.252, and S.253, 95th Congress, 1st
Session, 1977 (hereafter cited as 1977 Senate
Hearings); and U.S. Congress, House, Committee
on Interstate and Foreign Commerce, Clean Air
Act Amendments of 1977, Hearings Before the
Subcommittee on Health and Environment of the
Committee on Interstate and Foreign Commerce on
H.R.4151 and H.R.4758, 95th Congress, 1st
Session, 1977 (hereafter cited as 1977 House
Hearings).

200. There were some sections of the 1976 bill which
underwent more extensive committee markup prior
to its report in 1977. The most significant one
was the section dealing with growth in areas
which, unlike PSD areas, would not attain the
ambient standards by the then-1977 deadlines.
See 1977 Legislative History, pp. 1376-77.
Also, in introducing S.252, Muskie retained the
Hot Springs National Park exemption which
Senator Bumpers had inserted, with Muskie's
support, during the 1976 floor debate.

201. Ibid, pp. 586-96 (marked-up version of S.252).

202. Ibid., p. 2474.

203. Ibid., pp. 1868-71 (introduction of language in
H.R.4151) and 2670-74 (committee report). A

full discussion of the visibility program is
beyond the scope of this review. It is
sufficient here to note that this provision
suddenly appeared in 1977 as an appendage to the
Rogers bill and was carried along by the
momentum of the 1977 amendments. It was
approved, in stark contrast to PSD, with almost
no debate in the House, and was incorporated in
the conference bill in the absence of any
comparable Senate provision (ibid., p. 3198).

204. Ibid., p. 2474. Also compare pp. 2283 and 2045.

205. Ibid., pp. 3144-84.

206. The one attempt by Andrew Maguire to strengthen
      Federal oversight of the so-called
      "discretionary Class I" lands was rejected
      without a roll-call vote (ibid., pp. 3139-43).

207. Ibid., p. 705.

208. Ibid., pp. 912-59 (debate), 943-45 (Carter-
      Costle letters), 959 (vote).

209. Ibid., pp. 1049-52.

210. For a description of the Colstrip controversy,
      see 8 Environment Reporter 268, 539-40 and 550.
      See also the two Montana Power vs. EPA
      decisions, 9 ERC 2096 (district court decision
      that Montana Power had commenced construction
      prior to June 1, 1975) and 13 ERC 1385 (appeals
      court reversal of the district court and
      upholding EPA).

211. 1977 Legislative History, pp. 1101-2.

212. Ibid., pp. 1110-14.

213. The delay was caused by a dispute on the House
      side about the conferees, and by the July 4th
      Congressional recess. See 8 Environment
      Reporter 339-40 (July 1, 1977). One result of

this controversy was that Congressman Breaux was added as a conference for the purpose of PSD only.

214. 8 Environment Reporter 509. Garn did threaten to repeat his 1976 filibuster, but was satisfied instead by an agreement with Muskie to enter into a colloquy on the Senate floor which reinforced the point that the 1977 amendments did contain additional flexibility for high terrain areas. 8 Environment Reporter 568; 1977 Legislative History, pp. 37173; 378-79.

215. Compare 1977 Legislative History, pp. 430-42 (H.R.6161, the 1977 conference bill) with pp. 4325-35 (1976 conference report on S.3219).

216. 1977 Legislative History, pp. 437-38 (conference bill); 533 (conference report). For comments on the variance provisions, see the House debate on the conference report, ibid., pp. 324, 330-31. Even with all the debate, the bill's managers in the House and Senate felt compelled to introduce a written "clarification of provisions" into the debate on the conference report.

217. Ibid., p. 435 (§165(a) of the conference bill).

218. Ultimately to no avail as far as Montana Power was concerned, however. Its initial victory in the District Court was overturned on appeal; meanwhile, the Cheyenne had successfully redesignated their reservation as Class I prior to the passage of the 1977 amendments. Ultimately, Colstrip was subject to PSD and did receive a permit, but only after agreeing to install 94% SO_2 removal technology. See note 209 above.
        Statutory citations are 1977 Legislative History, pp. 435 (§165(c) and (e)); 441 (§169(2)(B)).

219. 1977 Legislative History, p. 434 (§164(B)(1)(B)). As has been noted repeatedly

322   **Protect and Enhance**

above, greater State autonomy and control was a
central theme for both Muskie ("The provisions
in this bill: First. Place primary
responsibility and authority with the States,
backed by the Federal Government . . . the
Federal role is sharply restricted in
implementing this policy"--pp. 724-25) and
Rogers ("Section 108, prevention of significant
deterioration, restores broad authority to the
States for determining the future air quality in
presently clean air regions and strictly
curtails EPA's authority to veto States'
ultimate decisions"--p. 3037). No doubt both
sincerely felt that the bill would have this
effect, at least in certain areas, though Muskie
was honest enough to note in debate that "if
one's definition of a significant State role is
no Federal role at all, then we have not done
that" (p. 1040, Senate debate, June 10, 1977).
Yet given the many new constraints placed on
State action by the PSD provisions of the bill,
these statements certainly do not fully capture
the effect of the legislation. It is not my
intent here to debate the wisdom of this policy,
only to note that the appeals of the floor
leaders and the effect of the legislation were
at variance.

220. Ibid., p. 433 (§163(c)(1)(D)). This provision
appears to have been aimed at new Mexican
smelters, which would be potential large
emitters of SO_2.

221. Ibid., pp. 443-45 (§169A) and p. 535 (conference
report language). For this case, since the
visibility provisions covered existing sources,
the conference used the Senate definition of
"major emitting facility." This had the effect
of excluding strip mines--a source of great
concern to Western energy producers.

222. Ibid., pp. 378-79.

223. Ibid., pp. 330-31.

224. Ibid., p. 1403.

225. Ibid., p. 303.

CHAPTER VI

EPA RESPONDS TO CONGRESS

When Congress took up amendments to the Clean
Air Act in 1975, Administrator Train said that one
of EPA's objectives was to receive Congressional
guidance on PSD, because "implementation of a [PSD]
program should proceed without the uncertainties
caused by continuing judicial review or an unclear
position within the executive branch or Congress."[1]
The contention that PSD legislation would reduce
uncertainty was a key argument used by Senate and
House leaders in opposing amendments calling for
further study of the PSD provisions.[2] Whatever
their other effects, Congress appears to have
expected that the 1977 Amendments would provide
stability and certainty to a program which had been
operating under the cloud of judicial review for its
entire lifetime.[3]
    If this was indeed the expected effect of the
1977 Amendments, then both Congress and EPA
officials were in for a disappointment. Instead of
bringing stability to PSD, the next three years
would find the program in a state of constant
turmoil and regulatory change. These conditions
began to subside only after the publication of final
regulations in the Federal Register on August 7,
1980--three years to the day from the signing of the
1977 Amendments.
    In attempting to interpret and implement the
detailed provisions of the new law, EPA's advocacy
of a stringent and comprehensive program would run
afoul of the very courts whose previous support had
given birth and life to PSD. Partly in response to

325

these court mandates, partly in response to its own
environmental agenda, and partly because EPA wanted
to avoid reopening the legislative debate on the
Clean Air Act, EPA would embark on the same road of
compromise which Congress had traveled in 1975-77.
The consequence for EPA of this choice was the same
as it had been for Congress: the rules became
increasingly complex as Agency officials struggled
to preserve their policy objectives while
accommodating vocal and influential opponents. Only
now, the problem of complexity began to compound
itself, so that in 1981 Senator Gary Hart--a PSD
advocate in 1975-77--could say that only one person
in America fully understood PSD.[4]
     This chapter will trace EPA's efforts to
implement the 1977 Amendments through rulemaking,
and how the Agency's actions triggered, once again,
forceful judicial intervention in the PSD program.
The factors which contributed to the direction which
EPA took in the post-1977 period will be discussed,
along with a review of the key issues presented to
the court in the crucial <u>Alabama</u> <u>Power</u> case.
Finally, the effect of the case on EPA's 1980 final
rules will be discussed, along with a brief review
of the reasons why, despite widespread
dissatisfaction with these rules, the report of a
major national commission and an out of court
settlement with industry, the long-sought stability
in the PSD program has to everyone's surprise
finally occurred between 1980 and 1990.

EPA in 1977: Activists at Work

     EPA in 1977 was not the same agency it had been
in 1971. Part of this was simply that EPA had
matured in the intervening six years. Where meeting
statutory deadlines had been Administrator
Ruckelshaus' top priority for setting standards in
1971, internal Agency procedures as well as external

reviews of EPA decisions had taken hold by 1977 to ensure that a wide range of viewpoints was considered in EPA rulemaking.[5] Moreover, both industry and environmental groups had become much more sophisticated in using Agency procedures, external review by other Federal agencies, and the courts to challenge proposed EPA actions. It was no longer possible, for example, for an Administrator to meet a 90-day timetable for setting air quality standards as Ruckelshaus had done in 1971.

However, while a more mature EPA had perhaps lost some of its initial speed, the years had maintained and reinforced some elements of the original EPA culture fostered by Ruckelshaus at the beginning. The most important of these elements was the perceived independence of the Agency from political pressure. While this independence was perhaps exaggerated, the Train years had if anything reinforced the notion among EPA staff that while the Agency was subject to pressure from all manner of groups, it retained considerable freedom to make up its own mind. Certainly EPA gained some flexibility in this regard because, as Alfred Marcus has noted, the Agency was frequently in the middle of disputes between two well-organized adversary groups.[6] However, both Ruckelshaus and Train had cultivated the principle of independence as part of the Agency's culture, and both had acted in accordance with this principle on enough occasions to give it credibility.

Moreover, the maturing of the Agency had also increased its ability to provide credible technical analysis. "Credible" is of course a relative term; the Agency's analyses were still routinely criticized as inadequate by both groups dissatisfied with their results and by impartial reviews of the Agency's decision-making processes.[7] However, EPA's role as a provider of expert information in the Congressional debate on PSD illustrates the growth in the Agency in the kinds of analytic answers it could provide to specific questions about the impacts of its programs. As Harold Wilensky predicts, the effort EPA devoted to what he calls "the intelligence function" had increased as EPA

found itself more in conflict with other actors in
society, especially during the energy crisis.[8] EPA
responded to the increasing sophistication of its
adversaries with an increasing sophistication of its
own, and even debates within the Agency, at least on
the surface, focused more and more on competing
analyses.[9]

Added to these changes in the organizational
culture of the Agency by 1977 was the element of a
new and environmentally activist Democratic
Administration. This shift in political leadership
was to have a significant effect on EPA's policy on
PSD. For while the new EPA Administrator, Douglas
Costle, was not noted as an environmentalist and had
in fact served in the Nixon Administration as a
staff member of the Ash Council which created EPA,
the new second-level officials in EPA came from a
much more environmentally activist background.
Nowhere was this more true than in the case of the
new EPA Assistant Administrator for Air and
Radiation, a young lawyer from the National
Resources Defense Council named David Hawkins.

Hawkins' appointment was one of several in the
Carter Administration where representatives from
public interest groups were appointed to head
agencies with which they had previously been in
conflict.[10] Most of Hawkins' specific work and
testimony for NRDC had been in the area of
transportation controls, where he was regarded as a
genuine expert. He had played a critical role in
the landmark NRDC v. EPA case in 1973 which
overturned EPA's decision to give States more time
to produce transportation control plans and ordered
EPA to devise programs to maintain as well as attain
air quality standards.[11] This decision triggered
years of work by EPA (and years of litigation in the
courts).[12] However, Hawkins was also acquainted with
the debate over PSD even though he personally had
not been a leading participant in it.[13] Moreover,
Hawkins had a well-deserved reputation as an skilled
and thorough advocate.

Hawkins, as the political head of the office
with the primary responsibility for developing EPA's
approach to implementing the new PSD requirements,

was in the most influential position with respect to
establishing EPA policy on just how the requirements
would be carried out. However, the review process
discussed earlier ensured, even if nothing else did,
that the rules would not be issued without comment
from other perspectives in EPA. In particular, the
Office of Planning and Evaluation's (OPE) role in
the Carter Administration EPA remained strong. The
economists in this office remained concerned about
the economic impact of the PSD rules and carefully
examined the specific proposals for carrying them
out. This disposition was reinforced by the new EPA
Assistant Administrator for Planning and Management,
William Drayton. Drayton, though himself a lawyer,
was a strong advocate of the use of economic
incentives to promote pollution control and was
keenly interested in economic arguments about the
relative effectiveness (or lack thereof) of "command
and control" regulation.[14] Drayton also contended
that EPA should become known as a "public health"
agency, which implied that programs such as PSD
should receive less attention.[15]
    This inherent tension between the two offices
set the stage for EPA's consideration of the post-
Amendment revisions to its PSD regulations. The
other players in the earlier debates over PSD
regulations were still present--the attorneys in the
Office of General Counsel (OGC) and the Office of
Enforcement (OE). However, the principal conflict
within EPA was between Hawkins' air office and OPE,
with each trying to enlist the support of the other
groups to buttress its position.
    One other important contextual factor should be
noted. The 1977 Clean Air Act Amendments, though
described by Senator Muskie as a relaxation of the
1970 Act,[16] nonetheless maintained most of the basic
goals of the Act and (in the case of PSD) expanded
some. Yet EPA's new political executives had
watched Congress tinker with the statue in 1977 and
make additional relaxations on automobile standards
as well as PSD (e.g., the Breaux amendment). When
combined with the emphasis in the Carter
Administration on energy, deregulation and reducing
inflation, this experience made them reluctant to

publicly propose any amendments to the Clean Air Act
which might jeopardize the environmental
requirements preserved in the 1977 Amendments. It
also made them reluctant to take any steps which
could require the early reopening of the statute for
amendment. Thus, for example, Costle and Hawkins
stated on numerous occasions that the sanctions
established under Part D of the Amendments
pertaining to non-attainment areas, which John
Quarles had characterized as "a loose cannon on a
pitching deck," would probably not apply to very
many areas at all.[17] This perspective, however,
seriously constrained EPA's willingness to confront,
head on, difficulties with the statutory
construction of the 1977 PSD amendments.

Implementing the Law: A Rough Start

On August 9, 1977, two days after the passage of
the Amendments, EPA's Division of Stationary Source
Enforcement (DSSE) sent out a memo to EPA's ten
regional offices which said, among other things,
that insofar as PSD was concerned, "the existing
[EPA] regulations will remain in effect until the
required SIP revisions are made to implement the
requirements of these [PSD] sections of the bill.
Any regulation in effect which would be inconsistent
with provisions concerning mandatory Class I areas,
Class I increments and redesignations is deemed
amended to conform with these provisions. Thus,
before any PSD permits are issued, care should be
taken to conform with those requirements." The
memo, which also touched on several other
points related to enforcement of the 1977
Amendments' requirements, closed with the hope that
"we look forward to working with your staff to
smoothly effectuate the new law."[18] Unfortunately,
it was only a matter of weeks before a major

controversy erupted over EPA's interpretation of
just what Congress had done.

The focus of this controversy was on the
provisions Congress had made for the transition
between the old and new PSD requirements. It will
be recalled that the Senate and House bills had
contained two different approaches. The House, in a
provision which became §168(a), provided that EPA's
PSD regulations should govern the review and
permitting of new sources, with the exception of
certain provisions prescribed in §168(b). It was
these exceptions which were enumerated in the DSSE
memo. However, the Senate bill had provided, in
what became §165(a), that "no major emitting
facility on which construction is commenced after
the date of enactment of this part" (emphasis added)
could be built unless it met all of the review
requirements in §165. Since the conference had
expanded the definition of "major emitting facility"
well beyond that contained in EPA's regulations, the
result of this provision would be to make a large
number of new sources subject to the requirement the
requirement to use best available control technology
(BACT). Such a requirement could have forced some
major facilities to undergo major redesign. It
quickly became apparent to the EPA staff who had to
implement the law that these two interpretations
stood in direct conflict with each other. Following
the interpretation in §165 would immediately subject
a very large number of new sources to the PSD
requirements, while following the interpretation of
§168 would delay the effective implementation of the
new PSD requirements for at least fifteen months.[19]

As the DSSE memo suggests, EPA staff who were
working to revise EPA's regulations to implement the
amendments originally proposed to take the less
stringent interpretation allowed under §168(a).
This would have kept the BACT requirements for the
new universe of PSD sources from becoming
immediately effective. However, Hawkins overturned
this recommendation on the grounds that it was, in
his opinion, contrary to the statute's requirements.
Instead, in a memorandum to EPA's Regional
Administrators dated October 6 which Hawkins co-

signed with Marvin Durning, the Assistant
Administrator for Enforcement, Hawkins announced
that §165 required that the new review requirements
applied immediately to all sources which had not
commenced construction by August 7, 1977, even if a
source had already received a PSD permit from EPA.
In such cases, the permit was to be suspended and
the source re-reviewed by EPA.[20]

The memo noted that these new requirements "may
result in delays in processing permits which may
disrupt the schedules for sources whose permits are
pending or have recently been granted."[21]   Judging by
the reaction, this was a dramatic understatement.   A
storm of protest from sources, Congressional
representatives, and the new Department of Energy
greeted this announcement, and less than a month
later, Hawkins and Durning had to retreat.   On
October 27, a second memorandum to the Regional
Administrators announced EPA's intent to specify
that sources which received permits before March 1,
1978, and commenced construction before December 1,
1978, would be reviewed under the old rather than
the new PSD requirements.[22]

Why did EPA take this position, only to suddenly
and quickly reverse itself?   The Agency's action
suggests that at least part of its political
leadership saw an opportunity to take advantage of
an ambiguity in the law to press for an
environmentally stringent policy--perhaps one more
stringent than they could have achieved if the
debate on these provisions had been more open.   EPA
was aided in this attempt by the sources which had
worked so effectively during the Train years--the
Congressional committees.   An October 4 memo from
Hawkins to EPA Administrator Costle said that the
immediately effective interpretation was valid not
only because of the statute's language in §165, but
because the failure to include §165 as a referred
section in §168(b) resulted from an "oversight by
Congressional staff caused by renumbering of
sections during the last minute drafting process,"
and that a "technical amendment" would be introduced
in Congress to

rectify this oversight.[23]   In the ensuing controversy
which followed EPA's announcement, Muskie rushed to
the defense of this interpretation, telling Costle
in an October 17 letter that the conference had
indeed intended §165 requirements to apply
immediately.[24]

However, in this case the committee unanimity
which had served PSD so well in the past broke down.
Senator McClure wrote to Costle on October 24,
arguing that "only the specific provisions
enumerated in Section 168(b) were intended to be
immediately applicable."[25]   Even more damaging was
the position taken by the Rogers committee.   While
Rogers expressed his personal agreement with the
§165 position as consistent with the conferees'
intent, he also made it clear that he would not
include language clarifying this point in "technical
amendments" to the Act.   As he later explained, "on
this point . . . considerable controversy developed
. . . I believed that technical and conforming
amendments should not generate any significant
controversy."[26]

Faced with this lack of political support for
its position, the Agency was forced to back down.
Hawkins later observed that he had "not done [his]
homework on the practical and political
implications" of a decision to make §165 immediately
effective.[27]   A more complete explanation appears to
be that, having identified the opportunity to probe
for a more restrictive interpretation of an
ambiguous statute, the Agency's political executives
did so to test whether holding the line would take
an extensive commitment of political capital or a
reopening of the political debate over PSD.   When
confronted with the fact that both would be
required, the Agency quickly backed down.   Thus
Hawkins wrote to EPA Deputy Administrator Barbara
Blum on October 18 to recommend that the earlier
effective date determination be reversed because of
the failure of the Congressional committees to
propose the requisite "technical amendments".   This
was a reflection of the delicate political balance
which still surrounded PSD, notwithstanding the
seeming force of the 1977 Amendments.[28]

In conceding its original position, however, EPA
was able to propose an "acceptable compromise" which
was considerably more stringent than a literal
reading of §168(b) would have suggested.[29] The
October 27 memorandum did not leave the old rules in
effect until new SIPs were approved, but only until
dates and under conditions specified by EPA. The
Agency justified its authority to essentially craft
its own rules by pointing to the conflict between
the two parts of the statute and saying that EPA had
decided that "the most prudent course is to
implement Section 165(a) as quickly as possible, but
through the rulemaking process."[30] Later, EPA
elaborated on this point by stating that because of
the conflicting statutory provisions, "EPA had no
choice but to fashion a reasonable program for the
transition from the old to the new requirements."[31]
    It is instructive to see just what EPA actually
gave up in making this "concession." First, because
it would take at least 90 days for a permit
application to be reviewed, the real deadline for a
potential PSD source which had not filed for a
permit was December 1, 1977, for the source to stand
a chance of getting its permit approved by the March
1, 1978, deadline.[32] Second, the reason EPA picked
March 1, 1978, as the deadline was that the Agency
said it would promulgate final revised PSD
regulations by then.[33] In the event, EPA did not get
these regulations published until June 19, 1978, for
reasons that will be discussed further below.[34]
However, despite issuing a public notice in
December, 1977 which said that it would not meet the
March 1, 1978 date, EPA nevertheless left it in
place, with one exception, as the date by which
facilities had to have received their permits to
avoid the new PSD requirements of §165.[35]
    EPA claimed it needed to do this to minimize
increment consumption--which subjecting more sources
to PSD would do--thereby giving "the States a full
opportunity to revise and implement their own PSD
programs."[36] Of course, this logic argued for
retaining the earlier proposed effective date of
August 7, 1977, but EPA responded that this
imperative was overcome by the need to avoid "severe

economic disruption" and "disorderly
administration."[37] However, EPA also argued in the
same notice that despite foregoing control of
230,000 tons of particulate matter emissions and
570,000 tons of SO_2 emissions, the "potential
consumption of the increment beyond what [sources]
would have consumed under the new requirements was
not so great as to warrant denying them an
opportunity for exemption."[38]

It was true that some sources could (and did)
escape PSD because of the Agency's shift. However,
EPA argued that some such "escape" was inevitable
because of the demands of the administrative
process, and that the environmental risk associated
with these "escapes" was limited. The fact that EPA
adopted its "compromise position" only after
determining that it lacked the political support to
maintain its original view obscured the point that
only as compared to the option of applying the new
requirements to all sources which had not commenced
construction before August 7, 1977, did EPA make any
significant concession. Certainly the Agency's
position was more stringent than a literal reading
of §168 would have suggested.

While the controversy over the effective date of
the new requirements was still going on, the Agency
proceeded to propose new PSD regulations on November
3, 1977, which would incorporate these requirements
as well as other provisions of the 19767 Amendments.
The dispute over the effective date shifted into the
courts, where suits by both environmental groups and
industry were consolidated in one case, known as
Citizens to Save Spencer County v. EPA.[39] These
suits had an erratic, stop and start effect on the
permitting of sources under PSD. In the earlier
DSSE memo and again in the two Hawkins-Durning
memos, EPA had already indicated that PSD permits
for sources which had not commenced construction
before the Act was signed would have to be reviewed
to ensure consistency with the new Act.[40] This
effectively froze the issuance of new PSD permits
until such a review could be completed. Then, in
February 1978, the Environmental Defense Fund (EDF)
sued EPA on the effective date issue. In response

to this suit, EPA suspended the issuance of all PSD
permits until a hearing could be granted on EDF's
request for an injunction against the Agency to
prevent it from issuing more permits.[41]   The D.C.
District Court ruled on March 15 that it did not
have jurisdiction in the case, but prohibited EPA
from issuing any permits until March 17.[42] Finally,
this prohibition was lifted on March 28 by the
D.C.Circuit Court of Appeals, which denied EDF's
motion for an injunction.[43]   EPA in the meantime had
continued to <u>process</u> permits so that their
processing record would be set in regard to the
March 1 date even if EPA could not issue the
permit.[44]

In this instance, the D.C. Circuit Court of
Appeals eventually upheld EPA's decision to fashion
its own rules regarding the effective date of the
new regulations.[45] Despite having to back away from
its original position, this represented a victory
for the environmental advocates among EPA's
political executives. More importantly for our
purposes, however, it illustrates that despite two
and a half years of work, Congress could not write
rules which were sufficiently specific and
prescriptive to avoid major controversies over their
interpretations. Yet Congress' failure in this
instance does not appear to have been a result of
ignorance, at least on the part of the committee
staff. The argument later advanced by Senator
Muskie and others that the discrepancy resulted from
inadvertence during the conference is not
persuasive, given that the 1976 conference bill (on
which the 1977 Act was based) had included very
similar provisions.[46]

While inadvertent errors could certainly have
occurred in the process which produced the 1977
amendments, a more likely explanation is that the
committee staff, unable to reach a firm agreement
between their principals on this issue, left the
effective date ambiguous in hopes that
administrative or judicial action would succeed in
making a choice where Congress could not.[47]   Even
when the issue was fully and publicly aired in the
wake of the Hawkins October 6 memo, Congress still

could not make a decision, as evidenced by the
failure to resolve this issue through technical
amendments. The decision was left to EPA and the
courts, which were finally able to resolve the
matter through what the court described as rules "of
baroque complexity."[48] It is important to recognize,
however, that this complexity resulted from
Congress' unwillingness to make a choice, and EPA's
unwillingness to force a choice that might threaten
to challenge the gains it had won on PSD in the
legislative arena. While there may have been a
consensus on the value of PSD, this exchange
illustrates just how fragile this consensus was.

EPA Proposes To Change Its Rules

When the controversy over the effective date
made it apparent that the §165 requirements could
not be made immediately effective, EPA rushed ahead
with revisions to its rules to quickly incorporate
them. While some provisions (the ones specified in
§168(b)) did go into effect right away, the
remainder were subject to notice and comment
rulemaking with the hope that they could be
implemented as quickly as possible. Thus, on
November 3, 1977, EPA published in the Federal
Register a three part notice covering 1) provisions
which were immediately effective; 2) proposed rules
governing PSD SIP revisions (Part 51 rules); and 3)
proposed rules stating how EPA would run the PSD
program in the absence of an approved SIP (Part 52
rules).[49] EPA claimed in its notice that "this
proposal only sets forth the minimum requirements
enacted by Congress in the Clean Air Act Amendments
of 1977."[50] EPA made this claim to avoid having to
prepare an Economic Impact Analysis for the Office
of Management and Budget.[51] However, this assertion
glossed over a number of very significant and, as it

turned out, controversial choices which EPA had made in drafting the proposed rules.

To describe all of these choices would, as Shep Melnick has noted, "take an entire book."[52] What follows is a brief description of some of the big issues whose history was discussed in earlier chapters and whose subsequent development illustrates the approach taken by EPA in the conduct of the PSD rulemaking through its subsequent review by the courts. The choices described below were also key in addressing the fundamental questions raised about PSD in earlier chapters, especially those concerning which sources would be covered and what role State and local governments would have in determining "significant" deterioration. However, by this time in PSD's development these choices, though real, were largely obscured in highly complex debates among lawyers and technical experts over the meaning of specific words in the Clean Air Act.

POTENTIAL TO EMIT

The 1977 Amendments had specified that new PSD rules should apply to any "major emitting facility." A "major emitting facility" was defined as one with a "potential to emit" more than either 100 or 250 tons per year of "any air pollutant," depending on whether the source was listed as a regulated category in the Act.[54] It will be recalled that this definition of "source" resulted from the combination of the House and Senate approaches on source coverage under the Act, with a result more stringent than either approach on its own.

However, Congress had not defined the term "potential to emit" (PTE). In defining it, the Agency had two choices. The first choice would have defined potential to emit as the amount of pollution a source was expected to emit after the application of any pollution control devices. The second choice would define PTE as the amount of pollution a source was capable of emitting <u>in the absence</u> of any

pollution control devices. This latter definition
produced a much more comprehensive PSD program,
since standard pollution control typically reduced
the amount of pollution, especially of particulate
matter, by 90% or more. In other words, not giving
credit for these reductions would substantially
increase the number of sources which would have to
undergo PSD review. In the November 3, 1977,
Federal Register notice, EPA without explanation
proposed to use the more comprehensive definition of
potential to emit in determining whether sources
were subject to PSD.[55] As we shall see below, this
caused a great controversy.

MAJOR SOURCE AND MAJOR MODIFICATION

      Any new source whose "potential emissions"
exceeded the 100/250 tons per year (TPY) thresholds
was defined under the Act as a "major emitting
facility." However, the Act was not clear about
whether these emissions should be considered apart
from any other emissions reductions at a plant where
a "major emitting facility" was being constructed.
While this would not be an issue at a "greenfield"
site for a completely new plant, it could be a major
issue when the major emitting facility "was a
modification to an existing plant.[56] At such plants,
offsetting emissions reductions (i.e., from retiring
an old production unit) could mean that a
modification could result in a net decrease in
pollution even without the application of best
available control technology.
      EPA's 1974 PSD rules had exempted modifications
from PSD review when these modifications did not
result in net emissions increases. However, In its
proposal of November 3, EPA held that the new law
changed this policy to require that modifications be
subject to PSD and be required to use BACT even if
no net increase in emissions would result at the
source. While modifications which caused no net
emissions increase would be exempted from

calculating increment consumption, the imposition of BACT on such changes was a significant new control requirement.[57]

EPA proposed to replace the term "major emitting facility" used in the Act with the terms "major stationary source" and "major modification" in order "to reflect current EPA terminology."[58]   In defining "major modification," the Agency proposed to use the same 100/250 TPY cutoffs that applied for new sources to determine when a modification was "major."[59]   However, once a new source or a modification became subject to PSD review because of potential emissions greater than 100/250 tons, then several other requirements were triggered, in particular the BACT requirement described below.

BEST AVAILABLE CONTROL TECHNOLOGY (BACT)

Because of the way the conference committee combined the House and Senate proposals, BACT was applied much more broadly in the new PSD program than it was under EPA's old regulations.   In particular, not only was a much larger universe of sources now subject to BACT, but BACT was required for "each pollutant regulated under this Act emitted from, or which results from, such facility."[60]   This included not just sulfur oxides and particulate matter, but all pollutants regulated under any portion of the Act, including some regulated only under §111 and §112.[61]   Many sources emit more than one such pollutant. Power plants, for example, emit particulate matter, carbon monoxide, sulfur dioxide, nitrogen oxides, and if oil-fired, can give off volatile organic compounds through evaporation. The question the Agency had to answer in its rulemaking was whether BACT had to be applied to emissions of all such pollutants at a source, or only to some of them.

EPA addressed this question in its November 3 proposal by setting up a "de minimis" level of 100 TPY of potential emissions of a pollutant for a

major source or modification to be subject to BACT
for that pollutant. In other words, once a source
or modification was defined as "major" by meeting
the 100/250 TPY potential emissions cutoff for any
one pollutant, then the source would have to control
all pollutants whose potential emissions were
greater than 100 tons per year by applying best
available controls to their emissions.[62] The
potential stringency of this requirement was
increased by the change made in the 1977 Amendments
to the definition of BACT. Where EPA's 1974
regulations had defined BACT as equal to NSPS
wherever NSPS existed (and case by case only when
they did not), Congress in the amendments had
defined BACT as resulting from a case by case
determination in all instances, with NSPS serving as
a floor but with the implication that tighter
controls could (if not should) be required.[63] EPA
highlighted this change in the preamble to its
proposed regulations, noting that "BACT is always
determined on a case by case basis, rather than
automatically applying any applicable [NSPS], as was
the case under EPA regulations."[64]

BASELINE CONCENTRATION

     It will be recalled from the discussion of
baseline concentration in Chapter 5 that several
amendments had been offered and accepted during
Congressional debate on the 1977 amendments to
include sources in the baseline and exempt them from
increment consumption. In particular, an extensive
set of exemptions had been included in the House
bill. However, in the conference bill, these
exemptions were allowed only to "any State which has
a plan approved by the Administrator for purposes of
carrying out this part."[65]
     If EPA had taken the approach envisioned in the
House bill of requiring SIPs to be submitted before
the new PSD rules went into effect, these exemptions
would have been available at the same time that

other parts of the rules took effect.
Alternatively, EPA could have chosen to include
these exemptions in its own rules and applied them
to areas which had not developed their own SIPs.
EPA, however, took neither approach. Instead, while
proposing to make the exemptions available to States
in the guidelines proposed for State PSD SIPs, EPA
argued that the Act did not "make such exemptions
available to EPA in implementing its own PSD
regulations; thus, such provisions are not included"
in EPA's regulations.[66] Moreover, in choosing a
baseline date, EPA went beyond its old regulations
by holding that air quality impacts from projected
emissions from all sources <u>commencing construction</u>
after January 6, 1975, were to be counted against
the increments. EPA had specified previously that
sources which had obtained <u>permits</u> by January 1,
1975, were included in the baseline as long as they
commenced construction by June 1, 1975.[67] Again, the
Agency had adopted a stringent construction of the
new statutory provisions.

EPA was able to make these choices because the
statutory definition of baseline concentration was
not completely clear. The confusion in this
definition can be traced back to the different
concepts of increment consumption in the House and
Senate bills. If increment consumption was
conceived of as an accounting procedure based on
modeling, the baseline <u>date</u> and the "commenced
construction" definitions were all that mattered.
These would allow the Agency to tell which sources
should and should not be included in modeling
increment consumption. However, if increments were
conceived as reflecting real changes in air quality,
having a baseline <u>concentration</u> was important. The
definition of baseline concentration adopted in the
amendments came from the Senate bill and, despite
the Senate's general reliance on a modeling
approach, appeared to treat the baseline and
increments as real, measurable air quality limits
and changes. In so doing, however, the definition
specified January 6, 1975, as the "commenced
construction" date, which meant that emissions from
all sources which began construction after this date

would consume increment. However, in a confusing
section, the statute also provided that the baseline
<u>concentration</u> was to consist of "the ambient
concentration levels which exist as of the time of
the first application for a plant in an area subject
to this part."[68] This meant that the baseline <u>date</u>
could vary from area to area, depending on when the
first eligible source applied for a PSD permit.
Thus the "commenced construction" date and the
"baseline" date were not necessarily the same,
creating both a subtle distinction and the potential
for enormous confusion. In its November 3 proposed
regulations, EPA tried to ignore this possibility
and attempted to make these dates the same, which
was the most stringent interpretation. Yet complex
as this issue already was, it would become even more
difficult later on.

MONITORING REQUIREMENTS

Another part of the statute which proved
troublesome to EPA was the issue of requiring
sources to submit ambient monitoring data along with
their application for a permit. Once again, the
problem arose over the issue of just what the
"baseline" and "increments" represented. In this
case, however, EPA's concern appears not to have
been over whether a requirement would produce a more
environmentally stringent result, but over whether
the requirement established by Congress could be
implemented at all.

It will be recalled that EPA, in developing its
1974 regulations, had debated whether sources should
be required to conduct ambient air quality
monitoring to determine what baseline air quality
was in the source's proposed location.[69] EPA
rejected such a requirement on the grounds that
monitoring data were not needed to track the
consumption of increment. The House of
Representatives, however, had inserted such a
requirement, though its reasons for doing so were

not very clear.[70] This requirement was included in
the conference bill in 1976 and again in 1977.[71]
Including the requirement in the law, however,
did not increase EPA's fondness for it. The
proposed regulations did contain the statutory
requirements, but limited them to pollutants for
which a NAAQS existed and which the source had the
potential to emit in amounts greater than 100 tons
per year.[72] In commenting on this requirement in the
preamble to the regulations, EPA reemphasized its
skepticism.

> In actual practice, assessment of the available
> increment is normally accomplished through an
> accounting procedure whereby atmospheric
> modeling of individual sources will be used to
> keep track of the available (or "unused")
> increment as sources or emissions are increased
> or decreased . . . Monitoring should emphasize
> the establishment of a background air quality
> level to be used primarily in the review against
> the applicable ambient ceiling, rather than for
> tracking the use of the increment.[73]

Reaction to the November 3, 1977 Proposal

The monitoring requirements were the exception
to the overall approach of the November 3 proposal.
While many of the features of the proposal did
reflect the provisions which Congress had written
into the law, EPA nevertheless took advantage of the
law's ambiguity, as it had in the dispute over the
statutory effective date, to make these new
provisions relatively more environmentally stringent
than they might otherwise have been. In defining
such terms as "potential to emit," "major stationary
source," "major modification," and "baseline
concentration," the Agency increased the expected
scope of the PSD program to cover more industrial
sources than it might otherwise have done. By doing
so, EPA's November 3 proposal made it quite clear
that despite the claims in Congress that the

amendments offered States additional flexibility,
the amendments were expected to have a very
constraining effect on States, and reinforced the
notion of PSD as a program driven by Federal goals
and requirements. A measure of how far PSD had come
from allowing substantial flexibility to the States
can be seen in the following comment in the preamble
to the Part 51 State guidelines.

The Act does not appear to allow States the
option of developing new, innovative approaches
to prevent significant air quality
deterioration. That is, States are required to
work within the numerical air quality
"increment" and preconstruction review
framework, and have no option to consider other
regulatory strategies (such as an emission
density approach), notwithstanding that such
schemes may be equivalent in accomplishing PSD.
The Administrator, however, would continue to
recognize the inherent right of a State to be
more restrictive than the requirements proposed
today.[74]

One of the reasons for the character of the
November 3 proposed rules was that they had moved
through the Agency very quickly, with Hawkins, OGC
attorneys and OAQPS staff playing a very strong role
and with little review by the economists in OPE who
were concerned with the "reasonableness" of the
regulations. Even within OAQPS, many of those who
were critical of the focus, scope and complexity of
the PSD program which emerged from Congress had
either left the Office or gone on to other things.
The absence of strong internal advocates for a more
limited program accounts in part for the stringency
of the regulations; no one in the Agency was pushing
back. The force of the new law, the skill of
Hawkins' advocacy and his stature as a new political
appointee, and the fact that Carter Administration
had not firmly set new review mechanisms in place
either within or outside EPA all combined to create
a climate in which the November 3 proposal could go
through the Agency relatively unchallenged.
Moreover (and paradoxically), the controversy over

the effective date of the rules may have made it
easier for a tight set of proposed regulations to be
approved, in that it could be plausibly argued that
a retreat on time was an acceptable trade-off for
tough controls.

This "environmental honeymoon," however, did not
last. Within a year of coming to the office, the
Carter Administration was coming under increasing
criticism for its approach to dealing with the twin
problems of the energy crisis and inflation. In
response, the Administration began to adopt the
theme of regulatory reform as one solution to these
problems. It was only a matter of time before the
pressures for such "reform" hit PSD.[75]

Reviews of EPA regulations by other Federal
agencies began to reappear in the winter and spring
of 1978. Having abolished the Nixon-Ford "Quality
of Life Review", the Carter Administration now found
itself reconstituting the same kinds of mechanisms,
albeit under different names and in slightly
different forms. The most significant of these was
the Regulatory Analysis Review Group (RARG), an
interagency group chaired by the Council of Economic
Advisers. RARG was constituted to review the
regulatory analyses which agencies, under a March
1978 Carter executive order, were required to
prepare on major regulatory actions.[76] Thus, when
the predictable attack on the November 3 proposal
came, a receptive audience both inside and outside
the Agency was ready to hear it.

The same industrial groups which had fought PSD
in the Congress were the most vocal in objecting to
the November 3 rules. The volume of comments forced
EPA in December, 1977 to extend the public comment
period on the proposal to the end of January, and to
warn that in light of the extension that EPA "may
not be able to meet the March 1, 1978, date" for
promulgating final regulations.[77] In their comments,
the oil, steel, chemical, electric utility and
forest products industries strongly attacked EPA's
interpretations as inconsistent with the Act and a
threat to economic growth and energy independence.[78]
The March 1 date for avoiding the BACT requirement
came under particular fire, with industries

requesting a delay until at least December 1, 1978.[79]
Also attacked were EPA's definition of "potential to
emit" and "commence construction," with the
protesting industries arguing that these and other
provisions in the rules enabled EPA to engage in ex
post facto regulation and create costly construction
delays on multi-year projects.

Industry's comments were echoed by those from
the new Department of Energy. Though the names and
players had changed, the disputes between EPA and
DOE, though not as public as the old Train-Zarb
battles, had much the same flavor.[80]

DOE was critical of EPA's regulations and made
recommendations for changes on several specific
points. These included:

o   Adopting a literal interpretation of the
    provision from the Senate bill that the baseline
    concentration should be determined as of the
    date of the first application for a PSD permit
    in an area (as opposed to EPA's proposal of a
    uniform baseline date of January 6, 1975).

o   Exempting Federally mandated fuel switches from
    PSD review under EPA's rules, and exempting
    other voluntary fuel switches from increment
    consumption. EPA had proposed that while fuel
    switches at sources which could burn an
    alternate fuel prior to January 6, 1975 would be
    exempt from PSD review, emissions from such
    switches would consume increment. EPA had also
    said that it lacked authority under the Act in
    its own rules to exempt Federally-mandated
    switches from PSD, though States could choose to
    do so in their implementation plans.

o   Reviewing and applying BACT to only those
    pollutants emitted at a rate of 250 TPY for non-
    listed sources. EPA had proposed that when a
    non-listed source would have the potential to
    emit more than 250 tons per year of any
    pollutant, then all potential emissions greater
    than 100 tons per year would have to be
    controlled through the use of BACT.[81]

DOE also joined industry in raising, as its
biggest objection, EPA's interpretation of
"potential to emit". While favoring the post-
control definition, DOE argued that, at a minimum,
the 50-ton exemption (added in the 1977 Senate bill)
should be expanded. On its face, this exemption
appeared to only exempt Class II modifications from
increment consumption if their "allowable" emissions
were less than 50 tons per year. DOE at a minimum
favored the expansion of this exemption to Class III
areas.[82]
    The issue of the definition of "potential to
emit" was the most controversial element of the
November 3 proposed regulations, and became the
focus of the attack by Carter Administration
"regulatory reformers" on PSD. The impact of the
definition in the November proposal, to be sure, had
not escaped attention even within EPA. OAQPS,
alarmed at the number of air pollution sources with
"negligible" air quality and emissions impacts which
would become subject to PSD review under the
proposed definition, prepared a memorandum in
December 1977 which suggested a "two-tier" approach.
The intent of this approach was to reduce the number
of sources which had to go through the complicated
review of increment consumption, while nevertheless
requiring as wide a universe of sources as possible
to put on BACT. OAQPS proposed to do this by
retaining the definition of potential to emit in the
November proposal (i.e., uncontrolled emissions),
but expanding the exemption provision in the Act to
exempt from increment review all sources whose
emissions after the application of BACT controls
would be less than some cutoff levels (initially
suggested to be 100 tons per year). The memorandum
noted that the legal justification for this approach
was "difficult," but suggested that virtually all of
the emissions reduction which would occur under the
November proposal would still occur if the two-tier
exemption were built in. However, there would be a
considerable reduction in the number of sources
subject to "the difficult and time consuming review
against the increments."[83]

Adopting a definition of potential to emit as post-control emissions would, of course, have reduced the number of sources subject to PSD even more. However, Hawkins had rejected such an approach in the November 3 proposal and, with the strong support of attorneys in the Office of General Counsel and staff in the Office of Enforcement, continued to oppose it in considering what the final PSD regulations should be.[84] This support persisted despite OAQPS' warning that a definition based on controlled emissions was "preferred by those that must actually implement the new source review programs."[85] Eventually, however, Hawkins did agree to the proposal to incorporate the "two-tier" approach suggested by OAQPS into the final PSD regulations, despite the presumed "legal risk," and the OAQPS staff proceeded to draft final regulations based on this approach.

In the meantime reviewers at the Council on Wage and Price Stability (COWPS) and the Council of Economic Advisers (CEA), two of the most active and influential RARG members, had focused their attention on the definition of "potential to emit." A series of memos and meetings between EPA and its Executive Branch critics occurred in March and April, 1978, in which CEA and COWPS insisted that EPA should abandon the "uncontrolled" definition of potential to emit in favor of a post-control definition.[86] CEA and COWPS focused their arguments on EPA's economic impact assessment of its PSD rules, arguing that such an assessment, properly done, would show that while the emissions benefits of the uncontrolled definition were almost zero, the costs (particularly administrative costs) would be quite large. Their conclusion was that since the benefits of an uncontrolled definition were outweighed by the costs, that "the national interest would be served by defining potential as allowable [controlled]."[87]

A RARG meeting to discuss the CEA/COWPS concerns occurred on May 2, 1978. Prior to this meeting, however, Hawkins and OAQPS had developed another alternative which retained the uncontrolled definition of potential to emit but expanded the

scope of the "two-tier exemption" previously
developed by OAQPS and incorporated in the proposed
regulation. Instead of applying just to increment
consumption analysis, sources whose post-control
emissions (referred to as "allowable emissions")
were less than 50 tons would now also be exempt from
having to use BACT. Hawkins formalized this
proposal in a memorandum back to CEA and COWPS,
stating that EPA believed that a "50 TPY Allowable"
system "could eliminate the need for over 2000
sources to obtain PSD permits each year" with very
little effect on the expected emissions reduction
which PSD would cause.[88] This memo also made it
clear, however, that this was EPA's final offer, and
observed that "confusion regarding PSD is growing in
the absence of regulations."[89]

CEA did not accept this as an adequate
concession and continued to press the issue, both
with Hawkins and with William Drayton, who as noted
earlier was in charge of EPA's economists in the
Office of Planning and Evaluation. When these
efforts proved unsuccessful, a meeting was held
between Charles Schultze, chairman of the Council of
Economic Advisers, and Administrator Costle in which
these arguments were repeated.[90] However, EPA would
make no further concessions, stating that the Agency
had already responded to CEA by using the 50 ton
exemption to eliminate 2400 of a prospective 4000
reviews. EPA also argued that adopting the CEA
approach would result in a "significant increase in
emissions compared to the stricter statutory
approach," with 20% higher particulate emissions,
10% higher SO_2 emissions, and 16% higher hydrocarbon
emissions.[91] Possible emissions increases had not,
of course, stopped EPA from backing off from its
earlier position in the debate over the effective
date. However, in this case there was one
additional factor: EPA's lawyers continued to
insist that the CEA approach was "much less legally
defensible" in addition to being less
environmentally protective.[92] While the CEA/COWPS
economists could argue with EPA about the relative
merits of being "environmentally protective," trying
to argue the law with EPA officials who were

themselves lawyers left CEA's economists at a
disadvantage. Costle rejected the CEA arguments and
the package proceeded to promulgation. Last-minute
objections to the final regulations by the
Department of Energy also failed to derail EPA, and
the "final" PSD regulations were finally promulgated
on June 19, 1978.[93]

The June, 1978 "Final" Regulations

    In addition to the expansion of the 50 ton
exemption, the June 1978 final regulations contained
other changes which accommodated some of the intense
criticism of the November proposal. The theme of
the changes was that once again EPA, rather than
change a general rule to accommodate objections,
instead left the rule intact but created exemptions
to it. In case after case, EPA's June, 1978 final
regulations repeated the approach used to apply the
50 ton exemption to the definition of "potential to
emit," where objections were accommodated not by
changing the definition, but by retaining one which
"caught" a broad spectrum of sources, then allowed
exemptions from the substantive requirements.[94]
    One of the most significant changes was in the
definition of "modification." The November proposal
had defined "major modifications" as applying to
individual emitting units and subjected such
modifications to PSD review. However, despite EPA's
arguments in November that the Clean Air Act
required such an approach, by June the Agency had
managed to change its mind. The final regulations
retained this definition, but went on to create an
exemption from the BACT and ambient impact analysis
requirements if any increased emissions associated
with the modification were offset by decreased
emissions elsewhere at the source. Such an
exemption was strongly favored by industry and by
staff in EPA's Office of Planning and Evaluation.

Faced with this pressure, EPA's attorneys were able
to construct a creative legal argument to justify
the exemption for such modifications. The argument
turned on the fact that EPA had earlier defined
"modifications" this way for NSPS sources. While
EPA ultimately lost in court on this definition for
NSPS purposes, this occurred after the 1977
Amendments had passed. EPA therefore argued that
there was "no reason to believe that the Congress in
late 1977 did not regard the [expanded] definition .
. . as being well suited to its purposes in the PSD
program."[95]
     The pattern occurred in other areas as well.
For BACT, in addition to the 50-ton and major
modification exemptions from BACT review discussed
above, EPA resolved the question posed in the
November proposal by agreeing with comments which
contended that sources which qualified for PSD under
the 250 TPY criteria would only have to apply BACT
for pollutants for which this potential to emit
exceeded 250 tons per year (not 100 tons as the
proposal suggested).[96] In the area of fuel switches,
EPA used a legal argument about Congress' intent
similar to the one developed for major modifications
to reject environmentalists' arguments that
voluntary fuel switches should be treated as
modifications and subject to PSD review (though it
did agree that such switches would consume
increment).[97] EPA also accepted DOE's comments and
backed off its contention in the November, 1977
proposal that certain exemptions from increment
consumptions would only be available in State
implementation plans and not in EPA's rules.
Instead, such exemptions would be available under
EPA's rules as well, though only if a Governor asked
for them and held a public hearing on the request.
Even then the exemptions would only apply for nine
months.[98] Finally, EPA added what was referred to as
the "fugitive dust" exemption. It is perhaps better
described as the strip mine exemption, since its
intent was to exempt strip mines from increment
consumption (though BACT was still to be required
where applicable). Hawkins is reported to have
commented that the battle to regulate strip mines

would have to be left to another day, and the June
1978 <u>Federal Register</u> notice observed that EPA only
intended this exemption to apply "on an interim
basis."[99]
    As EPA's rules became more and more precise
about just what sources did and did not consume
increment and as the associated exemptions grew, the
concept of "baseline concentration" became more and
more problematic. EPA's June, 1978 final rulemaking
shows a growing frustration with the idea of a
"baseline" value. The legal notion that preventing
"significant deterioration" meant preventing changes
in ambient air quality from existing actual levels
had run afoul of the difficulty of implementing such
a scheme while applying the sometimes conflicting
concepts and exemptions which EPA and the Congress
had built in.
    In the 1978 rules, EPA changed its 1977 proposal
and set the "baseline date" at August 7, 1977,
instead of January 6, 1975, as earlier proposed.
EPA noted that a "strict interpretation" of the
Act's language "would require the baseline to be
triggered only when the first source applied for a
PSD permit, but argued that this would create
"thousands of different areas each with different
baseline points" and was administratively
unworkable.[100] However, the baseline date took on
less importance because, in its June final rule, EPA
argued that baseline <u>concentration</u> no longer needed
to be established. The reason for this was that
increment consumption could be tracked adequately
using models, with no need for an actual
establishment of what a baseline level might be.
EPA noted that "data to establish baseline air
quality in an absolute sense would be needed only if
increment consumption were to be tracked using
ambient measurements." While the House committee in
particular appeared to believe this could be done,
EPA's technical experts did not.[101]
    The absence of any need to formally establish an
air quality baseline concentration called into
question the main rationale for the House-imposed
ambient monitoring requirement. EPA's confidence
that such a requirement could be implemented had not

increased since the November proposal. In the June,
1978 final regulations, EPA stated its intention to
largely ignore the monitoring requirements and to
use "existing air quality data to the maximum extent
practicable" and require preconstruction monitoring
only "as necessary." The Agency further stated that
if a source did not threaten to violate a NAAQS, EPA
would exempt the source from the monitoring
requirements.[102]

The press release which announced the final PSD
regulations reflected EPA's sensitivities to critics
inside and outside the Administration who charged
that the Agency was insufficiently sensitive to the
costs of its regulations. The release highlighted
the reduction in the number of sources subject to
PSD as a result of the 50 ton exemption, and also
noted the major modification exemption which would
allow such modifications to escape PSD review if
offsetting emissions decreases occurred elsewhere
within a plant. Administrator Costle's statement
cited these features of the regulations as "examples
of our efforts to streamline new regulatory programs
without sacrificing environmental objectives," and
claimed credit for the regulatory options analysis
done "to ensure that the approach we finally
selected is cost-effective and consistent with our
goal of maintaining clean air."[103]

Certainly compared to the November 1977 proposal
these were true statements. Though the RARG
reviewers were unable to overcome the combined
opposition of Hawkins and the OGC attorneys to
changing the definition of potential to emit, the
expansion of a 50-ton exemption was a victory of
sorts. Much the same can be said of the major
modification exemption, which represented a bow in
the direction of those both inside and outside EPA
who wanted to expand the flexibility of sources to
use less costly controls. The other exemptions and
changes in the June, 1978 regulations reflected
EPA's approach to satisfying PSD's critics by
building in exemptions for sources whose regulation
under PSD appeared particularly troublesome (e.g.,
strip mines; small sources; sources which had pre-
March 1 permits but had delayed construction).

Finally, EPA had created general exemptions from
provisions which the statute appeared to require but
which, as a practical matter, could not be
implemented easily if at all (baseline date;
baseline concentration; ambient monitoring).

However, the price for these exemptions was that
the complexity of the regulations continued to grow.
Evidence of this can be seen in the ever-expanding
length of the <u>Federal Register</u> notices required to
publish and explain the regulations. While EPA's
August 27, 1974, proposed regulations had been 10
pages long and the December 5, 1974, final
regulations were only 8 pages long, the November 3,
1977, proposal (which was "just" supposed to
incorporate Congress' changes) was 18 pages long.
The June 1978 final rules occupied no less than 31
pages in the <u>Federal Register</u>.[104] While the rules
may have been getting more comprehensive, they were
simultaneously getting more complex.

EPA fully anticipated that the June 1978
regulations would be challenged in court. They were
not disappointed, as both industry and environmental
groups filed massive petitions for review of the
rules in the D.C. Circuit Court of Appeals.[105] This
case, known as <u>Alabama Power vs. Costle</u>,[106] would
have a tremendous effect on PSD.

Alabama Power: The Courts Rewrite PSD

Even the hearing in the <u>Alabama Power</u> case was
exceptional. It took two days in the D.C. Circuit
to present oral arguments before a three-judge
panel. Literally thousands of pages of briefs and
supporting evidence were submitted to the court.
The final opinion in the case was ultimately so
complex that each of the three judges had to be
responsible for a separate part of it.

Following EPA's success in the D.C. Circuit's
March, 1979 decision on PSD's effective date

(<u>Citizens to Save Spencer County vs. EPA</u>), EPA's
attorneys may have been optimistic about the outcome
of the <u>Alabama Power</u> litigation. If so, they must
have been disappointed when the court issued its <u>per
curiam</u> (summary) opinion in June, for in its
decision the court rejected many of the key concepts
around which EPA had built its June 1978 final
regulations.

The distinguishing characteristic of the <u>Alabama
Power</u> decision was that the court showed little
deference to the Agency in reading the statute and
its legislative history. The court did this again
and again, beginning with the controversial
definition of "potential to emit." Hawkins and
EPA's lawyers in the Office of General Counsel had
argued that even the 50 ton exemption was something
of a legal "stretch" and that the uncontrolled
definition of potential to emit was unambiguously
mandated by the Act's legislative history. However,
the D.C. Circuit, in an ironic twist, agreed with
the CEA economists that "the fairly discernible
meaning of the statute" was that "potential to emit"
referred to <u>post-control</u> emissions and remanded this
portion of EPA's regulation for revision.[107] The
court dismissed the 50-ton exemption as "academic"
in light of their ruling, although it commented that
the spirit of the exemption exceeded EPA's authority
under the Clean Air Act "to create exemptions based
on cost-effectiveness."[108]

The court also criticized and remanded EPA's
definition of "source." EPA had tried to specify
that PSD should apply to emission increases at
individual pieces of "process equipment," though as
noted above it had included an exemption for
modifications which would not increase total
emissions from a source. The Court reviewed EPA's
attempts to define the term "source" and the
associated terms, "building, structure, facility,
and installation" and, while arguing that EPA had
"flexibility" to define these terms, also concluded
that by including the words "equipment" and
"operation" in the definition of stationary source
EPA had exceeded its statutory authority. The court
based this finding on the non-existence of these

words in EPA's earlier definition of "source" for
NSPS purposes and the same court's earlier finding
in the <u>Asarco</u> case.[109] The court did, however, open
up another avenue for EPA to pursue by suggesting
that the term "facility" was susceptible of a
broader interpretation than EPA had given it.[110]
This seemed to direct EPA to use <u>changes in
definitions</u> (as opposed to exemptions) to achieve
its objectives--changes which in practice would
reduce the number of "sources" subject to PSD. This
suggestion appeared to tell EPA that it had more
flexibility in interpreting terms undefined in the
statute than the Agency had previously used.
However, it also further increased the degree to
which substantive decisions on PSD would turn on the
interpretation of ambiguous words and phrases in the
statute.

Perhaps the clearest example of the court's
literal approach can be seen in its treatment of
another key definition, "major modification." The
court struck down EPA's definition because it
established the same exemption criteria for
modifications--an increase in "potential to emit" of
100/ 250 tons--that were established for new major
stationary sources. EPA, of course, had meant
potential to emit <u>before</u> control, and would have
allowed exemptions for the 50-ton rule and
offsetting emissions decreases. However, the court
read §169(2)(c) to require that, in contrast to new
sources, <u>all</u> modifications that resulted in <u>any</u>
increase in air pollution would be subject to PSD
and that the 100/250 ton exemption was illegal for
modifications.[111] The court gave EPA only the
flexibility to set administrative "de minimis"
exemptions for modifications. The court also struck
down the EPA scheme to subject modifications to
review and exempt them if offsetting decreases
occurred, holding that such modifications should be
<u>completely</u> exempt from PSD.[112]

The logic behind this reasoning bears
examination, as it shows both how literally the
court read the Act and, even more importantly, how
seemingly inconsequential wording changes could have
major effects on PSD's scope. The section on which

the court based its modification ruling reads as
follows:
> (c) The term "construction," when used in
>   connection with any source or facility,
>   includes the modification (as defined in
>   section 111(a)) of any source or facility.[113]

This sentence was not part of the Clean Air Act
Amendments of 1977. Instead, it was added later as
one of the noncontroversial "technical amendments"
to the Act in November 1977.[114] Its effect was to
trigger for PSD the definition of modification used
for NSPS, which provided that:
> (4) The term "modification" means any physical
>   change in, or change in the method of
>   operation of, a stationary source which
>   increases the amount of any air pollutant
>   emitted by such source or which results in
>   the emission of any air pollutant not
>   previously emitted."[115]

It was a literal reading of this provision,
triggered by the "technical" amendment of November
1977, which led the court to conclude that "the
language of the statute clearly did not enact such
[100/250 ton exemption] limit into the law," and
pronounce itself "constrained to follow the clear
language."[115]

The same logic, however, was then turned around
to justify striking down EPA's provision for the
review and subsequent exemption of modifications
with offsetting pollution decreases. Because the
offsets in question were offsets within a "source";
because the language of section 111(a)(4) cited
above did not preclude the word "increases" from
meaning "net increases;" and because an explicit
purpose of PSD was to ensure "that economic growth
occurs in a manner consistent with clean air;" the
court argued that allowing offsetting decreases as a
part of the definition of modification was
"precisely suited" to PSD.[117]

Legal students have questioned the validity of
the court's legal reasoning in attempting to
reconcile its rulings on "facilities," "sources" and
"modification" in Alabama Power with earlier rulings
in ASARCO vs. EPA, where the meaning of the terms

were defined for the NSPS program.[118] What is
significant, however, is how the court looked for
guidance in the detailed language of the Act rather
than the judgment of the Agency. Only "de minimis"
exemptions would be allowed to a literal reading of
the statute's words. Such a approach is consistent
with the view that the courts, in reviewing agency
implementation of detailed statutes, should ensure
that agencies do not overstep the bounds created by
these statutes. It does not, however, necessarily
simplify the administration of these same statutes--
a fact acknowledged by the court itself.[119]
Establishing defensible "de minimis" values would
become one of EPA's chief difficulties in revising
its regulations in the wake of Alabama Power.

In each of the other three areas discussed
earlier--BACT, baseline and the monitoring
requirements--the Alabama Power decision made
comparable changes based on the same principle that
regardless of EPA's judgment, a close reading and
interpretation of the statute's text by the court
took priority. On BACT, the court struck down EPA's
exemption for pollutants at a major stationary
source emitted in amounts less than 100/250 TPY,
arguing that the provision in §165 requiring BACT
"for each pollutant subject to regulation under this
Act emitted from, or which results from, such
facility" meant that it did "not exempt pollutants
emitted at quantities less than" the cutoff
levels.[120] Again, the court told EPA it could
specify "de minimis" exemptions, but these would
have to be "rationally designed to alleviate severe
administrative burdens, not to extend the statutory
100 or 250-ton threshold to a context where Congress
clearly did not apply it."[121]

In a different section of the opinion, the court
was even more forceful in reversing EPA's judgment
on the issue of baseline date. Criticizing EPA for
its "remarkable assertion of administrative power to
revise what Congress has wrought," the court
forcefully asserted that "EPA has no authority to
overrule a clear, consistent congressional
directive" and required EPA to trigger separate
baseline dates depending on the date of the first

PSD permit application. This was the interpretation of baseline which EPA had most feared.[122]

The court justified this decision by noting that the conference committee had explicitly adopted the Senate definition of baseline which contained this requirement.[123] The court failed to note, however, that this definition of "baseline" had been attached to a PSD program quite different in concept from the one which ultimately emerged from the conference committee. While the Senate "baseline" definition made some sense in the context of the Senate bill, it created an administrative nightmare when combined with the House approach which included specific types of sources within the "baseline" and did not specify that only major emitting facilities would consume increment. Adding to the complexity was the inclusion of emissions from sources which "commenced construction" before January 6, 1975, but were not "in operation" before the "baseline date" was established were to be included in the "baseline concentration" only complicated matters further (though the court did uphold EPA's rules on this point).[124] The court again showed little deference to the implementation concerns expressed by EPA, adopting instead a literal statutory reading regardless of the confusion which would result.[125]

Nor was administrative confusion the only concern whose value was discounted by the court. In treating the monitoring requirements, the court argued that EPA had improperly limited its application of the pre-construction monitoring requirement in the statute because this requirement was "technologically infeasible." Instead, the court agreed that the statute had a "technology-forcing objective" in three respects. First, the court argued that the monitoring requirements would serve to discipline modeling techniques (though this made no sense because preconstruction monitoring cannot validate emissions modeling of a source not yet constructed). Secondly, it would stimulate the development of monitoring techniques for pollutants other than the criteria pollutants covered by EPA's regulations. Finally, the court argued that the need to develop and submit accurate ambient data would further "the development of sophisticated monitoring techniques."[126] While upon later reflection the court did limit its requirement for monitoring data to criteria pollutants,[127] it nevertheless rejected EPA's attempt to limit pre-construction monitoring and ordered the Agency to require such data in permit applications. Again, the basis for this decision was a literal reading of the statutory text which said that the permit analysis "shall include continuous air quality monitoring data . . ."[128]

Other examples of the court's approach exist (i.e., the determination of how PSD review and nonattainment review related to each other). However, the issues discussed above clearly show the direction taken by the court in reviewing EPA's June 19, 1978, regulations. The court's opinion amounted to a total rewrite of the PSD regulations, in painful detail. Interestingly enough, the court showed no particular "environmental" or "industry" bias; some decisions (such as potential to emit and modification offsets) cut against environmental interests, while others (such as modification exemptions, BACT application and monitoring) ran counter to industry arguments. The deciding factor in each decision was a literal reading by the court of the statute's words. This approach has been criticized as "mechanistic,"[129] and indeed it seems that the court in the Alabama Power opinion was more concerned with syntax than with practicability or the implementability of some of its decisions. The approach taken in the case stands in stark contrast to both the opinion in the 1972 Sierra Club vs. Ruckelshaus decision, where the district court overturned an Agency rule but said little about what to do to fix it, and the 1976 Sierra Club vs. EPA decision where the same D.C. Circuit affirmed EPA's 1974 regulations in their entirety. In Alabama Power, the court felt confident that the statutory language told the Agency exactly what it was supposed to do.

It is worth remembering that only the existence of a detailed agency-forcing statute made such a literalist reading possible. The logic of the

<u>Alabama Power</u> decision is a consequence of such
highly prescriptive legislation. Whether it was a
desirable consequence is less clear. The <u>Alabama
Power</u> decision threw EPA and the regulated community
back into another extended period of uncertainty
over just what the rules were. Moreover, by showing
so little deference to EPA's technical judgments
about the feasibility of such things as the
monitoring requirements and the determination of
baseline concentration, the court reinforced the
tendency within the regulated community to focus on
PSD as an opportunity for endless litigation over
the program's particulars rather than as a
requirement for air pollution control. Still, a
somewhat disappointed EPA had little choice but to
once again take up the task of revising its
regulations.

EPA Tries Again: The 1980 PSD Regulations

     In issuing its preliminary opinion in the
<u>Alabama Power</u> case, the D.C. Circuit took the
unusual step of giving the parties to the suit an
opportunity to submit "narrowly focused petitions
for reconsideration" to the court.[130]   EPA petitioned
on only one issue, however--the applicability of PSD
to sources located in a non-attainment area and
emitting a pollutant for which the area was non-
attainment, but which might have an effect on an
adjoining attainment area.   There was apparently no
consideration by EPA of appealing the broader
aspects of the <u>Alabama Power</u> decision.[131]
     Instead, EPA staff from OAQPS, OGC and OPE
feverishly worked through the summer of 1979 to
prepare a set of proposed revisions to EPA's rules,
in the hopes of influencing the final opinion which
the Court had promised to issue "before the end of
this summer."[132] Having been criticized by the court
for failing to adopt a <u>literal</u> reading of the Act,

EPA staff were reluctant to do anything other than
take the same literal approach to the Alabama Power
decision which the court had applied to the statute.
On the other hand, because the court had intervened
in so many interrelated areas, it was difficult to
make changes in one part of the regulations without
having unintended effects on other parts. The
complexity of the court's opinion and the difficulty
of sorting out the interrelated changes required
marathon meetings and an enormous staff commitment
in the summer of 1979. Hawkins reportedly captured
the frustration of this process by wondering in the
midst of one of these sessions if all the
participants had died and that this task represented
hell.[133]

Pushed by Hawkins, EPA produced a new set of
proposed PSD regulations in early September, less
than three months after the court's preliminary
opinion.[134] Due to the speed with which the proposal
was developed, it was not accompanied by a RARG-
required economic impact analysis, though the Agency
did promise that one would be conducted and made
available for public comment prior to the
promulgation of final regulations.[135]

Despite the specificity of the Alabama Power
decision, EPA was still faced with interpretations
which affected the stringency of the regulations.
For example, while the decision on "potential to
emit" seemed clear, EPA found a loophole which it
proposed to eliminate in the September proposal.
The June 1978 regulations had allowed a source which
was a candidate for PSD to limit its emissions and
possibly escape review by accepting "enforceable
permit conditions which limit the annual hours of
operation."[136] However, in the September, 1979
proposal, EPA claimed that the court in the Alabama
Power decision "plainly thought" that potential to
emit "should be based on [a source's] full design
capacity, and proposed to remove this exemption.[137]
This expanded the number of plants possibly subject
to PSD, since few plants operate 24 hours a day, 365
days a year as EPA proposed to presume they would in
assessing "full design capacity."[138]

In defining "source," EPA also adopted the court
ruling, but again added a new twist. EPA argued
that the combined effect of the court's ASARCO and
Alabama Power decisions was that EPA had
"substantial discretion" to define the term "source"
differently for different regulatory purposes under
the Act so long as they were based on a "reasoned
application of the terms of the statute."[139] This
led EPA to conclude, with the court, that a "bubble
approach" should be used by defining "source" as
equal to an entire plant for PSD purposes.[140] This,
as noted above, allowed the use of offsetting
emissions decreases to exempt modifications from PSD
review. However, in a shift from its earlier
approach, EPA took advantage of the Alabama Power
decision to modify its definition of "source" for
non-attainment areas so that it referred to
individual pieces of process equipment and did not
allow the use of offsetting decreases to exempt
modifications from review in such areas. EPA argued
that this definition was required because "non-
attainment programs, in contrast to PSD programs,
must positively reduce emissions."[141]

This change, which became known as the "dual
source definition," provoked controversy within EPA,
especially in OPE where it was opposed on the
grounds that it would reduce the flexibility of
industry to comply with the Act and increase the
complexity of the rules regarding the review of new
plants. In a memo to Hawkins concurring reluctantly
with the September, 1979 proposal, OPE cited this
change in definition as one which they would "agree
to because of its potential safeguards, but we are
not at all convinced of its merits."[142] However, the
dual definition enjoyed support from both OGC and
the Office of Enforcement, and this was sufficient
to enable the Air office to prevail on this issue.

One of the most difficult aspects of the
September 5, 1979 proposal proved to be dealing with
the court remands of the exemptions from review of
modifications, BACT and the monitoring requirements.
While invalidating EPA's exemptions, the court had
said in each area that EPA could create "de minimis"
exemptions if it could demonstrate administrative

necessity.   However, the decision gave no guidance
on how this was to be done.

Faced with this situation, EPA proposed in each
case to allow exemptions based on whether the
increased emissions (for modifications and BACT) or
projected ambient impact (for monitoring) would be
"significant."   "Significant" was defined in two
tables of values, one for emissions (Table 1) and
one for ambient impacts (Table 2), in the preamble
to the regulations.   In the case of modifications
and BACT, only if a source projected that emissions
of a pollutant would increase by more than the value
in Table 1 would the change be "significant" and
thus subject to review and controls.   Air quality
review and modeling were similarly only to be
required if projected ambient impacts exceeded the
values in Table 2.[143]   The values in both tables
covered all pollutants regulated under the Act, not
just criteria pollutants, and in general were very
conservative.   They were developed through a quick
analysis by OAQPS staff, and EPA in its proposal
acknowledged that because of the time constraints
the tables were "not supported by extensive
analysis," and could change based on "public comment
or followup investigation."[144]   The development of
these significance or "de minimis" values bore a
striking resemblance to EPA's development of the
original increment values in 1973-74, only this time
it was done for even more pollutants and on a more
compressed time schedule.

While a logic trail can be constructed for the
various changes made by EPA in the September
proposal, it is more important for our purposes to
note that they continued the trend of increasing the
regulations' complexity.   This was especially true
for the new rules on modifications, "significant"
increases and "de minimis" exemptions.   Even worse,
the program was now so splintered and hedged about
with exceptions that it was beginning to produce
absurd results.   Perhaps the best illustration of
this can be seen by looking at the examples
developed by EPA of just how the new rules would
work.   These examples showed that the same source
might or might not be subject to control

requirements depending on whether it a) was a new
source or a modification, and b) was located in an
area which was classified as attainment or non-
attainment for the pollutant emitted by the source.
This could lead to the perverse result that a source
might be subject to <u>more</u> control if it were located
in a PSD area than if located in a non-attainment
area.[145]
    Such outcomes seemed to stand the purposes of
the Clean Air Act on their head. They led OPE to
issue a warning that the complexity and
inconsistency of the regulations were getting out of
control.

> . . . We should place greater weight on
> eliminating unnecessary complexity in the Act,
> seeking options that are administratively simple
> while providing necessary safeguards. We
> continue to complicate the program by providing
> environmental safeguards for problems of unknown
> magnitude. We should develop a better
> understanding of the consequences before we risk
> political backlash against the Act due to its
> complexity . . ."[146]

This warning, however, had little effect. The
development of the PSD regulations seemed to have
reached a point where major policy decisions seemed
to turn more on the precise definition of particular
words than on the substance of the policy itself.

THE AUGUST 1980 "FINAL" REGULATIONS

    The court was no more successful than EPA in
meeting PSD deadlines. Although it had promised a
final opinion by the end of the summer of 1979, the
opinion was not issued until December 14, 1979.[147]
The final opinion changed little of substance from
the <u>per curiam</u> opinion, though in a bow to
technological feasibility it did give EPA
flexibility not to require monitoring for pollutants

for which monitoring techniques did not exist.[148] In
the meantime, EPA had proceeded to conduct public
hearings and develop an economic impact analysis on
the proposed rules.[149] When the final opinion was
issued, EPA and other parties to the suit petitioned
the court to stay its effect until June 2, 1980 so
that EPA could finish its rulemaking. Even this
extension turned out to be insufficient, and EPA had
to request a further extension until the end of
July.[150] In the meantime, EPA issued a stay of its
PSD requirements with respect to sources which would
have been subject to the pre-_Alabama Power_
requirements, but which it appeared would not be
subject to the new regulations.[151]

EPA received the usual barrage of comments on
the September 1979 proposal (375 in all). What
changes did occur followed the past pattern of
loosening the proposal, though with a few important
exceptions. For example, EPA reversed itself on
"potential to emit" by allowing "federally
enforceable" restrictions on "hours of operation or
on the type or amount of material combusted, stored,
or processed" to restrict a source's potential to
emit and thus affect whether the source was subject
to PSD.[152] A highly technical change was made at
OPE's urging in the definition of "source" which
restricted the effect of the proposed definition in
making co-located industries constructing
simultaneously subject to PSD because of the broad
definition of "facility."[153] However, an exception
to the general trend of loosening the September
proposal also occurred in defining "source," as EPA
not only retained the "dual definition" proposed in
September, but tightened it by extending its
application to non-attainment areas with and without
approved demonstrations of attainment. The final
preamble stated that while the "use of different
definitions . . . adds to the complexity of the
permitting process . . . this complexity is
outweighed by the need for a more inclusive
definition of source in non-attainment areas in
order to assure attainment of standards."[154]

Among the changes to make the regulations less
restrictive, EPA increased the _de minimis_ values for

modification, BACT applicability and monitoring
which it had proposed in September in response to
"public comments" which favored such an increase.
The degree to which industry focused on commenting
on PSD can be seen in the 68 to 1 ratio of comments
favoring increased <u>de minimis</u> levels.[155] Faced with
this overwhelming sentiment, EPA presented an
elaborate technical justification for its decision,
but also added a <u>caveat</u> which said that even <u>de</u>
<u>minimis</u> sources near Class I areas might be subject
to PSD review.[156]

    Finally, EPA made a number of other changes
based on the public comments and its reading of the
final <u>Alabama Power</u> decision in the rules governing
the relationship between PSD and nonattainment
review, baseline area, the use of actual and
allowable emissions in calculating increment
consumption, and the provisions governing how
sources which already had PSD permits under the old
rules might go about getting those permits
modified.[157] No general conclusions can be drawn
about the effect of these changes on the relative
stringency of PSD. Some (for example, the
transition provisions on requiring monitoring data)
simply reflected administrative necessity and a
desire to give sources ample notice of the
applicability of the new provisions. Others (e.g.,
the expansion of PSD review in areas which were
attainment for at least one criteria pollutant
(almost everywhere in the country) represented an
expansion of PSD. Still others (e.g., a pollutant-
specific baseline based on impact area) had the
potential to relax PSD. The one thing they shared
in common is that, together with the other PSD
provisions discussed earlier, they had become
immensely confusing even to the air pollution
control professionals responsible for PSD policy.
By the time these final regulations were published,
one of the strongest sentiments which EPA staff
could muster was horror at the fact that the final
<u>Federal Register</u> package of rules and preamble was
48 pages long.[158]

Epilogue: PSD Today

EPA staff hoped that the August 1980 promulgation would end the cycle of litigation surrounding PSD. However, this was not to be, as industry groups challenged the 1980 regulations.[159] Following the election of Ronald Reagan as President and the appointment of Anne Gorsuch as EPA Administrator, EPA consented to a settlement agreement which required the Agency to propose changes favored by industry in EPA's PSD rules.[160] While EPA did uphold its end of the settlement agreement and _proposed_ changes, the settlement proved to be very controversial both inside and outside the Agency, and EPA has not as of this writing taken final action on all of these proposals. As a result, the August 7, 1980, rules are still in place.[161]

However, industry's main hope for substantive relaxations in the PSD rules lay not with the Agency or the courts, but with the Congress. The Clean Air Act was scheduled for reauthorization in 1981, and in anticipation industry had prepared a sophisticated lobbying campaign aimed at persuading Congress that substantial changes were needed in PSD. The chief spokesman for industry, ironically, was John Quarles, the former EPA Deputy Administrator who had signed the Agency's PSD proposal in August 1974.[162]

Industry was not alone in calling for reform of PSD. EPA's own Carter-era Regional Administrators charged that PSD "has resulted in an extended, complex permit process which has done little to improve air quality," and that the program was "too dependent on modeling, difficult to administer, time-consuming and expensive."[163] State air pollution control officials adopted resolutions calling for the elimination of the Class II and III increments and raising the _de minimis_ levels for modifications to 100 tons per years--positions very

similar to those taken by industry.[164] Finally, in
the spring of 1981, the National Commission on Air
Quality--whose establishment had been the source of
such controversy in the 1976 Congressional debate on
Clean Air Act Amendments--issued its report. The
Commission recommendations on PSD were similar to
those of the States--change the "de minimis"
exemptions to 100 tons, eliminate Class III and
Class II (except for mandatory or State-designated
Class II areas), require case by case BACT only for
sources with emissions greater than 500 tons per
year, and eliminate the preconstruction monitoring
requirement.[165]

Thus, when the Senate Environment and Public
Works Committee opened oversight hearings in April
1981, it seemed reasonable to expect that more
changes in PSD would be forthcoming. The
requirements contained in the August 1980
regulations had few defenders outside of the
environmental groups--the Sierra Club, the NRDC, and
the Environmental Defense Fund--who had fought to
create and expand PSD over the preceding ten years.
In the anti-regulation mood which accompanied the
Reagan election, these groups seemed as much on the
defensive as they had been earlier in 1974 and 1975.

Yet despite this seeming consensus, Congress
made no changes in the PSD requirements in the early
1980's. In large measure this was because of the
stalemate which developing over making any change in
the Clean Air Act. In the absence of an action-
forcing deadline such as the auto standards of 1977,
Congress was unable to agree on any basic framework
for Act revisions.[166] Neither environmental groups
who advocated increased controls on acid rain or
toxic air pollutants, nor industrial critics who
wished to relax auto emissions controls were able to
muster the political support necessary to produce
positive action, although were able to block
initiatives by the other.[167]

The resulting stalemate has preserved PSD in its
1980 form. In that form, the implementation of PSD
proceeded. Once it became apparent that the rules
were not going to be changed again by Congress and
under some pressure from EPA, most States eventually

took on the responsibility for administering PSD.
In so doing, they have been able to make PSD work,
though EPA audit reports suggest that confusion
still exists about such questions as how to assess
increment consumption. However, in general the
States have become more successful over time in
applying the complex requirements of PSD.[168]
Moreover, available data suggest that the States are
making practical decisions which have the effect of
reducing the administrative burden of PSD. For
example, few sources actually have to conduct their
own pre-construction ambient monitoring, but use
existing representative data instead, with both
States and EPA adopting relatively generous
interpretations of what constitutes "representative
data".[169]

  In the late 1980's, there was a new round of
regulatory activity on certain aspects of the PSD
program. In two areas, this activity was prompted
by lawsuits. In 1985, environmental groups in
California sued EPA in the Ninth Circuit Court of
Appeals to comply with the provisions of Section 166
regarding increments for oxides of nitrogen.
Although Section 166 required that these increments
be set by August, 1979, EPA had abandoned any
efforts to comply with this requirement early in
1981 for both technical reasons and because of
management decisions that other air programs had
higher priority in times of limited resources.
Although the Agency raised both of these defenses in
the suit, the Ninth Circuit gave them little weight,
and ordered EPA to comply with the terms of Section
166 in a very short period of time. Consequently,
EPA finally did promulgate nitrogen oxide
increments, which were calculated as a percentage of
the NO_x ambient standard--the same approach followed
in the original House bill for the SO_2 and TSP
increments. However, these increments are not
expected to have a great deal of impact on the PSD
regulatory system, since major NOx sources were
already required to apply BACT regardless of their
incremental air quality impact.[170]

  A second litigation front remained open on the
question of whether surface coal mines were subject

372   **Protect and Enhance**

to PSD because of fugitive emissions from the mines.
It will be recalled that this issue had been left
open in the 1980 rules. The Sierra Club sued EPA on
this question, and in response, the Agency undertook
a series of rulemakings which culminated in a
determination that for strip mines, fugitive
emissions alone would not subject the mines to
regulation as a major source under PSD. One of
EPA's chief rationales for this decision was that
the environmental impacts of such mines were already
sufficiently controlled by the Department of the
Interior. Further litigation in this area appears
likely.[171]

In these two areas, the timing if not the
substance of EPA's actions was largely dictated by
court requirements. However, other areas of PSD
controversy in the late 1980's reflected new
initiatives by the Agency. The first resulted from
EPA's decision in 1987 to drop the total suspended
particulate (TSP) ambient standard in favor of a
form of that standard which limited only those
particles smaller than 10 microns in diameter, and
standard known as "PM-10". With the disappearance
of the TSP standard, EPA concluded that it made
little sense to maintain a dual regulatory structure
by retaining TSP increments, and initiated a
rulemaking to establish PM-10 increments which would
be of equal stringency to the existing TSP
increments and would allow for a unified regulatory
scheme for particulate matter. This rulemaking was
not complete as of this writing but seemed to be
proceeding as of this writing and was specifically
authorized in the 1990 Clean Air Act Amendments.

EPA's policy on the issue of just what level of
control constitutes Best Available Control
Technology (BACT) has proved more controversial. A
1987 EPA task force concluded, among other things,
that PSD permitting authorities were not following
the intent of the statute to provide for case by
case determinations of BACT at facilities subject to
PSD. As a result, permitting authorities were
treating applicable NSPS standards more as a ceiling
than a floor, and permit applicants were not
adequately justifying decisions to require less

stringent controls than might otherwise be deemed "available."

In a December 1, 1987 memorandum from Assistant Administrator J. Craig Potter to EPA's Regional Administrators, EPA directed that more emphasis be given to the quality of these BACT analyses. In particular, such analyses were to start with the most stringent technologically available control alternative, and then proceed to look at less stringent alternatives only if the most stringent alternative was explicitly determined to be available considering the criteria of cost, energy, and environmental impacts as identified in Section 165 of the Act. To implement this approach, which received the name of "top down BACT", EPA's Regional offices were directed to begin exercising closer review of State BACT determinations.[172]

This approach produced an uproar. While EPA argued that the memorandum merely reflected and reinforced the existing policy and requirements of the statute, some States initially complained because they believed that the policy undermined State prerogatives on BACT determinations. However, State complaints were mild compared to those coming from industry, which argued that top down BACT represented a radical departure from the law and the 1980 regulations, and amounted to rulemaking by policy memorandum. The American Paper Institute and the Utility Air Regulatory Group, both of which were old opponents of PSD, filed suit against the Agency in 1988 on these grounds. As of this writing the case has not been settled. It is true that the debate over BACT has now narrowed and shifted from one over whether major sources in attainment areas should have good technological controls to one over just what level of controls should apply. However, this dispute simply reinforces yet again the principle that even highly detailed statutes and Agency rules cannot resolve highly technical disputes in areas where technical judgments and expertise matter greatly.

Finally, a new wrinkle emerged in the debate over the meaning of the concepts of modification and potential to emit. Some observers had thought that

the seeming lull in the arguments over PSD which
occurred in the early 1980's was a function of the
economic recession and declines in projected growth
in the electric utility sector, and that the debate
would reemerge in full force when utilities which
had overbuilt capacity in the early 1970's began to
look again at constructing new facilities. Events
in the late 1980's seemed to suggest some truth to
this, but with an unexpected twist. In the late
1980's, it began to appear that utilities were
adopting a conscious strategy of delaying the
retirement of old, unregulated electric utility
generating units because of the difficulty and cost
of constructing large new units. Such new units
would unquestionably have been subject to NSPS and
PSD controls. Older units, however, could escape
review under either of these requirements so long as
the repairs needed to keep the older units on line
were not so extensive as to trigger the modification
or reconstruction provisions of the PSD or NSPS
regulations.

In 1988, the Wisconsin Electric Power Company
(WEPCO) proposed such a project at its facility in
Port Washington, Wisconsin. The project was billed
as a major "life extension project" at the plant and
included, among other things, replacements of major
capital equipment at one unit (which was not then in
operation), and very extensive repairs at other
units at the same plant, which for safety reasons
were then operating well below their design
capacity. Upon review of the project, EPA
determined that it was subject to PSD requirements,
because it constituted a major modification which,
by increasing the potential ability of the plant to
generate electricity over existing unrepaired
levels, would result in a significant increase in
the plant's potential emissions when compared to
present-day actual emissions levels (a test known as
the "actuals to potentials" test). WEPCO, on the
other hand, argued that EPA should not use current
actual emissions as the baseline from which to
measure the projected increase in future emissions.
WEPCO, with the support of the utility industry and
the Department of Energy, held that since the

project would merely restore the plant to its
previously existing rated capacity, the baseline
should be the previous potential emissions level and
that these emissions would not change. WEPCO,
moreover, argued that the project was more in the
nature of repairs than a modification. For both
these reasons, the company denied that the project
should be subject to either NSPS or PSD.

Litigation between the company and EPA ensued.
The specific case resulted in a compromise on the
issue of the actual/potential baseline emissions
which allowed the project to go forward with some
level of additional controls. These controls
enabled the facility to reduce its net emissions
increase below the threshold which would make it a
major modification for PSD review purposes.
However, the interest of other utilities in pursuing
their own "life extension projects," along with
concern in the utility industry and in the
Department of Energy about the possible effects of
the WEPCO decision on DOE's Clean Coal Technology
demonstration projects, meant that the issue of the
appropriate baseline for utility modifications did
not die with the settlement of the WEPCO case. In
fact, the issue grew to the point that it became the
PSD concern which received the most attention when
the stalemate over the Clean Air Act broke at long
last in 1989-90.

PSD AND THE 1990 CLEAN AIR ACT AMENDMENTS[173]

The Clean Air Act Amendments of 1990 represent
by far the most sweeping U.S. air pollution control
legislation since the 1970 amendments. New
requirements are added in the areas of
nonattainment, mobile sources, acid rain, air
toxics, stratospheric ozone control, national
operating permits, and enforcement. Though it is
still far too early to tell just how they will work
out, it seems likely from past experience to expect
that these amendments will set the path for air

pollution control in the U.S. for the next twenty
years. In this context, what is most significant
about PSD in the relation to the Clean Air Act
Amendments of 1990 is that the amendments barely
mention PSD at all.

This stark contrast to the expectations of 1981-
82 was no accident. By 1989, the dominant agenda
for Clean Air Act amendments had changed
significantly. While in 1981-82 the dominant theme
for amendments had been regulatory relief, by 1989 a
new upsurge in attention to the environment had
increased the political leverage of groups favoring
stronger air pollution control laws. Environmental
issues had become a significant issue in the 1988
Presidential election, with both candidates
promising stronger programs than those of the Reagan
Administration. George Bush came into office
promising to be the environmental President, and
appointed the head of the Conservation Foundation,
William K. Reilly, to be the new Administrator of
EPA. The Administration's position on amendments to
the Clean Air Act came to be seen as an early test
of the Administration's commitment to environmental
protection.

Other forces also contributed to the breaking of
the long stalemate over amendments to the Act.
House and Senate committees in the 100th Congress
had considered a number of proposed amendments, but
neither House nor Senate leaders had been able to
successfully approve legislation in their respective
chambers. In the House, the longstanding battle
between Congressmen Dingell and Waxman kept any
proposal from even making it out of the Energy and
Commerce Committee. In the Senate, the opposition
of Senator Robert Byrd, the Senate Majority Leader,
kept any legislation concerning acid rain from
coming to the Senate floor. Since it was generally
felt that some kind of acid rain program would be a
component of any amendments, this effectively
foreclosed Senate action.

However, in late 1988 Senator Byrd announced he
would be stepping down as Majority Leader to assume
the chairmanship of the Senate Appropriations
Committee. In the ensuing election, Senator George

Mitchell of Maine was selected as the new Senate
Majority Leader. Following in the tradition of
Edmund Muskie, Senator Mitchell had been the
chairman of the Environmental Pollution Subcommittee
of the Senate Environment and Public Works
Committee, where he had worked hard in the 100th
Congress to advance Clean Air Act amendments. Upon
his election as Majority Leader, Mitchell made it
clear that he expected amendments to be among the
top priorities for the Senate in the 101st Congress.

The combination of political change in the
Senate and the election of a more environmentally
oriented President created the essential conditions
to break the logjam on amendments. Other factors
added momentum as well. The nonattainment
provisions of the old Act were increasingly out of
date. Cities like Los Angeles and Chicago, which
were supposed to attain clean air standards by 1987
but had not, were finding themselves subject to
litigation under the old Act to require them to
implement difficult measures in a very short time.
The tragic accident in Bhopal, India, where over 200
people were killed in an accidental release of toxic
methyl isocyanate gas, focused heightened attention
on the U.S. toxic air pollutant control program and
on the slow pace of national regulation, with only 7
chemicals covered in the 18 years since the 1970
amendments. New concerns about global warming and
stratospheric ozone depletion heightened public
awareness about air pollution. Finally, automobile
manufacturers came under continued pressure from
California for tighter control of emissions from
cars and trucks. While California maintained its
own research and regulatory programs to demonstrate
that additional reductions could be achieved in this
area, other States, especially in the Northeast,
began to look at adopting the California standards
in their area, thus presenting the automobile
manufacturers with the increasing prospect of a
patchwork of emissions standards nationwide.

While the 101st Congress opened early in 1989 by
reintroducing many of the proposals developed and
introduced in the 100th Congress, all groups waited
to see what the new Bush Administration would do.

The Administration, after an intense internal debate, announced on June 12, 1989 a comprehensive Clean Air Act amendment proposal covering acid rain control, nonattainment, air toxics, and mobile sources. Also included were new authorities for enforcement and for air pollution operating permits for major sources.

The President's proposal, however, said almost nothing about PSD. This absence reflected two things. First, the President's proposal already encompassed a large number of significant new air pollution control initiatives. The development of these initiatives and their explanation to the significant policy actors in the new Administration over a period of 5 months had taken an enormous amount of time and energy. These initiatives were extremely complex in and of themselves. Adding PSD to them would simply have overloaded the system.

Second, there were no effective advocates for changes in PSD law. Environmental groups which might have sought to tighten PSD were preoccupied with acid rain proposals, as were utility groups. Business groups which had supported changes to PSD law in 1981-82, such as John Quarles' National Environmental Development legislation, saw air toxics, nonattainment, and permitting changes as higher priorities for attention. There was no independent Congressional interest in PSD by either the Senate or the House committee staff--in fact, there was active disinterest by key Congressional staff who felt that the amendments already covered enough ground, and who remembered that PSD had been one of the reasons for the collapse of the 1982 effort to amend the Act. Finally, EPA had no desire to reopen controversies over PSD which if not settled in principle were working in practice.

Thus the President's proposal contained only a relatively small number of changes to PSD which had been advanced by EPA staff as housekeeping measures. The first was to eliminate the requirement under section 166 to set PSD ambient measures, equal at least in effect to increments, for other air pollutants such as ozone and carbon monoxide. The second was to explicitly authorize EPA to replace the existing TSP increments with equivalent PM-10 increments. The third was to fix an arcane problem--to allow the Class I area boundaries of mandatory Class I areas such as national parks to expand to match the geographic boundary of the area whenever the geographic boundary expanded because of addition land acquisition around the borders of the park. The fourth was to fix the problem which was not settled by the strip mine litigation--to exempt strip mines from consuming increment in areas where the baseline date had been triggered even if the strip mine itself was not considered a "major" source.[174] The fifth, supported strongly by DOE, exempted Clean Coal Technology demonstration projects from meeting PSD requirements.

Ultimately, only the provisions on PM-10 increments, Class I area boundary changes, and Clean Coal Technology projects were finally included in the 1990 amendments. The proposed deletion of the section 166 requirements was rejected by the Waxman Subcommittee and deleted from the bill. The strip mine provisions were the subject of last minute negotiating between Senate and House members, but in the rush to complete action on amendments, final agreements could not be reached, with the result that all relevant language was dropped from the conference report.

During the eighteen months in which the 1990 Clean Air Act amendments were consideration by the Congress, only two other matters pertaining to PSD received much attention. Both concerned electric utilities.

The first was an old controversy. Senator Alan Simpson of Wyoming, along with other Western Senators, saw in the acid rain title of the bill an opportunity to repeal of the so-called "percentage reduction" requirement. This provision had required EPA to set a New Source Performance Standard (NSPS) which forced all large new coal-fired electric power plants to use scrubbers, even plants burning low-sulfur Western coal.[175] Added in the 1977 amendments, this requirement was anathema to Western interests which felt that it limited their competitive advantage over higher sulfur Eastern

coal. In the Senate Environment and Public Works
Committee markup of the 1990 amendments, Simpson
successfully added a provision deleting percentage
reduction and requiring EPA to revise the NSPS in 3
years so that it did not require percentage
reduction but still had the same environmental
effect.[176]

Although pleased with this development, Western
interests were still concerned that even though the
NSPS might not require scrubbing, a "top down" BACT
requirement could. Therefore, language was added to
the 1990 amendments whose intent was to ensure that
case by case BACT requirements would not be
interpreted to require the use of scrubbers if the
NSPS was modified to avoid scrubber requirements.
While this closed the issue for the moment, whether
this provision will have any practical impact on
utilities remains to be seen, especially in light of
1) the new acid rain control requirements, 2) the
fact that since 1979 scrubbers have become a well
demonstrated control technology, and 3) concerns
about the impact of large power plants on Western
visibility.

The other area of debate over PSD in the 1990
amendments was a consequence of EPA's action in the
WEPCO case discussed earlier. The Department of
Energy, reflecting the concerns of the electric
utility industry about the impact of the WEPCO
decision on other planned life extension projects at
large electric utility plants, argued strongly both
within the Administration and in Congress for
statutory language which would limit the degree to
which such projects would be subject to PSD. After
extensive discussion, an Administration proposal was
developed and sent to Congress which addressed this
problem and gave additional exemptions to life
extension projects. However, despite considerable
effort and interest, ultimately the Congressional
negotiators were unable to resolve this issue, and
instead punted the matter back to EPA and DOE to
resolve through an interpretive rule.

While these controversies were real enough in
themselves, the absence of changes to PSD in the
1990 amendments is striking nevertheless. Although

clearly the scope and importance of the other issues
at stake in the 1990 amendments helped keep PSD
issues off the legislative agenda, this development
may also suggest that at last PSD has reached a
greater level of maturity. The principle of BACT
controls on major sources has become a matter of
conventional wisdom, even if debate continues over
just what BACT is in particular cases or just what
constitutes "considering cost." EPA, States and
industries are more skilled at handling the
difficult questions of applicability, baselines,
actual vs. allowable vs. potential emissions, and
"equivalent" monitoring data, so that when the
opportunity for legislative change finally arrived,
PSD concerns were overwhelmed by nonattainment, air
toxics, and acid rain control. One possible
conclusion from these events is that when left alone
by Congress for a long enough period of time, EPA,
States, environmental groups, and industry can
resolve conflicts without abandoning either
statutory direction or being captured by regulated
interests, even when these interests are strong and
the conflict is substantial. Certainly PSD's
history from 1980 to 1990 was more stable than its
history from 1972 to 1980! If true, however, this
has rather striking implications for Professor
Lowi's advocacy of the need for detailed statutory
instructions for regulatory agencies.

**Implementing the 1977 Amendments: Some Concluding
Thoughts**

     In passing the 1977 Amendments, Congress did not
eliminate uncertainty but, at least in the short
run, increased it. An environmentally activist EPA
initially took advantage of this uncertainty and,
together with its Congressional allies, attempted to
implement a stringent PSD program as rapidly as
possible following the 1977 Amendments. Though

forced to back off from its initial stringent interpretations in almost every area, the Agency did so in 1977-78 by carving out a series of narrow exemptions which preserved the program's broad scope while giving some relief to industry. Regulatory reformers both inside and outside EPA were able to influence the course of the regulations and gain partial victories, but were not successful in fully overcoming objections by EPA lawyers and program advocates that their reform proposals were illegal.

Ironically, on the key issue of "potential to emit" the economists were sustained as opposed to the lawyers. Yet this outcome in the <u>Alabama Power</u> case is less significant than the general approach taken by the court of adopting the most literal reading possible of the statute and its requirements. This literal reading placed enormous interpretive weight on certain phrases and even words in the Act, so that the definitions of these words became the key means by which the scope of PSD would be decided. Especially in the area of modifications, the court's opinion forced EPA to develop "de minimis" exemptions which, like the increments themselves, are somewhat arbitrary and enormously complicated. Following Congress' lead, the court interjected itself into the most detailed aspects of EPA's rules and ordered the Agency to look first to the words of the statute, rather than its own sense of an administrable air pollution prevention program, to determine what the contents of PSD should be. While these two perspectives were not always opposed, they conflicted enough in such areas as the monitoring and baseline date requirements that they added to the complexity of a set of rules that were already complex indeed.

Faced with these pressures, and having made a basic political decision that it was unable or unwilling to return to Congress for "repairs" to the Act, EPA proceeded as quickly as possible to incorporate the court's mandate. By this time, however, the relationship between PSD and non-attainment area new source review had become a further complicating factor. Moreover, as the full implications of the court's decision were drawn out,

the results appeared less and less rational in
environmental terms, drawing distinctions between
new sources and modifications, and attainment/non-
attainment locations which made little environmental
sense. Nevertheless, despite the growing
unhappiness with the outcome of the PSD rules, EPA
proceeded to promulgate final regulations which, as
a result of political stalemate over the Clean Air
Act, remain in effect today.

From the standpoint of "juridical democracy," it
could be argued that the behavior of the D.C.
Circuit in the Alabama Power case reflects precisely
what one might want a court to do--restrain a
wayward Agency from exercising excessive discretion
in the face of a clear statutory requirement. What
is less clear is whether this outcome is desireable
in a case like this. Depending on one's point of
view, one can argue that EPA went too far or not far
enough relative to "Congressional intent" in its
final 1978 regulations in building in exemptions
from PSD. However, as vividly illustrated by the
"effective date" controversy, it can be quite
difficult to tell what "Congressional intent" is,
especially when that intent seems to be largely
determined by a relatively small handful of
Congressmen and their staff. Few would disagree
that it is the special province of the courts to
judge such "intent." However, this case suggests
that even the most finely-tuned statute will have
significant ambiguities which must be addressed by
an implementing agency. Where the agency's role
stops and that of the court starts is a matter of
degree and balance. It can be argued that in
Alabama Power, the court took advantage of
opportunities to look for "literal readings" (for
example, the "net increase" phrase associated with
modifications) where greater deference to the
Agency's implementation concerns would have produced
a less cumbersome program.

Lowi hypothesized that literal court readings of
statutes would have a salutary effect on Congress by
forcing it to specify just what it wanted in
legislation. However, this case suggests that the
main burden of such interpretations falls not on

Congress but on the administrative agency, even in
cases where statutes seem to be quite specific. One
could assume, of course, that an agency faced with
an unworkable statute ought to then return the
burden to Congress by seeking relief. Yet while in
theory this is possible, both political and
practical constraints inhibited this in the early
1980's. By the time the opportunity for legislative
change reappeared in the late 1980's, many of what
had seemed to be important issues a few years
earlier had receded, to be replaced by others. This
occurred not because PSD was incorporated in such
detailed legislation that Congressional guidance was
clear, but because the EPA, along with other
affected parties, was able to take the legislation
and make it work despite the flaws which the
detailed legislation contained.[177] Over time, the
"system" has worked, and people have accommodated to
the flaws in the PSD system embodied in the
legislation and amplified by the Alabama Power case,
just as they do to any entrenched but inefficient
system. Yet it is hard not to wonder if there might
not have been a better way.

NOTES

1. 1975 House Hearings, p. 41.

2. See, for example, 1977 Legislative History, pp.
    1403 (1977 Senate Report on S.252); 2644-45
    (1977 House Report on H.R.6161); 5338 (statement
    of Senator Buckley opposing the 1976 Moss
    Amendment); 6294 (statement by Congressman
    Rogers opposing the 1976 Chappell amendment).

3. The Supreme Court had granted certiorari in
    April 1977 to industry groups appealing the
    August 2, 1976, decision of the D.C. Circuit
    Court of Appeals which upheld EPA's PSD
    regulations. 7 Environment Reporter 1835 (April
    8, 1977). In the wake of the passage of the
    1977 Amendments, EPA petitioned the Supreme
    Court to dismiss the case. The Court responded
    by remanding the case to the Appeals Court on
    October 3, 1977, for consideration of the
    effects of the amendments and the possibility of
    mootness. 8 Environment Reporter 851-52
    (October 7, 1977).

4. U.S. Congress, Senate, Committee on Environment
    and Public Works, Clean Air Act Oversight:
    Hearings Before the Committee on Environment and
    Public Works, 97th Cong., 1st sess., 1981, p.
    139. (Hereafter referred to as 1981 Senate
    Hearings).

5. On the evolution of these procedures, see
    Marcus, "Environmental Protection Agency," op.
    cit., pp. 289-90. The procedures in effect at
    the beginning of 1977 are described in the
    National Research Council report, Decision
    Making in the Environmental Protection Agency
    (Washington: National Academy of Sciences,
    1977), pp. 198-203. (Hereafter cited as NRC
    Report.)

6. Marcus, "Environmental Protection Agency", p. 296.

7. NRC Report, pp. 25-36.

8. Harold Wilensky, Organizational Intelligence (New York: Basic Books, 1967), pp. 10-16. Wilensky's distinction between "contact men" and "facts and figures men" fits a dichotomy that appeared in EPA during the Congressional debate over PSD. Barbara Brown of the Air office and Cheryl Wasserman of OPE played the role of "contact men," who took to Congress the results of studies done by the technical "facts and figures" men in OAQPS.

9. Ackerman and Hassler give a vivid example of this in their description of the internal EPA debate over the 1979 Subpart Da NSPS. See "Beyond the New Deal," pp. 1537-54.

10. Other such appointments were Joan Claybrook to head the National Highway Traffic Safety Administration, Michael Pertschuk to chair the Federal Trade Commission, and Gus Speth as a member of the Council on Environmental Quality. See 8 Environment Reporter 649-50 (August 26, 1977).

11. See the discussion of Hawkins' role in Melnick, Regulation and the Courts, pp. 312, 324-25. See also Hawkins' testimony in, for example, 1974 Senate Oversight Hearings, pp. 403-20; and 1975 House Hearings, pp. 969-74.

12. This saga is described in Melnick, Regulation and the Courts, pp. 320-42.

13. Richard Ayres had generally taken on this role for NRDC.

14. See, for example, 7 Environment Reporter 1907 (April 15, 1977); William Drayton, "Economic Law Enforcement," 4 Harvard Environmental Law Review

(1980); statement by William Drayton in <u>1981 Senate Hearings</u>, pp. 484-88, 579-603. These observations on Drayton and on OPE in general are also derived from the author's own experience as an employee of the Office of Planning and Evaluation from December 1977 through September 1983.

15. In addition to interview data, see for example Costle's statement on EPA's proposed FY79 budget stressing this point. 8 <u>Environment Reporter</u> 1451-52. Part of the reason for the emphasis by Drayton and Costle on EPA as a public health agency stemmed from concerns about the executive branch reorganization studies being conducted by the Carter Administration. One of the proposals under consideration was the creation of a Cabinet Department of Natural Resources which would combine EPA and the Interior Department, among other things. Costle had opposed such an idea when it surfaced in the Ash Council work in 1970 (see Marcus, <u>Promise and Performance</u>, pp. 34-37), and he and Drayton continued to oppose it at this time. The public health emphasis was one way of attempting to distinguish EPA's mission from that of the Interior, Agriculture, and other natural resources agencies. See 8 <u>Environment Reporter</u> 789, 820, 855, 1238, 1316, 1353, 1677. However, part of the reason for Drayton's attitude was also his belief that environmental goals would not continue to command public support unless they were tied in to public health benefits.

16. Cf. Marcus, "Environmental Protection Agency," pp. 296-98; Muskie remarks in debate on the final bill, <u>1977 Legislative History</u>, pp. 341-44; Lemart Lindquist, <u>The Hare and the Tortoise: Clean Air Policies in the United States and Sweden</u> (Ann Arbor: University of Michigan Press, 1980), chapter 7; Christopher Davis, Jeffrey Kurtok, James Leape, and Frank Magill, "The Clean Air Act Amendments of 1977: Away from

388   **Protect and Enhance**

Technology Forcing?" <u>Harvard Environmental Law Review</u> 2 (1977), pp. 103-99.

17. See, for example, 8 <u>Environment Reporter</u> 1818-19 (March 24, 1978), and 1908-9 (April 7, 1978). In contrast, the Chamber of Commerce embarked on a major campaign to convince businesses that "alarming" consequences would flow from the sanctions requirements. 8 <u>Environment Reporter</u> 1930 (April 7, 1978).

18. Director, Division of Stationary Source Enforcement to Enforcement Division Directors Regions I-X, "Clean Air Act Amendments of 1977," August 9, 1977, reprinted in 8 <u>Environment Reporter</u> 622-23 (August 19, 1977).

19. See the discussion in <u>Citizens to Save Spencer County v. EPA</u>, 12 <u>ERC</u> 1970-73. The fifteen month minimum assumed that EPA would promulgate new regulations in six months and that the States would have nine months to revise their plans. See the discussion in EPA's first proposal of regulation governing PSD State Implementation Plans in 42 <u>Federal Register</u> 57471 (November 3, 1977).

20. Interview data; David G. Hawkins and Marvin Durning to Regional Administrators, Regions I-X, "Changes to PSD and Emission Offset Requirements," October 6, 1977, reprinted in 8 <u>Environment Reporter</u> 931-32 (October 14, 1977).

21. Ibid.

22. 8 <u>Environment Reporter</u> 963 (October 28, 1977). For the rationale of why the March 1 and December 1 dates were chosen, see the discussion in 42 <u>Federal Register</u> 57479 (November 3, 1977); basically, these were the dates by which a) EPA expected to promulgate final PSD regulations, and b) PSD SIPs were supposed to be due from the States. EPA's November 3 notice (42 <u>Federal Register</u> 57459) making these requirements

immediately effective was unclear on how sources
who were not subject to PSD under the 1974
regulations but would be under the new ones
should be handled. On December 8, 1977, EPA
issued a notice which clarified this point (42
Federal Register 62020, December 8, 1977). See
also 8 Environment Reporter 1239 (December 16,
1977).

23. Citizens to Save Spencer County v. EPA, 12 ERC
1965, fn. 19 (quotation from October 4, 1977,
Hawkins to Costle memorandum).

24. 8 Environment Reporter 963-64 (October 28,
1977). From later developments, it seems clear
that EPA officials had talked extensively with
the committee staffs before deciding to proceed
with the original announcement.

25. 8 Environment Reporter 1002 (November 4, 1977);
also cited in Citizens to Save Spencer County,
1966, fn. 22.

26. 8 Environment Reporter 1002 (November 4, 1977).

27. Interview data.

28. Citizens to Save Spencer County, 1966, fn. 26
(paraphrasing Hawkins-Blum memorandum).

29. This characterization is Hawkins'. Ibid.

30. 8 Environment Reporter 1002-3 (November 4, 1977)
describes the Hawkins-Durning memo. This memo
also candidly notes that EPA's earlier
interpretation was "based on assurances that . .
. a technical amendment would be adopted . . . "
but that it "now appears that no technical
amendment will be offered on this subject."
Citizens to Save Spencer County 1966-67, fn 27
citing the Hawkins-Durning memo. EPA's
invocation of the rulemaking process is
contained in its proposed revisions to the

Federal PSD regulations in 40 CFR 52.21, 42
Federal Register 57479 (November 3, 1977).

31.   43 Federal Register 26389 (June 19, 1978). Not
surprisingly, some of the more vocal partisans
of PSD did not agree with this reasoning.
Senator Gary Hart pronounced himself
"distressed" that EPA "bowed to industry
pressures that were reported by Congress during
two years of struggle." An unnamed Senate
staffer (probably Leon Billings) called EPA's
reconsideration "a cave-in to the utility
industry." 8 Environment Reporter 963-64.
Environmentalists took much the same approach.
8 Environment Reporter 1033 (November 11, 1977).

32.   See the discussion in 42 Federal Register 57479
(November 3, 1977).

33.   Ibid.

34.   43 Federal Register 26389 (June 19, 1978).

35.   42 Federal Register 58542 (December 23, 1977).
The one exception is worth noting because it
supports the point that EPA backed off from its
hard line only to make necessary concessions to
politically effective customers. On March 8,
1978, EPA issued a notice which said that in the
case of PSD permit which would have been issued
before the March 1 deadline, but for an
extension of the public comment period on
meritorious grounds, the deadline for an
approved permit could be extended to March 18.
This last minute exception--which came only
after the Agency had done another reversal akin
to the October 1977 incident on the effective
dates--affected only two permits. One was
Colstrip, which has been discussed before. The
other was an oil refinery proposing to locate in
Maine which was where Senator Muskie had asked
for an extension of the comment period. In both
cases, the sources were eventually permitted
under pre-§165 requirements because of this

exemption. See 8 <u>Environment Reporter</u> 1684
(March 3, 1978) and <u>Citizens to Save Spencer
County</u>, 1968-69.
    EPA also changed the date by which sources
had to commence construction. The original
date, December 1, 1978, was 9 months from March
1, and was the date by which State PSD SIPs
would have been due. The final 1978 regulations
postponed this date to nine months from their
publication, or March 19, 1979. 43 <u>Federal
Register</u> 26390 (June 19, 1978).

36. 43 <u>Federal Register</u> 26390.

37. Ibid.

38. Ibid., 26390-91.

39. <u>Citizens to Save Spencer County</u>, 1961. The case
     got its name from an Indiana environmental group
     that was the first to file suit against EPA on
     this issue.

40. 8 <u>Environment Reporter</u> 623, 931, 1003. Both the
     October 6 and 27 Hawkins-Durning memos
     especially stressed that PSD permits not
     reviewed for commence construction dates and
     applicability of the new provisions were invalid
     and should be suspended pending review.

41. 8 <u>Environment Reporter</u> 1680 (March 3, 1978).

42. 8 <u>Environment Reporter</u> 1767 (March 17, 1978).

43. 8 <u>Environment Reporter</u> 1860-61 (March 31, 1978).

44. 43 <u>Federal Register</u> 9529 (March 8, 1978).

45. <u>Citizens to Save Spencer County</u>, 1962

46. See U.S. House of Representatives, <u>The Clean Air
     Act of 1976</u> H.Rpt. 94-1742 to accompany S.3219,
     94th Congress, 2nd session, 1976, §160(j)(2),

reprinted in <u>1977 Legislative History</u>, pp. 4333–34.

The 1976 conference report does contain a drafting error, as §160(e)(2)(c)(ii)(III), cited in §160(j)(2), does not exist in the bill. However, it appears that the intended reference was to §160(e)(1)(c)(ii)(III), which dealt with the procedures for resolving disputes between a Governor and a Federal Land Manager over sources with a potential impact on a Class I area. If a drafting error was made in 1977, it was that this reference was omitted from §168(b), not any broader reference to §165. Ironically, this section in the 1977 law which contained the Governor-FLM dispute resolution provisions also contained the Breaux amendment.

47.   It has been difficult to completely corroborate this hypothesis, as the committee staff have been reluctant to discuss it in interviews. Absent a conclusive finding on this point, one must conclude with the Court in <u>Citizens to Save Spencer County</u> that "it may never be known whether the members of the conference committee, while at conference, were aware of the inconsistencies they were writing into the law." 12 <u>ERC</u> 1976. It is hard to make this same argument about the staff, however, who had been following the details of these issues for months and were quick to advise the Agency and issue statements after the fact on what the "intent of the committee" had been.

48.   Ibid., 1970. In rejecting the arguments of both industry and environmental groups, the court said that while it was "impressed by the ingenuity and industry of counsel for both Groups," it was not convinced by either one. Fourteen briefs were filed on the case totaling 1175 pages, as well as five volumes of appendices and 2072 pages of legislative history, thus making prophets out of Congressmen Ashbrook and Devine who predicted the Amendments

would be "a lawyers' bonanza" (<u>1977 Legislative History</u>, p. 317).

49.   42 <u>Federal Register</u> 57459; 57471; 54779 (November 3, 1977). EPA proposed to impose its Part 52 rules on States by renewing its disapproval of all State plans for failing to include approvable procedures for preventing significant deterioration of air quality (57488).

50.   42 <u>Federal Register</u> 57474; 57483 (November 3, 1977).

51.   Ibid.

52.   Melnick, <u>Regulation and the Courts</u>, p. 104.

53.   Clean Air Act as amended, §165 (citations will be to the act as amended using the public law citations as to sections, since these are the citations commonly used by Agency staff in referring to the Act).

54.   CAA §169(1).

55.   42 <u>Federal Register</u> 57480, 57483.

56.   Unlike the failure on §168, EPA was successful in getting included in the November 1977 "technical amendments" to the Clean Air Act a provision that made it clear that modifications <u>were</u> subject to PSD, and not just completely new construction projects. See §14 (a)(54) in "Technical and Conforming Amendments to the Clean Air Act," added subparagraph (c) to §169(2) of the Act which stated, "The term 'construction' when used in connection with any source or facility, include the modification (as defined in section 111(a) of any source or facility." Reprinted in 8 <u>Environment Reporter</u> 1022 (November 4, 1977). This is discussed further below in relation to the <u>Alabama Power</u> decision on modifications.

57. 42 _Federal Register_ 57480; 57483.

58. 42 _Federal Register_ 57480.

59. 42 _Federal Register_ 57480; 57483.

60. Clean Air Act §165(a)(4).

61. Examples of such pollutants were fluorides, total reduced sulfur, sulfuric acid mist (§111) and mercury, beryllium, asbestos and vinyl chloride (§112) as well as the so-called "criteria pollutants" (PM, SO_2, NO_x, VOC's, CO, and lead).

62. 42 _Federal Register_ 57481; 57485 (November 3, 1977).

63. Clean Air Act, §169(3) (definition of best available control technology).

64. 42 _Federal Register_ 57481.

65. Clean Air Act, §163(c)(1).

66. 42 _Federal Register_ 57480 (compare the guidelines at 57475-76 with EPA's regulation at 57484). Further confusing the issue was the treatment of fuel conversions, one of the categories identified as eligible for exemption in §163(c) of the ACt. EPA, in both its regulations and the State guidelines, proposed to exempt such conversions from BACT review "if prior to January 6, 1975, the source is designed to accommodate such alternative use" (57483). However, EPA did _not_, in its proposed regulation, exempt sources ordered to convert later under a Federal Power Commission order (relating to natural gas shortages) or an ESECA order (relating to power plant coal conversions), although it did note in an

understatement in the preamble that whether such
exemptions should be subject to PSD review was
"an important issue" (57482). This proposal
created a confused situation whereby a mandated
conversion could be required to use BACT, but
might or might not consume increment depending
on whether an approved State plan was in effect.
Since such conversions had been a key element of
energy policies designed to stimulate the
increased use of coal, EPA's proposals were
bound to create controversy within the Carter
Administration, which had adopted the need for a
national energy policy as a key theme.

67. 42 Federal Register 57480; 57484.

68. Clean Air Act §169(4).

69. Chapter 4 above, p. 72.

70. The monitoring requirement received only passing
mention in two widely scattered paragraphs in
the House Report. See 1977 Legislative History,
pp. 2612 and 2638. A participant in the
development of the House bill acknowledged in an
interview that the issue of a "monitoring
requirement" "wasn't raised very clearly at the
time," and that to the extent it was considered,
monitoring was treated primarily as a necessary
means of validating the results of EPA's models.

71. 1977 Legislative History, pp. 244 (1977
§165(e)(2)), 4330 (1976 §160(c)(1)(D)(ii)).

72. 42 Federal Register 57477 (Part 51 guidelines);
57486 (Part 52 regulations).

73. 42 Federal Register 57472.

74. 42 Federal Register 57473.

75. See, for example, the comments of Carter
Administration anti-inflation chief Robert S.
Strauss on including environmental regulations

as one of three targets in the anti-inflation drive (<u>Washington Post</u>, April 20, 1978, p. 1). EPA and Congressional environmental advocates reacted with predictable hostility, but this sensitivity shows the sense that their influence, which had seemed so strong in 1977, had begun to fade. 8 <u>Environment Reporter</u> 2045-47, 2069-70 (April 28, 1978).

76. For a description of RARG, see Robert E. Litan and William D. Nordhaus, <u>Reforming Federal Regulation</u> (New Haven: Yale University Press, 1984), pp. 69-71.

77. 42 <u>Federal Register</u> 64378 (December 23, 1977). However, in this same notice, EPA warned that it would not extend the March 1 deadline date for applying the new PSD requirements.

78. See the description of a January 9, 1978, public hearing on the rules, conducted by EPA and chaired by Hawkins, in 8 <u>Environment Reporter</u> 1373-74. In contrast to the intense interest of industrial groups, only one environmental group testified at the January 9 hearing.

79. Ibid.

80. Ironically, the director of the new DOE Office of Coal and Utility Policy, which had the lead in developing DOE's comments on the proposed regulation, was James Speyer, a former analyst in the Train EPA's Office of Planning and Evaluation who had been largely responsible for the EPA-FEA report which Senator Muskie and Congressman Rogers used in Congressional debate to prove that PSD would not cause massive economic disruption.

81. 8 <u>Environment Reporter</u> 1531 (February 2, 1978).

82. Ibid.

83.   Walter C. Barber to David G. Hawkins,
       "Definition of Potential Emissions," draft dated
       12/15/77 found in OAQPS files.

84.   Interview data. Citing the exemption provision
       in §165(B) as evidence of Congress' intent, OGC
       was reportedly absolutely convinced that any
       definition of potential to emit other than
       uncontrolled would not withstand judicial
       scrutiny. As the Agency's legal spokesman this
       view carried considerable weight. Of course,
       this suited Hawkins' policy objective of an
       expansive PSD program very nicely.
            Office of Enforcement staff supported OGC
       because they had traditionally tracked sources
       using an "uncontrolled" definition. See 43
       <u>Federal Register</u> 26392 (June 18, 1978).

85.   Barber to Hawkins, "Definition," 12/15/77. See
       also Thomas W. Devine to Richard Rhoads,
       "Significant Deterioration Regulation," December
       28, 1977 ("if the agency's position on size of
       source covered is not revised to reflect a
       minimum level for coverage of emissions of 100
       tons after control then the States are not going
       to accept implementation of the PSD program,"
       and OAQPS' reply indicating that an after-
       control definition was still being considered
       along with the two-tier approach (Darryl Tyler
       to Thomas W. Devine, "Significant Deterioration
       Regulations," January 25, 1978).

86.   A chronology found in EPA files shows that
       William Nordhaus of CEA and Barry Bosworth of
       COWPS wrote to Drayton and Hawkins on March 30,
       1978, expressing concern on this issue, and that
       a meeting between the groups occurred on March
       31.

87.   William Nordhaus and Barry Bosworth to David
       Hawkins and William Drayton, "Analysis of PSD
       Economic Input Document," April 21, 1978. The
       "economic impact assessment," of course, was one

of the new RARG regulatory review requirements.
EPA had originally opposed doing such an
analysis for the PSD regulations and had not
done one prior to the November proposal, but was
forced by RARG to develop such an analysis for
the final regulations. See "Impact of Section
165, Requirements for the Prevention of
Significant Deterioration," OAQPS, June 5, 1978
(final analysis; the draft was much debated and
discussed between EPA and the RARG reviewers).

88.   David G. Hawkins to William Nordhaus and Barry
      Bosworth, "Impact of PSD Regulations," May 4,
      1978. Also see 9 <u>Environment Reporter</u> 35-36
      (May 12, 1978).

89.   Ibid.

90.   William D. Nordhaus to David G. Hawkins, "Impact
      of PSD Regulations," May 11, 1978; letter from
      Charles Schultze to Douglas Costle, May 27,
      1978.

91.   "Talking Points for PSD Meeting with Schultze,"
      n.d.(but about May 30, 1978).

92.   Ibid.

93.   Letter to David Hawkins from Al Alm and Jim
      Liverman, Department of Energy, June 7, 1978.

94.   43 <u>Federal Register</u> 26395-96; 26407.   40 CFR
      52.21(i), (j)(2)(3) and (4), and (k) (1978)
      contain the major exemptions created by EPA.

95.   43 <u>Federal Register</u> 26394 (June 18, 1978).

96.   43 <u>Federal Register</u> 26397; 26406 (§52.21(i)(1))
      (June 18, 1978).

97.   43 <u>Federal Register</u> 26397-98 (June 18, 1978).
      This exemption applied to voluntary fuel

switches by sources which could use an alternate
fuel prior to January 6, 1975. This issue was
principally of concern in the Gulf Coast area of
Texas and Louisiana, where it was feared that
large-scale voluntary fuel switching between
natural gas (which was a cleaner fuel but was
scarce in the late 1970's) and higher-sulfur oil
could cause the consumption of that area's
entire increment and drastically limit growth.
This problem is discussed and dealt with more
explicitly in later EPA rulemakings,
specifically 44 <u>Federal Register</u> 51942
(September 5, 1979) and 45 <u>Federal Register</u>
52720-21 (August 7, 1980).

    This problem was exacerbated by a late
shift by OAQPS in the 1978 regulations which
changed the bases of increment consumption from
<u>actual</u> to <u>allowable</u> emissions. While noting
that this shift "enjoys the support of OE and
the Regional offices," OAQPS also observed that
a "major drawback" was that "some areas may not
be able to grant certain PSD permits without
first revising their SIP." See Walter C. Barber
to David G. Hawkins, "Final PSD Rulemaking,"
April 21, 1978.

98. 43 <u>Federal Register</u> 26401-2; 26405 (June 19,
1978). This is a very clear example of a
concession that was not much of one; the
procedural requirements made it very unlikely
that such a request would ever be made.

99. 43 <u>Federal Register</u> 26395 (June 19, 1978).
Though beyond the scope of this dissertation, it
may be of interest to note that EPA was later
sued by the Sierra Club over the strip mine
exemption, and rulemaking is currently underway
by EPA to address this suit.

    Hawkins' comment was reported in an
interview.

100. 43 <u>Federal Register</u> 26400 (June 19, 1978).

101. Ibid.

102. 43 <u>Federal Register</u> 26399 (June 19, 1978).
      OAQPS' files contain staff notes of a meeting
      between Assistant Administrator Hawkins and
      House and Senate staff on May 4, 1978, at which
      time a draft of the PSD regulations and <u>Federal
      Register</u> preamble were being reviewed. While
      the Congressional staff's general reaction was
      that EPA had overall done a "good job working
      with [a] nasty beast," the staff (perhaps
      reacting somewhat defensively) criticized EPA's
      critique of the monitoring requirements as
      "detrimental to the program" and recommended
      "toning [it] down." It is not clear whether EPA
      took this advice. See notes of Dave Dunbar,
      "Subj: May 4, 1978 Meeting on PSD Regulations
      with Congressional Staff."

103. "Environmental News" (EPA Press Release), "EPA
      Announces New Rules on Industrial Growth in
      Clean Air Areas," June 13, 1978.

104. The rules are at 39 <u>Federal Register</u> 31000-31009
      (August 27, 1974); 39 <u>Federal Register</u> 42510-17
      (December 5, 1974); 42 <u>Federal Register</u> 57471-88
      (November 3, 1977); and 43 <u>Federal Register</u>
      26380-410 (June 19, 1978).

105. Under section 307(b)(1) of the Clean Air Act,
      suits against EPA actions under §110 of the Act
      could be filed only in the D.C. Circuit if the
      Administrator determined that the action in
      question was "of nationwide scope or effect."
      This was done in the case of the PSD
      regulations, 43 <u>Federal Register</u> 26403 (June 19,
      1978). Shep Melnick comments on this procedure
      and some of its consequences in <u>Regulation and
      the Courts</u>, pp. 55-56 and 362-67.

106. Two opinions were issued in the <u>Alabama Power</u>
      case, as will be discussed below. The first, a
      summary (<u>per curiam</u>) opinion, can be found at 13

ERC 1225, June 18, 1979; the second complete
opinion is at 13 ERC 1993, December 14, 1979.

107.   13 ERC 1227-28.

108.   13 ERC 1228. The court did say EPA could create
exemptions based on administrative necessity so
long as these exemptions were based on "de
minimis" circumstances. Calculations of "de
minimis" exemptions would become a major issue
in EPA's post-Alabama Power rulemaking.

109.   13 ERC 1229. A fuller discussion occurs in the
full opinion, 13 ERC 2039. The ASARCO Case can
be found at 11 ERC 1129.

110.   13 ERC 1229.

111.   13 ERC 1232 (pp. 19-20).

112.   13 ERC 1232. The logic of the offsetting
modification rulings is much more extensively
set forth in the full opinion, 13 ERC 2044-45.

113.   Clean Air Act, §169(2)(c).

114.   Compare P.L. 95-95, §127 (the PSD provision)
with the Clean Air Act §169 and the Technical
and Conforming Amendments, a copy of which can
be located at 8 Environment Reporter 1021-23
(November 4, 1977). Recall that Muskie
attributed the need for the amendments to the
rush to produce a conference report which
precluded "the detailed proofreading that
usually accompanies the production of a
conference report," but that the effort to use
this mechanism to amend the Act with regard to
PSD's effective date had proven quite
controversial indeed. 9 Environment Reporter
995-96, 1002-3 (November 4, 1977).

115.   Clean Air Act, §111(a)(4).

116.   13 ERC 2042. See especially footnote 47, where
       the technical amendments, which passed with
       virtually no debate on the strength of Senator
       Muskie's assurance that they were merely
       "technical" reflections of the conferees'
       intent, override Senator Buckley's contrary
       assertions in the 1976 Senate debate on the
       bill.

117.   13 ERC 2044. The court described these changes
       the modification rules as applying a "bubble
       concept." This term refers to the regulation of
       a single plant as if a giant "bubble" were
       placed over it, with the intent of giving plant
       managers to tighten or relax emissions control
       on various points of emissions within a plant so
       long as overall emissions loadings from the
       plant remained the same. While the concept had
       been discussed at EPA for some time, the use of
       the term "bubble" was growing in the Agency's
       lexicon in 1978 and 1979, and a separate staff
       in the Office of Planning and Evaluation had
       been established to promote its use. PSD was
       only one of several areas in the air program
       where OPE staff were trying to force a "bubble"
       approach to regulation on a reluctant Hawkins
       and OAQPS.

118.   Adam W. Glass, "The EPA's Bubble Concept After
       Alabama Power", 32 Stanford Law Review (1980)
       603-9. ("Although the court's attempt to
       discern legislative purpose through careful
       linguistic inference is a valid approach, it is
       not convincing. The differences in statutory
       language examined by the courts are too
       inconsequential to justify different treatment
       of the bubble concept . . .")

119.   "EPA does have discretion . . . to exempt from
       PSD review some emissions increases on the
       grounds of the de minimis or administrative
       necessity. The exemption in question, however,

has not been so justified, and thus cannot stand
. . ." Implementation of the statute's
definition of "modification" will undoubtedly
prove inconvenient and costly to affected
industries; but the clear language of the
statute unavoidably imposes these costs except
for <u>de minimis</u> increases." 13 <u>ERC</u> 2042.

120.   13 <u>ERC</u> 2046.

121.   Ibid.

122.   13 <u>ERC</u> 2022; 43 <u>Federal Register</u> 26400 (June 19,
        1978).

123.   13 <u>ERC</u> 2022.

124.   13 <u>ERC</u> 2024-27. The opinion notes at 2026-27
        that the industry petitions for the exemptions
        of voluntary switches from increment consumption
        would have been on firm ground if <u>either</u> the
        House or Senate baseline definition had passed,
        but noted the combination adopted by the
        conference committee ruled this out.

125.   The discussion above is taken form the final
        full opinion of the court in <u>Alabama Power</u>. The
        <u>per curiam</u> opinion evidences more confusion over
        just what a "baseline" is. For example, in
        remanding EPA's regulations, it states that
        "Congress may reasonably have concluded that the
        accuracy of the determination of 'baseline
        concentration'" is of paramount importance,
        since it forms the basis for calculation of
        allowable increments which . . . may determine
        whether a particular source will be permitted to
        construct and to commence operations in a
        particular area." 13 <u>ERC</u> 1239.
        However, as EPA had pointed out on numerous
occasions (and at length in the June 19, 1978,
preamble) that baseline concentration had nothing to
do with increment consumption and was important only
on rare occasions when a TSP or SO_2 NAAQS would be

threatened by the addition of a new source. See 43
<u>Federal Register</u> 26400 (June 19, 1978).

126.   13 <u>ERC</u> 1238.

127.   13 <u>ERC</u> 2019.

128.   13 <u>ERC</u> 2019 (citing §165(e)(2) of the Act.   The
       emphasis is in the opinion.)

129.   Ackerman and Hassler, "Beyond the New Deal," p.
       1560 (fn. 389).

130.   13 <u>ERC</u> 1242-43.

131.   Interview data.

132.   13 <u>ERC</u> 1227 (note 7).

133.   Interview data.

134.   44 <u>Federal Register</u> 51924 ff. (September 5,
       1979).   The push to get this proposal out so
       fast caused friction between the air office and
       OGC on the one hand, and OPE on the other.   In
       an August 17, 1979, memo, OPE chief Roy Gamse
       noted that while he was "sympathetic" to the
       need for "rushing this package out the door," he
       would have "preferred to have had more time to
       develop and push for a strong Agency consensus
       position on this proposal." Roy N. Gamse (for
       William Drayton, Jr.) to David G. Hawkins,
       "Revised PSD and Nonattainment Requirements in
       Response to <u>Alabama Power</u>, August 17, 1979.

135.   44 <u>Federal Register</u> 51925 (September 5, 1979).

136.   43 <u>Federal Register</u> 26404 (June 19, 1978)
       (§52.21(b)(3)).

137.   44 <u>Federal Register</u> 51929-30 (September 5, 1979)
       (emphasis in original).

138. Ibid.

139. 44 <u>Federal Register</u> 51931 (September 5, 1979).

140. 44 <u>Federal Register</u> 51931-32.

141. Ibid. The only exception to this requirement was if a State could demonstrate that attainment could be reached without the use of the more restrictive definition of "source."

142. Gamse to Hawkins, cited above in n. 134.

143. 44 <u>Federal Register</u> 51937-38.

144. Ibid; interview data.

145. 44 <u>Federal Register</u> 51941.

146. Gamse to Hawkins, cited above in n. 134.

147. <u>Alabama Power vs. Costle</u>, 13 <u>ERC</u> 1993.

148. 13 <u>ERC</u> 2019.

149. 45 <u>Federal Register</u> 52679 (August 7, 1980). A discussion of some of the reactions to the proposed rules can be found at 10 <u>Environment Reporter</u> 1423-25 (October 19, 1979).

150. 45 <u>Federal Register</u> 52679-80; 10 <u>Environment Reporter</u> 2147 (March 21, 1980).

151. 45 <u>Federal Register</u> 7800 (February 5, 1980).

152. 45 <u>Federal Register</u> 52688-89, 52737 (§52.21(b)(4)).

153. 45 <u>Federal Register</u> 52694-95.

154. 45 <u>Federal Register</u> 52696-98.

155. 45 <u>Federal Register</u> 52706.

156. 45 <u>Federal Register</u> 52706-10. EPA in fact
      resurrected the old "buffer zone" bugaboo
      despite the Act's prohibition, as it specified
      that any source (even de minimis ones) located
      less than 10 kilometers from a Class I area
      "must be prepared to demonstrate that no 24-hour
      impact greater than 1 ug/m^3 would occur in the
      Class I area.

157. See the summary of changes at 45 <u>Federal
      Register</u> 52680-81. Geographic and pollutant
      applicability is discussed in greater detail at
      52710-12; baseline area at 52713-17; increment
      consumption at 52717-21; and the transition
      provisions for permitted sources at 52681-86.

158. The author was present in the summer of 1980 at
      a seminar where these final regulations were
      being presented to the EPA Regional staff who
      would have to implement them. The common
      reaction at this session was that absolutely no
      one could possibly understand the new rules.

159. Chemical Manufacturers Association vs. EPA, No.
      791112 and Consolidated Cases (D.C. Circuit).

160. 48 <u>Federal Register</u> 38742 (August 25, 1983).

161. Interview data. A separate discussion would be
      needed on fugitive emissions, where EPA was sued
      by the Sierra Club for not including strip mines
      as a source from which fugitive emissions should
      be counted in determining "potential to emit"
      for PSD applicability purposes. Regulatory
      action in this area is also still proceeding as
      of this writing.

162. "Clean Air Act An Inviting Target for Industry
      Critics Next Year." <u>National Journal</u>, vol. 12,
      November 15, 1980, pp. 1927-30.

163.   "EPA Regional Heads Assess Current Air Act, See
        'Chaos' and 'Uncertainty.'" Inside EPA, November
        14, 1980, pp. 2-3.

164.   "Recommended Changes to the Clean Air Act,"
        State and Territorial Air Pollution Program
        Administration (Adopted 12/10/80), reprinted in
        1981 Senate Hearings, pp. 31-33.

165.   National Commission on Air Quality, To Breathe
        Clean Air, Washington, D.C., (typewritten copy),
        March 1981, pp. 2.2-13-15. At the time the
        Commission was created, industry groups had
        expressed concern that the Commission and its
        staff were dominated by environmentalists.
        However, when the Commission's report came out,
        the vote to accept it was nine to three, with
        the three strongest environmentalists
        dissenting. Disagreement with the
        recommendations on PSD was one of the stated
        reasons for this dissent. See "Dissenting
        Statement of Commissioners Richard E. Ayres,
        Annemarie F. Crocetti, and John J. Sheehan," pp.
        5-42-51. Even these dissenters, however, felt
        compelled to offer suggestions for reducing
        "certain unnecessary complexities" of PSD in the
        areas of baseline date, monitoring requirements
        and common de minimis potential to emit
        thresholds for new sources and modifications.
        Reportedly, the Commission's vote on whether to
        retain the Class II increments was a tie. 1981
        Senate Hearings, p. 140.

166.   There was one failed attempt by the Reagan
        Administration to create such an event by trying
        to impose construction and funding sanctions on
        areas which did not meet the 1982 attainment
        date. Congress passed an appropriations rider
        banning the use of EPA funds for such purposes,
        but this only symbolized the degree to which the
        action lacked the political support it would
        have needed to succeed. EPA's policy on this
        subject was reversed by William Ruckelshaus

shortly after succeeding Anne Gorsuch as EPA
Administrator in May 1983.

167.   "Congress Likely to Ignore Reagan's Request for
Clean Air Act Passage," National Journal, vol.
14, November 27, 1982, pp. 2027-28, and Michael
Barone, "Tactics of an Ace in the Congressional
Air Wars," Washington Post, December 14, 1982,
document some of the political twists and turns
of the debate over amending the Act in 1981 and
1982, when this possibility seemed most real.

168.   U.S. EPA, National Air Audit System FY 1984
National Report (EPA: Research Triangle Park,
N.C., 1984), Section IV.

169.   Ibid., pp. iv-7.

170.   One consequence of this was that unlike SO_2 and
TSP, there is no short term NO_x increment since
there is no short term averaging time for the
nitrogen oxide ambient standard, but only an
annual average standard. Since annual averages
are not normally very restrictive for a point
source, this is the reason that the NO_x
increments are not expected to have a great deal
of impact on the PSD regulatory system. They
would be most likely to have an effect only if
there were true increment tracking for minor
sources in a high-growth area.

171.   However, this decision did not settle one
ambiguity. Since increment consumption is
supposed to be calculated based on minor as well
as major source growth, the potential exists for
operations at surface coal mines to be
restricted based on increment concerns. The
most recent developments in this area have
focused on disagreements between mine operators
and EPA over the types of models used to predict
the air quality impact of mine emissions;
studies in this area are continuing as of this

writing. See also the discussion on the 1990
Clean Air Act Amendments which follows.

172.   Memorandum, J. Craig Potter, Assistant
       Administrator for Air and Radiation to Regional
       Administrators, December 1, 1987.

173.   The following description is based on the
       author's observations. It is emphatically <u>not</u>
       intended to be a history of the Clean Air Act
       Amendments of 1990, so it will be necessarily
       sketchy and selective.

174.   A rather involved story lay behind the strip
       mine proposal. complicated. The President's
       proposal was made before the strip mine decision
       was made pursuant to the Sierra Club litigation.
       One original thought behind the provision in the
       President's proposal was to render the
       litigation moot. In the event, the legislative
       language in the President's proposal did not
       reach the issue in the Sierra Club litigation
       and rulemaking, but only addressed the narrower
       issue of increment consumption.

175.   The percentage reduction requirement is the same
       one which was briefly discussed on pp. 251-252
       and is fully discussed in Ackerman and Hassler,
       "Beyond the New Deal," <u>op. cit.</u> EPA published
       regulations on the percentage reduction
       requirement in 1979.

176.   How EPA will interpret this ambiguous
       requirement remains to be seen. The final
       wording of the provision reflects a classic
       Congressional compromise. On the one hand, the
       standard is not supposed to require scrubbing.
       On the other hand, the requirement is supposed
       to have an equivalent environmental effect as if
       scrubbing had been required. The apparent
       intent of this provision is to require EPA to
       lower the emissions rate cap on the NSPS from
       the current 1.2 lbs. SO_2/MM Btu to some lower
       number in the .3 - .5 lb. range. The difficulty

is that some power plants using scrubbers and low sulfur Western coal have reduced emissions to the .1 - .2 lb. range. The 1979 rulemaking on percentage reduction was extremely controversial; the new rulemaking promises to be equally contentious.

177. EPA did make one major change to its new source review requirements, though this change did not affect PSD. Shortly after the change in Administrations, EPA proposed to eliminate the dual definition of source, a proposal which was finalized in October 1981 (46 Federal Register 50766, October 14, 1981). NRDC sued the Agency, and in 1982 succeeded in the D.C. Circuit in having EPA's revision overturned (NRDC vs. Gorsuch, 17 ERC 1825, August 17, 1982). However, this time EPA appealed, and in 1984 the Supreme Court in a unanimous decision overturned the D.C. Circuit and upheld EPA's revision as a legitimate use of its discretionary authority. Chevron vs. NRDC, 21 ERC 1049, June 25, 1984.
    Notable in this decision is the observation that "we are not persuaded that parsing of general terms in the text of the statute will reveal an actual intent of Congress" (p.1059). Also notable in the opinion is the rebuke issued to the D.C. Circuit for giving insufficient deference to the views of responsible policy officials. The Supreme Court argued that "the Court of Appeals, rather than Congress or any of the decision makers who are authorized by Congress to administer [the Clean Air Act], that was primarily responsible for the 1980 position taken by the Agency." Having conceded this, the Supreme Court criticized the judges of the Appeals Court for reversing a decision made by the Agency after appropriate notice to change that policy. Where Congress was silent on the law, the Supreme Court held, it was the Agency's responsibility, not the Court's to make such policy judgments (pp. 1061-62). While it is

still too early to tell what the full
ramifications of this decision will be, it is
the author's sense that since 1984, the <u>Chevron</u>
decision has already begun to have a healthy
effect in correcting the kind of judicial fine
tuning which characterized the <u>Alabama Power</u>
decision and in restoring some much needed
discretion to EPA.

CHAPTER VII

PSD, JURIDICAL DEMOCRACY, AND ADMINISTRATIVE DISCRETION

The preceding chapters have described the development and implementation of a national policy to prevent the significant deterioration of air quality in areas with clean air. From its simple conceptual beginnings, this policy and the accompanying program to carry it out have become one of the most complicated elements of Federal air pollution control. Along the way, PSD changed from a policy which was largely ignored to one which was a major focus of concern by environmental and industry groups alike. Efforts to define and implement PSD have imposed substantial costs on Federal, State and local governments that had to develop and respond to federal rules for the program, and to industries which had to comply with these rules. Not the least of these costs have been those incurred simply trying to understand just what the rules required.

It is not the purpose of this review to attempt to determine whether these costs are worth the benefits that PSD brings.[1] However, it is worth seeing what effects PSD has had on the overall air pollution control program. This will lead to the larger question of how these effects relate to the administrative practice which underlay the creation and development of PSD. To the extent this practice

413

conforms to the philosophy laid out by Professor
Lowi, it suggests certain conclusions with respect
to what the actual effects of "juridical democracy"
might be.

PSD's Effect on Air Pollution Control

     Consensus exists both within and outside EPA on
PSD's complexity. This feeling is so widespread
that even senior career EPA air pollution control
officials will avoid PSD because they do not want to
take the time and trouble to understand it. The
result is that even within EPA, PSD has become the
province of a relatively small number of staff who
have been with it for many years and understand the
subtleties which have accompanied its development.
This has two effects. First, it is very difficult
for senior Agency career or political managers to
understand issues related to PSD or the impact of
proposals to change it. In the face of this
difficulty and giving an already overwhelming agenda
of air pollution concerns, there is a tendency
within EPA to postpone dealing with PSD issues.
Second, when such issues present themselves in ways
which force them to the attention of senior
officials (usually through a court suit), these
officials are hard pressed to do anything other than
accept the recommendations of the small group of PSD
experts within the Agency. In particular, the
combination of complex rules and the literalist
approach to the Act in the Alabama Power ruling has
given special weight to the opinions of Agency legal
experts, especially those in EPA's Office of General
Counsel, who by virtue of their position and
experience with PSD can maintain a status as the
authoritative interpreters of what the statutes and
the regulations mean.
     Perhaps the most lasting effect of PSD on the
field of air pollution control is the general

acceptance of the principle that "best available
control technology" should be required on large new
sources of air pollution, regardless of whether the
site where the source will be located presently has
an air pollution control problem. To be sure,
arguments persist about what a "major" source is, or
what control technology is "best," but these are
largely arguments at the margin. While the 1970
Clean Air Act had specified that new sources would
have to meet New Source Performance Standards
(NSPS), these had to be set on an industry by
industry basis, with the burden on EPA to justify a
particular level of needed control. Not
surprisingly, the establishment of NSPS has been
difficult, costly and slow. PSD, in contrast,
places the burden on the source to demonstrate
through the permit process that BACT will be
applied. Moreover, even under the post-Alabama
Power definition of potential to emit, PSD embraces
a wide universe of sources based on the sole
criterion of whether they will produce increased
emissions of air pollution. This characteristic
means that as time goes by and more and more sources
are subject to PSD (or its companion, nonattainment
new source review), regulation under the Air Act
will become less and less linked to the ambient
standards, and will more and more come to resemble
the technology-based approach taken in the Clean
Water Act (and proposed, ironically enough, by NAPCA
officials in 1966 only to be killed by Senator
Muskie). While the ambient standards will probably
never disappear, the development of PSD suggests
that, over time, they may lose much of their
importance as an air pollution regulatory tool.
This acceptance of technological availability as a
basis for national air pollution control made it
that much easier for the EPA, the Administration,
and the Congress to accept the extension of this
principle to new and existing sources of toxic air
pollutants in the Clean Air Act Amendments of 1990.
    The effects of the increment scheme which was at
the heart of EPA's original PSD proposal are less
clear. Calculation of increment consumption has
been at the heart of the most vexing and confusing

elements of PSD, and many of the theoretical
elements which would be required to turn the
increments into real tools of regulatory control
remain quite unsettled. The concept of "baseline,"
for example, has led to such actions as the State of
Massachusetts designating more than 100 separate
"baseline areas" to avoid having one source trigger
the "baseline date" for the entire State.

Moreover, increment tracking has strained the
capabilities of both EPA and State air pollution
control agencies, and available evidence suggests
that to the extent it occurs at all it happens in
ways different from those envisioned in the rules.
An EPA report on State practices in 1984 noted that
"most agencies have no specific plans to
periodically assess PSD increment consumption beyond
the analysis accompanying the PSD application for
major projects," and that "there is a general
uncertainty as to how such periodic assessments are
to be done."[2] The report went on to note that "the
absence of EPA guidance in terms of developing
increment tracking procedures, particularly with
respect to short-term averaging periods, needs to be
addressed before State and local agencies can be
expected to do much developmental work of their own
in this regard."[3] What this means is that far from
establishing an air "budget," the increments are
considered only in conjunction with an application
for a PSD permit, and even then the increment
tracking tests which an applicant must meet may vary
substantially from one agency to another. EPA notes
in this connection that "agencies should generally
be giving more attention to their own technical
documentation of the modeling analyses provided by
permit applicants," but that "this issue may be
difficult to address in the near term because of in-
house limitations on resources and expertise."[4]
Those responsible for implementing the increment
provisions of PSD appear to be limited by both
technical constraints and by the availability of the
resources needed to do the job. As a result, to the
extent increment consumption is being evaluated now,
it is being done by industry in analyses which may
or may not receive careful scrutiny.

This may account in part for the strongest indictment of the increments, that though they cannot be assessed without extensive analysis, they make almost no difference in the ultimate air pollution control required at most PSD sources. While there has been some willingness even by industry to acknowledge that the Class I increments may serve a special purpose by affording protection to unique areas such as national parks, the Class II increments have come under special criticism as requiring extensive additional analysis for little benefit. Estimates of the percentage of PSD permits issued where emissions limits were affected by the Class II increment constraints range from almost none to 13%.[5] Not surprisingly in light of the negotiations over the increment levels, the 24 hour SO2 increment has turned out to be the most restrictive.[6] Very few if any examples exist where general area growth has resulted in increment consumption approaching the statutory levels. Where the increments have had any constraining effect at all, this has been attributed to the use of conservative air quality models, to the use by the source of very short smokestacks for aesthetic or air traffic safety reasons, or to the location of the proposed source in an area of hilly terrain so that "plume impaction" (a smokestack plume hitting the side of a hill) became a problem.[7]

Environmentalists have argued that the increment system has had little effect to date only because the PSD requirements are still relatively new.[8] Since it is hard to predict the future with certainty, this is a difficult assertion to disprove. It is true that where the increments have made any difference, it has principally been in cases involving large power plants or other energy developments near national parks, which was one of the major concerns of the environmental groups that lobbied for PSD. However, while the increments may have had some effect on individual cases, in general they have not been the driving force behind PSD that EPA staff envisioned when the increment system was first created, especially in Class II areas.

The increments are the most troublesome part of PSD because of the difficulty of determining what they are and how to calculate them. They remain dependent on procedures--air quality modeling--which are inherently uncertain, especially for the relatively small concentrations of pollutants at issue in determining increment consumption. While they may give a "protection" bias to PSD, they do so at a considerable cost to States, EPA and industry in terms of time, money and uncertainty.

It is these costs, taken collectively, which are the most disturbing about PSD. Administrator Ruckelshaus, who first had to deal with PSD, was also the most articulate of EPA's Administrators in expressing the concern that PSD would divert EPA from the more pressing concern of cleaning up the air in areas where human health was at risk. It can, of course, be argued that as this task proceeds, a program such as PSD becomes even more necessary to ensure that problems such as those created in the past by industrial growth do not recur, and that America's future industrial base is well controlled. Such choices, however, are rarely absolute; the real questions turn on the relative levels of effort to be devoted to each task. Few would argue that either Federal or State air pollution control officials should completely neglect either "clean" or "dirty" air areas at the expense of the other, and most people would probably agree with the desirability of providing some special protection in areas where small additional concentrations of air pollution could have major effects on treasured national values such as visibility in the Grand Canyon.

However, as we have seen, the PSD program ultimately created by Congress, the Agency and the courts is far greater in scope. In their efforts to add such objectives as promoting land use planning, reduction of total atmospheric pollution burdens and prevention of "pollution havens" and "economic blackmail," the Agency and Congress created a PSD program which goes well beyond the original focus of the 1970 Act on cleaning up the air. Even bypassing as beyond our scope the larger question of the

societal costs and benefits of keeping clean air
clean, the implications of the PSD program as it
exists today are troubling solely from the
perspective of the relatively fixed and scarce
resources which society currently chooses to make
available for pollution control in general, and air
pollution control in particular. If one accepts
that air pollution control programs will always be
faced with resource needs which exceed their
availability, this means that there is a tradeoff
between the attention which can be devoted to those
areas where air is "clean" and those where it is
not. To the extent that PSD is complex to
administer in ways that produce little environmental
benefit, aims at objectives little related to air
pollution control, provokes time-consuming arguments
over what Congress meant in obscure phrases of the
law, and focuses the attention of pollution control
agencies on textual analysis instead of realistic
planning to reduce pollution, it takes away from
efforts that could otherwise be aimed at improving
the lot of people living in areas with unhealthy
air. While the concept of the "public interest" is
elusive, it seems difficult to argue that this kind
of outcome serves it. PSD has had its benefits, but
air pollution control has paid a price for some of
them.

The Effect of "Juridical Democracy" on PSD

At the beginning of this review, it was
suggested that the making of policy for the
prevention of significant deterioration of air
quality resembled the process which Theodore Lowi
predicted would characterize a "juridical
democracy." Lowi suggested that three reforms were
needed to make "juridical democracy" work. First,
Congress had to write specific laws which stated
what it wanted and avoided overly broad delegations

of authority to administrative agencies. Doubting
that Congress would impose such discipline on
itself, Lowi argued that the courts would have to
resume the practice of declaring statutes invalid
when Congress made excessively broad grants of
authority to administrative agencies. This would
have the effect of forcing Congress to do the
necessary work of specifying, with greater clarity,
what it wants and how it expects things to be done.
Finally, recognizing that even the best acts of
Congress could not eliminate all uncertainty in the
delegation of power, agencies had to make increased
use of formal administrative rulemaking, so that
whatever "bargaining" occurred would be over a rule
rather than over specific cases. Lowi anticipated
that if Congress had done its job adequately in rule
formulation, most of the bargining over rules would
occur there. Even if it did not, dissatisfaction
with specific rules would lead aggrieved parties
back to Congress instead of producing "logrolling on
the case" with administrative agencies. This would
have the healthy effect of reinforcing the
discipline on Congress to improve the quality of its
legislative draftsmanship.

Did policymaking on PSD meet these tests? To
answer this requires looking at PSD policymaking in
two phases, the first culminating in EPA's 1974
final rules, the second in the 1980 post-<u>Alabama
Power</u> final rules.

In the first phase, while Congress wrote very
specific goals and requirements into the 1970 Clean
Air Act in most areas, it did not do so for PSD.
Instead, the entire problem which PSD was supposed
to address--the treatment of new pollution sources
in areas where air was relatively clean--was treated
vaguely, if at all, in statutory deliberations.
This enabled a small group of policy advocates, who
themselves had little idea of what the true
ramifications of a significant deterioration policy
might be, to build general statements about PSD into
various policy documents, testimony, and legislative
history. These statements, though vague, were
enough to enable advocates to make a credible
argument that although Congress had not spoken with

certainty or clarity on the subject, its "intent"
had been that a policy of preventing significant
deterioration be incorporated into the national air
pollution control program.

Advocates first tried to press this view
following the passage of the 1970 Amendments in
formal agency rulemaking. Not only was this effort
unsuccessful, it also began to illuminate just how
unclear the concept of preventing significant
deterioration was. Having failed in formal
rulemaking, however, advocates took their case to
the courts. Here another major deviation occurred
from the pattern which would occur in a "juridical
democracy." Instead of forcing the advocates of PSD
to return to Congress on the grounds that
legislative intent was not specified with sufficient
clarity, the courts instead accepted the advocates'
arguments and ordered EPA to develop and implement a
program to carry it out. Even worse, the courts at
all levels followed the lead of Congress by failing
to provide the slightest bit of guidance to the
Agency about just what problem it was supposed to
solve or how it was supposed to do it.

This would seem to have created precisely the
situation decried by Lowi of the excessive
delegation of authority to an administrative agency
which creates strong opportunities for capture of
agencies by regulated interests. Certainly efforts
were made by such interests, both directly and
through sympathetic Federal agencies, to weaken any
potential PSD program. However, in a return to
"juridical democracy" principles, EPA chose to
proceed along a formal rulemaking route in
describing and carrying out a policy on PSD. In
doing so it explicitly rejected options which would
have given more discretion to regulating agencies
(both itself and States) to define "significant
deterioration" on a case by case basis in favor of
formal rules using explicit criteria (the increments
and the classification system) to make these
determinations.

This course of action produced a set of detailed
rules which the courts ultimately upheld (though
since the Supreme Court accepted a case on EPA's

1974 regulations but did not rule on it, we will
never know definitely if that Court would have
upheld EPA's exercise of discretion in this
instance). "Logrolling on the rule" did occur, as
Lowi would have predicted, on items such as the
value of the three hour Class II SO_2 increment.
Moreover, as compared to later efforts, EPA's 1974
rules were quite limited in scope, as they would
have applied only to an estimated 165 sources per
year (vs. 4000 for the November, 1977 proposal and
1600 for the June, 1978 final regulations). Still,
they represented a response which seemed to meet
Lowi's tests of both specificity and general
applicability. The 1974 rules also had another
effect which Lowi predicted would occur in
"juridical democracy--they stimulated attempts to
make legislative adjustments. Thus the apparent
failure of Congress and the courts in <u>Sierra Club
vs. Ruckelshaus</u> to conform to the principles of
"juridical democracy" was offset by EPA's use of
formal rulemaking authorities to implement the vague
mandates of the statutes and the courts. This
approach appears to have worked relatively well in
the first phase of PSD.

However, the process of legislative review did
not result in the simplification of the task of
administration as Lowi might have predicted. This
failure hardly resulted from a lack of willingness
by Congress to write specific rules. While Congress
took the rules developed by EPA as a starting point
for their review, they added on to and went beyond
these rules in several key respects. Yet the effect
of these additions was to <u>increase</u> rather than
decrease the uncertainty faced by administrators
after the 1977 Amendments. The most striking
example of this, of course, is the debate over which
sources were subject to PSD, a debate which Congress
could not settle when it was brought out into to
open and which ultimately had to be resolved (after
numerous adjustments) by EPA and the courts.
Moreover, though the expected "logrolling on the
rule did occur in Congress, it happened in such
convoluted ways (such as the change in the
definition of "commenced construction," aimed at the

Colstrip plant, the Bumpers amendment to exempt Hot
Springs from classification as a Class I area, or
the Breaux amendment which would allow the
construction of large power plants in Utah) that it
became very difficult to distinguish logrolling on
the rule from logrolling on the case.

The conduct of EPA's formal rulemaking the
second time around, far from being made simpler by
the explicit Congressional delegation of authority,
in fact became more difficult. Though the law was
more specific, major areas of ambiguity remained.
These were reflected (for example) as EPA lawyers
and program advocates argued with economists about
the precise meaning and utility of terms such as
"potential to emit." Uncertainty over the rules
also grew as the Agency faced up to the recognition
that the literal application of statutory language
in such areas as the monitoring requirements made
little sense. Finally, the Agency traveled down the
same path as Congress in that the complexity of the
rules made it difficult to distinguish between
logrolling on the rules and logrolling on cases.
The extension of the March 1, 1978 deadline for
permits with "significant public comment"
illustrates this point, since this seemingly general
extension was known to apply to only two sources:
the Colstrip power plant, and a Pittston, Maine oil
refinery of interest to Senator Edmund Muskie. More
recently, EPA has been faced with requests from the
Department of Energy, the Council of Economic
Advisers, and OMB to prepare interpretative rulings
when these agencies want EPA to change its decisions
on specific projects like WEPCO-Port Washington.

The Alabama Power decision exacerbated these
problems. By adopting a literalist approach to the
interpretation of the statute, the court forcefully
intervened in the rulemaking process, almost going
so far as to set itself up as an administrative
agency in its own right. In doing so, however, the
court imposed requirements which went beyond the
technical and administrative ability of EPA to
implement them. Even where EPA was eventually able
to craft provisions which appeared to conform to the
court's ruling, they were so complicated (i.e., the

424 Protect and Enhance

de minimis rules for modifications) that they
further increased the confusing surrounding PSD even
after final rules were promulgated. While after ten
years EPA and State air pollution control agencies
appear to be doing the best they can to carry out
these rules, it is hardly surprising that inconsistencies in their implementation have appeared.

In an ideal world, court rulings on specific
laws and regulations need not have this effect on
administrative agencies. Agencies can appeal to a
higher court, or seek legislative change in
Congress. As a practical matter, however, only
limited opportunities exist for exercising these
options. The political and technical resources
which an agency can devote to such appeals are
limited, and this creates a strong incentive for
agencies to accept even irrational court rulings
unless they are absolutely disruptive to an agency's
programs. The solution of going back for
legislative review neglects the powerful incentives
which mitigate against its routine use by
administrative agencies.[9] Moreover, this case
suggests that agency caution in seeking legislative
review is quite understandable. While EPA sought
such review in the hope of getting its PSD
regulatory program endorsed, what it got as a result
was far different. The expectation that this might
happen again gives advocates of the regulatory
status quo a powerful argument against actively
pursuing even needed legislative corrections.

ARE COMPLEX RULES NECESSARY?

It can be argued that the uncertainty which
accompanied PSD from 1975 until 1980 was the
necessary and predictable result of the move to a
formal administrative system. Under such a system,
sufficient time had to be allowed for "logrolling on
the rule" to take place. Clearly, as noted above,
this phenomenon occurred both in Congress and in
EPA. By this reasoning, the criticism of the PSD

rules as complex misses the point.   If the rules are
complex because they move from abstractions to
specific cases, then complexity should not be a
cause for concern because it simply reflects the
need to formulate rules which are sufficiently
specific that they will prevent administrative
officials from bargaining away the objectives which
the rules and the law were intended to achieve.
PSD's advocates have in fact raised precisely this
point in defending the rules.   David Hawkins,
perhaps PSD's strongest defender, noted in a
discussion on PSD that the rules could not
simultaneously be comprehensive, rigorous and
simple.[10]   Given these choices, simplicity was the
value which should be sacrificed in the public
interest.

It is certainly possible to concede the need in
principle for specific, generally applicable rules.
To use a homely example, it would clearly be unwise
to leave the issue of automobile speed limits up to
negotiations between individual motorists and
policemen.   While the existence of different speed
limits for residential areas and interstate highways
arguably complicates the traffic laws, most people
would concede that this "complexity" is both
bearable and sensible.   In this case, it is
important to remember that the argument about the
complexity of PSD is hardly an argument against the
value of specific, directive law in principle.   To
cite only the most relevant example, despite the
faults which are routinely found with the Clean Air
Act, its effectiveness is generally conceded to have
been vastly improved by its reformulation in 1970
along these lines.

However, the example of PSD suggests that there
is a limit to the detail which ought to be embodied
in law.   The purpose of legislation and formal
rulemaking is, after all, to ensure that fixed rules
result which can be applied consistently and with
certainty.   Such rules prevent the kind of
"logrolling on cases" which Lowi condemned as
antithetical to the rule of law and even to
representative democracy itself.   Yet if, as in the
case of PSD, the rules are so complex that the

agencies responsible for administering them cannot
understand them and consequently cannot apply them
consistently, then what has effectively occurred is
the same kind of delegation without direction which
was of such concern to Lowi in the absence such
rules. Under these conditions, formal rulemaking
does little to reduce the phenomenon of "interest
group liberalism" with which Lowi was so concerned,
since only the affected interest groups will make
the necessary investment of time and resources to
understand the rules. To the extent that the
development of PSD from 1975 to 1980 produced this
situation, it is possible to argue that there was
"less law" on PSD after the 1977 Amendments than
there was before under EPA's 1974 rules, even though
the statute obviously spoke to the issue in far more
detail. Excessively complex rules restrict the
benefits of formal rulemaking while also reducing
the advantages of case by case review--the ability
to identify solutions appropriate to particular
problems when the problems do not precisely fit the
categories envisioned in the rules. Excessively
complex rules force officials to spend their time
trying to figure out obscure provisions of the rules
rather than addressing the facts of the case at
hand. This distorts decision-making and leads
officials to pay more attention to legislative
histories which purport to give guidance on these
obscure points. This not only reinforces the power
of those who write such histories but, as Ackerman
and Hassler suggest, it can also lead agencies to
neglect the identification of real problems and
rational solutions to them.[11]

To Lowi, the whole point of having specific laws
and formal administrative rules is to provide the
basis for the predictable exercise of power in
accordance with authoritative, publicly formulated
decisions. In the case of laws passed by Congress,
this presumes that decisions on these laws are
public matters. In looking at PSD, it was certainly
the case that there was extensive debate over both
the concept and specific provisions. Open committee
meetings and conferences certainly leave the
impression that decisions on PSD were arrived as in

as public a way as possible. Certainly the
committees are to be commended for this effort,
especially when the reward for committee members
(such as Senator Muskie) was sometimes to be
attacked during reelection campaigns by industry
experts who tried to put the worst possible face on
committee staff proposals.

Yet a "publicly formulated" decision is more
than one arrived at in an open forum. It presumes
that the "public" is in some way able to understand
what is going on. No doubt there was some
understanding by most Congressmen that PSD involved
a debate between environmentalists and industry.
Perhaps this is all which can be asked of a group
whose agendas are enormous, and where the overload
of demands leads to the specialization in and
corresponding deference to committees which occurred
in this case. However, this system creates the
opportunity for a relative handful of insiders
(Congressmen, Congressional staff, agency experts
and interest group lobbyists) to affect highly
technical, complex and specific laws in ways that
few if any outsiders can understand. This ability
is exaggerated when, as occurred in both 1977 and
1990, final versions of laws must be put together
with great haste to meet some outside deadline. The
effects of such insider interventions may be aimed
at the scope of the general rules (as in the
extension of BACT to a larger universe of facilities
in the conference report than either the House or
the Senate had envisioned) or they may be aimed at
particular cases (the Colstrip example). In the
latter case the distinction between logrolling on
the rule and logrolling on the case tends to break
down. More importantly, with laws as complex as
PSD, this phenomenon makes it little more than a
semantic exercise to say that "the public" knows
what is going on or that "the Congress" has spoken
authoritatively on such issues in passing a law.
This is one of the prices to be paid for excessive
complexity in statutes.

Attempts to make laws even more specific will
only make this problem worse. The number of true
experts on a particular subject will always be

428 **Protect and Enhance**

samll; Congressmen cannot know everything; and often
action cannot be delayed until everyone fully
understands a particular piece of legislation.
Given these constraints, it is important to
recognize that increasing the specificity of the
laws passed by Congress makes the role of experts
with access even more important. Such laws may well
achieve their objective of reducing the discretion
of officials in administrative agencies, but they do
so only by increasing the importance of the
discretion exercised by these alternative groups.
Whether their actions will be more accountable to
the public than the actions of officials in
administrative agencies is an open question.[12]

Moreover, the complexity which can accompany the
increased specificity of law can have another
consequence. Lowi argued that specific laws and
formal rules would be likely to lead agencies back
to Congress more frequently.[13] As noted earlier,
this happened in the case of EPA's 1974 rules.
However, in the wake of the 1977 Amendments and
EPA's subsequent rulemakings, Congress has shown
signs of overload. While the ten year delay by
Congress in revising the Clean Air Act was certainly
attributable in large measue to the lack of
political consensus on such issues as acid rain, the
complexity of the Act was a deterrent in its own
right. Senator John Chafee, chairman of the Senate
Subcommittee on Environmental Pollution from 1981 to
1986, once remarked that "few things make the
committee's eyes glaze over more than launching into
the Clean Air Act" because of its complexity.[14]

PSD bears its share of responsibility for this
reaction. Without the pressure of an action-forcing
deadline such as the automobile standards in 1977
and in the absence of a strong initiative from the
Administration, Congress was unable to revisit the
Act for many years, as environmental groups, in
alliance with committee chairmen, successfully
blocked any attempt to streamline PSD (or any other
part of the Act) through the legislative process.
PSD's complexity aided these groups in this effort,
as time-consuming hearings and markup sessions are
required to assess amendment proposals which appear

minor but which may have major program consequences.
This was especially true in the Clean Air Act
debates of 1981-82, when strong interest groups
branded any effort to revise the details of the
statute as an attempt to destroy a piece of
legislation whose principles retained strong public
support.[15]

Seen in this light, complexity becomes a
conservative political value, rendering statutes
highly resistant to change. Though in the case of
PSD it is now a "conservatism" in the service of
objectives thought of as "liberal," both sides in
the debate over PSD have used this tactic. Whether
the values under attack are those of industry or
environmental groups, however, the complexity of PSD
certainly has not facilitated legislative review.
From this standpoint, it is no surprise that even
when the political forces changed in 1989-90 and
amendments to the Clean Air Act were at last
proposed by the Admiistration and approved by
Congress, significant about PSD did <u>not</u> occur and
few changes were made in PSD law.

Administrative Rules and Administrative Discretion

The arguments advanced by Lowi in favor of
greater specificity in legislation and greater
formalism in administration are really arguments
over how to control administrative discretion. Lowi
argues strongly that without clear standards
incorporated in statutory and administrative law,
public administration degenerates into unrestricted
bargaining among groups, with the strongest and best
organized groups influencing the conduct of the
state to the detriment of the public interest, and
administrators accountable primarily to private
groups rather than to the public through the
President, the Congress, or other elected officials.
Limiting administrative discretion through the use

of explicit, detailed, and authoritative standards
furthers the application of policies developed using
democratic forms of government, as opposed to the
oligopolistic control fostered by interest group
liberalism. The importance of such laws and
standards in limiting administrative discretion,
then, goes beyond the importance of improving public
administration and becomes essential to the
maintenance of democracy in America.

If explicit laws and standards are the measure
of whether government will be controlled by the many
or the few, then an observer applying these criteria
would be heartened by the prevention of significant
deterioration program. Yet for reasons outlined
above, it is not clear that for all their
specificity, the PSD rules represent an optimal
solution to the problem of administrative control.
Attempts to control PSD through Congress suffer from
the limited attention which most Congressmen can
give to air pollution issues, leaving this process
subject to domination by a relative handful of
expert committee members and their staff. Attempts
to apply control through the courts are subject to
the limits of court expertise, not only on technical
matters but also, as Shep Melnick has pointed out,
on issues of practical public administration.[16]
Neither court nor Congressional control proved very
satisfying in the case of PSD.

A third possible source of control which was
clearly at work in this case is the administrative
agency itself. On the surface this seems like a
contradiction in terms, especially in an Agency such
as EPA which is headed by a single Administrator.
However, a closer look at the development of this
case shows many control mechanisms which the Agency
has imposed on itself, reinforced by other elements
of the executive branch and State governments and by
the differences in professional norms in different
EPA organizations.

The existence of three major groups within EPA--
the air pollution control professionals in the
Office of Air and Radiation, the lawyers of the
Office of General Counsel, and the economists and
planners of the Office of Planning and Evaluation--

shaped the development of the PSD rules at every step. Each office had its own reporting chain to the Administrator, and thus was not constrained to accomodate policy choices with which they did not agree short of the highest levels within the Agency. More importantly, each office had an independent external base of power. The Office of Air and Radiation, and particularly the Office of Air Quality Planning and Standards, drew its authority from the mandates contained in the statute, for which it was ultimately responsible. This office was the chief beneficiary of explicit and clear Congressional direction. OAQPS also gained influence as the final arbiter of "technical" and implementation issues. Although challenged on occasion by the Office of Planning and Evaluation, which could purchase outside expertise, the rest of EPA ultimately depended on OAQPS to lay out the limits of what could practically be done, even if these limits were not always heeded.

In contrast to the legislative/expertise base of the Air office, the economists of the Office of Planning and Evaluation (OPE) derived their influence from the inevitable push from the White House and other Executive Branch agencies to judge pollution control requirements in the context of broader macroeconomic policies. Because of the authority which the White House could exercise (at least in theory) over EPA, this was a very potent power source. To the extent that OPE could form alliances with other Executive Branch agencies such as the Council of Economic Advisers, the Federal Energy Administration or the Office of Management and Budget, its influence could be strengthened even further. Moreover, since OPE could select the issues on which it would intervene (as opposed to the Air office, which as keeper of the regulatory package had to worry about everything), its efforts could be focused and effective. On the other hand, OPE's influence was offset to the degree that EPA relied heavily on Congressional support, as was clearly the case under Administrator Train and to a lesser degree under Administrator Costle. Moreover, the presence of strong political leadership in the

Air office, as was the case under Assistant
Administrator Hawkins, could weaken OPE's relative
influence over the course of PSD. Still, as keeper
of the Agency's central control system for all
regulations, OPE had powerful tools at its disposal
to make its views known and considered.

The Office of General Counsel, the third major
internal actor, derived its influence from its
position as official interpreter of what the law
was, both with respect to statutory law and
regulations. Its influence was greatest when
Congressional intent was most vague, because in such
cases OGC became the authoritative spokesman for
what the Agency legally could or could not do. To
the extent that anticipated court reaction was a
concern (which was almost always the case in PSD),
OGC's influence was further enhanced as it alone
possessed the institutional authority to speak
definitively on this issue. This had a lasting
effect on the broad policy structure of the PSD
program (the use of the increment system). It also
affected the crafting of fine points of wording in
the regulations themselves, which became
increasingly important in the wake of the
definitional arguments triggered by the 1977
Amendments and the <u>Alabama</u> <u>Power</u> decision. In light
of this, it is interesting to note that although the
upholding of the 1974 regulations in their entirety
must be regarded as a major success for OGC, the
office was not without its legal setbacks. The two
most notable were the original defeat in <u>Sierra Club
vs. Ruckelshaus</u>, and the loss on the definition of
"potential to emit" in the <u>Alabama Power</u> case. This
suggests that administrators would be well advised
to retain a certain skepticism about the correctness
of their legal advice. However, even when OGC's
predictions of outcomes went astray, their position
benefitted from the relevant expertise of the
Agency's senior political executives. Most were
attorneys and shared to a considerable degree the
professional norms of the OGC staff attorneys, if
not necessarily their political values.[17]

As a result of this division of authority within
EPA, much of what is classically considered control

of Agency discretion occurred inside the Agency
itself. Each of these offices was able to develop
staff experts who understood the ins and outs of
PSD. Because of their different outlooks and
sources of influence, if the staff in the three
offices agreed on how to resolve an issue, this
resolution would generally be accepted by the
Agency's senior political executives. The use of
formal administrative rulemaking, along with
attendant formal intra- and inter-agency reviews,
reinforced the effectiveness of such internal
controls by requiring explicit decisions to be made
about specific language in a specific document.
While on occasion one office could be "railroaded"
by the combined efforts of the other two, this was
not generally possible over the long term.

The political sources of external influence on
EPA's internal organizational units--Congress on the
Air office, the Executive Branch on the Policy
office, and the courts on OGC--parallel the
Constitutional separation of powers. That the
separation of powers would have this kind of effect
even within an administrative agency is an outcome
of the use of formal rulemaking which Lowi did not
explicitly foresee. From the standpoint of
"juridical democracy" this should be an additional
benefit, in that it makes it even more likely that
agencies will face opposition even within their own
ranks to actions which are not clearly mandated by
law. Organizational structures in which internal
groups are deliberately established along
independent lines of authority, oriented primarily
toward different sets of outside influential
political actors, reinforced by differences in group
professional norms, and set in competition with each
other over the desire to influence the policy
decisions embodied in formal administrative actions
may be one of the most effective safeguards against
the problem of excessive discretion which was of
such concern to Lowi.

Yet every solution has its price. Bargaining
among internal groups may result in outcomes similar
to those of Congressional bargaining--regulations in
which the complexities obscure who "won" and who

"lost", or where a complex compromise is deemed
preferable by agency heads anxious not to alienate
any group completely. The fifty ton exemption in
the 1978 regulations is an example of this.
Moreover, given sufficient time and outside support,
a determined administrator can override the
objections of other agency groups, as William
Ruckelshaus did in 1971 and David Hawkins did to a
lesser extent in 1978 and 1979. Finally, unless
senior administrators make clear choices among the
competing policy perspectives of the groups on any
given issue, action may be stalled in futile
attempts to achieve compromise until it is forced by
outside events such as court deadlines. While such
delay may sometimes be in the public interest, there
is no guarantee that the delays inherent in an
organizational structure which stimulates internal
competition will meet this test.

     All of these results are most likely to occur
when actors who might otherwise be concerned about
the course of public policy are foreclosed from
participation in it. Such foreclosure can, of
course, result from deliberate efforts at secrecy.
However, foreclosure can also result from
complexity, which "makes it difficult for many of
these actors to invest the time necessary to
understand the issues that executive agencies
commonly confront." Complexity thus works in much
the same way as secrecy to "prevent other
participants in the policy process from giving
attention to decisions that bureaucratic
organizations may be making."[18]

     This points up a weakness of "juridical
democracy." The case of PSD suggests that to a
greater extent than Lowi believed, specific rules
must also be complex. Yet this complexity prevents
the public and their elected representatives from
understanding the law and its application. This
hardly constitutes increased public control of
administrative agencies. To the extent that Lowi's
specific laws and formal administrative rules turn
into complex laws and regulations whose effect
cannot be understood, they may make no greater

contribution to democracy than the unbridled discretion they are supposed to replace.

The conclusion this leads to is that while "juridical democracy" offers some attributes which contribute to making and administering public policy in a democratic society, these attributes have risks of their own and, when taken to extremes, can defeat the very purpose for which they are used. The legislative cure for unbridled administrative discretion may be worse than the disease if it forces public officials to do irrational things in the name of conformance with the letter of a statute whose exact provisions were developed in last-minute bargaining and are understood, if they are understood at all, by only a few. Formal administrative rules, developed through the use of public notice and comment rulemaking, can help inform the public of actions under consideration by administrative officials and allowing interested groups to mobilize. This virtue can be offset, however, if the "publics" who participate in this process are limited to those who can afford the time and resources to become sufficiently educated to participate as experts and to invoke the power of the courts if advocacy before the agency is unsuccessful.

The existence of "public interest" organizations which can mobilize both technical and legal expertise in the cases such as PSD is significant as an offset to the influence of expertise which would otherwise rest solely with industry. The easy access to the courts which the Clean Air Act provides to "public interest" groups has also been important both as part of the political struggle over the larger values which PSD symbolizes and in increasing the role of the courts as policy-making institutions. Certainly the Sierra Club has had as much influence on PSD, if not more, than the National Coal Association (though the influence of either has probably been less than that of the D.C. Circuit Court of Appeals). Yet the existence of offsetting groups by itself does not necesarily mean that the public interest will be served. Even "public interest" groups and courts can have agendas

which are not any more readily subject to public
review and scrutiny than those of industrial groups
or administrative agencies.

For all the checks that exist, the case of PSD
suggests that the wise exercise of discretion and
judgement by responsible Congressional and
administrative officials is still necessary to limit
potential abuses of authority or the public
interest. Lowi's "juridical democracy" is a useful
concept in that it suggests how administrative
mechanisms can be established to reinforce the
tendency to use such authority wisely. Yet those
who write rules, especially in new areas such as
PSD, will never be able to anticipate all possible
needs and contingencies. Moreover, the story of PSD
shows that the attempt to write very detailed rules
into the statute resulted in a number of perverse
effects which could have been avoided by allowing
administrative officials greater discretion in
determining what "significant deterioration of air
quality" is. The desire to tie this elusive concept
down so firmly that it was fixed for all time is
responsible for many of the problems which affect
PSD today.

A major theme in The End of Liberalism was the
phenomenon of agency capture by the interests it is
supposed to regulate. Given this emphasis, it is
significant that capture is one pattern of agency
behavior which is not displayed in this case. The
principles embodied in "juridical democracy" and
exemplified in this case may be assigned some of the
credit for this outcome. Admittedly, it is
difficult to measure both the precise degree to
which "capture" was avoided. Adjustments to PSD
were made to avoid bringing certain activities
(e.g., strip mining; smaller new sources and
modifications) within PSD's scope. These
adjustments, however, hardly seem to constitute
"capture" as described by 1960's reformers, unless
one takes the position that any deviation from a
strict environmentalist position on PSD constituted
"capture." It is also difficult to measure the
effect of "juridical democracy" principles on the
avoidance of capture as compared to the effect of

such factors as the culture of independence
established by EPA's first Administrators.
Nevertheless, it is fair to give legal formality and
specificity some of the credit for avoiding capture
by providing forums in formal rulemaking and
judicial review for issues to be fully and publicly
aired.

"Juridical democracy" cannot be said to have
failed in the case of PSD. However, the case
suggests that Lowi's model of "juridical democracy"
is worth pursuing only up to the point at which the
complexity of the resulting rules overwhelms their
purpose. While the issues associated with
preventing significant deterioration are complex,
they are not so much so as to have required the set
of rules which exist today. A clearer and simpler
protection scheme could have been devised, though as
Melnick suggests it would have required greater
clarity about which of several possible values were
of primary concern.[19] Yet surely this is not too
much to ask of decision-makers, whether they are in
Congress or the Executive Branch. While such an
approach no doubt would have had to give some
additional discretion to administrative agencies,
the excessive specification of detailed requirements
has given administrators that discretion anyway, by
overloading the technical and administrative
capabilities of oversight organizations (either
Congress or EPA) to review or correct aberrant
administrative behavior by implementing
organizations. In addition, the demands of the PSD
program have diverted attention from finding
solutions to other, more pressing environmental
problems, and by its complexity has called into
question the overall benefits of air pollution
control. Future attempts to apply the principles of
"juridical democracy" would do well to learn the
lessons of the potential risks of this approach
which are embodied in the history of PSD.[20]

NOTES

1. I am not aware of any systematic attampt to do
    this. Industry and EPA attacks on PSD instead
    criticize certain elements of the PSD program as
    adding complexity and costs while producing
    little or no change in total required emissions
    reductions. See Dames and Moore, <u>An
    Investigation of Prevention of Significant
    Deterioration (PSD) of Air Quality and Emission
    Offset Permitting Processes</u>, Report to the
    National Commission on Air Quality, Contract No.
    NCAQ 1-AQ-7133, June, 1980, Staff Summary pp. 1-
    4; A.D. Little, <u>The Effects of Prevention of
    Significant Deterioration</u> of Air Quality on
    Industrial Development, Prepared for the
    <u>Business Roundtable Air Quality Report</u>,
    November, 1980, pp. iii-vii; <u>1981 Senate
    Oversight Hearings</u>, Testimony of John Quarles,
    pp. 108119; 245-259 (prepared statement).

2. U.S. Environmental Protection Agency (EPA),
    <u>National Air Audit System FY84 National Report</u>,
    p. IV-7.

3. Ibid., p. IV-9

4. Ibid.

5. Business Roundtable, <u>Effects</u>, pp. v, xi, 86;
    EPA, <u>Analysis of New Source Review (NSR)
    Permitting Experience</u>, June, 1982, p.39;
    National Commission on Air Quality (NCAQ),
    <u>Report</u>, pp. 3.5-43-44.

6. EPA, <u>Analysis</u>, p. 38

7. Dames and Moore, <u>Investigation</u>, pp. 5-2-3

8. See the statement of Richard E. Ayres, et al.,
    in the NCAQ <u>Report</u>, pp. 5-44-46, and his
    statement before the Senate at <u>1981 Senate
    Oversight Hearings</u>, pp. 130-132.

9. Thus a National Research Council report on EPA
    would observe,
        "As a matter of policy, EPA leadership
        decided not to ask Congress to amend the
        Agency's stated mission in its early years.
        The first imperative was to give the new
        approaches to pollution control a fair chance
        of proving effective. The Agency has
        promoted legislation giving it new authority
        in areas where it saw a need, but a
        reluctance to request statutory alteration in
        existing programs still persists. There is
        concern that requests to Congress to correct
        unworkable provisions might lead to the
        unraveling of others that the Agency feels
        are sound"
    The National Research Council, <u>Decision-Making
    in the Environmental Protection Agency</u>
    (Washington: National Academy of Sciences,
    1977), p. 2.

10. Interview data.

11. Ackerman and Hassler, "Beyond the New Deal," pp.
    1555-1561.

12. See the discussion in Ackerman and Hassler,
    "Beyond the New Deal," pp. 1513-14 and Melnick,
    <u>Regulation and the Courts</u>, pp. 37379.

13. Lowi, <u>The End of Liberalism</u>, p. 301

14. "Chafee Dismisses Chances of CAA
    Reauthorization, Looks At Environmental
    Priorities for the 1980's," <u>Air and Water
    Pollution Report</u>, vol. 24, no. 4, January 27,
    1986. See also the comments of former EPA
    Administrator Douglas Costle, cited in Melnick,
    <u>Regulation and the Courts</u>, p. 384

15. See U.S. Senate, Remarks of Senator Stafford,
    <u>Congressional Record</u> (daily edition), September
    10, 1981, pp. S9424-26; "Clean Air Act Rewrite
    Tangled in Thicket of Conflicting Interests,"

<u>Washington Post</u>, August 2, 1982, p. A6; Michael
Barone, "Tactics of an Ace in the Congressional
Air Wars," <u>Washington Post</u>, December 14, 1982,
p. A27.

16. Melnick, <u>Regulation and the Courts</u>, pp. 387-89

17. Administrators William Ruckelshaus, Russell
     Train, Douglas Costle and Anne Burford were all
     attorneys, as were Air Assistant Administrators
     Roger Strelow, David Hawkins, Joseph Cannon,
     Craig Potter, and William Rosenberg. Current
     Adminstrator William K. Reilly also has a law
     degree, although he differs in that his
     professional career has been spent primarily as
     director of various conservation organizations.
     Of EPA's Adminstrators, only Lee Thomas (1985-
     1989) was not an attorney. Of EPA's Air
     Assistant Administrators, only Kathleen Bennett
     (1981-1983) was not an attorney.

18. Francis E. Rourke, <u>Bureaucracy, Politics and
     Public Policy</u>, 2nd ed. (Boston: Little, Brown,
     1976), p. 81-83.

19. Melnick, <u>Regulation and the Courts</u>, pp. 81-83.

20. As of this writing, it seems very likely that
     these lessons have not been learned. In 1984,
     Congress passed amendments to the laws governing
     hazardous waste treatment, storage and disposal
     which in spirit seem quite related to PSD in
     their detail and specificity, with the added
     dimension the in the intervening seven years
     Congress has become more adept at developing
     sanctions to force EPA to act. The 1986
     extension of the 1980 "Superfund" law passed
     Congress under conditions similar to the 1976/77
     conferences on the Clean Air Act. Many
     parallels to PSD can be found in these laws, and
     the outlook is not hopeful for an approach which
     would restore a balance between central
     legislative direction and sensible discretion in
     the administration of programs to protect the

environment. The difficulties which EPA has
encountered since 1986 in administering both
RCRA and Superfund reflect this inability to
achieve a more appropriate balance.

While it is too soon to tell how the 1990
Clean Air Act amendments fit into this paradigm,
thre are elements of both hope and concern. The
Administration bill attempted to expand some of
the discretion available to the EPA in
comparison to the RCRA and Superfund amendments,
and since the final bill was based in large
measure on the Administration proposal, many of
these elements were retained in some form.
However, Congress in its consideration of the
bill imposed many additional specific mandatory
duties on EPA. In the present budget climate it
seems unlikely that EPA will be given resources
commensurate with these added requirements. How
the Congress, the Agency, the Administration and
the courts respond when EPA fails to meet some
of these deadlines will be the next significant
test of "juridical democracy".

SELECTED BIBLIOGRAPHY

I. INTERVIEWS AND DOCUMENT SOURCES

The following people were interviewed during the course of research for this work. As each was promised anonymity, their comments, where cited, are not identified by name unless permission to do so was specifically requested (which occurred in only one case). However, the assistance and candor displayed by the interviewees is gratefully acknowledged.

> Irwin Auerbach
> Robert Baum
> Kent Berry
> Jack Farmer
> David Hawkins
> John Middleton
> Hugh Miller (deceased)
> Joseph Padgett
> Richard Rhoads (deceased)
> William Ruckelshaus
> Jeffrey Schwartz
> Bernard Steigerwald (deceased)
> Roger Strelow
> Bruce Terris
> Michael Trutna
> Edward Tuerk
> Cheryl Wasserman

In addition, this work makes extensive use of notes and internal EPA memoranda in tracing the history of PSD. I am especially indebted to Cheryl Wasserman for her carefully maintained record of the events which are described in Chapter IV, and to Michael Trutna for allowing me to use his records of the events described in Chapters III and VI. Finally, I also used documents found in the files of EPA's Office of Air Quality Planning and Standards to assist in describing the events of Chapter III.

444   **Protect and Enhance**

I gratefully acknowledge the assistance provided to me in gaining access to these records, as the dissertation could not have been written without them.

II. GOVERNMENT DOCUMENTS

<u>Federal Register</u>, various issues

U.S. Congress. House. <u>Air Quality Act of 1967</u>.
    H. Rpt. 728 to Accompany S.780, 90th Congress,
    1st sess., 1967.

U.S. Congress. House. Committee on Interstate
    and Foreign Commerce. <u>Clean Air Act Oversight:
    Hearings Before the Subcommittee on Public
    Health and the Environment of the Committee on
    Interstate and Foreign Commerce</u>. 92nd Congress,
    2nd sess., 1972.

U.S. Congress. House. Committee on Interstate
    and Foreign Commerce. <u>Clean Air Act Oversight--
    1973, Hearings Before the Subcommittee on Public
    Health and Environment of the Committee on
    Interstate and Foreign Commerce</u>. 93rd Congress,
    1st sess., 1973.

U.S. Congress. House. Committee on Interstate and
    Foreign Commerce. <u>Clean Air Act Amendments--
    1975, Hearings Before the Subcommittee on Health
    and the Environment of the Committee on
    Interstate and Foreign Commerce</u>. 94th Congress,
    1st sess., 1975.

U.S. Congress. House. <u>Clean Air Act Amendments of
    1976</u>. Report of the Committee on Interstate and
    Foreign Commerce to accompany H.R. 10498. 94th
    Congress, 2nd sess., 1976

U.S. Congress. House. <u>The Clean Air Act of 1976</u>.
    H.Rpt. 94-1742 to accompany S. 3219. 94th
    Congress, 2nd sess., 1976.

U.S. Congress. House. Committee on Interstate and
Foreign Commerce. Clean Air Act Amendments of
1977, Hearings Before the Subcommittee on Health
and Environment of the Committee on Interstate
and Foreign Commerce on H.R. 4151 and H.R. 4758.
95th Congress, 1st Session, 1977.

U.S. Congress. House. Clean Air Act Amendments of
1977. H.Rept. 95-294 to Accompany H.R. 6161.
95th Congress, 1st sess., 1977.

U.S. Congress. Senate. Committee on Public Works.
Hearings Before the Subcommittee on Air and
Water Pollution of the Committee on Public
Works. 90th Congress, 1st sess., 1967.

U.S. Congress. Senate. Air Quality Act of 1967.
S. Rpt. 403 to Accompany S. 780. 90th Congress,
1st sess., 1967.

U.S. Congress. Senate. National Air Quality
Standards Act of 1970. Report of the Committee
on Public Works to Accompany S. 4358. 91st
Congress, 2nd sess., 1970.

U.S. Congress. Senate. Committee on Public Works.
A Hearing Before the Subcommittee on Air and
Water Pollution of the Committee on Public
Works. 92nd Congress, 2nd sess., 1972.

U.S. Congress. Senate. Committee on Public Works.
Nondegradation Policy of the Clean Air Act,
Hearings before the Subcommittee on Air and
Water Pollution of the Committee on Public
Works. 93rd Congress, 1st sess., 1973.

U.S. Congress. Senate. Committee on Public Works.
The Fuel Shortage and the Clean Air Act, Hearing
before the Subcommittee on Air and Water
Pollution of the Committee on Public Works.
93rd Cong., 1st sess., 1973.

U.S. Congress. Senate. Committee on Public Works.
A Legislative History of the Clean Air
Amendments of 1970. 93rd Congress, 2nd sess.,
1974. 2 vols.

U.S. Congress. Senate. Committee on Public Works.
Clean Air Act Oversight, Hearings Before the
Subcommittee on Environment Pollution of the
Senate Committee on Public Works. 93 Cong., 2nd
sess., 1974.

U.S. Congress. Senate. Committee on Public Works.
Implementation of the Clean Air Act--1975,
Hearings before the Subcommittee on
Environmental Pollution of the Committee on
Public Works. 94th Cong., 1st sess., 1975.

U.S. Congress. Senate. Committee on Public Works.
Clean Air Amendments of 1976. Report of the
Committee on Public Works, S.Rept. 94-717 to
accompany S.3219. 94th Congress, 2nd sess.,
1976.

U.S. Congress. Senate. Committee on Environment
and Public Works. Clean Air Act Amendments of
1977: Hearings Before the Subcommittee on
Environmental Pollution of the Committee on
Environment and Public Works on S.251, S.252,
and S.253. 95th Congress, 1st sess., 1977.

U.S. Congress. Senate. Committee on Environment
and Public Works. A Legislative History of the
Clean Air Act Amendments of 1977. Committee
Print, 95th Congress, 2nd sess., 1978. 6 vols.
(numbered vol. 3 - vol. 8)

U.S. Congress. Senate. Committee on Environment
and Public Works. Clean Air Act Oversight,
Hearings Before the Committee on Environment and
Public Works. 97th Congress, 1st sess., 1981.

Council on Environmental Quality. Environmental

Quality 1974: The Fifth Annual Report of the Council on Environmental Quality. Washington: Government Printing Office, 1974.

U. S. Department of Health, Education and Welfare. Public Health Service. *Proceedings: The Third National Conference on Air Pollution, Washington, D. C., December 12-14, 1966*.

U.S. Department of Health, Education and Welfare. Public Health Service. "Guidelines For the Development of Air Quality Standards and Implementation Plans." May 1969.

U.S. Environmental Protection Agency and Federal Energy Administration. *An Analysis of the Input on the Electric Utility Industry of Alternative Approaches to Significant Deterioration*. October, 1975.

U.S. Environmental Protection Agency. Office of Air Quality Planning and Standards. "Guideline on Air Quality Models." June 1978.

U.S. Environmental Protection Agency. Office of Air Quality Planning and Standards. *National Air Audit System FY84 National Report*. December 1984.

III. COURT CASES CITED

Note: ERC stands for *Environment Reporter--Cases*, published by the Bureau of National Affairs, Washington, D.C. All cases were decided in the D.C. Circuit Court of Appeals except for the 1972 *Sierra Club* case, which was originally decided in the D.C. District Court.

Sierra Club et al., vs. Ruckelshaus, 4 *ERC* 1205 (1972).

Sierra Club vs. EPA, 9 *ERC* 1129 (1976). (Also cited as *Dayton Power and Light vs. EPA*)

ASARCO vs. EPA, 11 ERC 1129 (1978).

Citizens to Save Spencer County v. EPA, 12 ERC 1965 (1979).

Alabama Power vs. Costle, per curiam opinion, 13 ERC 1225 (1979).

Alabama Power vs. Costle, final opinion, 13 ERC 1993 (1979).

IV. SECONDARY REFERENCES--PERIODICALS, NEWSLETTERS
    AND NEWSPAPERS

Air and Water Pollution Report
Environment Reporter
Inside EPA
National Journal
New York Times
Wall Street Journal
Washington Post

V. SECONDARY REFERENCES--BOOKS AND ARTICLES

Ackerman, Bruce and Hassler, William. "Beyond the
    New Deal: Coal and the Clean Air Act." Yale
    Law Journal 89 (1980): 1466-1571.

A. D. Little. The Effects of Prevention of
    Significant Deterioration of Air Quality on
    Industrial Development. Prepared for the
    Business Roundtable Air Quality Report,
    November, 1980.

Asbell, Bernard. The Senate Nobody Knows.
    Garden City, N.Y.: Doubleday, 1978.

Bernstein, Marver. Regulating Business By
    Independent Commission. Princeton: Princeton
    University Press, 1955.

Berry, Jeff. <u>Lobbying for the People</u>. Princeton: Princeton University Press, 1977.

Blackburn, W. Stanley; Roj, William H.; and Taylor, Ralph A. "Review of EPA's Significant Deterioration Regulations: An Example of the Difficulties of the Agency-Court Partnerships in Environmental Law." <u>Virginia Law Review</u> 61 (1975): 1115-1186.

Crenson, Matthew. <u>The Un-Politics of Air Pollution</u>. Baltimore: The Johns Hopkins University Press, 1970.

Dames and Moore. <u>An Investigation of Prevention of Significant Deterioration (PSD) of Air Quality and Emission Offset Permitting Processes</u>. Report to the National Commission on Air Quality, Contract No. NCAQ 1-AQ-7133, June, 1980.

Davies, J. Clarence and Davies, Barbara S. <u>The Politics of Pollution</u>. 2nd ed. Indianapolis: Bobbs-Merrill, 1975.

Davis, Christopher; Kurtok, Jeffrey; Leape, James and Magill, Frank. "The Clean Air Act Amendments of 1977: Away from Technology Forcing?" <u>Harvard Environmental Law Review</u> 2 (1977): 103-199.

Downs, Anthony. "Up and Down With Ecology--The Issue Attention Cycle." <u>The Public Interest</u> 28 (Summer 1972): 38-50.

Esposito, John C. <u>Vanishing Air: The Ralph Nader Study Group Report on Air Pollution</u>. New York: Grossman Publishers, 1970.

Freeman, A. Myrick. "Air and Water Pollution Policy." In Portnoy, Paul M., ed. <u>Current Issues in U.S. Environmental Policy</u>. Baltimore: The Johns Hopkins University Press, 1978.

Glass, Adam W.   "The EPA's Bubble Concept After
    Alabama Power."   32 Stanford Law Review 603
    (1980).

Gotbaum, Joshua.   "Non-Degradation, the Courts, and
    the Clean Air Act."   Kennedy School Case
    Program, No. C95-77-164, 1977.

Jacoby, Henry D. and Steinbruner, John D.   Clearing
    the Air: Federal Policy on Automotive Emission
    Control.   Cambridge, Mass.:   Ballenger, 1973.

Jones, Charles.   Clean Air: The Policies and
    Politics of Pollution Control.   Pittsburgh:
    University of Pittsburgh Press, 1975.

Kneese, Allen V. and Charles L. Schultze.
    Pollution, Prices, and Public Policy.
    Washington: Brookings, 1975.

Lundquist, Lennart.   The Hare and the Tortoise:
    Clean Air Policies in the United States and
    Sweden.   Ann Arbor: University of Michigan
    Press, 1980.

Litan, Robert E. and Nordhaus, William D.   Reforming
    Federal Regulation.   New Haven: Yale University
    Press, 1984.

Lowi,Theodore.   "American Business, Public Policy,
    Case Studies, and Political Theory."   World
    Politics 16 (July, 1964): 677-715.

_____.   The End of Liberalism.   New York:
    W. W. Norton, 1969.

Marcus, Alfred.   "Environmental Protection Agency."
    In Wilson, James Q., ed.   The Politics of
    Regulation.   New York: Basic Books, 1980.

_____.   Promise and Performance: Choosing
    and Implementing An Environmental Policy.
    Westport, Conn.:   Greenwood Press, 1980.

McConnell, Grant. <u>Private Power and American Democracy</u>. New York: Alfred A. Knopf, 1966.

Melnick, R. Shep. <u>Regulation and the Courts: The Case of the Clean Air Act</u>. Washington: Brookings, 1983.

Mihaly, Marc Bremer. "The Clean Air Act and the Concept of Non-Degradation: Sierra Club vs. Ruckelshaus," <u>Ecology Law Quarterly</u> 2 (1973): 801-836.

Morgenthau, Hans. <u>Scientific Man vs. Power Politics</u>. Chicago: University of Chicago Press, 1946.

Nadel, Mark V. "The Hidden Dimensions of Public Policy: Private Governments and the Policy-Making Process." <u>Journal of Politics</u> 37 (February, 1975): 2-34.

National Commission on Air Quality. <u>To Breathe Clean Air</u>. Washington: Government Printing Office, 1981.

National Research Council. <u>Decision-Making in the Environmental Protection Agency</u>. Washington: National Academy of Sciences, 1977.

Pressman, Jeffrey and Wildavsky, Aaron. <u>Implementation</u>. Berekley: University of California Press, 1973.

Rosenbaum, Walter. <u>The Politics of Environmental Concern</u>. New York: Praeger, 1973.

Rourke, Francis E. <u>Bureaucracy, Politics and Public Policy</u>. 2nd ed. Boston: Little, Brown, 1976.

_____. <u>Bureaucratic Power in National Politics</u>. 2nd ed. Boston: Little, Brown, 1972.

Sabatier, Paul. "Social Movements and Regulatory

Agencies: Toward a More Adequate--and Less
Pessimistic--Theory of Clientele Capture."
<u>Policy Sciences</u> 6 (1975): 311.

Vietor, Richard K. <u>Environmental Politics and the
Coal Coalition</u>. College Station, Texas: Texas
A&M University Press, 1980.

Wellford, Harrison. "On How To Be A Constructive
Nuisance." In de Bell, Garrett, ed., <u>The
Environmental Handbook</u>. New York: Ballantine
Books, 1970.

Wiehl, Peggy. "William D. Ruckelshaus and the
Environmental Protection Agency," Kennedy School
of Government Case No. C16-74-027, 1974.

Wilensky, Harold. <u>Organizational Intelligence</u>. New
York: Basic Books, 1967.

Wilson, James Q., ed. <u>The Politics of Regulation</u>.
New York: Basic Books, 1980.

Zuckerman, Elias, "Senator Muskie and the 1970
Amendments to the Clean Air Act," Kennedy
School of Government Case Study C94-76-140,
1976.

THE ENVIRONMENT

BRIAN BAKER. *Groundwater Protection from Pesticides.*

JOHN BEEKER, JR. *Implementing Tailpipe Tests: What Factors Influence States to Respond to National Environmental Goals?*

KENNETH T. BOGEN. *Uncertainty in Environmental Health Risk Assessment.*

BRIAN CLOWES. *Simplified Framework Evaluation of Large Water Resource Project Impacts.*

KAREN COLLIGEN-TAYLOR. *The Emergence of Environmental Literature in Japan.*

LETICIA P. CORTÉS. *A Survey of the Environmental Knowledge, Comprehension, Responsibilty, and Interest of the Secondary Level Students and Teachers in the Philippines.*

MARILYN DUBASEK. *Wilderness Preservation: A Cross-Cultural Comparison of Canada and the United States.*

SEZAI DEMIRAL. *Pollution Control and the Patterns of Trade: Germany and the United States.*

JEFFRY FAWCETT. *The Political Economy of Smog in Southern California.*

JUAN J. FERRADA. *Hazardous Chemical Waste Management.*

SUMITRA M. GURUNG. *Beyond the Myth of the Eco-Crisis in Nepal: Local Response to Pressure on Land in the Middle Hills.*

JONATHAN M. HARRIS. *Environmental Limits to Growth in World Agriculture.*

JAMES K. HAMMITT. *Probability is All We Have: Uncertainties, Delays, and Environmental Policymaking.*

DANIEL S. IACOFANO. *Public Involvement as an Organizational Development Process.*

ELLEN HUENING MAKOWSKI. *Scenic Parks and Landscape Values.*

LAURA L. MANNING. *The Dispute Processing Model of Public Policy Evolution: The Case of Endangered Species Policy Changes from 1973 to 1983.*

A. STANLEY MEIBURG. *Project and Enhance: "Juridical Democracy" and the Prevention of Significant Deterioration of Air Quality.*

A. RICHARD MORDI. *Attitudes Toward Wildlife in Botswana.*

ROBERT W. MORESCHI. *Tort Liability Standards and the Firm's Response to Regulation.*

USHA MUNSHI. *An Integrated Approach to Pollution Control.*

RICHARD B. OLOWOMEYE. *The Management of Solid Waste in Nigerian Cities.*

COLLEEN K. O'TOOLE. *The Search for Purity: A Retrospective Policy Analysis of the Decision to Chlorinate Cincinnati's Public Water Supply, 1890–1920.*

ROBERT B. OLSHANSKY. *Landslide Hazard in the United States: Case Studies in Planning and Policy Development.*

KENNETH B. SEWALL. *The Tradeoff Between Cost and Risk in Hazardous Waste Management.*

SMITA K. SIDDHANTI. *Multiple Perspectives on Risk and Regulation: The Case of Deliberate Release of Genetically Engineered Organisms into the Environment.*

ROBERT N. STAVINS. *The Welfare Economics of Alternative Renewable Resource Strategies: Forested Wetlands and Agricultural Production.*

ELAINE VAUGHAN. *Some Factors Influencing the Nonexperts Perception and Evaluation of Environmental Risks.*

LEAH J. WILDS. *Understanding Who Wins: Organizational Behavior and Environmental Policies.*

DAVID K. WOODYARD AND JONATHAN HAUFLER. *Risk Evaluation for Sludge-Born Elements to Wildlife Food Chains.*